The Great Violinists

By the same author:

Dolmetsch: The Man and his Work

Margaret Campbell

The Great Violinists

Foreword by Ruggiero Ricci

Doubleday & Company, Inc.
Garden City, New York
1981

First published in Great Britain in 1980
by Granada Publishing in Paul Elek Ltd 1980

ISBN: 0-385-17565-5
Library of Congress Catalog Card Number 80-2904

Foreword

by Ruggiero Ricci

The violin is probably the most hellish invention ever conceived by man, a beautiful and treacherous work of art that demands our constant attention but can never be completely dominated. We must adapt to her individual characteristics and hope that she will respond with a gracious nod to *our* own uniqueness. 'Treat her right, and she'll treat you right,' Jascha Heifetz once told me.

The problems, even for the high priests, are considerable: 'I used to sleep on the chin rest,' confided David Oistrakh as we recalled the slavish hours of practice required. 'How do you keep the violin from going out from under your chin when you downshift?' asked Szigeti. We all have some nightmare gremlin waiting to pounce during that elusive perfect performance. 'You mustn't pay attention to my fingerings,' Kreisler warned me, 'I never could play in first position.' Why do we go on? The gratification that comes if one can melt a heart or draw tears is worth the countless hours spent trying to play double harmonics and blistering our fingers with *pizzicato*.

The hallmarks of some of today's performers are over-sweetness and excessive feelings, as compared to the dry sound, bad shifting, and eccentricities that characterized many of our forebears. Every violin player thinks he's the greatest. If he doesn't, then forget him. Paganini, Wieniawski, Ysaÿe, Kreisler, Heifetz, Oistrakh — all were great and all were different. None was conformist. And yet, as we see in this book, every great violinist embodies in his playing the influence of his predecessors; this shared inheritance, added to and subtly transformed by his own unique stamp, becomes in turn a legacy to future generations.

v

The gipsy, the jazzman, and the Hochschule professor are all branches of the fiddler's family tree; Margaret Campbell's remarkable work now shows us the fascinating pattern of its growth.

Contents

		Page
	List of Illustrations	x
	Author's Acknowledgements	xiii
	Publisher's Acknowledgements	xv
	Author's Preface	xvii
	Prologue: Tools of the Trade	xxiii
1	Beginnings	1
2	The Archangel and the Red Priest	4
	Arcangelo Corelli; Antonio Vivaldi	
3	Master of the Nations	12
	Giuseppe Tartini	
4	Viotti and the French Trio	18
	Giovanni Battista Viotti; Pierre Baillot de Sales; Pierre Rode; Rodolphe Kreutzer	
5	'Nightingale of Violinists'	28
	Louis Spohr	
6	The Catalyst	36
	Niccolò Paganini	
7	Disciples of Paganini	45
	Camille Sivori; Heinrich Wilhelm Ernst; Antonio Bazzini; Ole Bull	
8	Age of Transition	53
	Joseph Böhm; Ferdinand David; Charles Auguste de Bériot	
9	The Hot-Bed of Liège	60
	Lambert Joseph Massart; Martin Marsick; César Thomson	
10	'He holds you in a magic circle'	64
	Henri Vieuxtemps	

11 The Slavonic Wizard   69
    Henri Wieniawski
12 Servant of Art   74
    Joseph Joachim
13 Lady of the Bow   84
    Wilma Norman-Neruda
14 Incomparable Charmer   88
    Pablo Sarasate
15 The Great Teachers   94
    August Wilhelmj; Leopold Auer; Otakar Ševčik; Jeno Hubay;
    Carl Flesch
16 'As the birds sing'   108
    Eugène Ysaÿe
17 Symbol of an Epoch   117
    Fritz Kreisler
18 The French Phenomenon   128
    Jacques Thibaud
19 To Dance in Chains   132
    Georges Enesco; Jan Kubelik
20 The Unbridled Individualist   139
    Bronislav Huberman
21 'Our Own Albert'   144
    Albert Sammons
22 The Russian Vanguard   150
    Efrem Zimbalist; Mischa Elman
23 The Scholarly Virtuoso   159
    Josef Szigeti
24 'King of Violinists'   167
    Jascha Heifetz
25 Child of the Revolution   176
    Nathan Milstein
26 The *Bel Canto* Virtuoso   182
    Alfredo Campoli
27 The Entertainers   187
    Albert Sandler; Tom Jenkins; Max Jaffa; Reginald Leopold;
    John Georgiadis
28 The Violin 'Hot'   197
    George Morrison; Eddie South; Stuff Smith; Joe Venuti;
    Stephane Grappelli
29 More Ladies of the Bow   206
    Marie Hall; Maud Powell; Erica Morini; Gioconda de Vito

30 The Enkindling Spirit   213
    David Oistrakh
31 A Man for all Music   223
    Yehudi Menuhin
32 The Born Virtuoso   233
    Ruggiero Ricci
33 Aim high — aim at beauty   239
    Ginette Neveu; Ida Haendel
34 The Elder Statesman   249
    Isaac Stern
35 The Musician's Musician   255
    Arthur Grumiaux
36 The Diplomat and 'The Polish Boy'   262
    Henryk Szeryng; Josef Hassid
37 Great Teachers of America   269
    Louis Persinger; Josef Gingold; Ivan Galamian
38 The 'Galamian Trio'   276
    Itzhak Perlman; Pinchas Zukerman; Kyung-Wha Chung
39 The English Phenomenon   288
    Ralph Holmes
40 Great Quartet Leaders   294
41 The Way Ahead   306

    Notes   313
    Bibliography   329
    Discography   333
    Index   354

Illustrations

Pupil-teacher links from Corelli
The modern violin
Arcangelo Corelli: portrait by Hugh Howard
    Royal College of Music
Antonio Vivaldi: engraving by F.M. La Cave, 1724
Giuseppe Tartini *Mansell Collection*
Giovanni Battista Viotti: engraving by Fremy after
    Vigée Le Brun *RCM*
Pierre Baillot de Sales
Rodolphe Kreutzer *Mary Evans Picture Library*
Louis Spohr: lithograph by Stott *RCM*
Niccolò Paganini:
    daguerrotype, 1840 *BBC Hulton Picture Library*
    drawing by Ingres *MC*
    painting after Isola *MC*
Heinrich Wilhelm Ernst: painting formerly in the possession
    of W.E. Hill & Sons
Ole Bull *RCM*
Joseph Böhm *Archiv für Kunst und Geschichte, Berlin*
Ferdinand David: lithograph by Prinzhofer, 1845 *RCM*
Charles Auguste de Bériot: lithograph by Baugniet, 1838 *RCM*
Martin Marsick
Henri Vieuxtemps: lithograph by Baugniet, 1845 *MC*
Henri Wieniawski: lithograph by Pressow after Mora *AKG*
Wilma Norman-Neruda (Lady Hallé) *RCM*
Joseph Joachim:
    in 1868 *BBCHP*
    the Joachim Quartet *MC*

Pablo Sarasate *BBCHP*
August Wilhelmj: wood engraving after drawing by Koegler,
  1878 *AKG*
Leopold Auer *AKG*
Otakar Ševčik *Juliette Alvin*
Jeno Hubay *RCM*
Carl Flesch *Carl Flesch Jr*
Eugène Ysaÿe *MC*
Jan Kubelik *RCM*
Fritz Kreisler, Georges Enesco and Jacques Thibaud
  Helen Dowling
Bronislav Huberman *BBCHP*
Albert Sammons Mrs M.C. Boswell-Cumming
Efrem Zimbalist *BBCHP*
Mischa Elman *MC*
Joseph Szigeti *RCM*
Jascha Heifetz *MC*
Nathan Milstein *Clive Barda*
Alfredo Campoli *Alfredo Campoli*
Albert Sandler
Reginald Leopold *Ken Thomas*
Stuff Smith
Joe Venuti *Culver Pictures/Decca Record Company Limited*
Stephane Grappelli *Jean-Pierre Leloir*
Maud Powell
Erica Morini *Erica Morini*
Gioconda de Vito *Gioconda de Vito*
David Oistrakh
Yehudi Menuhin *Klaus Hennch, Zurich*
Ginette Neveu *BBCHP*
Ida Haendel *Clive Barda*
Ruggiero Ricci *photo Ken Saunders; copyright The Guardian*
Isaac Stern
Arthur Grumiaux *Arthur Grumiaux*
Henryk Szeryng *Henryk Szeryng*
Josef Hassid *Paul Fishman*
Louis Persinger with his pupil Yehudi Menuhin
  Yehudi Menuhin
Josef Gingold *Josef Gingold*
Ivan Galamian: painting by Wayman Adams, 1958
  Ivan Galamian

Itzhak Perlman *Clive Barda*
Pinchas Zukerman *Clive Barda*
Eugene Fodor *Clive Barda*
Ralph Holmes *Jeremy Grayson*
Kyung-Wha Chung *Clive Barda*
The Amadeus Quartet *Decca Record Company Limited*
The Guarneri Quartet *RCA Records*
Albert Markov *Maxim Gershunoff, Inc.*
Vladimir Spivakov *photo Reg Wilson; copyright EMI Limited*
Mayumi Fujikawa *Sophie Baker*

RCM   *Royal College of Music*
MC   *Mansell Collection*
AKG   *Archiv für Kunst und Geschichte, Berlin*
BBCHP   *BBC Hulton Picture Library*

Author's Acknowledgements

My first acknowledgement must be given to Mr Harold C. Schonberg, although I have never met him. His witty and informative *Great Pianists* and *Great Conductors* have been a constant source of enjoyment to which I turn again and again. I could not compete with either his experience or his knowledge — this book is my own — but his writing has inspired me, and for that I am most grateful.

I should like to express my gratitude to all the violinists and other musicians who assisted me by giving me interviews: many personal touches would have been impossible without their cooperation. In this respect I should like to make special mention of Professor Josef Gingold, who, despite forty hours weekly teaching at Indiana University, found the time to make and send me a most evocative cassette describing his earliest meeting with Ysaÿe; and Helen Dowling for her vivid reminiscences of Enesco.

Jennifer Wilkins has assisted me in French translations and Jeanne Huckstepp and Sylvia Rotter have worked tirelessly as honorary research assistants: without their help this book would certainly not have appeared so soon. In addition, Sylvia Rotter has not only translated from the German but it is to her that I am indebted for the meticulous typing of the final manuscript.

My thanks also go to Dr Baird and her staff at the Music Library at the University of London, to Mr Philip Robinson at the County Music Library, Welwyn Garden City, the staff of the British Library at Colindale and at the Public Library, Hemel Hempstead, the Society for Cultural Relations with the USSR, and Old Town Records, Hemel Hempstead. Erich Gruenberg, Emanuel Hurwitz and Nicholas Roth have given me valuable advice on matters of technique and I have benefited from Patricia Naismith's expert knowledge and experience on the construction and development of the violin itself. Edmund Kurtz and Ian White have remained a constant source of inspiration throughout the writing and John Bishop has painstakingly read every word of the typescript: many of his suggestions have been advantageously incorporated into the text.

In addition I would like to acknowledge the help I have received from the following during my researches: Dr Gerald Abraham, Miss Juliette Alvin, Mr Toby Appel, Mr Philip Bate, Mr Hugh Bean, Mr Charles Beare, Professor Karl Beckson, Miss Suzanne Bloch, Sir Adrian Boult, Mr Norbert Brainin, Mr Frank A. Clarkson, Professor Robert Donington, Mr Paul Fishman, Professor Ivan Galamian, Mr Brian Hedley, Mr and Mrs V. Hochhauser, Mr Edgar Hunt, Mr Alexander Knapp, Sir Robert Mayer, Mr Yehudi Menuhin, Professor Jean Mongredien, Madame Bernadette Morand, Miss Ursula Müller, Miss Jessica Nasmyth, Miss Mavis Oswald, Mr and Mrs Sergio Peresson, Mr Barrie Perrins, Prem, Dr Stanley Sadie, Mr Lionel Salter, Mr Joseph Saxby, Mr Peter Schidlof, Mr Istvan Somos, Miss Hope Stoddard, Mr John Thomson, M. Hervé Thys, Professor Alan Tyson, Professor Chappell White, M. Antoine Ysaÿe.

My husband has been a continual source of help and encouragement throughout the growth of this project, and his patience and understanding have gone a long way towards making it a reality.

Margaret Campbell
Piccotts End, 1980

Publisher's Acknowledgements

Acknowledgement is made to publishers and copyright-holders for their kind permission to quote from the following:

Leopold Auer, *Violin Playing As I Teach It*, Duckworth & Co. Ltd, 1960.

Dr Herbert R. Axelrod, *Heifetz*, Paganiniana Publications, 1976 (by permission of Herbert R. Axelrod).

Hector Berlioz, *The Memoirs of Berlioz*, translated and edited by David Cairns (translation and original material copyright © David Cairns 1969), Alfred A. Knopf, Inc., 1969.

Sir Adrian Boult, *My Own Trumpet*, Hamish Hamilton Ltd, 1973.

Donald Brook, *Violinists of Today*, Barrie & Rockliff Ltd, 1948.

Carl Flesch, *The Art of Violin Playing*, Carl Fischer, 1924 (by permission of Carl F. Flesch).

Carl Flesch, *Memoirs of Carl Flesch*, translated by Hans Keller, Bois de Boulogne: W. Reeve/Rockliff, 1957 (by permission of Mrs Joan H. Hartfield and Carl F. Flesch).

Ivan Galamian, *Principles of Violin Playing and Teaching*, Prentice-Hall, Inc. and Faber & Faber Ltd, 1962.

Grove's *Dictionary of Music and Musicians*, edited by Eric Blom, 5th edition, Macmillan Publishers Ltd, London and St Martin's Press Inc., New York, 1954: articles by C.R. Halski, D. Heron-Allen, P. Donostia and Eric Blom.

Ida Haendel, *Woman With Violin*, Victor Gollancz Ltd, 1970.

Eduard Hanslick, *Vienna's Golden Years of Music: 1850–1900*, translated by Henry Pleasants III (Copyright © 1950 by Henry Pleasants III), Simon & Schuster, a Divison of Gulf & Western Corporation.

Louis Lochner, *Fritz Kreisler,* Macmillan Publishing Co., Inc., New York, 1951.

Yehudi Menuhin, *Unfinished Journey* (copyright © 1977 by Yehudi Menuhin and Patrick Seale and Associates Limited), Macdonald & Jane's and Alfred A. Knopf, Inc., 1977.

Roger North on Music, edited by John Wilson, Novello & Co. Ltd, 1959.

Marc Pincherle, *Vivaldi, Genius of the Baroque,* Victor Gollancz Ltd and W.W. Norton & Company, Inc., 1958.

M.J. Ronze-Neveu, *Ginette Neveu,* Barrie & Rockliff Ltd, 1957.

Joseph Szigeti, *With Strings Attached: Reminiscences and Reflections,* 2nd edition, revised and enlarged (© copyright 1947, 1967 by Alfred A. Knopf, Inc.), Alfred A. Knopf, Inc., 1967.

Antoine Ysaÿe, *Eugène Ysaÿe,* Editions Ysaÿe, 1974 (by permission of Jacques Ysaÿe).

Penguin Books Ltd for permission to reproduce on page xxviii figs 23 and 25 (pp 104 and 109) from Anthony Baines: Ed *Musical Instruments Through the Ages* (Revised edition 1969). Copyright © Penguin Books 1961, 1966, 1969.

Author's Preface

This is a book about violin players — it is not a history of violin playing. In tracing the careers of the great violinists from the inebriate Thomas Baltzar, who 'drank more than was ordinary' at the court of Charles II, to the enchanting Kyung-Wha Chung and other players of today, I have traced links that extend through three centuries in master-pupil relationships: this is the skeleton upon which the flesh and blood of my book grew.

It has been interesting to draw unbroken lines from Corelli and Vivaldi through to Viotti, who brought the classical Italian style of playing to Paris and became the pivot from which all modern schools evolved. The subsequent French, Belgian, Czech, Viennese and Russian schools each had their roots in Viotti. Artists as widely differing in style as Heifetz, Kubelik, Kreisler, Sarasate, Huberman, Ysaÿe and Menuhin have been reared in many varieties of soil, but all share the same parent plant.

The word 'school', which I use a great deal in this book, can have a variety of meanings and some definition might be helpful. I use the term to refer to the principles or style of playing as laid down by the founders and disciples of a particular method. Auer's school, for example, was founded at the Conservatoire in St Petersburg before the Revolution. In 1917 he fled the country and brought his school to Western Europe and later to America. When his pupils imparted the Auer principles to their students, they were perpetuating a 'school', whether it was in a studio in New York or a village in Belgium. Sascha Lasserson immortalized Auer's principles in a modest terraced house in North Kensington.

I also use the word 'classic' or 'classical' fairly frequently in the pages that follow, and feel that some explanation of my use of the term is in order here. When referring to the period, I say 'Classical'; when to the traditional Italian method of violin playing stemming from Corelli, 'classical'; when to the indisputably greatest works, 'the classics', 'the classic repertoire'.

The story that this book tells is how the solo performer progressed from court employee to concert hall virtuoso, from downtrodden private servant to public idol. Through examining personalities and individual styles of playing, one becomes aware of the many changes in style, fashion, public taste and in the instrument itself, that have taken place during the centuries this book covers. I have endeavoured to show how these changes have influenced violinists. At the same time I have tried to give some indication of what each was like as a human being. Many diverse characteristics have emerged, but there is a common denominator: in varying degrees, technical talent, musicality and personal magnetism are present in every great violinist, and it is this amalgam that holds the audience rapt. How it happens remains as inexplicable as the violin itself.

Margaret Campbell
Piccotts End, 1980

Teacher-pupil relationships from Corelli to the present day

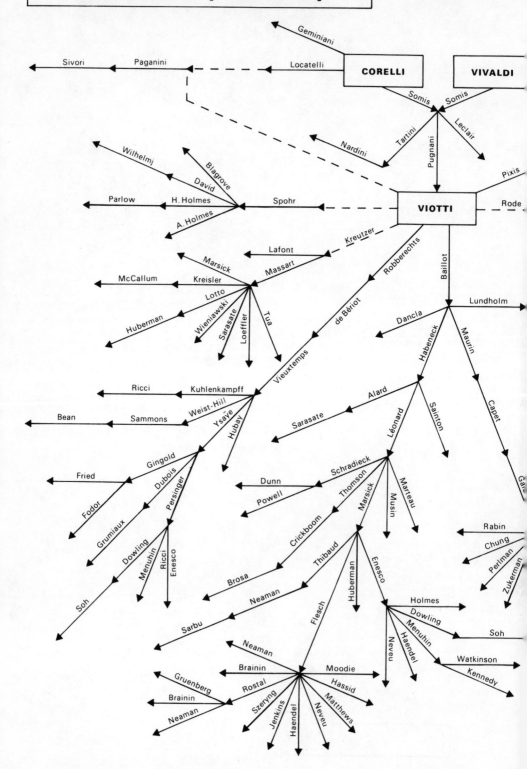

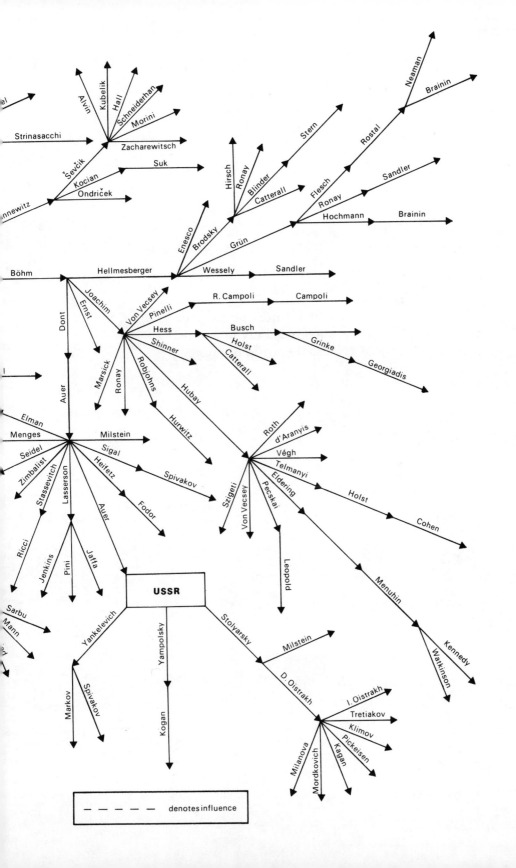

denotes influence

To the memory of my father
who guided my first steps
into the world of music.

Prologue: Tools of the Trade

The history of the violin has long been associated with myth and legend, and antiquity holds the secret of its origins. The earliest and most primitive examples of stringed instruments played with a bow come from the Middle East and Arabia, and the pear-shaped, three-stringed medieval rebec is probably the violin's most likely immediate ancestor. This instrument was brought to Italy in the ninth century by the invading Arabs. From it stemmed the miniature form that survived to the end of the eighteenth century as the 'kit' or dancing-master's fiddle, in France called *pochette*, a term derived from the habit of its being carried in a dancing-master's tailcoat pocket.

In medieval times we have the fidel — also known as *fidula*, *vythule* and a variety of related names. Three-stringed like the rebec, this instrument was played with a *fydelstyk*, a clear indication that it was bowed, not plucked. Since it was used by 'those who make a living from it through their labour', [1] by playing for dancing and at banquets and other social events, it was not considered respectable.

During the Renaissance a fairly short-lived but direct development of the medieval instrument was the *lira da braccio* ('arm-lyra'), a violin-shaped bowed instrument with seven strings, held low against the shoulder and supported by the upper arm. This distinguished it from the viols, which are held downwards between the knees.

About the middle of the sixteenth century a fourth string was added to the medieval three-stringed instrument. The tuning was in fifths — g below middle c, d, a, e. Thus the violin had come into being.

Gasparo da Salò (c.1540–1609; his real name was Bertolotti after his birthplace on Lake Garda), who settled in Brescia in northern Italy, is one of the earliest known craftsman in the records of violin making. The instruments made by these early Brescian makers — of which there were a number — were generally robust, often on the large side and sometimes roughly built, with an extremely powerful tone. But the violins made by Gasparo da Salò's most famous pupil, Giovanni Paolo Maggini (1581–c.1632), are uncommonly elegant; they also have a distinctive large tone. The Belgian virtuoso Charles de Bériot (1802–70) owned two Magginis. After the death of Maggini the Brescian school went into a decline.

The most important centre of violin making was in the neighbouring city of Cremona where it had flourished since the middle of the sixteenth century. The first of its celebrated makers was Andreas Amati who is believed to have worked there as early as 1550 and died about 1580. He was followed by his two sons, Antonio and Hieronymus, and they in turn by Nicola Amati (1596–1684), the best known in the family that became the most powerful dynasty in the history of the instrument. It was in Cremona that the violin reached its peak of perfection.

In the second half of the seventeenth century, schools of composition and violin-playing were emerging at centres all over Italy, the most important being at Bologna, Venice, Rome and Modena. This development was clearly linked with the growing popularity of the violin itself. Nicola Amati experimented for many years to achieve a combination of the sweetness of tone and brilliance demanded by the new and proliferating breed of musician, the 'soloist'.

Amati had many famous pupils, some of whom settled in Cremona. Others set up workshops and took on pupils in other parts of Italy. Francesco Ruggieri, Giovanni Rogeri and Paolo Grancino had all been apprenticed to 'Old Amati', as had Andreas Guarneri, founder of the other great Cremonese dynasty. And, finally, there was Nicola's most celebrated pupil — Antonio Stradivari (1644–1737).

Stradivari is believed to have been a woodcarver before he entered Amati's workshop. After his training was over he continued to live and work with his master, and his first violin is dated 1666. In 1667 he married and in 1680 left Amati to start up on his own in the Piazza San Domenico in Cremona, where the craftsmen lived side by side in the 'violin makers' quarters'. These old three-storey houses were built with a *seccadour*, or 'open room', on the top floor, exposed on all sides to the Italian sun. It was here that the women hung the linen and the fruit to dry alongside the maturing unvarnished violins and selected pieces of seasoning wood.

For some time Stradivari followed his master's design with only an occasional deviation, but after Amati's death in 1684 he began a series of experiments in his search for richer tone. By the turn of the century he appears to have arrived at his ideal, and the instruments he completed between 1700 and 1725 are acknowledged to be his best. Although they can convey *pianissimo* with absolute clarity, they can also make their powerful voices heard over a large orchestra. At this time orchestras were gradually expanding their forces beyond the scope of the baroque chamber groups, but the solo concerto as we know it today had not come into being. It was almost as if Stradivari could anticipate what would be asked of his instruments a hundred years hence.

Great players have always been attracted to Stradivari instruments. Mischa Elman played one dated 1721 which had once belonged to Joseph Joachim; David Oistrakh owned a Stradivari made in 1706; Milstein and Perlman both prefer instruments by this great maker.

Many of these 'Golden Age' Stradivaris have been named after their owners. The 'Viotti' of 1709, for example, was played by the Italian virtuoso until his death in 1824. The most famous of all named instruments is the 'Messiah', which owes its nickname to an unusual set of circumstances.

Early in the nineteenth century, a young Milanese carpenter-turned-collector, Tarisio, travelled all over Italy driving hard bargains for forgotten treasures, and he accumulated a valuable store of master violins, including one superb example from the estate of Count di Salabue, one of the most famous eighteenth-century collectors. The violin had been purchased in 1775 in perfect condition from Stradivari's son Paolo. Tarisio went to Paris, offering some of his less valuable pieces for sale, which were snapped up by one dealer after another. Finally he approached Vuillaume, the best-known Parisian dealer and maker of the nineteenth century, and found his most enthusiastic customer. He tantalized Vuillaume with descriptions of the Salabue Stradivari which 'he would bring next time'. Tarisio frequently reappeared, but never with the promised instrument. On one occasion Delphin Alard, Vuillaume's son-in-law, overheard the conversation and exclaimed: 'Really, Monsieur, your violin is like the Jews' Messiah! We always wait, but he never comes!'

When Tarisio died, Vuillaume rushed to Italy and bought the entire collection from the unsuspecting heirs for a fraction of what it was worth. When he finally owned the 'Messiah', he fell victim to the same disease and could never part with it. Ironically, the 'Messiah' has always retained its unattainable image. Over the years it changed hands several times, but was never actually used by a performer: even when it was owned by the French virtuoso Alard, he scarcely ever played it. Eventually it became the property of Hills of London, who gave it to the Ashmolean Museum at Oxford. The 'Messiah' can be seen today in a glass case, immaculate and still unplayed.

The most brilliant of the younger generation of the Cremona School was Joseph Guarneri. Born about 1683, he was known as del Gesù because he inscribed his instruments IHS (Jesus Hominum Salvator — Jesus, Saviour of Mankind).

If Stradivari is seen as the refined aristocrat of his profession, del Gesù could be regarded as the drunken ruffian, the wayward genius who worked in fits and starts, especially towards the end of his short life. Del Gesù's instruments reflect the variation which was the natural outcome of his unpredictable and individual genius. He is the one maker who is considered the equal of Stradivari, and his instruments are celebrated for their ravishing beauty of both form and tone. His varnish, amber in colour, with a translucent red overlay, gives off a luminous effect which has been compared with the 'dying glow of the evening sun on the waves of the sea'.[2]

Many great players today prefer Guarneri instruments to any others, on account of their pungent tone. Fritz Kreisler owned a del Gesù of 1733, and Heifetz played on the 'Ferdinand David' of 1742. Kyung-Wha Chung plays a Guarneri dated 1735. Paganini played a Guarneri. He named it the 'Cannon' on account of its exceedingly powerful tone, and in his will he bequeathed it to his native city of Genoa, where it rests in a glass case, as mute as the 'Messiah'.

The only German-speaking master violin maker, Jacob Stainer (1621–83), came from Absam in the Austrian Tyrol. He was a wood-carver by trade and a first-class violinist. Stainer's work shows some influence of Amati and it is possible that he studied in Cremona. Musicians of the time were enthralled with the 'Stainer' tone, and in seventeenth- and eighteenth-century Germany he was considered the greatest of all makers. His instruments — distinguished by their high arching — then fetched far higher prices than those of Stradivari. In 1800, Count Salabue placed Stainer's name at the top of a list that included all the most celebrated Cremona masters. J.S. Bach and Mozart both had Stainers. In his famous *Violinschule* (a tutor on violin technique), Mozart's father Leopold does not mention the existence of Italian violins.

During the Thirty Years War, Bohemian violin makers escaped across the border and settled in Saxony, where they set up a collective cottage industry. Similar methods were employed in Mittenwald, a small town in the Bavarian Alps, and made famous by the work of Matthias Klotz (1653–1743), who worked in Italy as a young man.

Nicolas Lupot (1758–1824) of Mirecourt was the first master craftsman in French violin making. He was followed by Jean-Baptiste Vuillaume (1798–1875), of the same town, who later set up in Paris and became the most famous, both as maker and dealer. Copying was Vuillaume's greatest strength and he successfully imitated the work of the greatest masters. When repairing the Guarneri 'Cannon' for Paganini, Vuillaume made a copy so perfect that at first sight it deceived its owner. Paganini was so impressed that he offered a high price for it, but the astute Vuillaume presented the instrument as a gift on receiving Paganini's assurance that he would play on it at a public concert.

The phenomenal advances in violin making technique in the seventeenth century were not reflected in the development of the bow. The first performers on the violin used the bows already in use for viols, the principles of which had not changed since medieval times. A convex wooden stick strung with horsehair at a fixed, slack tension, slightly modified it came to be called the 'Corelli' bow, after Arcangelo Corelli (1653–1713), the Italian virtuoso-composer. Eminently suited to the baroque performing style, the old bow could produce beautifully clear, short unaccented strokes. However, with the development of the Classical symphony and the solo concerto, new musical demands were made upon both composers and violinists. The emphasis on *cantabile*, or 'singing tone', especially in a long phrase, called for a longer bow and a wider spread of hair. The new accented *martelé*, or 'hammer-stroke', needed a greater tension than that of the old bow, staccato was difficult to achieve with the less perfectly balanced stick.

Tartini carried out intensive study of the bow resulting in certain modifications. But the solution to the problems just mentioned was provided by the Parisian Tourte family, culminating in the work of François Tourte (1747–1835). His standards for curvature of the stick and tapering of the head towards a fine point, so as to attain the correct balance together with the most desirable length, were established about 1780 and have been accepted as perfect right up to the present day. He justly earned the title 'Stradivari of the Bow'. Tourte never stamped his bows with his name, but to the connoisseur they are clearly recognizable by their finely tapering heads. They were frequently embellished with beautiful tortoiseshell nuts mounted in gold.

It is entirely logical that the bow should have been developed in France and not in Italy. The latter country brought the violin and

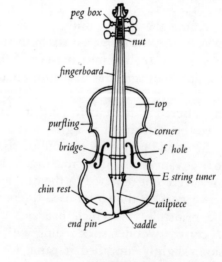

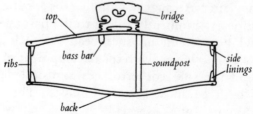

The modern violin

its baroque performing technique to a peak of perfection. But around the time of the deaths of Bach (1750) and Handel (1759), the baroque style of playing declined. When Viotti went to Paris in 1782, he took with him a fusion of the past and future virtuoso styles. He passed on his ideas to pupils who became the leaders of the new French school of violin playing which was to dominate Europe for most of the nineteenth century.

I

Beginnings

Paganini is the name that naturally springs to mind as the archetypal virtuoso of the violin. But mountain peaks do not fall from the sky. Although they may not have reached such dazzling heights, there were many accomplished performers a century and more before Paganini was born. The explorations of these early violinists, who were also of necessity composers, laid the foundations on which all techniques of future generations were based.

The first-known 'virtuoso' seems to have been the Italian Carlo Farina, born in the latter half of the sixteenth century. His reputation for performing tricks on the violin, from the mewing of cats to the imitation of fife and drum, earned him the contempt of serious musicians. Nevertheless it is of interest that even at this early date he employed advanced techniques such as double-stopping and pizzicato.

The diarist John Evelyn, in an entry of 4 March 1656, tells us that Thomas Baltzar (1630–63), a native of Lübeck in Germany, at one time employed at the Court of that great patron of music, Queen Christina of Sweden, was 'incomparable': his 'wonderful dexterity was admirable . . . there was nothing, however cross and perplexed, brought to him by other artists, which he did not play off at sight with ravishing sweetness and improvements to the astonishment of our best masters.' Baltzar's success earned him the coveted appointment of Leader of the 'Twenty-four Violins of the King' under Charles II. But his popularity encouraged him to 'drink more than ordinary',[1] the consequence of which brought him to an early though distinguished grave. He was buried in Westminster Abbey.

During his exile at the Court of Louis XIV, Charles had acquired a taste for everything French. At his restoration in 1660 he formed his 'Twenty-four Violins', in an attempt to emulate Louis XIV's 'grande bande'. His less reverent subjects called them his 'four and twenty fiddlers'.

John Banister (1630–79), Baltzar's successor as leader of the King's Band, was instructed, in the manner of Louis' Italian-born director of music, Jean-Baptiste Lully, to 'make choyce of twelve drawn from our four and twenty violins to be a select band to wayte on us whensoever there should be occasion for musick'. He was given 'full power to instruct and direct them for better performance of service, without being mixed with the other violins unless the King orders the twenty-four'. Banister is mentioned favourably in Pepys' Diary, both as performer and composer, but he fell from grace when it was discovered that he had misappropriated funds entrusted to him for paying the musicians' wages. It was John Banister who gave the first public concerts in London at his house in White Friars off Fleet Street, on the site where the Guildhall School of Music and Drama stood until its recent removal to the Barbican.

The aristocratic patrons of music in the seventeenth century and the first half of the eighteenth century also often employed their own private bands. The leader of the group could be a violinist or a keyboard player, and generally he had to fulfil some additional function, such as steward, secretary, or even valet. At worst, musicians were regarded as servants and at best as tradesmen who supplied a commodity: namely an endless output of new compositions to divert their patrons. There were special occasions, both sacred and secular, but mostly the music was provided as background for supper or card-playing: Wagner called it 'the clatter of princely plates'. More than one distinguished musician was reprimanded by his patron for allowing the music to drown the card-calling.

By the late seventeenth century there were in Germany a number of violinist-composers seriously exploring the virtuoso potentialities of their home-produced instruments. The most important of these was Heinrich Franz von Biber (1644–1704), from Wartenberg in Bohemia, a country with a continuing association with the violin right up to the present day. Biber was Konzertmeister at the Court of the Prince Archbishop of Salzburg. Burney, the eighteenth-century musician-historian, wrote: 'Of all the violin players of the last century, Biber seems to have been the best, and his solos are the most difficult and the most fanciful of any Music I have seen of the same period.'[2] Biber's powers of execution must have been extraordinary and his knowledge of the violin considerable. He made extensive use of *scordatura* (mis-tuning) to obtain special effects — strings tuned in thirds and fourths instead of the usual fifths, which made certain passages easier to play and facilitated the execution of double-stopping. The different tension on the strings also brought about a change in tone colour which Biber developed to an advanced degree. In his set of 'Rosary' sonatas, for example, depicting fifteen episodes in the life of Christ, Biber employs a different tuning for each sonata. There is a fine recording of these sonatas by Eduard Melkus playing a baroque violin in original state.

Among others who used *scordatura* was Johann Jakob Walther (1650–1717), first violinist and chamber musician at the Saxon Court. He was renowned for his feats of virtuosity, one of which was said to be that of playing a sustained melody with the bow whilst he accompanied himself pizzicato with the left hand. The German Nikolaus Bruhns (1665–97) went one better. His audience were said to have been astonished by his two-part improvisations on the violin whilst he played the bass with his feet on the organ pedals.

Nicolo Matteis came to England in 1672 and was first noticed by Evelyn, who wrote in his diary for 19 November 1674:

> I heard that stupendous violinist, Signor Nicholao, whom I have never heard mortal man exceed on that instrument. He had a stroke so sweet·and made it speak like the voice of a man, and when he pleased, like a concert of several instruments ... he played such ravishing things as astonished us all.

Roger North, in his *Memoirs*, says that though many gifted amateurs had heard Matteis play solos, yet none would attempt

> to do the like, for none could command that fulness, grace and truth of which he was the master ... His staccatos, tremolos, divisions, and indeed his whole manner was surprising, and every stroke was a mouthfull.

Although poor when he came to England, Matteis amassed a fortune, apparently through his concerts and publication of his compositions. North tells us that he 'took a great house, and after the manner of his country lived luxuriously, which brought diseases upon him of which he died'.[3]

Arcangelo Corelli, the 'Father of Violin-playing'

Antonio Vivaldi, versatile genius of the Italian baroque

THE DEVIL'S SONATA.

Giuseppe Tartini, founder of the Paduan school, dreams of hearing the Devil playing the 'Devil's Trill' Sonata

2

The Archangel and the Red Priest

Arcangelo Corelli; Antonio Vivaldi

The first important influence on violin playing, to say nothing of his impact on early eighteenth-century music in general, was that of Arcangelo Corelli (1653–1713). A native of Fusignano who spent most of his working life in Rome, he received his earliest musical training under a priest in Faenza. At the age of thirteen he went to Bologna, one of the oldest and greatest centres of learning in Italy. There he had his first lessons on the violin from the two well-known teachers Benvenuti and Brugnoli.

Corelli enjoyed much eminent patronage, including the ex-Queen Christina of Sweden, but the most important for him was that of Cardinal Pietro Ottoboni, who employed him as Director of his Private Music and also became his personal friend. Corelli lived comfortably in his own apartments in the Cardinal's Palace, composing, teaching and conducting the Monday Concerts which were attended by the élite of Roman Society. Corelli was a hard-working, simple man who lived frugally. Handel tells us that Corelli's wardrobe was ostentatiously shabby and he could never be persuaded to take a carriage. 'His favourite pastime was to look at pictures which cost him nothing.'[1] Corelli, in fact, acquired a fine collection of paintings and became recognized as an authority on art.

Corelli was constantly asked to perform to people of high rank, but he was not above meeting his superiors on equal terms. Once, during a private concert at the Ottoboni Palace, some guests began talking: Corelli put down his violin and moved away to sit amongst the guests. When questioned he replied that he was afraid his playing might interrupt the conversation.

In the early eighteenth century it was difficult to find a violinist who did not lay claim to have studied with Corelli. Pietro Locatelli (1695–1764), was perhaps one of the most famous. Through his teaching and writing for his instrument he laid the foundation of violin playing, and his solos were seized upon immediately they appeared. Important enough in their own time, Corelli's compositions today remain a permanent influence in violin literature. He took the best ideas of his predecessors and synthesized them into a form which exploited the possibilities of the violin, both in ensemble and as solo instrument, in an entirely new way. It was Corelli who first extensively exploited the violin as a melodic, singing instrument. Before the middle of the seventeenth century, composers appear to have been more concerned with writing violin music that contained scale passages, figurations and special effects. Corelli provided variety by the use of small ensembles in a dialogue with the larger body of strings, as exemplified in his twelve Concerti Grossi Op. 6. Corelli is best known for his twenty-three variations on the popular theme 'La Folia di Spagna'.

The main objective in Corelli's violin playing was the production of a beautiful tone, variety and elegance in bowing, full expression in slow movements and a well developed left-hand technique. He was particularly noted for his insistence upon not allowing his pupils to use the fingers of the left hand — to stop the strings — before they could master the slow sweep of the bow across the open strings. This practice is endorsed by all the best teachers of the present day. Furthermore, Corelli's sonatas contain some of the best bowing exercises to be found anywhere, even up to the present time.

As a performer, Corelli was said to be a serious and dignified artist, but occasionally, when carried away with the music, 'his countenance was distorted, his eyes red as fire, and his eyeballs rolled as if he were in agony'.[2] His sense of humour is manifest in an encounter with the German virtuoso Struñgk (1640–85), whose brilliant reputation was somewhat dimmed by his notorious bragging. Strungk is said to have performed well-nigh impossible feats of *scordatura* without difficulty and then awaited the master's acclamation. Instead, Corelli smiled and said quietly: 'I am called Arcangelo, but you one might justly call Archidiavolo.'[3]

When Corelli died he left a considerable fortune and a fine

collection of master violins. His paintings went to Ottoboni, who showed his gratitude by placing Corelli's remains in the Pantheon near the tomb of Raphael.

If Corelli laid the solid foundations of violin playing, it was Antonio Vivaldi (1678–1741) who decorated them with sparkling ideas and an inventiveness that, through his pupils and imitators, provided the eighteenth-century virtuosos with their stock-in-trade.

The son of a violinist in the orchestra at St Mark's Cathedral in Venice, Vivaldi was born into a city where music was ever present and enjoyed by all classes of society. At the age of ten the young Antonio was said to play well enough to assist his father with the music at St Mark's. He entered the priesthood at fifteen. On account of his bright red hair, he was nicknamed 'The Red Priest'. In line with prevailing custom, he combined his church duties and musical studies.

In 1703, Vivaldi was appointed violin master at the Ospedale della Pietà, where, apart from sporadic leaves of absence, he stayed for almost forty years. The Pietà was one of the four asylums in Venice established in the fourteenth century for the protection of orphaned or foundling girls. Apart from general education the girls were given a good musical training and had their own choir and orchestra. Concerts were given to raise funds for running costs, and during Vivaldi's time the Pietà was known throughout Europe for its high standards of performance, many of the girls becoming professional musicians.

Vivaldi wrote over forty operas and managed to get most of them produced in leading Italian cities. He acted as his own impresario, choosing singers, dancers and orchestral players. Unfortunately it was his interest in opera that ultimately led to his downfall. On his one absence from the Pietà, when employed by the Margrave Philipp of Hessen-Darmstadt in Mantua, Vivaldi met Anna Giraud, a singer who was first his pupil and later the most popular *prima donna* of his operas. When Anna's sister, Paolina, became Vivaldi's nurse, the relationship grew closer and finally all three set up house together. Vivaldi's association with the Giraud sisters gave rise to much gossip and eventually the Church took a stand. Because of his association with Anna who, was known as 'mistress of the Red Priest', Vivaldi was forbidden by the Papal Nuncio to put on his operas in Ferrara. The ban gained momentum and his popularity in Venice declined. Other composers were commissioned to write for the Ospedale, and in 1740 Vivaldi could no longer stand the neglect and left the city for Vienna. He died there alone and unknown in a lodging house and was buried in a pauper's grave. So passed the great Vivaldi, who once boasted: 'I have the honour to be in correspondence with nine high princes and my letters travel throughout all Europe.'[4]

Vivaldi's fame and influence as a virtuoso-violinist and composer during his lifetime had been immense, but the dimming of his reputation in his final years was followed by a neglect of almost a century. His name seldom appeared in the eighteenth-century violin tutors and, although there were sporadic efforts in Germany to play and publish his music, the great masters of the French school of violin playing at the turn of the century totally ignored him. Nevertheless, his ideas survived in the works of his pupils. By the same token he vicariously supplied eighteenth-century performers with their basic technique.

Although we do not have precise accounts from those who studied with Vivaldi, many contemporary performers and players show evidence of his influence. 'La Chiaretta', one of his girls at the Pietà, is said by Marc Pincherle to have been among the best violinists in all Italy. A pupil of his later years was the violin virtuoso Santa Tasca, who was employed by the Emperor Francis I of the Holy Roman Empire. German, Czech and French violinists came to Venice to pay him homage. It is extremely unlikely that they left without receiving some instruction from the master.

Vivaldi's most important pupil was the German Georg Johann Pisendel (1687–1755), already a professional violinist with an established reputation when he was sent by his employer, the Elector of Saxony, to have lessons with the Venetian. Pincherle considers that his 'work most openly bears the impress of Vivaldi's teaching', and that there was a 'pre-established harmony between their personalities'.[5] Pisendel and Vivaldi became close friends and the composer dedicated many violin concertos — the most famous being the one in A major (RV 29) — to his pupil.

Vivaldi was a prolific composer whose ideas were so rapidly committed to paper that he said himself he could compose a concerto with all its parts faster than a copyist could write it out. Besides his forty operas he wrote almost four hundred violin concertos. Pincherle maintains that Vivaldi, almost by instinct, 'hits upon the runs that lie best under the fingers, the multiple stops on which the open strings supply the surest points of support, and the most sonorous registers'.[6]

His violin music involves wide leaps from one string to another: many examples demand a jump from the lowest string (G) to the highest (E), an operation calling for deft bowing. His *cantabile* passages show his innate understanding of his violinistic craft and he uses many effects that are close to vocal techniques, such as contrasting the *legato* passages of the soloist with the orchestra playing pizzicato.

Few accounts of Vivaldi's performances as a violinist survive but it is clear from the music itself, and the post he held, that he must have been able to play his own compositions. He was always spoken of as a virtuoso. The most important piece of evidence of Vivaldi's part in the development of violin technique comes from a German pupil, von Uffenbach. In his Journal of 1715 he writes of a visit to the opera:

> Towards the end Vivaldi played a solo accompaniment admirably, adding at the end a free fantasy which quite frightened me, for it is scarcely possible that anyone ever played or will play this way, for he placed his fingers but a hair's breadth from the bridge, so that there was barely room for the bow, doing this on all four strings with imitations at incredible speed.

Von Uffenbach was a violinist himself and other accounts of musical matters in his Journal are regarded as trustworthy. Even if a 'hair's breadth' was an exaggeration, it is sufficient to prove Vivaldi's virtuosity and that he employed fingering positions quite unfamiliar to the informed observer. What is also interesting is that, if this account is correct, Vivaldi may have played in much higher positions than would have been possible on the short fingerboard of the time: the only logical explanation must be that he had a longer fingerboard fitted for his own personal use.

Johann Joachim Quantz (1697–1773), flautist and musician to the Court of Frederick the Great, attributes the invention of the cadenza to Vivaldi. In the Dresden Library is a Vivaldi MS where an original cadenza thirty-nine bars long is inserted just before the orchestra enters for the finale. It begins with rapid scale passages, frequently changes key and then soars into the high positions, and looks forward to the cadenzas of Mozart, Beethoven and later.

A man of great human contrasts, Vivaldi was on the one hand

very devout, described as never having the rosary out of his hand unless it was to take up his pen, and on the other, hot-tempered, easily irritated and as quick to regain tranquillity. His music magnificently reflects these contrasts.

In England the art of violin playing in the early eighteenth century was still primitive compared with the rest of Europe. It was due to the teaching of Italians such as Francesco Geminiani (1687–1762) that this situation greatly improved. Geminiani was a pupil of Corelli in Rome and started his career as leader of the orchestra in Naples. But according to the eighteenth-century writer Busby, his tempo was said to be so erratic that he 'disordered their motions, embarrassed their execution and, in a word, threw the whole band into confusion'.[7] The penalty for this crime was to be demoted to the viola section. It was a common saying at the time that no good music was written for the viola because there were no good viola players, and vice versa. Although Geminiani's talents may not have been suited to the orchestral ranks, he made a fine reputation for himself as a soloist and was said to use techniques which employed double-stopping and the shift (quick moving with the left hand from one position to another), together with a brilliant style that far exceeded anything previously heard. Sonya Mono-soff, a specialist in baroque performing styles, has made an excellent recording of Geminiani sonatas playing on a baroque violin in original state.

But Geminiani's greatest contribution to violin playing was his book *The Art of Playing the Violin*, published in 1740. It contains the essence of Corelli's teaching and was one of the best instruction books of the time. Geminiani was also the first to advocate holding the violin as it is held today, with the chin to the left of the tailpiece. At this time the violin was held against the neck, with the chin resting upon the right side of the tailpiece but with little support from the chin itself: the chin-rest had not been invented. The main support came from the left hand holding the rather thick neck (modifications to the instrument came later). The hand was held much lower than it is today, so that the scroll was lower than the tailpiece. For simple dance accompanying these holds were adequate, but in more sophisticated music, requiring shifts up and down the fingerboard, bracing of the neck and bending of the head were unavoidable. Geminiani's change allowed the player to keep his head straight and permitted more freedom in shifting.

Leopold Mozart, in his tutor published in 1756, adhered to the established practice of the chin resting on the right of the tailpiece.

A small but significant link between the 'classical' and 'modern' schools of violin playing is provided by the Italian Giovanni Battista Somis (1676–1763). A pupil of both Corelli and Vivaldi, he combined the teaching of the two great masters to form a style of his own which marked a considerable step forward in violin technique. Students throughout Europe were attracted to the school he established in Turin. Among his most famous pupils were Jean Marie Leclair (1697–1764), through whom Somis exerted a considerable influence on French violin playing, and Gaetano Pugnani (1731–98). A contemporary writer, Hubert le Blanc, says that Somis 'had the most beautiful stroke of the bow in Europe' and that he achieved a great victory on the violin: 'He can play a whole note in one bow [so] that it takes one's breath away when thinking of it.'[8]

3

Master of the Nations

Giuseppe Tartini

By the end of the seventeenth century the violin was capable of a brilliance of tone and range of expression that went hand-in-hand with its growing popularity. Consequently different styles of playing had begun to assert themselves. The fiddler who provided accompaniments for dancing could not be compared with the soloist whose playing was on a more sophisticated level. About the middle of the seventeenth century playing styles had become associated with national characteristics and the contrast between the Italian and the French styles became more apparent. Violin playing in other countries largely followed the lines of these two schools.

The virtuoso techniques of the Italian school were developed to suit the newest forms of composition, the sonata, the variation, and later, the solo concerto. The Italians also favoured the *cantabile* style of playing — a logical development in the land where musical sound had always been associated with the human voice.

The French perfected a highly sophisticated style of bowing which suited the clearly accented dance rhythms with which they were preoccupied. The Germans created an advanced virtuoso style of playing, modelled on Italian principles, which exploited the extended range of the violin, double-stopping, and *scordatura*. Their bowing techniques were correspondingly advanced.

This high degree of development is reflected in the music of J.S. Bach. As Kapellmeister of the court orchestra for the Prince Leopold of Anhalt-Köthen, he composed his violin sonatas, two violin concertos (in E major and A minor), and the Double Concerto in D minor. It was also at Köthen that he wrote his unaccompanied suites for solo violin which remain today among the most demanding music ever written for the instrument. There are no contemporary accounts of Bach's violin playing, but in a letter dated 1774 to the German musicologist Johann Forkel, C.P.E. Bach mentions his father's life-long interest in the violin:

> In his youth, and until the approach of old age, he played the violin cleanly and penetratingly, and thus kept the orchestra in better order than he could have done with the harpsichord. He understood to perfection the possibilities of all stringed instruments.[1]

By the beginning of the eighteenth century the violin was to be found in all classes of society and had finally lost its 'rogue and vagabond' image. Its new respectability was largely due to the increase in amateur playing.

It was Giuseppe Tartini (1692–1770) who formed the most significant link between the baroque and Classical periods, and his style contained elements of both. He may be seen as 'the most important figure in the violin concerto between Vivaldi and Viotti'.[2]

Tartini's family were rich Florentines who had settled in Istria on the Adriatic (now part of Yugoslavia), and much of their wealth found its way into the church, which gave the young Tartini his first musical instruction and lessons on the violin.

When Tartini reached the age of seventeen, his father was determined he should enter the priesthood. Tartini was equally convinced he would not. His preference was for law. Despite strong pressure from the Bishop of Istria, whose monastery had been promised a handsome donation if his persuasion was successful, Tartini won his point. In 1709 he entered the University at Padua as a law student, but it is doubtful if he was over-zealous in his legitimate studies: fencing, art and music all held greater claims on him. At this time he seriously considered opening a fencing school to subsidize his career as a violinist.

But in his final year, Tartini fell in love with the fifteen-year-old Elisabetta Premazone, a dependant relative of an eminent Paduan Cardinal. Their elopement and secret marriage caused family fireworks: Tartini's father stopped his allowance and the Cardinal issued a warrant for his arrest. Tartini fled from Padua and, disguised as a monk, wandered from city to city, finally reaching Assisi where he stayed for two years under the protection of the Franciscan Friars.

During this time he received instruction in theory and composition from Bohuslav Matej Cernohorsky, a distinguished Czech composer and teacher, who no doubt assisted him in his own early writing. In the Czechoslavakian monasteries the violin was employed both in string ensembles and as a solo instrument, and the music composed for it in this setting shows a high degree of technical development.

It was at this time also, through scientific experiments with the violin, that Tartini first became aware of what he called *terzi tuoni*, or 'third sound'. It is what we recognize today as the phenomenon of 'differential' notes, which have been investigated and detailed by acoustical experts such as Helmholtz. The differential note can clearly be heard as a 'third' sound which is not being played, when two notes on the violin are stopped in perfect intonation. On his own admission, Tartini's mathematical calculations contained errors and, although he published a Treatise on Harmony in 1754, he was never able to prove his theory. Nevertheless authorities are agreed that it was he who made the initial discovery. Tartini was also the first to experiment with a thicker gauge of violin string to obtain a richer tone; this was later taken into general use.

It was at Assisi that Tartini wrote the 'Devil's Trill' sonata. It is said that he had a dream in which he sold his soul to the devil: whereupon the devil took up his violin and played the most exquisite sonata imaginable. In the words of the eighteenth-century writer Lalande, to whom Tartini related his dream:

> I felt enraptured, transported, enchanted; my breath failed me ... I awoke ... I tried to reproduce the sounds I had heard. But in vain. The piece I then composed, 'The Devil's Sonata', although the best I ever wrote, how far was it below the one I heard in my dream.[3]

In exchange for his food and lodging Tartini provided a valuable source of revenue to the Friars, as his playing attracted large audiences to the concerts in the monastery chapel. He was, of necessity, hidden behind a curtain and spoken of as 'The Mystery Violinist of Assisi'. It was in 1715, on the annual Feast of St Francis, when pilgrims came from all over Italy to worship at the tomb, that a deacon accidentally moved the curtain and revealed the identity of the performer. Paduans in the congregation immediately recognized Tartini. The Cardinal was informed but he dropped his original charges and Tartini and Elisabetta were reunited.

Tartini's career as a violinist became established and his fame spread throughout Italy. Socially, he and his wife moved only in aristocratic circles. This state of affairs may well have continued but for an invitation extended to Tartini and the great Florentine violinist Veracini in 1716 to compete at Venice in honour of the visit of the Elector of Saxony. It was common practice in the eighteenth century to invite artists to outdo each other for the benefit of eminent guests. But Tartini was never to meet this challenge. By chance he happened to hear Veracini play in Cremona, was immediately convinced of the Florentine's superiority, and withdrew from the contest.

Shaken by this eclipse, Tartini once again caused a marital separation by removing himself to Ancona, where he vowed to stay until he had reached the perfection he desired. How long he resided there is uncertain, but the records show that he was appointed to the post of first violin at the Capella del Santo at Padua in 1721. He was described as an 'extraordinary' violinist and was to receive an annual stipend of 150 florins, a handsome sum at the time. He was also excused from the need to show proof of his excellence: a singularly high honour since each member of the choir and orchestra was annually subjected to a strict re-audition. The ultimate concession was that he should be allowed to appear elsewhere. He did not take advantage of this opportunity until 1723, when an irresistible invitation to play in Prague at the Coronation of Charles VI came from Count Kinsky, the Chancellor of Bohemia — a passionate devotee of music. Tartini's performance caused a furore in Prague, and he accepted an offer to stay on to lead Count Kinsky's private band. But he was fated never to enjoy prosperity for long. Three years later, when his brother became involved in financial difficulties, Tartini left Prague, in the belief that 'the skin is nearer than the purse'.[4]

In 1728, at the age of thirty-six, Tartini set up his 'School of the Nations' in Padua and saw it become one of the most respected of its time. It was renowned for its excellence of teaching and pupils came from all over Europe. As 'Master of the Nations', Tartini became even more famous than he had been as a performer.

Many great violinists studied at the 'Nations', including Gaetano Pugnani (1731–98), who was also a pupil of Somis, and the legendary Maddalena Lombardini, the young girl to whom Tartini wrote a letter (dated 1760) on the art of bowing which has passed into musical history as the sole and classic example of

Tartini's detailed instruction of his method.

Tartini stresses that at first practice should be confined to the 'use and power of the bow', in order to learn

> the true manner of holding, balancing and pressing the bow lightly, but steadily, upon the strings; in such a manner as that it shall seem to breathe the first tone it gives, which must proceed from the friction of the string, and not from percussion, as by a blow given with a hammer upon it. This depends on laying the bow lightly upon the strings, at the first contact, and on gently pressing it afterwards, which, if done gradually, can scarce have too much force given to it, because if the tone is begun with delicacy, there is little danger of rendering it afterwards either coarse or harsh.

Tartini also advocates that his pupil should master the art of the swell on an open string from *pianissimo* to *fortissimo* by exercising for an hour each day until perfection is attained. 'When you are a perfect mistress of this part of a good performer, a swell will be very easy to you; beginning with the most minute softness, increasing the tone to its loudest degree, and diminishing it to the same point of softness with which you began, and all this in the same stroke of the bow.'[5]

Tartini wrote some two hundred violin concertos and an equal number of sonatas; few of these are ever heard today, with the exception of the 'Devil's Trill' and 'Didone Abbandonata'. But the fifty variations on a theme by Corelli, 'The Art of Bowing', constitute one of the best exercises for the right arm in the repertoire. Tartini, far more than any of his predecessors or contemporaries, undertook an intensive study of the bow. He made the stick itself narrower and was the first to modify its outward curve. He also altered the shape of the head and discarded the fluting.

As a performer Tartini was considered to be one of the most accomplished virtuosos of the day, rivalled only by Veracini. Pierre Lahoussaye, the great French violinist and pupil of Tartini at Padua, wrote: 'Nothing could express my astonishment and admiration caused by the perfection and purity of his [Tartini's] tone, the charm of expression, the magic of his bow, the all-round perfection of his performance.'[6] Tartini hated virtuosity for its own sake. Most contemporary accounts remark upon the beauty of his *cantabile* passages, not only for their depth of expression, but for a certain reserve which would seem to point more to the style that was later to be echoed in the playing of Spohr and Joachim. Tartini possessed both the talent and the physical equipment for a virtuoso and yet he was singularly unambitious, a trait not conducive to the egotistic demands of a soloist at the top of his profession. He lacked respect for money. And fame, though readily accepted at the time, passed lightly over his shoulders. He rejected countless offers to play abroad. Sir Edward Walpole and Lord Middlesex both tried hard to tempt him to play in London — the latter, to the tune of 3,000 lire. And neither the Prince of Condé nor the Prince of Clermont could persuade him to appear in Paris.

Elisabetta Tartini receives little credit from any of Tartini's biographers. It seems that when they finally settled in Padua, she became possessive and would not let him out of her sight. Peevish and nervous, she seemed always to be suffering from some small, imaginary illness. She is clearly blamed for Tartini's refusal of so many lucrative offers to play abroad. Nevertheless, as is common in such cases, he was absolutely devoted to her to the end of his days.

4

Viotti and the French Trio

Giovanni Battista Viotti;
Pierre Baillot de Sales;
Pierre Rode; Rodolphe Kreutzer

'Viotti, it is true . . . astonishes the hearer; but he does something infinitely better — he awakens emotion, gives a soul to sound, and leads the passions captive', wrote a critic in the *Morning Chronicle* on 10 March 1794, after one of Viotti's London concerts.

A pivotal figure in violin playing, linking the Corelli tradition, through Locatelli, to the nineteenth-century French school which he established, Giovanni Battista Viotti (1753–1824) was 'the most influential violinist between Tartini and Paganini'.[1] His playing — and his compositions — had a brilliant and romantic element which belonged to the nineteenth century.

Viotti was born at Fontanetto da Po, the son of a blacksmith and amateur horn player. His first violin lessons were from a roving lute player, and as a boy he was fortunate in coming under the patronage of the Prince Alfonso dal Pozzo della Cisterna, who chose him as a student-companion to his son. Viotti lived with the family and the two boys became pupils of Pugnani, who had studied with Somis, thus forming a link with Corelli. In 1775, Viotti became a member of the orchestra of the royal chapel in Turin. Here 'for five years he occupied the last desk of the first violins, drawing one of the lowest salaries in the orchestra'.[2]

At the end of this period Pugnani took Viotti on a concert tour of Europe, introducing him as 'his pupil'. They first visited Switzerland, then Dresden and Berlin, and encouraged by their success extended their itinerary to include Warsaw and St Petersburg. In the latter city, Catherine the Great, notorious for her susceptibility to young men, showered gifts upon Viotti and tried to persuade him to join her court orchestra. But women played little or no part in Viotti's life, and he declined the Empress's offer by saying he did not care for the Russian climate.

From St Petersburg Viotti travelled to London. Here his playing was well received and compared favourably with that of Geminiani, then considered the finest violinist to have crossed the Channel. But it was at a concert in Paris in 1782 that Viotti achieved his greatest triumph. It immediately established him as a leading virtuoso and he enjoyed this success for almost two years, acclaimed by critics and public alike. During this time he set up house with his friend the composer Cherubini, and their soirées became the centre of Parisian musical life. Then he suddenly retired from the concert platform without explanation. The mystery of this defection at the height of his powers has remained unsolved.

A year later he entered the service of Marie Antoinette at Versailles and in 1788, under the patronage of the Count of Provence, produced a brilliant season of Italian opera at the Théâtre de Monsieur. But this venture, too, was short-lived. The Revolution of 1789 disrupted all Viotti's plans for future productions.

Employment in royal service did not curb Viotti's democratic ideas. Once, during a private concert at Versailles, when he was playing one of his own compositions, there was an interruption, followed by whispering among the guests. As murmurs of 'Make way for the Duke' heralded the late arrival of the Duke d'Artois, Viotti stopped playing, tucked his violin under his arm and left the salon. Moreover, unlike his venerated predecessor Corelli, when faced with a similar situation at the Ottoboni Palace, Viotti resolutely refused all entreaties to return.

On another occasion, in 1790, Viotti accepted an invitation to play in a charity concert which was arranged to take place on the fifth floor in the house of a friend. 'I will play', said Viotti, 'but only on one condition . . . that the audience shall come up here to us — we have long enough descended to them; but times are changed.'[3] When the aristocrats had climbed the stairs, they found that the only ornament on display was a bust of J.J. Rousseau, whose democratic ideas were so feared that his remains, together with those of Voltaire, were removed from the Panthéon and secretly disposed of when the Bourbon monarchy was restored some twenty-three years later. However, in 1792, on the eve of the arrest of the King and Queen, Viotti decided, democrat or not, that his views could be open to question. He fled without a sou to England.

In contrast to the turbulent events in France, Viotti's life in England was tranquil, and he earned a reasonable living. His success on the concert platform — especially at the Hanover Square Rooms — attracted an ever-widening circle of influential and cultured friends, and he took on a number of pupils, many of whom were from the upper echelons of society. The Duke of Cambridge was one of the most celebrated. It was through one of his young pupils, Walter Chinnery, that he became acquainted with the family who were to become his life-long friends. Chinnery was an employee of the Treasury, and his wife Caroline a gifted pianist. In 1794 Viotti took over the post of acting-manager of the Italian Opera at the King's Theatre (now Her Majesty's).

In 1798 the British government, unjustly suspecting his involvement in a revolutionary plot, ordered Viotti to leave the country. In exile he was given the use of the country house of a friend at Schoenfeld, near Hamburg, and spent the time composing and corresponding with his beloved Mrs Chinnery. It was here that he wrote the duets for two violins, Op. 5, which bear the inscription: 'This work is the fruit of leisure which misfortune procured for me. Some of the pieces were dictated by Pain, others by Hope.'

Viotti took on a few pupils, one of whom was the young Friedrich Wilhelm Pixis (1786–1842) of Mannheim, a brilliant young violinist who was himself to become a significant figure when the Prague Conservatoire opened in 1811. This institution has since played an important part in the history of violin playing and given to the world many who have influenced the development of their art; Antonin Bennewitz, Otokar Ševčik, Karel Ondřiček and Jaroslav Kocian are among the most prominent.

The Czechs have always possessed a natural instinct for music. Burney, when travelling in Bohemia in 1773, was amazed to find in simple village schools throughout the country, children of both sexes from six to eleven years old, 'reading, writing, playing on violins'[4] and other instruments. Pixis brought to Prague the traditions of the Mannheim school allied to Viotti's teaching. The Mannheim traditions stemmed from the group of virtuoso musicians who formed the court orchestras in the reign of the Duke Carl Theodor during the third quarter of the century. The founder and leader of this school of violinists and conductors was the Czech Johann Stamitz (1717–57). The main features of their style of playing have been described as 'perfect team-work, fiery and expressive execution, uniform bowing, exciting dynamic effects and accuracy in phrasing in orchestral performance'.[5] In 1772 Burney called them 'an army of generals'. Through Viotti Pixis would have learned that violin playing was not only concerned with technical brilliance but must also emphasize tonal beauty, power and expression.

With Napoleon firmly in power in France, it was seemingly safe in 1801 to allow Viotti to return to England. But he had temporarily lost interest in concert giving and, acting upon Mrs Chinnery's encouragement, reinforced by her financial support, he opened a shop in London as a wine merchant. Music was not a lucrative profession. Many of Viotti's Italian contemporaries had similar commercial interests. Geminiani bought and sold pictures; Clementi made a fortune out of making pianos. The parsimonious Clementi and his pupil John Field would wash their own shirts and socks when on tour in St Petersburg. At first Viotti probably made a living from his business for he declined at this time to take on any pupils. He even refused Ludwig Spohr, who had long held Viotti as his model. In his autobiography Spohr bitterly laments the fact that he was denied the chance to study with the master. Spohr always maintained that no better test existed for a fine player than the execution of Viotti sonatas or concertos. Spohr relates the tale of a friend who, by chance, entered Viotti's shop and was surprised to find the great man behind the counter. He reproached him for denying the public the pleasure of hearing him play. Viotti replied: 'My dear Sir, I have done so simply because I find that the English like Wine better than Music.'[6]

Unfortunately the wine shop never prospered sufficiently to keep Viotti out of financial difficulties, and he later made several attempts to re-establish himself in the musical world. In 1802 he visited Paris to present some of the works he had written at Schoenfeld. Viotti's pupil, the celebrated Pierre Baillot, wrote of this particular performance: 'Everything seemed to flow without effort, softly yet powerfully. With the greatest élan he climbed the heights of inspiration. His tone was magnificent, sweet, but metallic, as though the tender bow were handled by the arm of Hercules.'[7]

Later Viotti was appointed director of the Opéra in Paris at a high salary but, as in previous years, misfortune seemed to attend every undertaking and he returned to London in 1822. The previous year he had made his will, a pathetic document revealing the underlying sadness in a life that once held so much promise:

> If I die before I can pay off this debt [he owed Madame Chinnery 24,000 francs which she had lent him to finance the wine business] I pray that everything I have in the world may be sold off, realized, and sent to Madame Chinnery or her heirs . . . [8]

He died at the Chinnerys' house in Berkeley Street, Portman Square, in 1824.

Viotti seems to have been a man of extreme sensitivity and too vulnerable for the hazards of a public career. He was liked by his contemporaries and remained unspoiled by the decadence of the French court. According to a friend, 'No one ever attached so much value to the most simple gifts of nature . . . Everything struck his imagination; everything spoke to his soul and his heart overflowed with warm and affectionate feelings.'[9]

The critics were unanimous in their praise of Viotti's handling of the bow. The *Allgemeine Musikalische Zeitung* of 3 July 1811 described the principles of Viotti's school: 'A large, strong, full tone is the first; the combination of this with a powerful, penetrating, singing *legato* is the second; as the third, variety, charm, shadow and light must be brought into play through the greatest diversity of bowing.'

Viotti was one of the first violinists to use the Tourte bow, which had a lightness, firmness and elasticity that the older bows lacked. He would therefore have had a considerable advantage over his predecessors. According to Fétis, during his time in Paris from 1782 or thereabouts, Viotti gave advice and guidance to François Tourte in his efforts to perfect the bow.

Although Viotti abandoned his career so unaccountably at such an early age, his influence on tone production and expression has remained one of the most important of the eighteenth century. As a violinist, Viotti was not only regarded as the greatest player of his day in the classical Italian style, but the founder and originator of the modern school of violin playing.

As a composer he was prolific though not remarkable for his originality. He was one of the first violinist-composers to expand the violin concerto by adopting, as far as possible, the symphonic form of Haydn, with well-contrasted themes. In our own time there has been a welcome revival of his music. A recent record of four of his concertos, played by Menuhin and the Menuhin Festival Orchestra, is proof that he is a composer whose work has been too long neglected.

One of Viotti's most prominent pupils was the Belgian violinist André Robberechts, who in turn became teacher of Charles de Bériot, father of the great nineteenth-century Belgian school. When the young de Bériot played for the aging Viotti, the master told him that he had already acquired an original style that needed only cultivating, and that he could do nothing more for him. In his maturity, when confronted with the seven-year-old Henri Vieuxtemps, de Bériot passed on the same piece of advice.

It was through his trio of French disciples — Baillot, Rode and Kreutzer — that Viotti's influence on performing style was firmly established early in the nineteenth century. All three became professors at the Paris Conservatoire, which had been opened in 1795. Their *Méthode*, first published in Paris in 1804, was based on the principles of Viotti's teaching in its insistence on refinement, excellence of bowing, and power and beauty of tone. The attention paid to detail in left-hand technique looks forward to the late nineteenth and twentieth centuries. The range of three octaves and a tone known to Geminiani and Mozart is increased to more than four octaves, besides which the directions for holding the instrument are considerably in advance of the earlier methods. Baillot mentions the 'Tourte' grip and his bowing directions are much nearer our own than those concerned with the outcurved bow. It is also clear that the violin is now universally held with the chin to the left of the tailpiece. On the production of a good tone there is a piece of advice which is as relevant today as the day it was written: 'Aspirants should search no further than their own sensitivity, which they should try to draw out of the depths of their soul, for it is there that they will find its source.' The *Méthode* subsequently developed into *L'Art du Violon* (published in 1834), and remained the standard text of the Conservatoire during its greatest era.

Pierre Baillot de Sales was born in Passy, a suburb of Paris, in 1771, the son of a schoolmaster. He first learned to play the violin with a pupil of Nardini. He heard Viotti play in Paris when he was only ten and, although twenty years elapsed before he heard him again, the experience was cataclysmic. Viotti remained his model for all time.

Giovanni Battista Viotti took the Italian
tradition to Paris

Pierre Baillot de Sales, chief disciple of Viotti

Rodolphe Kreutzer, reluctant dedicatee of
Beethoven's famous sonata, and first violin in
Napoleon's Private Band

Louis Spohr, much travelled virtuoso-
violinist–composer

Viotti helped Baillot to secure a place in the orchestra at the Théâtre Feydeau, but he abandoned the post to become a government official. However, he continued to play in private. In 1795, Baillot decided to return to the music profession and studied theory and composition with Cherubini. He then travelled extensively as a soloist throughout Europe, achieving considerable success. Baillot was last in the line of the classical French school of violin playing. After him, Paganini's style dominated the scene. Paul David writes: 'His playing was distinguished by a noble, powerful tone, great neatness of execution and a pure, elevated, truly musical style.'[10]

Baillot was said to have been one of the few players who retained his skill and freshness to the end of his career. Mendelssohn considered the performance of his octet led by Baillot finer than he had ever heard it. Hiller wrote in 1831 that, at a Conservatoire concert, 'Baillot, though growing old [he was sixty] still played with all the fire and poetry of youth.'[11] Spohr also speaks highly of Baillot's technique as being 'unrestricted by the narrow limits of mere virtuosity'.

As a teacher, Baillot was greatly respected, and of his many pupils the most celebrated are Charles Dancla and François Habeneck, the latter being the teacher of Hubert Léonard, François Prume and Prosper Sainton.

Pierre Rode, second of the French trio, was born in Bordeaux in 1774. In 1788, when he was fourteen, his teacher sent him to Paris with an introduction to Viotti, who, struck by the boy's exceptional talent, taught him for two years. Rode toured as a virtuoso and held leaderships in a number of theatre orchestras including that of the Paris Opéra where he remained until 1799. In 1800 he was appointed solo violin to Napoleon.

In 1803, Rode went to St Petersburg as first violin to the Tsar Alexander at a salary of 5,000 silver roubles, with the sole obligation to play at Court and the Imperial Theatre. He met Spohr en route at Brunswick and the German virtuoso was so enchanted with his playing that he tried for many years to emulate Rode's style.

The constant pressures and intrigues of five years at the Russian Court had a harmful effect both on Rode's playing and his health. He became increasingly nervous in disposition and when he returned to Paris, his playing was said to have deteriorated. Rode never succeeded in his attempt to re-establish himself as an artist and died of a stroke in 1830.

In his better days Rode was a true artist. His profoundly musical nature shows itself in his compositions which are particularly suited to the nature of the instrument itself and are of a higher standard than those by most of his contemporaries. He published a considerable number of concertos, quartets, sets of variations and duos for two violins. The twenty-four 'Caprices' or studies remain today indispensable for a sound study of the violin. He also had many pupils. Although his wandering life was not conducive to teaching for long periods, there were those who benefited greatly from sporadic instruction from him, the most famous being Joseph Böhm, teacher of Joseph Joachim.

The third of Viotti's great pupils, Rodolphe Kreutzer (1766–1831), was born at Versailles, where his father was a member of the Royal Chapel; he was also his first instructor. Later Kreutzer studied with Anton Stamitz, son of the famous Johann Stamitz of Mannheim. He was also a pupil of Viotti. At the age of thirteen Kreutzer played one of his own compositions in Paris, and before he was sixteen was regarded as equal to the greatest virtuosos of the day. Following the death of his father the same year, Kreutzer took his place at the Chapel Royal. Through Viotti's influence he became first violinist at the Théâtre Italienne. Later he undertook a concert tour of Europe with great success and was subsequently appointed professor of violin at the Conservatoire with Baillot and Rode. He also was first violin in Napoleon's private band and received from the emperor the title of 'Chamber Virtuoso'. Napoleon's 'musique particulière' was an élite group who played exclusively for the emperor, following him around to his various residences. As first violin Kreutzer was paid only 4,000 francs, whilst the first tenor received 20,000. However, Madame Paër, also a singer, was considered worth 30,000.

At the height of a brilliant career Kreutzer broke his left arm and retired from the concert platform, after which he confined himself to composing, conducting and teaching. His numerous works include nineteen violin concertos and forty-two studies which include every possible aspect of technique.

As a man Kreutzer was arrogant and unpopular with his colleagues; as a performer, he was an artist in whom warmth, feeling and liveliness were well blended. Often compared to Viotti, he was said to be almost equal to him in the sweetness of his cantilena and broad full tone. He was considered less elegant in style than Rode, but his playing had more impetuosity and fervour.

To most people his name is known in connection with Beethoven's Kreutzer Sonata, Op. 47. This was originally written for the mulatto George Bridgetower, whose training in Vienna had been sponsored by the Prince of Wales. Bridgetower created a great impression in this city, not only because of his eminent patron but on account of his stylish playing. At the first performance on 24 May 1802, Beethoven accompanied Bridgetower on the piano. However, when Beethoven later fell out with Bridgetower, he dedicated the sonata to Kreutzer. Unfortunately, this most passionate of Beethoven's sonatas was not to Kreutzer's taste, and he never played the work. At the time, Beethoven's music was certainly not popular in Paris. Most music from beyond the Rhine suffered a similar neglect. When Kreutzer heard a rehearsal of Beethoven's second symphony in progress, he is said to have rushed away with his hands over his ears.

François Antoine Habeneck (1781–1849), a contemporary of the French trio and pupil of Baillot at the Conservatoire, is principally remembered as a great conductor, but he started his career as a brilliant violinist at the age of ten. As director of the Concert Society at the Paris Conservatoire, he gave in the 1820s accomplished performances of Beethoven, which had hitherto met with great prejudice in France. He taught many gifted violinists such as Léonard, Prume and Sainton (who brought his art to England). Habeneck's most celebrated pupil was Delphin Alard, in turn the master of the great Spanish virtuoso Pablo Sarasate.

So began the great French school of violin playing which stood for elegance and grace in bowing as well as brilliance of left-hand technique. Rode, like his master Viotti, excelled as a performer and demonstrated his influence through his playing, whilst Kreutzer and Baillot consolidated his principles through their writing and teaching. Kreutzer's pupil Lambert Joseph Massart was the teacher of Fritz Kreisler.

5

'Nightingale of Violinists'

Louis Spohr

A giant of a man, well over six feet in height, and of herculean constitution, Ludwig — he preferred the French 'Louis' — Spohr (1784–1859) dominated the violin world of Germany at the beginning of the nineteenth century and his reputation spread throughout Europe.

When the twenty-year-old Spohr made his début in Leipzig, Rochlitz wrote:

> Perfect purity, security, precision, the most beautiful finish, every type of bowing, all varieties of violin tone, the most natural ease in the execution of all such things, even in the most difficult passages — these render him one of the most skilfull of virtuosos.[1]

The English composer C.V. Stanford, who died in 1924, could recall the time when Spohr was considered a better composer than Beethoven. Spohr's output was tremendous; yet except for the Nonet Op. 31 in F major, for string and wind ensemble, his violin music is rarely heard. And as a virtuoso violinist he is virtually forgotten.

Spohr's posthumously published autobiography, although exasperatingly egotistical, is a valuable account of contemporary social conditions for the musician. His own achievements are recounted in pompous language, but when he turns to travel, self-aggrandisement gives way to evocative description.

Louis Spohr was born in Brunswick, the son of a physician and amateur flautist; his mother sang and played the piano. At the age of four he taught himself to play a small fiddle bought at a local fair, and received his first lessons from Dufour, a French amateur musician. As a child he showed a natural gift for composition which led to further study with Kunisch, a member of the Duke of Brunswick's Band, and lessons in counterpoint.

The rigid discipline of a strict father may have influenced Spohr's struggle for identity. If Dr Spohr saw his son crossing out to re-write, he would shout to his wife: 'The stupid boy is making windows again!'. Spohr remembered all his life: 'That is perhaps the reason why I acquired early the habit of writing a clean score straight off without erasing anything.'[2]

When he was fifteen, Spohr was taken on as Kammermusikus (chamber musician) to the Duke of Brunswick at a salary of 100 thalers. The band gave concerts once a week in the Duchess's apartments. As the music disturbed her card playing, the Duchess ordered a thick carpet to be spread underneath the musicians to deaden the sound. Spohr tells us that the words 'I play' or 'I stand' were often louder than the music. When the Duke was present, the carpet was discreetly removed. One evening, when playing one of his own compositions, Spohr got carried away, and a lackey took hold of his sleeve: 'Her Highness sends me to tell you not to scrape away so furiously.'[3] The enraged Spohr played even more loudly and was reprimanded by the Court Marshal.

But Spohr's truculence earned him the Duke's approval. He offered to give him a proper musical education, and asked Spohr to name his choice of teacher. Unfortunately, his idol, Viotti, was then running his wine shop in London, so Franz Eck (1774–1804) agreed to take him on a tour of Germany and Russia and give him lessons *en route*.

Eck was born in Mannheim and probably came under the influence of Karl Stamitz. At any rate he would have been well grounded in the Mannheim school with its insistence upon clean bowing and expressive execution. Spohr says of Eck that his style was 'powerful without harshness, exhibiting a great variety of subtle and tasteful *nuances*, irreproachable in his execution of difficult passages, and altogether possessing a great and peculiar charm in performance'.[4]

The couple set out in April 1802, just after Spohr's eighteenth birthday. The first lesson left Spohr discouraged, when he found he could not play a single bar to his teacher's satisfaction. However, he practised for ten hours each day and within two weeks, he tells us in his autobiography, was confident that for him 'nothing in the violin literature of the time was too difficult'.[5]

In St Petersburg, although he did not appear in public, Spohr met all the visiting celebrities, among them the famous pianist Clementi with his pupil John Field. On the less pleasant side of life at court, he witnessed his teacher's involvement in a scandal with the daughter of a member of the Imperial Band. Eck was deported. Through his wanderings and privations in the Russian winter he went insane and eventually died in a lunatic asylum in Strasbourg about 1810. Spohr returned home by sea, alone.

In 1803 Spohr made his début in Brunswick as a violinist-composer and was given a place in the first violins in the Dukes's band at twice his previous salary. It was at this time that Spohr first heard Rode play and was greatly affected by the experience. Spohr modelled himself on the master's style, and freely admitted that he eventually became one of the most faithful imitators of Rode among the young violinists of the day. Later, Spohr developed his own individuality, but the pure style of Viotti and Rode always remained the main source of his inspiration.

From this point onwards, Spohr's career achieved the same kind of success we associate with present-day virtuosos, but lacking the advantage of modern transport. Journeying by road or on the water, Spohr visited almost every important city in Europe and made a number of trips to London. After his marriage in 1806 to the harpist Dorette Scheidler he designed a special passenger coach to accommodate their music, instruments and personal belongings.

In 1812, Spohr fulfilled a lifelong ambition to visit Vienna, the city where Mozart and Haydn had lived and worked and where their successor, Beethoven, in the full strength of his creative powers, still lived. To succeed here, at the centre of the musical world, was the ultimate test. Spohr took Vienna by storm. One musical journal described him as 'unquestionably the nightingale of all the living violinists ... In fast tempi he masters difficult passages including the most extended reaches with incredible ease, thanks partly, no doubt, to the size of his hand.'[6]

A year later Spohr was appointed leader of the orchestra at the Theater an der Wien (National Theatre), and moved with his wife and family to Vienna. Shortly after his arrival, Spohr was approached by Johann von Tost, a wealthy Moravian textile merchant who was also a passionate music lover. They made an agreement whereby von Tost would purchase everything that Spohr wrote and retain the manuscripts for three years. After this time they would be returned unconditionally. A sliding scale of payment according to the number of instruments involved was agreed upon: thus thirty ducats for a quartet, thirty-five for a quintet, and pro rata for further combinations. (It was for von Tost that Spohr wrote his nonet.) In return, von Tost would supply the music for parties or concerts, but only if he were present. It was a clever plan, for as a mere manufacturer von Tost would never have been admitted. The hosts had no option but to invite him. He would arrive with his portfolio, quietly place the music on the stands and sit silently throughout the performances. When it was over, he picked up the music and retired. Eventually, he became such a familiar figure in musical circles that he was automatically invited even when Spohr's music was not being played.

It was at the Theater an der Wien that Spohr became acquainted with Franz Clement (1780–1842), the violinist and director of the theatre orchestra. His style of playing — known for its gracefulness and tenderness of expression — would have appealed to Spohr, who was opposed to virtuosity for its own sake. Beethoven thought so highly of Clement that he wrote his violin concerto for him, inscribing his manuscript to that effect. Clement played it at the first performance on 23 December 1806, but Beethoven, having only just completed the work a few hours before the concert, left no time for rehearsal. Clement was therefore obliged to sightread the entire solo part. Nevertheless, 'on account of its originality and manifold beauties', the critics received the piece well enough, but thought that 'the continuity often seems broken ... endless repetition of some trivial phrases may become tedious'. As for Clement, his 'proven skill, his grace, his power of [tone] and absolute power over his violin, which is indeed his slave, called forth the ringing cheers of the audience'.[7] In the second half, by way of ludicrous contrast, the same approval was given to Clement for performing a set of variations with the violin held upside down!

Spohr counted Beethoven among his friends, and his impressions of the composer are among the most vivid on record. Although always a champion of Beethoven's early quartets, he reacted against the later works, particularly the late quartets, seeing them as full of 'aesthetic aberrations' which he attributed to Beethoven's deafness. He considered the ninth symphony 'monstrous', 'tasteless' and 'trivial'. As to Beethoven himself, Spohr writes: 'He was a little blunt, not to say uncouth; but a truthful eye beamed from under his bushy eyebrows.'[8]

In 1815 Spohr left Vienna and visited Switzerland and Italy. When he made his début at La Scala, Milan, the Italians loved his 'singing' tone. But Spohr did not value their praise: he had a poor opinion of the Italians as musicians. He thought them good singers, but even so, criticized their over-ornamentation. He wrote: 'Italian virtuosi and dilettanti direct their whole attention to the acquirement of mechanical skill, but as regards a tasteful style of execution, they form themselves very little after the good models which their best singers might be to them; while our German instrumentalists generally possess a very cultivated style, and much feeling.'[9]

It seems romantically appropriate that Spohr and Paganini should meet for the first time in Venice. Spohr notes that the connoisseurs admit the wizard to be of 'great dexterity with the left hand in double-chords and in passages of every kind, but that the very thing by which he fascinates the crowd debases him to a mere charlatan'.[10]

Spohr was unwittingly involved in the pro- and anti-Paganini controversy when, without his knowledge, a letter appeared in the press comparing him favourably with the Genoese maestro. Spohr's playing reminded the writer of the style of Pugnani and Tartini, whose 'grand and dignified manner of handling the violin has become wholly lost in Italy, and had been compelled to make room for the petty and childish manner of the virtuosi of the present day'.[11]

Spohr was entertaining some friends when Paganini called to offer congratulations on his last concert. Spohr asked him to play, but Paganini declined, saying he had fallen and his arm was affected. When the friends had left, Spohr repeated the request but Paganini protested that his style of playing was for the great public only, and he must elicit a different manner for private performance.

Spohr was always curious to hear Paganini and almost despaired of ever having the opportunity. But in 1830, he heard him play in Kassel. Spohr commented: 'His left hand, and his constantly pure intonation, were to me astonishing. But in his compositions and his execution I found a strange mixture of the highly genial and childishly tasteless, by which one felt alternately charmed and disappointed.'[12]

Spohr rapidly became one of the most sought-after musicians in Germany. He successively held a number of leaderships in theatre orchestras and undertook some fifty-three concert tours travelling by horse and carriage, even in the Russian winter. At this time, festivals were becoming a regular feature of musical life in all the important German capitals, and few of them would be considered successful without Spohr as director. In 1820, at the invitation of the Philharmonic Society, he made his first trip to England. Not only was he well received, but he even managed to get the autocratic governing body of the society to waive rules which insisted that they should be in sole charge of selecting the programme. The music of Mozart, Haydn and Beethoven was traditionally preferred, but Spohr created a precedent at his opening concert by playing his own 'Gesangsscene'. An amusing incident occurred shortly after Spohr arrived in England. He decided to make an early call on his friend Ferdinand Ries, the great German violinist, pianist and composer, and one of the most important figures on the London musical scene. Spohr made himself very smart, donned a bright red Turkish patterned silk waistcoat, and set out to walk to his destination. As he proceeded he found everyone looking at him, and urchins shouting abuse, which, fortunately, through his lack of English, he did not understand. But by the time he arrived at Ries's house he had a trail behind him. Ries then explained that George III had just died and official mourning had been decreed. Ries assured Spohr that only his great height and serious bearing had protected him from a crowd who would certainly have tackled him had he been shorter and less formidable in appearance. Spohr was immediately taken back to his lodging, where the offending waistcoat was exchanged for one of the correct hue.

Spohr's most important appointment was that of director of the theatre at Kassel from 1822. It was here that he founded his school of violin playing which spread its influence so widely. Through Eck he had inherited the solid basic principles of the Mannheim school; with his adherence to the purity of Rode's example, combined with his own individuality, he produced the most important influence of his time.

Spohr had close on two hundred pupils who came from all over Europe, and there were even some from America. Henry Holmes, one of the most distinguished English violinists, was a pupil of Spohr at Kassel. The best known of Spohr's pupils, Ferdinand

David, was a close friend of Mendelssohn, and it was for David that the composer wrote his violin concerto.

Spohr possessed a hand of exceptional size so that he was able to execute double-stops and stretches with the utmost facility. His breadth and beauty of tone and refinement of expression were said to be almost unequalled. Spohr treated the violin pre-eminently as a singing instrument and his music is proof of this concept, particularly in the slow movements of his concertos and his beautiful 'Gesangsscene'. Spohr disliked tricks of any kind and condemned the use of artificial harmonics daringly exploited by Paganini.

The light, free style of bowing also introduced by Paganini, and which has been adopted by all modern players, did not meet with Spohr's approval. Nevertheless, his staccato was said to be brilliant, every note firmly marked by a movement of the wrist. When Mendelssohn heard Spohr play his own Concerto in E minor and introduce, by way of novelty, a staccato passage in one long stroke, he remarked to his sister: 'See, this is the famous Spohrish staccato which no violinist can play like him.'[13] This manner of bowing — exemplified in the salon piece 'Hora Staccato' — is achieved by a single stroke of the bow drawn in one direction as the notes are stopped. The result is that any number of notes can be sounded articulately without change of bow direction.

Spohr was also interested in the construction of the violin itself and made several experiments with stringing and tuning. His most famous contribution is the invention in 1820 of the chin-rest.

Spohr disapproved of the earlier method of holding the violin on the right side of the tailpiece. As early as 1803, in St Petersburg, he found the playing of Ferdinand Fränzel pure and clean but 'His posture displeases me ... He still holds the violin in the old manner, on the right side of the tailpiece, and must therefore play with his head bent.'[14] It is interesting that when Spohr heard Fränzel again in 1815, he found his playing 'antiquated' and wanting in purity of intonation. This is perhaps not so much a criticism as proof of the advance made in technique in one decade of the nineteenth century.

Spohr wrote over two hundred works, which include no fewer than fifteen violin concertos. His *Method*, completed in 1831, served successive generations of nineteenth-century musicians. His democratic attitude towards the nobility was no mean achievement in the early nineteenth century, and his insistence that a musician deserves to be given the hearers' full attention helped to establish a social respect for both music and musical performance which scarcely existed previously.

6

The Catalyst

Niccolò Paganini

Before we can hope to see clearly into the mystery of this man's art, we shall have to remove from our imagination all the preconceived notions that have been placed there by a couple of generations of gossips

writes Jeffrey Pulver about Niccolò Paganini.[1] This legendary figure was the quintessence of eccentric genius. Strange in physical appearance, brusque and often rude in manner, mean in his financial dealings, with a fatal attraction for women, he was also thought to be in possession of satanic powers. Such a combination, allied to playing powers without parallel among his contemporaries, could not fail to make him both famous and notorious in his lifetime..

A twentieth-century doctor has put forward the suggestion that Paganini was suffering from a connective tissue disorder known as Marfan's syndrome — not diagnosed until 1896. Symptoms include a tall, thin build, long arms, spider-like fingers, exceptionally extensible joints and a transparent skin. The description fits all the known accounts of Paganini's appearance.

Niccolò was born in Genoa in 1782, the son of a ship's chandler, a delicate child of nervous disposition. When he was five he received his first lessons on the mandolin and violin from his father who quickly recognized his son's talent and exploited it to the limit. At the age of eleven, he successfully appeared in public for the first time, playing not only pieces by Corelli and Tartini but also one of his own compositions, the 'Carmangole' variations on a popular air.

At the age of thirteen, having received the best instruction available in Genoa, Paganini was taken by his father to Parma to play to the distinguished violinist and composer, Alessandro Rolla (1757–1841). When they arrived, they were told the maestro had been taken ill and could not see them. Whilst waiting in the vestibule, Paganini's father spotted Rolla's latest composition lying on the table. He made a sign to his son, who proceeded to play the piece at sight. Rolla was so astonished that he rose from his sickbed to see for himself. Having decided that he could teach the boy nothing, Rolla recommended Paganini to take lessons in counterpoint. After some study with the Neapolitan Gasparo Ghiretti, Paganini's musical education was complete. 'Under his direction,' writes Paganini, 'I composed, as an exercise, twenty-four fugues for four hands, without any instrument — just with ink, pen and paper'.[2]

This example apart, Paganini gives little credit to any of his teachers, claiming that he was 'self-taught', and that 'great ideas sprang spontaneously from the inner flame that animated him'.[3] However, there would appear to be another influence. The nineteenth-century Belgian musicologist Fétis says that Paganini told him that some time in 1794 or 1795, he had an experience that 'revealed to him the secret of everything one could do on the violin'. He had heard the Polish Auguste Durand (1770–1834), a pupil of Viotti in Paris. Durand, whose natural gifts were said to be of an exceptional order, attracted attention solely by the execution of brilliant tours de force. Paganini confided to Fétis that 'many of his most brilliant and popular effects were derived to a considerable extent' from this artist. Certainly many contemporary accounts confirm Durand's virtuosity: 'that his technical facility was prodigious and he invented a multitude of technical tricks and devices that no-one but himself could play'.[4] Paganini would certainly have imitated those tricks.

Accompanied by his father, Paganini made his first concert tour of northern Italy in 1797, but for the next few years there are no records of any sensational appearances. He played at numerous 'private affairs' but in a modest way. What we do know is that his father kept him on a tight rein, supervising every minute of his daily practice. When he was eighteen, Paganini told Schottky, his friend and biographer, 'My father's excessive severity now seemed more oppressive than ever as my talent developed and my knowledge increased. I should have liked to break away from him so that I could travel alone; but my harsh mentor never left my side.'⁵

In the autumn of 1801, Paganini and his brother Carlo went to play in the Festival at Lucca. On the Feast of San Croce during High Mass, Paganini was invited to play a concerto after the Kyrie. He was audacious enough to play one that took twenty-eight minutes. A member of the cathedral orchestra gives an eye-witness account of his 'unusual and unprecedented ability and virtuosity. He imitated on his strings the songs of birds, the flute, trombone and horn. And though everyone admired his astounding bravura ... such mimicry ... aroused laughter even in church.'⁶ Paganini's unashamed playing to the gallery did him no harm. He was asked to play on several future occasions, and a few months later he was appointed first violin to the newly-formed Republic of Lucca.

There are few accounts of his public appearances at this time, but many stories of love affairs. In later life, Paganini invented and perpetuated a number of such tales, but always emerged as the victor. He was never able to admit failure. He seems to have been under the impression that all women were 'mad about him'. Doubtless he had his conquests, although it is unlikely that he was on intimate terms with all the high-born ladies that he and many of his biographers would have us believe. He had experienced the stiff yoke of a possessive and avaricious parent and was free — at the age of nineteen — to make his own decisions. It is not altogether surprising if he sometimes made the wrong ones.

The wildest accounts of gambling excesses date from this time. Paganini had inherited from his father a love of gambling, and would frequently risk the entire proceeds from a concert before it had taken place. The story of how he came by his famous 'Cannon' Guarneri del Gesù is the classic instance. On the eve of a concert in Leghorn, Paganini had gambled away his Amati violin. A rich merchant named Livron loaned him an instrument from his private collection. After the concert, Livron rushed up to Paganini begging him to keep it as a token of appreciation. Livron made the one proviso that the violin should be played only by Paganini himself. The artist kept his word and used it for the rest of his life. Curiously enough it was the 'Cannon' that caused Paganini to give up gambling. He was once offered a high price for it and was tempted to accept the offer to settle a debt. Instead he staked his last thirty francs and won. He never sat at the tables again.

In 1806 Paganini became Court Musician to Elisa Bacciochi, Napoleon's sister and Princess of Lucca and Piombino. It was whilst in the service of the princess that he wrote his famous 'Scena Amorosa' for two strings — E and G — only. Paganini described it to Schottky: 'The first string represented the girl, the second the man, and I then began a sort of dialogue, depicting little quarrels and reconciliations between my two lovers. The strings first scolded, then sighed, lisped, moaned, joked, express-ed delight, and finally ecstasy. It concluded with a reconciliation and the two lovers performed a *pas de deux* closing with a brilliant coda.' Paganini said he directed it to an unknown lady in the audience who rewarded him with 'the most friendly glances'.[7] The princess challenged him by saying that if he could compose for two strings, why not one? In response, Paganini composed his Military Sonata for the G string only, entitled 'Napoleon'.

During his leave of absence from court, Paganini continued to give public concerts. As his popularity with his audiences increased so his importance as a court musician diminished. He finally broke with the princess in 1813 and promised never again to become dependent upon a single patron.

As a free agent Paganini decided to try his luck in Milan and found his first overwhelming success. In the space of six weeks he gave eleven concerts at La Scala and other theatres and had the audiences at his feet. He then toured northern Italy, Venice, Rome and Naples, scoring triumphs everywhere. In a short while his fame shone like a blazing comet the length and breadth of Italy. But the light did not blind Paganini's eyes to the material benefit of such fame. He demanded higher fees than those asked by any other violinist, and his hypnotized audiences paid up without a murmur.

Some time in 1824 Paganini met the singer Antonia Bianchi. She became his mistress, bore him a son, Achilles, in 1826, and kept him tightly in rein by her possessive and jealous tempera-ment. Two years later, after much wrangling, a final settlement was made in Bianchi's favour in exchange for the custody of their son. Paganini was devoted to the boy and over-indulged him to the limit. Achilles turned out to be profligate and lazy, and remained a constant source of anxiety to his father for the rest of his life. Ironically, Paganini, exploited and ill-treated by his own father, was in turn tyrannized by his own son.

The other tyranny that overshadowed Paganini's life was

recurrent ill-health. If it was not the rages of tuberculosis — which eventually reached his larynx — it was the effect of taking mercury for syphilis, which he had contracted at the age of twenty-seven. In addition, he suffered from a stomach complaint. He was frequently prevented from undertaking concert tours because of a breakdown in his health.

It was poor health that prevented Paganini from appearing abroad until he was forty-six. Stories of his fame had reached every European capital and made audiences impatient to hear him. In 1828, Vienna was the first city outside Italy to witness the miracle. The initial concert took place on 4 April and the audience went mad with excitement. Next day these words appeared in the *Allgemeine Theaterzeitung*:

> To analyse his performance is sheerly impossible and numerous rehearings avail but little. When we say that he performs incredible difficulties with as clear and pure an intonation as another, when we say that in his hands the violin sounds more beautiful and more moving than any human voice . . . when we say that every singer can learn from him, this is still inadequate to give a single feature of his playing. He must be heard, and heard again, to be believed.

For months 'this god of the violin'[8] was the one topic of conversation which spread to all classes of the population. Fashion took advantage of this 'Paganini mania'. Shirts and neckties were 'à la Paganini', snuff-boxes were enamelled with his portrait, and Viennese dandies carried walking-sticks with his head carved on the handles. A good stroke at billiards was called 'un coup à la Paganini'. One enterprising cabman who had once conveyed the virtuoso for a short ride placed a notice in his cab which read 'Cabriolet de Paganini'. So remunerative was his warrant that eventually the cabman was able to set himself up in business as a highly successful hotelier.

From Vienna, Paganini toured Europe. On 9 March 1831 he gave his first long-awaited concert at the Opéra in Paris. An account of this concert comes from the artist Amaury-Duval, who had been invited by Ingres, his master and leader of the Neo-classicist school. Ingres had painted Paganini's portrait in Rome and was full of admiration for his playing, especially his interpretation of the works of the masters. Duval tells us that the curtain rose upon an empty stage without furniture or scenery. Then a tall, thin man dressed entirely in black entered, with features that were almost diabolical. The whole hall experienced a moment of sharp astonishment which was almost a shudder. At the first notes he drew from his instrument, he captivated every person in the theatre, and Ingres expressed his pleasure with little gestures of admiration. But when Paganini suddenly abandoned himself to exercises in virtuosity 'those tours de force that have given birth to such a ridiculous school'[9], Ingres' face flushed with anger. As the audience became increasingly delighted, he became more and more enraged. Finally, he stood up and cried out: 'It isn't him! Heretic! Traitor!'[10] Ingres' loyalty to the Classical tradition was violated by such exhibitionism. He saw in Paganini the antithesis of his own ideals, rooted in purity of line and intellectual application to art.

But there was another painter in the same audience who reacted quite differently. It was Ingres' most deadly enemy, the arch-romantic Delacroix. Delacroix was completely overcome. In his *Memoirs* he describes his reaction: '*There* is the inventor! There is the man who is truly fitted for his art!'[11]

From Paris, Paganini went on to London, where he repeated his phenomenal success. The first concert took place on 3 June 1831 at the King's Theatre in the Haymarket. 'The house was full, but not fashionably attended; very few ladies were present . . . the orchestra pit and gallery were crowded, while a large proportion of the boxes remained unoccupied.'[12] For *The Times*, Paganini was 'not only the finest player perhaps that has ever existed on that instrument, but he forms a class by himself.' Chorley, the most celebrated critic of the day, wrote: 'There is a relation between a unit and a million — none between him and his fellow men.'[13] Mary Shelley, wife of the poet, wrote to a friend that Paganini 'threw me into hysterics . . . his wild ethereal figure, rapt look — and the sounds he draws from his violin are all superhuman.'[14]

Paganini went on to play at Bath, Cheltenham, Norwich, Liverpool and Dublin. Altogether he netted £16,000 out of his appearances in the British Isles.

Over the years, Paganini amassed a considerable fortune, and in 1833 he purchased the Villa Gaione, a large estate at Vigatto, about four miles from Parma, where the soft air was beneficial to his condition. His fame was now world wide and, although he still appeared in concerts from time to time, the periods of inactivity became more prolonged. It was his intention at this time to devote himself to the publication of his compositions, but he asked too high a price from publishers and failed to come to terms with them. Paganini was very astute over the distribution of his music. At his concerts he would provide orchestral parts but no one ever saw the solo part. He always played everything from memory.

He died on 27 May 1840 in his fifty-eighth year. His post-humous history is remarkable. The accusations of his being in league with the devil during his lifetime were as nothing com-pared to the treatment meted out to his corpse by the church. In his last days a priest had called to give him the Last Sacrament, but Paganini refused, saying he was not ready to die. When death came he had still not received absolution. As no mortuary chapel could receive an excommunicated sinner, the coffin was placed in the cellar of the house in which he died. There followed a series of events in which the coffin was shunted from place to place and was once taken out to sea and back again. Meanwhile, a war between relatives and authorities raged for thirty-six years. In 1876 the Church's provisions were revoked and the body was finally transferred to consecrated earth at the cemetery at Parma.

Paganini left about 2,000,000 lire (£80,000), mostly in estates and securities. He also left a valuable collection of master stringed instruments; fifteen violins by Stradivari, Amati, Tononi and Ruggeri, and the 'Cannon' Guarneri del Gesù, which he bequeathed to the Civic Museum at Genoa; four cellos, two by Stradivari, an Andreas Guarneri and a Rogeri; a Stradivari viola and a Guadagnini guitar. The whereabouts of most of these instruments today is unknown, but a quartet of Stradivari instru-ments have remained together and are used by the members of the American Paganini Quartet.

For the most part, Paganini played only his own compositions and was a law unto himself. Therefore any comparison with contemporary virtuosos is irrelevant. What is important is that Paganini's devices were then unknown and came as a shock to the violinists who had been reared on classical tradition. Paganini often employed *scordatura* to facilitate the playing of certain intervals, and when performing works with orchestra, he fre-quently tuned his G string up half a tone, thus enabling him to play difficult passages with greater ease. This tuning was not only well-suited to harmonics but also produced a more brilliant sound on open strings. An eye-witness, Carl Guhr, says of his bowing: 'His ordinary staccato, played with a very tight bow, was prodi-giously loud and firm, like the strokes of a hammer, whilst his

Niccolò Paganini:
Daguerrotype taken shortly
before his death in 1840

Portraits classical and romantic —
by Ingres *(left)* and an unknown artist *(right)*

method of dashing the bow on the strings, and letting it leap through an infinity of tiny staccato notes with unerring precision, was wholly his own invention.'[15] In his 'Perpetuum Mobile' he played whole passages staccato on one bow up and down — with perfect articulation and intonation. This is what we know today as *saltato* bowing. Except when playing heavy broken chords near to the heel, he held his bow arm very close to his body. All the elasticity seemed to be controlled by the wrist.

Paganini's way of holding the violin was also extraordinary. His shoulder was so wide, the bone structure almost horizontal, that the violin rested upon it as if it had been designed for the purpose. Paganini was the last virtuoso violinist to play without a chin-rest.

His Twenty-four Caprices for solo violin remain today some of the most brilliant virtuoso music ever written for the instrument. The product of his youth — composed between 1801 and 1807 — they are the work of a genius. The devices involved — double-stopping, octaves, tenths, trills in thirds, sixths and harmonics of every variety — brought technique to its zenith. The twentieth century has said nothing that is not already said in these caprices.

In her biography *Paganini the Genoese*, Geraldine de Courcey shows some significant links between the caprices and Locatelli's *Arte de nuova modulazione*, which fell into Paganini's hands during his student days. Fétis tells us that Paganini told him that 'this work opened up to him a world of new ideas and devices that had never had the merited success owing to their excessive difficulty'.[16]

Paganini's 'miracles' of harmonics, double- and treble-stopping and left-hand pizzicato are now common practice among virtuoso performers. Consequently many great players have a healthy respect for his music. Grumiaux, Szeryng, Ricci and Perlman have all made recordings of Paganini concertos, and Ricci was the first to record all twenty-four of his caprices. There are still those who sneer at the 'mere virtuosity' of his music, but as one famous violinist was heard to remark: 'The only violinists who denigrate Paganini are those who can't play him.'

7

Disciples of Paganini

Camille Sivori;
Heinrich Wilhelm Ernst;
Antonio Bazzini; Ole Bull

Paganini, by his example, unquestionably revolutionized the art of violin playing. But because of his obsessive guarding of his manuscripts, his contemporaries had little chance to perform his music. The only works published in his lifetime were the Twenty-four Caprices, Op. 1, twelve sonatas for violin and guitar — an instrument of which Paganini was very fond — and six quartets for strings and guitar..

The one link between Paganini and the next generation of violinists was through his solitary pupil, the Genoese Camille Sivori (1815–94). A virtuoso of considerable gifts in his own right, Sivori received lessons from Paganini when he was six. As a young artist he travelled extensively in Europe, North and South America, and in 1846 came to England, where he gave the first British performance of the Mendelssohn concerto. *The Times* was unstinting in its praise of Sivori's execution but was non-committal in its assessment of the work itself: 'It is a great work, but we must listen to it again ere we venture on a detailed analysis.'[1]

Sivori enjoyed a long and successful career and naturally specialized in performing the music of Paganini. His master had written several works for him and the first two concertos were published soon after Paganini died. E. van der Straeten, writing in 1933, says that in the 1870s he heard Sivori at Cologne playing Paganini's B minor Concerto and 'Le Streghe'. He still remembered 'the wonderful impression his superb technique, faultless intonation and beauty of tone' made on him.[2]

Paganini and Sivori remained life-long friends, but according to

Sivori, it was not due to Paganini's pedagogic gifts — he was probably the worst teacher in the world. During lessons he was sarcastic and rude: he would scribble a few manuscript exercises on the spot, place them on the stand and expect Sivori to execute them from sight. Whilst Sivori struggled with the difficulties, Paganini paced up and down like a caged lion, with a sardonic smile on his face. When his pupil had finally battled through, Paganini would first sneer in silence, and then ask why he was not playing it as he had been shown. Sivori usually managed to answer a feeble 'No', whereupon Paganini, 'seizing the violin like a lion seizing a sheep would play the study again without even looking at the MS sheet on the stand'.[3]

Heinrich Wilhelm Ernst (1814–65), from Brno in Moravia, heard Paganini in Paris and became obsessive in his admiration of the master. A pupil of Joseph Böhm, Ernst went on tour as a fully-fledged virtuoso at the age of sixteen. He met de Bériot in Paris and studied with him for a further six years.

By observing Paganini perform, Ernst acquired many features of his technique, such as staccato runs, the use of harmonics and left-hand pizzicato. His playing was described by Berlioz as a 'fascinating display of virtuosity put to consistently tuneful ends, and performed with almost careless ease ... He is like a juggler whose counters are diamonds.'[4]

On the concert platform, Ernst — apart from his moustache — even looked like Paganini, with cadaverous features, high cheekbones and long, dark hair. But in character he was altogether different. Berlioz described him as: 'The most delightfully humorous man I know ... the complete rounded artist, profoundly and predominantly expressive in everything he does, yet never neglectful of the craft, the disciplining art of music.'[5]

Today Ernst is remembered mainly as a composer. For Leopold Auer he 'wrote for the virtuoso player ... His compositions have far more than mere technique to recommend them, his expressive "Elegie", his incredibly difficult transcription of Schubert's "Erlkönig", his "Otello" fantasy, no violinist can afford to ignore.'[6]

Another virtuoso who modelled himself on Paganini was the Brescian Antonio Bazzini (1818–97). Auer admired his playing and said that it was 'distinguished by the singing quality of his tone ... [He was] a virtuoso in the true sense of the word.'[7] Bazzini once played to Paganini and so impressed the latter that he advised him to tour as a virtuoso. As a result his fame spread throughout Europe and he was hailed as Paganini's successor.

Bazzini made considerable efforts to popularize the works of Bach and Beethoven in his own country: a difficult task since Italians were never well disposed towards German music. Perhaps the most blatant instance was the response to Spohr's suggestion to the famous Neapolitan conductor Zingarelli, that he should include the operas of Mozart in his repertoire: 'Yes,' said Zingarelli, 'he was not deficient in talent ... if he could only have continued to study ten years longer he would then have been able to write something good'.[8]

Also a composer, Bazzini's music was frequently performed in the church and in the theatre. Today he is remembered for 'La Ronde des Lutins' ('Goblins' Dance'), a show-piece employing every possible virtuoso technique, with lavish use of harmonics and left-hand pizzicato, that has remained one of the most popular in the violinist's repertoire.

Perhaps the most colourful figure among Paganini's disciples was the Norwegian Ole Bull (1810–80), whose virtuoso playing gained him the nickname 'The Flaxen-haired Paganini'.[9]

Bull was born in Bergen, the son of a physician who was also a good amateur musician, and his earliest memory was listening to his family playing string quartets. When Ole was five years old he taught himself to play the violin, and probably also received some instruction from the peasant fiddlers at the family's country home at Osteroy. The Norwegians had had little contact with the influences of European music until the Romantic movement touched them in the middle of the nineteenth century. But they possessed a rich store of folk music — and accompanied themselves on indigenous instruments. The most popular of these was the *hardingfele* or 'hardanger' fiddle, an eight-stringed violin with sympathetic strings — placed under the playing strings and which vibrate in sympathy when the upper strings are bowed or plucked.

Ole had his first music lessons from a Dane with an inordinate passion for brandy. As long as there was a drop in the bottle he was happy to teach or join in family music making. But when it was empty he would stagger on to the house of the next patron. One night he became too inebriated to continue playing in a string quartet and the eight-year-old Ole took his place.

In 1822 a visiting Swede named Lundholm, who had studied

with Baillot, gave Ole some thorough training in violin technique. A stickler for the established rules of posture, he insisted that when playing, his pupil should stand upright with his head against the wall: a practice advocated by Viotti and his school. In later years, Bull was noted for his repose and grace of bearing on the concert platform.

Bull's family opposed his ambition to become a performing violinist. His father wanted him to become a clergyman, but Ole failed his university examination. He immediately set out for Kassel to consult Spohr, who was then the most famous teacher in Europe.

The mighty Spohr was unimpressed, and declined to take on this wild, self-taught youth as a pupil. To make matters worse, Bull heard Spohr and his quartet play and was so overcome with their style and musicianship with its purity of line and depth of expression, that he temporarily gave up all idea of becoming a professional violinist. Five years later, Spohr admitted that he had been hasty in his previous judgement, albeit with some Spohrish reservations! He wrote: 'His wonderful playing and sureness of his left hand are worthy of the highest admiration, but unfortunately, like Paganini, he sacrifices what is artistic to something that is not quite suitable to the noble instrument.'[10]

In 1831 Bull went to Paris with two objectives: the first was to hear Paganini and the other to enter the Conservatoire. He failed in the latter but succeeded in the former. From this time on he took the master for his model. There is plenty of evidence to show that Bull attained a great deal of Paganini's technical facility and had a vast repertoire of similar inventiveness, which later gained him a tremendous public following.

At first life in Paris for Bull was adventurous. He suffered the inevitable poverty of the penniless artist, and once tried to commit suicide by jumping into the Seine, but he was rescued by a passer-by. On another occasion, through an absconding landlord, he lost all his possessions, including his violin. He had a fiery and impulsive temperament, so he never managed to find himself a job in the orchestra. Eventually, he was fortunate in meeting a violinmaker who exploited Bull's virtuosity to sell his fiddles, and who engaged him to play at a soirée given by the Duke of Riario, the Italian chargé d'affaires in Paris. Ole Bull is reported to have played magnificently, despite the fact that he was nearly asphyxiated by the pungent smell of the new varnish. His performance so impressed the Duke of Montebello, Marshal Ney's son, that he invited him to breakfast the following day. This introduction brought Bull into contact with Chopin, Ernst and other celebrated artists. Shortly afterwards, under the Duke's patronage, he gave his first public concert in the French capital and was again received with much enthusiasm.

Buoyant on the wave of success, Ole Bull travelled to Italy, and in Milan achieved a similar response from the audience at La Scala. But one critic found something adverse to say:

> M. Bull played compositions by Spohr, Mayseder, and Paganini without understanding the true character of the music, which he marred by adding something of his own. It is quite obvious that what he adds comes from genuine and original talent, from his own musical individuality; but he is not master of himself; he has no style; he is an untrained musician. If he be a diamond, he is certainly in the rough, and unpolished.[11]

Ole Bull's reaction is revealing. He sought out the critic, listened to more of his advice which he found invaluable, and for the next six months devoted himself to study under the guidance of good teachers.

Bull's sudden rise to fame was caused by a happy accident in Bologna. Auguste de Bériot and the singer Malibran had refused to appear at a concert because of a dispute over fees. Someone who had passed Ole Bull's window and heard him practising suggested that he might fill the bill. So late at night, Ole Bull was woken up and brought to the theatre. He rose to the occasion and played before a distinguished audience which included the Duke of Tuscany and his friends. Ole Bull's virtuosity caused a sensation and his charm of personality captivated the audience. After supper he reappeared and asked for a theme on which to improvize. He was given three and proceeded to take all of them, combining them in a brilliant display that had his audience loudly cheering. He was escorted to his lodgings by a torchlight procession in a carriage drawn by his admirers.

Bull repeated these triumphs all over Italy, and in London the audiences responded with equal enthusiasm. Like Paganini he asked high fees for his performances. In Liverpool he received £800 for one concert, and if that fee was representative, he must have made a fortune out of the 274 appearances he made in Britain in the space of sixteen months.

Heinrich Wilhelm Ernst, who modelled himself on Paganini

The Norwegian Ole Bull, 'The Flaxen-haired Paganini '

Ole Bull now repeated these successes in all the main cities of Germany where Spohr reigned supreme, and went on to Vienna and Budapest. At St Petersburg, he gave a number of concerts to audiences of over five thousand people. When he finally arrived in the Scandinavian countries he was fêted like a victorious monarch returning from battle.

America first saw Ole Bull in November 1843. He stayed for two years and gave two hundred concerts, playing in every important city, where his programmes were often printed on silk. He amassed a considerable fortune, making about $100,000, $20,000 of which he donated to charity.

Ole Bull always maintained a great feeling for his own country and was much concerned with the poverty existing there. On his second visit to the USA he tried to set up a colony for Norwegian immigrants and purchased a tract of land of some 125,000 acres in Potter County, Pennsylvania. Here he hoped to found 'A New Norway, consecrated to liberty, baptised with independence, and protected by the Union's mighty flag'.[12] Three hundred houses, stores and a church were soon built. A splendid castle for his own use was set on the top of a mountain. Hundreds of immigrants flocked to the new colony to take up residence. But during a concert tour he was summoned to Philadelphia with the news that he had been swindled by a confidence trickster who had sold him land owned by somebody else. There followed many years of litigation. The real owner agreed to let Bull have the land at a low price, but his fortune was already spent.

Travelling the length and breadth of the American continent, Bull gave concerts to regain the money he had lost, Although he was a victim of yellow fever, was caught in the cross-fire of a riot in California, and had his violin stolen when crossing the Isthmus of Panama, for five years he struggled to repay his debts. When he made his last appearance in New York, in 1857, he was so ill he had to be assisted in getting on and off the platform. On his return to Europe, all his debts honoured, he was restored to health and began concert-giving once more.

In appearance Bull was tall, athletic, with large blue eyes, the typical Viking. Like Paganini, his almost hypnotic personal magnetism attracted a large following. He never missed an opportunity to make full use of theatrical gestures. His sixty-sixth birthday, which occurred when he was in Egypt, was celebrated by his ascending to the pinnacle of the Pyramid of Cheops, where he played one of his own compositions, 'Saterbesog'. This event took place at the suggestion of the King of Sweden, to whom an account of the proceedings was duly telegraphed from Cairo next morning.

Ole Bull may have been criticized for his eccentricity but he never pretended to belong to the modern cultivated school of violin playing. Henry Lahee makes an apt point: 'He was a minstrel rather than a musician in the broad sense of the word, but he held the hearts of the people as few, if any, minstrels had previously done.'[13]

8

Age of Transition

Joseph Böhm;
Ferdinand David;
Charles Auguste de Bériot

The beginning of the nineteenth century saw a decline in private patronage. Although a few of the nobility still maintained their own orchestras, there was little support for the solo performer. An artist had either to find someone with money, or foot the bill himself. Apart from exceptions like Spohr and Paganini, artists were a poverty-stricken bunch. For instance, at the Paris Conservatoire there was never any question of anything as vulgar as a fee being paid to a soloist, however eminent. In his memoirs, Carl Flesch tells us that things were only slightly better at that establishment as late as the 1890s. Orchestras also suffered from a similar impecuniosity. They were under-rehearsed, seldom consisted of more than thirty players and were led by the first violin without a conductor. Standards were generally low. It is therefore not surprising that under such conditions Beethoven's symphonies were unpopular when first performed.

Inevitably, the implications of the system were echoed in the box office. The complete indifference of the early nineteenth-century public to anything but virtuoso tricks on the violin meant that concert-giving was a hazardous occupation. Concerts were by subscription only, so the sponsor had to be sought out before tickets could be purchased.

One of the important changes that had affected all musical instruments was the decision to raise pitch at the end of the eighteenth century. Mozart's 'A' would have been about 422 cycles per second, but the increasing popularity of the virtuoso was synonymous with a continued striving after brilliance and power. Paganini had used *scordatura* and employed thinner strings to obtain his effects, but eventually, a more general method had to be devised and the 'A' was raised a semitone to 435 cycles per second. As a consequence, the violin itself had to be modified to meet the new demands placed upon it.

When the pitch was raised, the pressure of the bridge on the belly increased, and the bass-bar (a strip of pine glued to the belly inside to retard the vibrations on the left side) had to be made longer and thicker.

One other change — by far the greatest since Stradivari — took place at the beginning of the nineteenth century. It concerned the proportions and position of the head and neck of the instrument. Until the late eighteenth century, few players exceeded the third or fourth positions (we have already seen that Vivaldi may have done so, but this was exceptional). The fingerboard now had to be lengthened, and as a result, the neck needed to be extended; it was also tilted back to accommodate the extra tension. Stradivari's longest fingerboard was 8½ inches in 1715 — the modern fingerboard is about 10½ inches. When a player uses a Stradivari or a Guarneri today, the instrument will certainly have undergone a neck operation, as well as an exchange of bass-bar. The necks of Stradivari's instruments were approximately ⅜ inch shorter and ⅛ inch narrower than those of the modern violin. In the current revival of playing baroque music on original instruments, in which Eduard Melkus in Austria and Sonya Monosoff in the USA are two of the leading exponents, there is a return to Stradivari's dimensions.

In the hands of the virtuoso performer, the modified violin could now reach the farthest corners of a large auditorium without difficulty. In one respect this was fortunate since the growing popularity of the solo performer attracted bigger audiences. On the other hand, large concert halls were scarce and it was difficult to find the right hall in which to perform. This shortage in large part explains why, until quite late in the nineteenth century, violinists performed solo concertos with piano or a string quartet.

It was inevitable that the modified violin, with its greater carrying power and Spohr's invention of the chin-rest (allowing greater freedom of the left hand), would call for more advanced teaching methods. Consequently the nineteenth century gave birth to some of the greatest teachers in the history of the instrument.

One of the most important of these was Joseph Böhm (1795–

1876), a Hungarian who through his teaching at the Conservatoire in Vienna attracted much Hungarian talent. His most prominent pupil was Jenö Hubay (1858–1937), also a pupil of Joachim, who put his principles into practice at the Conservatoire in Budapest.

Hungary has far-reaching associations with the violin. Her people are naturally musical and through their folk music have been playing on primitive instruments from the earliest times. Their long history of violin playing stems from the gipsy virtuosos. Böhm was the first Hungarian violinist who pursued more serious studies of the instrument.

Born in Pesth, he received his first instruction from his father, and in 1808 became a pupil of Rode when he was on his way home from a Russian tour. Böhm enjoyed considerable success as a soloist and toured Europe with the pianist Johann Peter Pixis, brother of the violinist who had studied with Viotti in exile.

When Böhm first played in Vienna in 1815, he met with such a warm reception that he decided to settle there. In 1819 he was appointed professor of violin at the Vienna Conservatoire, and in 1821 also became a member of the Imperial Chapel. He took over the leadership from Schuppanzigh — Beethoven's famous quartet player — in the quartet matinées at the Erste Kaffeehaus (First Coffeehouse). These took place at eight o'clock in the morning.

From 1827, Böhm played less and taught more. His technique, tone and style, were above reproach, but he was not temperamentally suited to performance. His exceptional talent as a teacher placed him as one of the most important links in the chain forged by Viotti and Rode from the classic to the modern school of violin playing. Through his pupil Joseph Joachim (1831–1907), a fellow Hungarian, the line remains unbroken to the present time since Joachim's pupil Leopold Auer was the master of Sascha Lasserson (1890–1978), who was teaching in Britain right up to his death. Virtuosos of the same line are Nathan Milstein, Mischa Elman and Jascha Heifetz. Jacob Dont (1815–88), a Böhm pupil at the Vienna Conservatoire, is another example of a fine soloist and chamber musician who is remembered as a gifted teacher. Dont's best-known pupil was Auer.

Through Spohr's pupil Ferdinand David (1810–73), we have another important link. David trained a number of young violinists at the Leipzig Conservatoire, including Joachim and August Wilhelmj.

David was born in Hamburg. His childhood was spent during the French occupation of the city, when life for the Germans was not easy. He went to Kassel in 1823. Two years later, he made his first appearance at the Gewandhaus in Leipzig. In 1827, when a member of the Königstädter Theater in Berlin, he first made the acquaintance of Mendelssohn. They became life-long friends, and each exercised a considerable artistic influence upon the other.

In 1835 Mendelssohn became conductor of the Gewandhaus Orchestra and a year later offered the leadership to David. Although Dresden was then the capital of Saxony, Leipzig was an important city. The centre of the book trade, people came from all over the world to attend its fairs, as they still do today. In the early nineteenth century it was also the most important musical centre in Europe, with the Thomaskirche and its choir school where Bach had been organist and choirmaster, a fine Sing-Akademie (singing school) and an excellent theatre.

Mendelssohn worked to develop the existing conditions, particularly in improving those of the musicians. It was through him that their wages were increased and a pension fund established. Under his direction the Gewandhaus Orchestra became a model for all Europe, as had the Mannheimers under Karl Stamitz a century before him. David often deputized as conductor.

In the summer of 1838, Mendelssohn wrote to David: 'I want to write a violin concerto next winter. One in E minor is running in my head, and the beginning of it never gives me a moment's peace.'[1] Constant letters passed between the two friends during the process of composition: hardly a passage in the work fails to reveal Mendelssohn's deference to David's taste and practical knowledge, especially from the violinistic point of view. It was first performed by David with the Gewandhaus Orchestra on 13 March 1845.

In 1843, when Mendelssohn opened the Conservatoire in Leipzig, he appointed David professor of violin. David's friendship with Mendelssohn endured, and he was one of those who sat at the composer's bedside in his last hours. He was also one of the pall-bearers at Mendelssohn's funeral in Leipzig on 6 February 1847, sharing the honour with the pianist Moscheles, Robert Schumann, and others.

David was also responsible for reviving the works of the old masters at a time when nothing but contemporary — and mostly inferior contemporary — music was played. He collected, edited and published, with accompaniments and marks of expression, classic works by eminent Italian, German and French composers: his arrangement of Tartini's 'Devil's Trill' is the popular version still used today. He also wrote a violin tutor.

André Robberechts (1797–1860) from Brussels is one of the two significant links between Viotti and the Belgian school of violin playing, the main influence in nineteenth-century violin playing; the other was through Baillot and the Liège branch.

In Paris Robberechts studied privately with Baillot and for many years with Viotti. His playing was distinguished by a combination of technical brilliance and beauty of expression with musicianship — all basic principles of the Viotti school. He became one of the most respected teachers of his time, and among his many pupils was Charles Auguste de Bériot, who is recognized as the founder of the Belgian school of violin playing.

Charles Auguste de Bériot was born in 1802 at Louvain into a noble but impoverished family and was orphaned at the age of nine. That same year he made his début at a public concert, playing a concerto by Viotti. De Bériot met Viotti in Paris, where the master told him: 'You have a fine style. Give yourself up to the business of perfecting it. Hear all men of talent, profit by everything, but imitate nothing.'[2] It was this piece of advice that de Bériot was later to give to the seven-year-old Henri Vieuxtemps.

On the concert platform, de Bériot enjoyed continuing success. He first appeared in London in 1826 at a Philharmonic Society Concert playing a concerto by Rode. The English audiences loved him, not only for his beautiful playing but for his aristocratic good looks. Nevertheless, it was fortunate that he made his début before Paganini arrived on the scene, for it is doubtful if he could have successfully competed with the eccentric genius of the Genoese maestro.

De Bériot's style was elegant rather than showy, and distinguished by its constant accuracy of intonation. But it was in the art of bowing that he was considered a master. Critics frequently praised the neatness and facility of his bowing, aspects that were helped considerably by the extra lightness and elasticity of the Tourte bow, by now in universal use. Unlike many virtuoso performers, de Bériot was uncomplex in character and equable in temperament. He also had many interests outside music. He was a talented painter and sculptor, wrote poetry, and was also in-

Joseph Böhm, the first important Hungarian teacher, and Joachim's professor at the Vienna Conservatoire

Ferdinand David first performed the Mendelssohn concerto in 1845

Charles Auguste de Bériot, Belgian disciple of Viotti

Martin Marsick, lady-killer and teacher of Flesch, Thibaud and Enesco

terested in violin making and repairing.

In Paris in 1828, de Bériot first met the beautiful opera singer Maria Felicita Malibran. She was already married to and separated from an elderly but supposedly rich French merchant who had wedded her with the idea of restoring his own failing fortune. Singers, in contrast to instrumentalists, earned very high fees. In one London season of forty appearances at Drury Lane, Malibran received over £3,200 — more than de Bériot could have earned in a year with violin playing.

The de Bériot-Malibran love affair was one of the great romances of the day. They toured together with much success and from about 1830 they set up house together in a villa on the outskirts of Brussels in the fashionable Ixelles district. Malibran obtained a divorce in 1836 and the couple were married. But six months later, Malibran fell from her horse and died from her injuries. She was only twenty-eight.

De Bériot retired from public life for four years, after which he was persuaded to return to the concert platform. He then resumed his European tours and met with all his former success. When Baillot died in 1842, de Bériot was offered the vacant post at the Paris Conservatoire. He refused because he preferred to teach in his own country, and in 1843 he was appointed professor of violin at the Conservatoire in Brussels, a post he held until 1852, when he resigned owing to failing eyesight. However, he continued to teach a few special pupils privately, one of whom was Emil Sauret. By 1858 he was totally blind and paralysed in one arm: he died in 1870.

De Bériot published seven concertos and many books of studies. His *Grande Méthode*, published in 1858, has been widely used by students ever since. His music was known in his day for its pleasing melodies and the way it brings out the most characteristic effects of the violin as a 'singing' instrument. It was often said that in his compositions his wife's singing could be heard.

9

The Hot-Bed of Liège

Lambert Joseph Massart;
Martin Marsick;
César Thomson

At the close of the eighteenth century, Flanders, allied to the Dutch, had been incorporated into France, and in 1815, Belgium and Holland were united to contain most of Flanders and the French-speaking Walloon districts. Much antipathy existed between the two peoples, and even when the Revolution of 1830 brought independence to Belgium, and a consequent leaning towards a more national spirit, the dichotomy persisted. Even today, everything from street names to concert programmes is printed in two languages.

In music, the Walloon influence predominates. From the eighteenth century onwards the Walloons have excelled in musical performance, particularly in violin playing, Liège being the most important centre: Carl Flesch called it a 'hot-bed'. A tradition of amateur violin playing and violin making had existed in this city for almost three centuries — not among the aristocracy, but among the artisans. It was the weavers and the barbers who had kept the tradition alive culminating in the foundation of the Conservatoire Royal de Musique de Liège in 1826. Most of the great violinists of the nineteenth-century Belgian school were born in or around Liège: Massart, Léonard, Vieuxtemps, Marsick, Thomson and Ysaÿe. At the beginning of the twentieth century it was said that the majority of the string players in the Paris orchestras were of Walloon birth and training.

Lambert Joseph Massart (1811–92) from Liège, who once performed the Kreutzer Sonata with Liszt, was a violinist of considerable talent who seemed to lack the desire to excel on the concert platform. He was awarded a municipal scholarship to study at the Conservatoire in Paris, but Cherubini, the then director, refused him without explanation. A chauvinistic attitude prevailed at the time, and doors were kept tightly closed to foreigners. Fortunately Kreutzer took him on as a private pupil.

As an artist he was received with the greatest enthusiasm, but shyness and nerves dogged every performance, and he decided to devote himself to teaching. In 1843 he was appointed professor of violin at the Paris Conservatoire, where he gained a world-wide reputation. He was known for his energy, and for his infinite care and thoroughness in considering the individual needs of each pupil. Few teachers of the time can boast as many celebrated pupils as Massart, either in direct line or second generation: Lotto, Wieniawski, Teresina Tua, Sarasate and Kreisler.

Hubert Léonard (1819–90) was born at Bellaire in Belgium, and studied as a child under Rouma at Liège. He entered the Conservatoire in Paris in 1836 as a pupil of Habeneck, and subsequently toured successfully throughout Europe. When de Bériot retired from the Brussels Conservatoire on account of ill-health, Léonard succeeded him. His most famous pupils were César Thomson, Henri Marteau, Martin Marsick and Ovide Musin. He was also an avid promoter of performances of music by contemporary composers, particularly that of Brahms and César Franck.

Martin Pierre Marsick (1848–1924) was born at Jupille, near Liège. He was a pupil of Léonard's at the Liège Conservatoire and also studied at both the Brussels and Paris Conservatoires; at the latter he was in Massart's master-class. In 1870 he was awarded a scholarship to take a final year with Joachim at the Hochschule in Berlin. In 1892, Marsick became professor of violin at the Paris Conservatoire and gained a reputation both as a teacher and string quartet player. A first class, all-round musician, Marsick was also a gifted organist and pianist.

As a performer, Marsick was greatly influenced by the poetic quality of Joachim's playing. Carl Flesch says that his right arm was a 'model . . . an absolutely perfect instrument'. His tone was 'enchanting', and he played with 'great imagination, constantly engaging one's interest without falling into mannerisms'[1]. Flesch had a high opinion of his teaching.

Marsick's exceptional good looks made him irresistible to women — and unfortunately womanizing overtook his teaching and performing career. After a disastrous affair with a married woman, Marsick, in his fifties, tried unsuccessfully to re-establish himself in Paris. He went to New York where he suffered a similar indifference, dying in poverty there in 1924.

But during the course of five years Marsick had three pupils whose names will always be synonymous with the development of their art: Carl Flesch, Jacques Thibaud and Georges Enesco.

The Liège-born Ovide Musin (1854–1929) gained a reputation for both solo and quartet playing of a high order. He toured extensively throughout the world and in 1874 formed a Quartet for Modern Music, mainly with a view to popularizing Brahms in Paris. After several successful appearances in New York, he returned to make his home in that city in 1908, and established a school for violin playing.

César Thomson (1857–1931) was also born in Liège, and studied with Léonard at the Conservatoire. He spent some years as leader of Bilse's orchestra (which later became the Berlin Philharmonic), for a short time sharing the leadership with Ysaÿe, then at the beginning of his career. From 1883 to 1897, Thomson taught sporadically at Liège Conservatoire, fitting his teaching in between extensive concert tours. In 1898 he settled in Brussels, where he succeeded Ysaÿe at the Conservatoire. At the height of his fame, Thomson seems to have been considered one of the most brilliant performers of the Belgian school. His good taste and excellent musicianship were assets in themselves, but by all accounts it was his extraordinary technique that 'fills the listener with wonder'.[2] He was particularly celebrated for his almost magical 'fingered octaves', which Flesch tells us 'rolled up and down under his fingers at the pace of a simple scale'. His performances are variously described as 'big, but inflexible and cold'[3] by Flesch, and by Henry Lahee: 'his command of all the technical resources of the violin is so great that he can play the most terrific passages without sacrificing his tone or clearness of phrasing, and his octave playing almost equals that of Paganini himself.'[4]

Thomson took his teaching seriously. Although dedicated to his pupils, he was also ruthless in his attempts to right a bad habit. One of the services he rendered to future generations of violinists was his method of correcting faulty *vibrato* through gymnastic exercises. This was the germ of an idea that was further developed by Achille Rivarde and finally perfected by Carl Flesch.

In the early nineteenth century the Belgian and French branches of violin playing developed independently although their roots were common. Nevertheless, many violinists considered it important to study in both schools, perfecting their bowing following de Bériot's principles in Brussels while developing a virtuoso technique in Paris.

It was Delphin Alard (1815–88) who took over at the Paris Conservatoire in 1843 when de Bériot declined the offer of professorship. A product of the classical school of Viotti through Baillot and Habeneck, he was the foremost representative of the French school then working in Paris. He had many pupils, the most distinguished being Sarasate. Alard's edition of collected classics, 'Les Maîtres Classiques', a valuable collection of sonatas, and his tutor, are still in use.

Prosper Philippe Catherine Sainton (1813–90) from Toulouse was another important product of the French school. A pupil of Habeneck, he followed a distinguished career touring Europe and for some time played in the orchestra of the Paris Grand Opéra. In 1844 he came to London, where he was appointed violin professor at the Royal Academy of Music, leader of the Queen's Band, Chamber Musician to the Queen and leader of the orchestra of Her Majesty's Theatre. In 1860 he married the famous singer Charlotte Dolby, who henceforth adopted her married name and became known as Madame Sainton-Dolby. She was a great favourite in the 'Pops' — a series of concerts founded in 1858 for the performance of chamber music. Sainton was much respected in Britain, where he was responsible for considerable improvement in the standards of violin playing. Robin Legge once wrote that 'at the last Birmingham Festival before his death, every violinist in the orchestra had been either a direct pupil of Sainton's or a pupil of a pupil'.[5]

IO

'He holds you in a magic circle'

Henri Vieuxtemps

Of the wealth of talent that existed in the mid-nineteenth-century Belgian school, one name is outstanding; that of Henri Vieuxtemps. As a virtuoso violinist, Vieuxtemps was one of the greatest of modern times. His staccato, both on the up and the down bow, was acclaimed as wonderful, and his intonation was said to be perfect. His use of strong dramatic accents and contrasts brought a new dimension to the art of violin playing. Paganini had shown the public how virtuosity as an end in itself could capture an audience. Vieuxtemps demonstrated that a more musical approach, allied to virtuosity, could achieve the same effect.

Vieuxtemps was also one of the first of the modern players to take a comprehensive approach to his art. Many of his predecessors and contemporaries had studied composition and were violinist-composers of considerable talent, but Vieuxtemps, like Spohr, investigated every possible aspect of his art.

The son of poor weavers, Henri Vieuxtemps was born in 1820 in Verviers, the centre of the wool trade in Belgium. His father played the fiddle and made musical instruments to raise extra money to feed his family (besides Henri, there was another brother who later became a cellist in the Hallé Orchestra in Manchester).

Henri had his first lessons from his father, and before he was five had outstripped his father's knowledge. A benefactor financed further lessons from a local teacher and Henri made such rapid progress that he appeared with success at his first public concert at the age of six playing the fifth concerto by Rode and the Variations with orchestra by Fontaine.

A year later, Henri went with his father on a tour of Belgium, Holland and the Netherlands. De Bériot heard him in Brussels and was so convinced of his genius that he agreed to teach him for nothing.

Henri studied with de Bériot for four years. In 1828 de Bériot took him to Paris. Here the eight-year-old child appeared in a number of concerts in which he was well-received. When de Bériot left Paris to settle in Italy, Vieuxtemps regarded it as a catastrophe. But it was then that de Bériot passed on the same advice to his young pupil that he had himself received from Viotti — that he should go his own way and imitate no-one. Vieuxtemps heeded that advice for the rest of his life.

Henri returned to Brussels, where he took lessons in harmony and studied the chamber music repertoire. Even as a young boy, Vieuxtemps had a predilection for this music, and had started his own quartet. When he was twelve he met Pauline Garcia, a contralto singer and pianist of considerable skill — sister of Malibran. Together the two young musicians undertook an intensive study of works by Mozart, Schubert and Beethoven, so that by the time Henri was fourteen, he was not only a fully-fledged virtuoso but was equipped with a mature repertoire.

Vieuxtemps' concert tours gained him esteem throughout Europe. Schumann, who heard him in Leipzig, wrote of his playing:

> When we listen to Henri, we can close our eyes with confidence. His playing is at once sweet and bright, like a flower ... From the first to the last sound that he draws from his instrument, Vieuxtemps holds you in a magic circle traced round you, and you cannot find the beginning or the end.[1]

In Vienna he came into contact with many of the great musicians of the day. Here he took lessons in counterpoint with Simon Sechter, professor at the Conservatoire and teacher of Anton Bruckner. Despite his extreme youth, Vieuxtemps played the Beethoven concerto in this city, and created musical history by being the first to perform it in the seven years which had elapsed since the composer's death in 1827. Vieuxtemps was praised both for his style and the beauty of his powerful tone; but more significant was that his playing was said to be impregnated with the Beethoven spirit.

From Vienna, Vieuxtemps went to London where he played in

a Philharmonic concert. It was also in London that he first met Paganini and received encouragement from the maestro.

On Vieuxtemps' return to Paris, he studied composition with Reicha, teacher of Gounod, Franck, Berlioz and Liszt. Although appearing continually on the concert platform, so boundless was his energy and concentration that he managed to fit everything in. After 1835 he began composing himself, and it was during a tour of Holland the following year that he first played his own compositions at his concerts. His works were first published in Vienna in 1836.

However, well trained as he was in harmony, counterpoint and composition, Vieuxtemps did not feel that he fully understood orchestration. His next step is one almost unprecedented for a conductor, let alone a violinist-composer: he returned for some months to Brussels and attached himself purely as a listener to the orchestra of the Théâtre de la Monnaie. He would seat himself beside players at different desks, absorbing every detail of the individual orchestral parts. He discussed the music with the players, looking at each of the various problems so he was able to learn the technique of all the instruments employed. It is therefore not surprising that Vieuxtemps' compositions show a comprehensive appreciation of the capabilities of each instrument. His colourful orchestration is proof of the valuable knowledge gained by this experience. Berlioz was particularly interested in his compositions and made this observation: 'Beethoven was the first to find a successful solution to the problem of how to give the solo instrument full scope without reducing the orchestra to a minor role, whereas the plan adopted by Ernst, Vieuxtemps, Liszt and one or two others . . . seems to me to strike the balance exactly.'[2]

In 1846 Vieuxtemps took up employment with the Tsar of Russia as director of violin studies at the Conservatoire in St Petersburg and 'Solo Violinist to the Imperial Court'. His six years in St Petersburg are important because it was at this time that he laid the foundations of the Russian school. Vieuxtemps brought to his pupils the lightness and elasticity of de Bériot's bowing and the perfection of his staccato. He also instilled in them the need to look into the music for the composer's intentions. The subsequent work of Henri Wieniawski and, later, Leopold Auer in the same city formed a direct link between Vieuxtemps and the present Soviet school, which has produced the Oistrakhs, Kogan, Kremer and Spivakov. Auer was himself heir to Vieuxtemps, the line strengthened through his own additional links with Dont, Böhm and Rode back to Viotti.

In 1871 Vieuxtemps was asked to take over the post vacated by the now blind de Bériot at the Conservatoire in Brussels. In 1873 he suffered a stroke which left him paralysed down the left side, but his determination to continue teaching became a source of both pity and amusement. He was quite unable to demonstrate how he wanted his pupils to play certain passages; as a consequence, frequent outbursts of rage would pour forth. If the student still did not take his advice, he would prod them with his iron-shod stick. When important visitors were brought into his class to see him at work, he would turn and smile sweetly to them, but on facing his pupils, he would scowl and grimace with all his usual fury, muttering under his breath about their incompetence.

In his memoirs, David Laurie, the nineteenth-century violin dealer, tells of a personal encounter with Vieuxtemps in Paris. He had been invited to the home of a M. Jansen, who was giving one of his regular musical afternoons. One of the late Beethoven quartets was being played. When the programme was in progress, Laurie observed a stocky, clumsy-looking little man enter. He bowed in greeting to certain members of the audience and sat himself next to Laurie. The leader of the quartet immediately became nervous, began to make mistakes, and was forever casting frightened glances towards the new arrival. The small man then began to make signs to the leader, shaking his arm to suggest more *vibrato* and throwing his right arm up and down as if to demonstrate how each passage should be bowed. He grimaced at every mistake and made wild gestures to indicate tempo. Laurie was so thoroughly incensed that when the music was over and the young leader ran towards the little man, he relished a confrontation. He was disappointed. The violinist was apologizing to the visitor, who proceeded to play the passages to perfection and then demanded why the leader could not play them like him. The embarrassed violinist retorted: 'Because I am not M. Vieuxtemps!'[3]

Vieuxtemps enjoyed a life of constant travel — and this had fatal results. In 1881 he went to Algiers for a period of convalescence. When travelling in his carriage he was hit by a stone hurled by a drunken Arab, and received severe injuries from which he died.

On 28 August 1881, Vieuxtemps' remains were brought back to his birthplace at Verviers. The grimaces and the scowls so characteristic of the man in life were forgotten, and pupils and friends turned out in their thousands. In spite of the sweltering heat, the streets were packed solid with the crowds. The cortège was drawn by four magnificent black horses and amongst the hundreds of mourners in the funeral procession was his favourite pupil, Ysaÿe, who had travelled from St Petersburg to pay his last respects. It was he who had been chosen to carry the black velvet cushion with silver tassels on which rested the violin and bow of his beloved master.

11

The Slavonic Wizard

Henri Wieniawski

The Slavs have always made a significant contribution to the history of violin playing. A virtuoso who lent considerable colour to the concert platform in the latter half of the nineteenth century was the Polish born Henri (Henryk) Wieniawski (1835–80). He was not only one of the greatest violinists in an age of virtuosos, but his warm, impetuous Slavonic temperament was transmitted to his audience from the minute he stepped on to the platform, and the fascinating, individual quality of his tone went straight to their hearts. His technique was miraculous: his fellow violinists said enviously that for him difficulties were non-existent.

Wieniawski's compositions are violinistically sound and possess great charm. He wrote about twenty-two works in all, including two violin concertos. No. 2 (Op. 22) in D minor became one of the most popular violin compositions of the day. Although Wieniawski's writings were conceived mainly to show off his own dazzling technique, this concerto, two of his polonaises and his 'Légende' are still an indispensable and greatly loved part of the present-day violin repertoire.

Born in Lublin, Wieniawski was fortunate in being reared against a cultured musical background. His father was an army surgeon and his mother the sister of the pianist Edward Wolff. When he was five Henri had lessons on the violin from Jan Hornziel, subsequently leader of the Warsaw Opera Orchestra. Later he became a pupil of Serwaczynski, who also taught the young Joachim.

Henri's success was phenomenal, even at a time when prodigies seem to have been abundant. When he was eight, he was

immediately accepted into Clavel's class at the Paris Conservatoire, and soon became a pupil of Massart. At eleven he carried off
the much coveted first prize for violin playing: this, for a
foreigner, was exceptional.

As a fully-fledged virtuoso the thirteen-year-old Henri went on
a tour of Poland and Russia, meeting everywhere with success.
Two years later, in 1850, he conquered audiences with his brother
Joseph — a pianist — in the Netherlands, France, England and
Germany.

At this time, the Russian Court was the Mecca of the great
players, and in 1860 Wieniawski was appointed solo violinist to
the Tsar at St Petersburg. He held that position for twelve years.

By the mid-nineteenth century, it was essential for great artists
to visit the USA. Not only were they likely to be well received,
but the financial rewards were tremendous. In 1872 Wieniawski
crossed the Atlantic for the first time, travelling with the world-
famous pianist Anton Rubinstein (a close friend), and a group of
instrumentalists. The tour was an historic one for a number of
reasons. They contracted to play in two hundred performances at
$200 a concert, and gave no fewer than 215 concerts in 239 days.
According to Harold Schonberg, Rubinstein complained that an
artist becomes 'an automaton' under such conditions, 'May
Heaven preserve us from such slavery!' But Wieniawski, in spite
of being 'a man of extreme nervous temperament' who on account
of recurrent ill-health had habitually missed appearances whilst in
St Petersburg, 'never missed one concert in America. However ill
he might be, he always contrived to find strength enough to
appear on the platform with his fairy-like violin.'[1] It seems that the
reason for this uncharacteristic punctuality was a clause in the
contract which demanded a fine of 1,000 francs for every non-
appearance.

Despite their friendship, under such pressure, Wieniawski and
Rubinstein suffered from strain. Tempers were often frayed and
heated arguments would be followed by long periods of icy
non-communication. One of the main bones of contention — as
far as Wieniawski was concerned — was that Rubinstein had his
name billed in larger type. Although they played the Kreutzer
Sonata on some seventy occasions, giving superb performances
which reduced the audience to tears, they privately maintained an
acrimonious silence which neither was prepared to break.

After his first appearance in the USA, a critic wrote: 'In

Above left: Henri Vieuxtemps, the Belgian who laid the foundations of the Russian school, in his virtuoso days

Above right: Henri Wieniawski, for whom his contemporaries claimed difficulties were non-existent; seen here with his brother Joseph with whom he performed

Wilma Norman-Neruda (Lady Hallé), whose success as a virtuoso encouraged other women to take up the violin

Wieniawski we have the greatest violinist who has yet been heard in America ... Of all now living Joachim alone can claim superiority over him.'[2] But in private life, Wieniawski drank heavily and was a compulsive gambler who thought nothing of sitting up all night playing roulette. Quite often he gambled away his earnings before the concert had taken place. Although this high living seemingly had no effect upon the quality of his playing, it had a disastrous effect upon his health which was not improved by extreme corpulence.

When Vieuxtemps was taken ill in 1873, Wieniawski took over his post at the Brussels Conservatoire for two years, in which time he proved to be a valuable teacher. The regular régime also led to an improvement in his health, but when Vieuxtemps had recovered sufficiently to take over again, Wieniawski resumed his former lifestyle that was to prove lethal. When in his thirties, Wieniawski was found to be suffering from a heart disease. He died, impecunious and alone, in a Moscow hospital at the age of forty-four.

There is a touching story concerning Joachim and Wieniawski. Always his ungrudging admirer, it appears that Joachim had recommended his pupils to attend a concert that Wieniawski was giving in Berlin. It was to be the first performance of his second violin concerto. When Wieniawski walked on to the platform he looked very ill and after playing for only a few minutes, stopped and asked for a chair. He continued to play, seated, but suddenly an attack of asthma almost suffocated him, and he had to be carried off the platform. Joachim rushed backstage and after a short delay returned carrying Wieniawski's violin. He apologized for being in morning dress and also for his inability to play his friend's wonderful concerto. Instead he would give them Bach's Chaconne for unaccompanied violin. The applause was tumultuous, but when poor Wieniawski staggered on to the stage and embraced Joachim, with tears of gratitude pouring down his face, the enthusiasm of the audience knew no bounds.

In his memoirs, Joachim said that 'no-one who had not witnessed Wieniawski's playing could imagine the feats of his left hand'.[3] This was praise indeed from one who was not over-generous in extolling the merits of his fellow artists. Wieniawski was said to perform double harmonics, swift passages in tenths, left-hand pizzicato and flying staccato, crystal clear and always with perfect intonation. His bowing was also said to be flawless. It is interesting that, according to Grove's he was 'one of the first, if not the first, to discover an important factor in the rational production of tone by means of a special grasp of the bow, in which the stress was laid on the function of the fore-finger and its ability to balance the weight of the bow'.[4] This would seem to be the earliest indication of a move towards the newest 'Russian' method of holding the bow as advocated much later by Carl Flesch and which is the grip most used at the present time. Wieniawski also perfected the rapid stiff-arm bowed staccato.

Wieniawski owned two exquisite violins, both of which he was forced to sell to pay gambling debts. One was the 'Wieniawski' Stradivari, made in 1719, when the maker was seventy-five and at the height of his powers. Ševčik, who heard Wieniawski play the instrument, said that of all the virtuosos he had heard in his long life-time, he had never heard anything like the tone of the 'Wieniawski'. In a rare burst of affluence during his last years, Wieniawski acquired a magnificent Pietro Guarneri violin. All who heard him said that his dazzling genius was admirably matched to the rare qualities of this instrument. Eventually, it came into the possession of Hubay, who played on it for many years.

12

Servant of Art

Joseph Joachim

It was on 28 March 1844, at Drury Lane Theatre in London, at a benefit for the manager, Alfred Bunn, that the 'Bohemian Girl' and the 'Hungarian Boy' appeared together on the same programme. The 'Girl' was Balfe's operetta, then all the rage, and the 'Boy' the twelve-year-old Joseph Joachim, making his 'first appearance before an English audience'. Sandwiched, as was customary, between the first and second acts of the operetta, the young performer had chosen to play Ernst's 'Grand Variations' on a theme from Rossini's '*Otello*', and brought the house down. Two months later, at a Philharmonic Society Concert conducted by Mendelssohn, he gave his first performance of the Beethoven violin concerto, with the cadenzas he had written himself. Mendelssohn wrote enthusiastically to Joachim's family of his 'unparalleled success'. The excitement was so great that the audience started applauding as soon as he stepped on to the platform. He played the opening bars 'so splendidly, with such certainty and pure intonation' that the public frequently interrupted him. At one point he had turned to Mendelssohn and said 'I really am very frightened.'[1] At the end they would not let him go and he had to return again and again to acknowledge the applause.

The seventh of eight children of a poor Jewish family, Joachim was born in the Hungarian village of Kitsee. When he was five he took lessons with Serwaczynski, Konzertmeister of the Opera and the best violinist in Pesth, and within two years he was playing duos with his master in public. A critic described him as 'a living marvel ... a second Vieuxtemps, Paganini or Ole Bull'.[2] Years later, when asked what he could remember of the occasion, he replied that it was his 'sky-blue coat with its mother-of-pearl buttons'.[3]

Later he studied in Vienna with the greatest teacher in that city, Hellmesberger the elder. Unfortunately, Serwaczynski's neglect of bowing arm exercises had produced what Hellmesberger considered insurmountable problems, but a second opinion was sought from Ernst, who recommended his own teacher, Josef Böhm. Apart from improving his bowing, it was Böhm who introduced Joachim to the chamber music repertoire.

Paris would have been the natural choice for further training, but a married relative was living in Leipzig, then an important centre of music. As we know, the Gewandhaus Orchestra had been thriving under Mendelssohn's direction since 1834, and the newly-opened Conservatoire was now providing another outlet for his energies. So in 1843 Joachim was auditioned by Mendelssohn who suggested study in counterpoint with Moritz Hauptmann, but considered that no further lessons in technique were necessary. 'Let him work by himself and play occasionally to David [then violin professor at the Conservatoire] for the benefit of his criticism and advice ... I myself will regularly play with him and be his adviser in artistic matters.'[4]

In a letter written in April 1844, Hauptmann wrote that young Joachim

> only needs to play about an hour [daily]. The other day ... he played Spohr's 'Gesangsscene' [Op. 47 Concerto for violin No. 8 in A minor] which he had only gone through with David a few days before the first time. It was an impromptu performance and, as the solo part was mislaid, he played it by heart, and in such a way that even Spohr would have been satisfied. The singing quality of his tone was of touching beauty, his intonation clear as a bell, and the most difficult passages unfailing in precision.[5]

The following year saw Joachim's great success in England, and on his return to Leipzig he took part in a performance at the Gewandhaus of Maurer's concertante for four violins. His co-artists were Ernst, Bazzini and David, world-famous and all very much his senior. At thirteen Joachim was now clearly on equal terms with the greatest artists of the day. But his family were against the exploitation of child prodigies, so he completed his general education and continued to study the classics with David.

Mendelssohn's powerful influence on the young Joachim was of

much benefit and many of his later attitudes stemmed from this
association. It was Mendelssohn who introduced him to the music
of Bach. Every Sunday, at the composer's home, the two would
play duos and sonatas for hours on end. The social advantages of
mixing with the musical élite at Mendelssohn's house must also
have been enormous. It was here that he met Robert Schumann
and his wife Clara, one of the greatest pianists of her day. Joachim
was to become closely associated with them and later he and Clara
were acclaimed on their recital tours.

Standards in Leipzig declined after Mendelssohn's death in
1847, and Joachim felt the need for a change. The opportunity
came by way of a suggestion from Liszt, who had now ceased
giving solo performances and was seeking a quieter life as
Kapellmeister at the Court of Weimar. Liszt offered Joachim the
post of Konzertmeister in the Grand Duke's orchestra, which he
accepted with enthusiasm. Until this time he had been rather
over-protected and, being of a naturally serious disposition, had
experienced little outside his restricted world of study. At
Weimar, where he stayed for three years under Liszt's powerful
personality, the transition from boyhood to maturity was undoubtedly effected. Joachim's compositions at Weimar show a
strong influence of Liszt. He composed his Violin Concerto in G
minor, Op. 3 there and dedicated it to Liszt, who returned the
compliment and wrote his Hungarian Rhapsody in C sharp minor
for Joachim.

Joachim's Weimar period was one of inner conflict. An admirer
and friend of Liszt on the one hand, he was, on the other,
governed by his own taste. For him the 'classics' predominated.
Liszt and the classics were oil and water. Furthermore, the
worship of Wagner's music permeating musical taste at Weimar
was to Joachim inordinate and unacceptable.

When the opportunity came to move on he relinquished his
post, although loath to leave Liszt and his other friends. He would
have been even more distressed had he known the part he was to
play in the dramatic battle between the progressive 'New German
School' and the conservative opposition. The 'new' movement
represented the 'music of the future', with Liszt and Wagner as
their idols. The opposition condemned all post-Beethoven music
(except that of Mendelssohn), holding the 'classics' as their
models. But it did not stop there. Music began to take on an
ethical significance. A composer indulging in chromaticism or
striking effects of orchestral colour was considered depraved,

whereas the work of those adhering more closely to the rules of Classical harmony represented high moral purpose.

When Liszt published what Joachim thought an arrogant preface to his 'Symphonic Poems' in 1857, Joachim wrote politely severing their relations but thanking him for his past friendship. This was followed by depositions in the *Neue Zeitschrift für Musik*, after which the opposition to the 'New German School' published the now famous manifesto of 1860, disagreeing with the 'new and unheard-of theories which are contradictory to the innermost nature of music'.[6] It was signed by Brahms, Joachim, the pianist Julius Otto Grimm and the conductor Bernhard Scholz.

When Joachim left Weimar in 1853, he became 'Royal Court and State Violinist' to the blind King George of Hanover, a great patron of music. Although he was on intimate terms with the King, Joachim's affairs did not always run smoothly. A perfectionist in everything he undertook, he constantly fought with the players to improve the standards of orchestral performance, but with minimal success. He frequently grumbled that musically he was preaching to the deaf and was obliged to make his own music at home. He stayed at his post until 1866, when Hanover became part of Prussia and the King went into exile.

In 1863, Joachim married Amalie Weiss, a beautiful contralto from the Hanover Opera. Six years later, when he was appointed director of the newly-opened Hochschule in Berlin, they moved with their young family to the city which was fast becoming the new Prussian capital. After Prussia's emergence as the leading German state following her defeat of Austria in 1866, Berlin played an increasing part in European politics and as a result the musical life of the city began to show signs of improvement. Famous artists could be heard there more often; Clara Schumann, Brahms and Wagner all visited Berlin with far greater frequency than before.

When Joachim arrived on their doorstep it was rightly sensed that a new era in the musical life of the city had begun. The Hochschule went from strength to strength and within three years the number of pupils had increased from nineteen to one hundred. Joachim instituted public students' concerts which were attended by the press and soon became major events in the musical life of the city, Joachim's own performances being the star attraction. In 1869 he founded a string quartet, establishing the medium as a specialized field and raising it to a high peak of achievement.

Joachim's violin teaching is best described by one of his most

Joseph Joachim in 1868

Pablo Sarasate, the greatest 'salon' virtuoso of the late nineteenth century

The Joachim Quartet: Joachim, Robert Hausmann, Emanuel Wirth, Karel Halir

famous pupils, a fellow Hungarian, Leopold Auer, who had lessons with him in Hanover in 1862. Because of the busy life of their master, students never had fixed lessons but were summoned by a servant at short notice. Auer says that Joachim rarely entered into technical details and never made suggestions as to how to attain technical facility; this was supposed to be taken care of at home. But he always had his violin in his hand throughout the lesson, and whenever he saw fit to criticize, he 'would draw his bow and play the passage or phrase in question himself in a manner truly divine'.[7] Divine or not, Carl Flesch — also a Joachim pupil — is highly critical of his master's bowing. He tells us that Joachim played with the upper arm in such a low position that a right angle was formed between the arm and the forearm at the nut. The bow was held by the finger-tips, the index finger touching the stick at the line of the top joint with the little finger remaining on the stick. When a change of bow at the nut was required, due to the stiffness of the fingers it could only be accomplished by a horizontal jerk of the wrist. Nevertheless, Flesch considers that: 'Joachim's bowing was a purely personal affair, an intuitive motional translation of a thoroughly expressive need.' It was only when his followers tried to establish a 'school' based on wrong and 'unnatural' principles that the trouble started. Flesch claims that the majority of his pupils, as violinists, were 'cripples for life' and for this reason Joachim 'never trained a single violinist who achieved world fame'.[8]

But in other respects Flesch agrees with Auer that Joachim was no ordinary teacher. Since he seldom made his meaning clear in detail, it was absolutely essential that the student should have considerable technical training before approaching the master. For those who understood him and could follow his inarticulate directions, much benefit could be obtained; the less gifted, who could not appreciate the inner expression of his ideas, were left unenlightened. This would seem to be one explanation for the controversy concerning Joachim's teaching gifts.

Joachim had tremendous reserves of mental and physical strength, and retained the buoyancy of youth well into his advancing years. His capacity for work was almost inexhaustible. After a twenty-hour journey he was quite likely to go home, change and within the hour would be at the Hochschule to give three or four lessons. After lunch he would probably conduct an orchestral rehearsal and then get into a carriage, drive to the Mendelssohns for dinner, and spend the remainder of the evening playing quartets with the other guests.

One of the most significant associations in Joachim's life was his friendship with Brahms, whom he first met in Hanover in 1852. Brahms had heard Joachim play the Beethoven concerto in Hamburg four years before, and the performance had left a deep impression. The friendship lasted over forty years. Their extensive correspondence shows that they frequently exchanged musical sketches for criticism and each respected the other's opinion on equal terms. In fact, Brahms considered Joachim to be a better composer than himself.

When Brahms turned to writing a violin concerto, it was naturally with Joachim in mind. He made the first sketches of the work at Wörthersee in the summer of 1878 and sent the solo part to his friend for comment. Joachim found it difficult to judge from an incomplete score and without being able to play it with an orchestra. However, he must have envisaged some of the problems for he wrote: 'Some of it is quite original, violinistically, but whether one can comfortably play all this in an over-heated hall is another matter.'⁹ The extended duration of solo passages in this concerto has always been a test of stamina for the soloist.

Their letters highlight the disadvantages suffered by the keyboard player writing for an instrument he knows little about. Curiously enough, Brahms was more willing to accept Joachim's advice on the composition itself than that relating to matters of technical difficulty in the solo violin part. It was only in the writing of the cadenza that Joachim had a free hand. One of the main points of disagreement concerned directions for *legato* phrasing where Brahms insisted upon pianistic slurs rather than bowing directions. Joachim writes: 'With so many notes on the same stroke [of the bow], it is better to divide the notes by several strokes. It can still sound as if it is played with one.'¹⁰ On another occasion Brahms is quite put out. 'With what right, and since when, and on whose authority do you violinists write the sign of *portamento* where it doesn't mean anything? . . . So far I've never given in to violinists and not accepted their damned slurs!' His parting shot is to the point. 'Why should ⌒ mean something else with us than it did with Beethoven?'¹¹

However, in a passage where 'the basses should play pizzicato, not sustained'¹² Brahms seemed happy enough to accept Joachim's modifications for making the solo part less taxing by providing a 'lighter' accompaniment. In another instance Brahms was persuaded by Joachim to cut down the strength of the woodwind so that the soloist would not be overpowered.

Brahms completed the work by December 1878 and it was given a try-out at the Hochschule. Almost without exception, Berlin critics condemned it as 'a barren production' and attacked Joachim for having compelled a student orchestra to accompany 'such unmitigated rubbish'.[13] On New Year's Day 1879, the first public performance was given at the Gewandhaus in Leipzig and the critics were no kinder.

The concerto was not published until the autumn of 1879. Brahms knew Joachim's technique and musicianship to be superior to any other living violinist's and resisted publication because he feared it would be too difficult for other violinists. So until then, Joachim carried the entire score, including the orchestral parts, in manuscript from city to city. At the first five performances he played with the music: only at the sixth — a Philharmonic concert in London — did he feel confident enough to play the concerto from memory.

Over the years Brahms and Joachim had occasional minor disagreements. Mostly these concerned the performance or non-performance of one of Brahms's compositions and did not greatly disrupt the course of friendship. But when Joachim brought an action against his wife, accusing her of an illicit relationship with the publisher Simrock, Brahms took Amalie's part. He wrote her a long personal letter confirming his belief in her innocence. The letter was read out in court and Joachim lost his case.

For a year all contact between the two men ceased. Then they corresponded on purely musical matters, addressing each other without intimacy. Brahms appears to have suffered most and constantly sought to patch up the quarrel. Joachim was personally more inflexible, although he never doubted Brahms's genius and continued to play his music.

In the summer of 1887 when Brahms was in Switzerland, he began work on the double concerto for violin and cello. This was composed for Joachim and Robert Hausmann, cellist from the Joachim Quartet, in an attempt at reconciliation. When Brahms sent the solo parts to Joachim and Hausmann they seized upon them excitedly. All three musicians came together at Clara Schumann's house at Baden-Baden in September, where they rehearsed with a piano. They also had a run-through with the Kursaal orchestra. The concerto received its first performance on 18 October 1887 with Brahms conducting. At a later performance, with the same artists at the Gewandhaus in Leipzig,

Tchaikovsky said: 'In spite of the excellent performance this concerto did not make the slightest impression on me.'[14]

The concerto succeeded in its purpose for Clara Schumann noted in her diary that Joachim and Brahms had spoken to each other for the first time in years. The two string players offered a number of suggestions for improvement, and many of Joachim's pencilled modifications remain on the manuscript score. But Brahms, intransigent as always, would not give way to their wishes until the work was finally published in 1888. Even then, in the Rondo finale, where the cellist has the main theme and is called upon to play a lively passage, the bowings in the score are Brahms's, not Joachim's.

The impressions of Joachim left by contemporaries range from idolatry to blunt, cold criticism. After a concert in Vienna in 1861 when Joachim was thirty, Edward Hanslick wrote:

> After the first movement [of the Beethoven concerto] it must have been clear to everyone that here was no stunning virtuoso but rather a significant and individual personality. For all his technique, Joachim is so identified with the musical ideal that he may be said to have penetrated beyond the utmost in virtuosity: anything suggestive of vanity or applause-seeking has been eliminated . . . What a flood of strength there is in the tone which his large, sure bow draws from the instrument![15]

Joachim's struggle to improve standards of musicianship had immeasurable influence throughout Europe. Although artists like Ernst and Vieuxtemps had made the public aware that virtuosity could be successfully allied to musicianship, it was Joachim who established it as a fact of performing life. He was the first of the nineteenth-century violinists to play the unaccompanied sonatas of Bach and his programmes invariably included works by Scarlatti, Tartini and Spohr. Before his introduction of the classics into his own programmes, the general repertoire contained an abundance of short items, pot-pourris and transcriptions. Other artists soon followed Joachim's example, and although there were sporadic bursts of empty virtuosity, the dignity that Joachim brought to the concert platform has remained until our own time. Flesch, although critical of his bowing, considers that it is 'Thanks to the high ethical ideals of Joachim's art' that 'the virtuoso developed, within a mere thirty years, from his early nineteenth-century position of an entertainer to that of an artist who wished to be primarily regarded as a mediator between the work and the listener'.[16]

Joachim was not an avid promoter of performances of new music, yet Brahms would probably never have had a hearing but for him. His own composing gifts were considerable. Carl Flesch considered that his 'Concerto in the Hungarian Style' is 'a work of genius ... the most outstanding creation that a violinist has ever written for his own instrument'.[17] His cadenzas, written before the Berlin period, have stood the test of time rather better than his concerto, which is rarely played.

Joachim was a complex character: outwardly very serious and a man of high ideals — some thought too high; inwardly, with depths of feeling that he seldom betrayed to his closest friends. But his response to an erring pupil could be fiery, and when competition showed itself from an unexpected quarter, he could be downright sarcastic. When the twenty-three-year-old Fritz Kreisler, who had scored a sensational success in Berlin in 1898, was brought by a friend to Joachim's class, he was greeted by the master with cold politeness and without a glimmer of recognition. The accompanist had failed to appear, and Kreisler, also an accomplished pianist, offered to take his place. He played perfectly. When he took his leave, Joachim said curtly, 'You certainly are a ready pianist'.[18] Yet in later years Kreisler admitted Joachim was one of the great influences in his life: 'He was a queer mixture of generosity and jealousy. He wanted everybody to do exactly as he desired it to be done and was very pedantic about it.'[19]

Joachim was honoured and fêted everywhere. In 1899, at his Golden Jubilee on the concert platform, a festival concert in the Philharmonic Hall in Berlin was given in his honour. An élite orchestra was formed from his most prominent pupils and he was presented with a Stradivari violin to add to his collection. He already possessed the 'De Barrau', the 'Alard' and the 'Dolphin'.

In a letter to his brother in 1849, when wrestling with a composition for his next London concert, he had written:

> It seems as though I were fated to do no good in music ... And I do mean well with my art, it is a holy thing to me ... But in spite of that I accomplish practically nothing; it seems as if some tragic fate hung over me, with which I am powerless to battle! Will this fate pursue me all my life? ... I shall yet conquer it. I should so like to be of some great service to art![20]

The contrast with his self-doubts of fifty years before was complete.

13

Lady of the Bow

Wilma Norman-Neruda

In King Henry VII's accounts there is an item dated 2 November 1495: 'For a womane that singeth with a fidell, 2s' whereas the queen's male 'fideler' of the period, 17 February 1497, was paid 'in rewarde' £1.6s.8d!'[1] The 'womane' would have been exceptional for her time, since we know that the fiddle was not thought to be respectable. Nevertheless, the existence of amateur women violinists can be traced throughout the history of the instrument.

The earliest professional would seem to be a Mrs Sarah Ottey, born about 1695 who performed 'solos on the harpsichord, violin and bass viol'[2] frequently at concerts about 1721–2. Another was 'La Diamantina', born around 1715, and described by the poet Thomas Gray in 1740: 'A famous virtuosa who played on the violin divinely, and sung angelically'. We have already learnt of Maddalena Lombardini Sirmen (b.1735) through the letter she received from Tartini. She enjoyed a considerable reputation and was thought to rival Nardini.

Regina Strinasacchi (1764–1823), a product of the della Pietà at Venice, where the standards were high, has also been mentioned previously; a highly successful soloist in her own right, she is immortalized by her association with Mozart in the historic performance of his Sonata in B flat major (K.454), when the composer accompanied her from a blank sheet of paper, having written only the violin part.

Around the turn of the eighteenth century we find an increasing number of women violinists, some of whom were child prodigies well known in their own time but whose names today mean nothing. The sisters Milanollo, child prodigies of exceptional talent, were the best known. Natives of Savigliano in Piedmont, they caused a furore wherever they appeared. Nicknamed Mlle Staccato and Mlle Adagio, they travelled extensively through France, Belgium, Holland and England. Teresa, elder of the two, went to Paris in 1836, when she was only eleven, to study with Lafont. Afterwards she took some lessons from Habeneck, and finished under de Bériot in Brussels.

Despite these sporadic successes, the violin was still not considered to be fit for ladies, and certainly we know that Spohr discouraged his wife from playing such an unbecoming instrument. Of the women born during the early part of the century, only two names can be remembered today. One was Camilla Urso (1842–1902), a French violinist of Italian parentage who travelled extensively throughout the world as a virtuoso and finally settled in New York. The other was the Czech Wilhelmina Neruda, who became better known as Wilma Norman-Neruda, and later as Lady Hallé, wife of Sir Charles Hallé, whose name is perpetuated by the oldest of the great British orchestras, which he founded in 1858.

Wilhelmina Neruda (1839–1911) was born in Brno, Moravia, into a distinguished family of violinists and musicians dating from the seventeenth century. She could play the violin before she could walk and was given her first lessons by her father, Josef Neruda, a professional violinist and organist. She later had further instruction from Leopold Jansa, a distinguished Bohemian violinist and Imperial Chamber virtuoso in the Court Chapel in Vienna. In 1849 Wilhelmina made her début in Vienna with her pianist sister Amalie, and astounded even that severe critic, Edward Hanslick, who said 'the little Neruda is wonderful indeed in bravura music, in musical intelligence, and finally in her remarkable accuracy'.[3]

Josef Neruda caused a stir when he brought his talented children to London in April 1849 — a 'remarkably clever trio' (the nine-year-old Wilhelmina, her sister, aged twelve, and Victor, their eleven-year-old brother), second violinist and cellist respectively. Wilhelmina was the star. *The Times* music critic wrote: 'Her performance of Vieuxtemps' "Arpeggio" and Ernst's "Carnaval de Venise" are wonderful, nor does it require any apology on the score of her tender age.' The juvenile trio, booked originally for two nights only, were re-engaged for a further sixteen performances.

The following month, Wilhelmina was engaged to play a de

Bériot concerto at the Philharmonic Society's Concert, an account of which comes from William Bartholomew (English librettist and violinist), who wrote to a friend the next day:

> A little girl, a child in years and person, but a perfect miniature Paganini, played last night to the Philharmonic audiences a concerto of de Bériot's on the violin. Her tone, her execution, especially with the bow hand, were all perfect — the latter is beautiful: her graceful and elastic wrist produced some of the most sparkling staccatos by up and down bowing that I have ever heard.[4]

In 1864, Wilma (as she now preferred to be called) made a great success in Paris where she played in the Pasdeloup (a famous series of popular concerts founded by the composer, Jules Pasdeloup), and Conservatoire concerts. In musical circles she was dubbed 'The Queen of Violinists'. Wilma Neruda favoured the 'classic' style of playing and consequently was considered by many to be the female counterpart of Joachim. She was a child prodigy who, unlike so many others, fulfilled the promise of early talent. Her performances were always considered to be synonymous with all that is good in musical art, and her programmes were examples of the 'classic' influence of Joachim. She was also a fine quartet player and was for many years first violin of the Philharmonic Quartet in London. She also played in the Joachim Quartet, and in 1896 she appeared with Joachim playing Bach's D minor concerto for two violins. Indeed, it was Joachim who, after having heard her as a child, first recognized her talent. He remarked to Charles Hallé, who had not then met her, 'I recommend this artist to your careful consideration. Mark this, when people have given her a fair hearing, they will think more of her and less of me.'[5]

In 1864 she married the Swedish Opera conductor Ludwig Norman, and was for the duration of their marriage professor of violin at Stockholm Royal Academy of Music. When they separated, in 1869, she came to London and appeared in concerts with both the Philharmonic Society and the Monday 'Popular' series. Her husband died in 1885 and three years later she married Sir Charles Hallé.

The late Archie Camden and Sir Robert Mayer could recall hearing Lady Hallé in their youth, and both remarked upon her fine presence and beautiful tone. She also possessed a sense of fun. Alfred Gibson, an English violinist who played occasionally with the Joachim Quartet, writes that Lady Hallé used neither chin-rest nor shoulder-pad. When she was in the artists' room with Joachim, she would tease the members of the quartet by saying 'Now put on your little pincushions'.[6]

There is no doubt that Lady Hallé's success encouraged other women to take up professional violin playing, a field which until this time had been virtually dominated by men. But the struggle was to remain uphill for some time to come.

14

Incomparable Charmer

Pablo Sarasate

By the middle of the nineteenth century, Spain had fallen behind her Latin-speaking neighbours and was one of the most musically backward countries in Europe. It was not until the end of the century, for example, that Spaniards had the opportunity to hear all the Beethoven symphonies. Few therefore sought a career in music, and those who were gifted enough to try were obliged to go to Paris. One of Spain's most famous émigré musicians was Pablo Sarasate, favourite pupil of Alard at the Conservatoire in Paris and whose 'Spanish Dances' perpetuate his memory with music-lovers the world over.

'Pablo' — his real name was Martin — Sarasate was born in Pamplona, northern Spain, in 1844, the son of a bandmaster, who gave him his first violin lessons at the age of five. Later he studied with Manuel Rodriguez Sáez in Madrid and here he played at Court to Queen Isabella. She not only gave him a magnificent Stradivari violin dated 1724 but also provided the means for him to study at the Conservatoire in Paris. He was then twelve years old. After only three years' study, Sarasate carried off the first prize for violin playing. When asked by Alard what he would like as a personal gift from him, the boy replied without hesitation 'A box of tin soldiers'.[1] This direct simplicity was characteristic of the man who was to become Joachim's most serious rival.

After completing his studies, Sarasate undertook some concert tours, but achieved very little success other than as a salon virtuoso. His style of playing was somewhat affected, and his programmes consisted of variations on opera themes arranged for the violin. He never touched the classical repertoire — a surprising lack of development for one who had shown such early promise.

Then in 1867 there came about a complete change both in his playing and in his choice of programme. There is no evidence of any academic influence which could have brought about this transformation, but the cause could have been an emotional one. At the age of twenty, Sarasate fell deeply in love with Maria, a pianist and daughter of Louis Lefébure-Wély, organist of the Church of Saint Sulpice in Paris. Three years later they had planned their wedding, but Sarasate returned one day from a concert tour to find Maria was to marry another. Sarasate never recovered from the shock and, although throughout his life he was followed everywhere by women who even fought over his cigarette stubs, he remained a life-long bachelor. He had also experienced a great tragedy in his childhood that could have been linked with this later event. At the age of eleven, when *en route* to Paris with his mother, they stopped overnight in Bayonne. On entering his mother's room to kiss her good-night, he found her dead from cholera.

From this time, he started playing the classics and his style took on a seriousness which had hitherto been totally absent. His technique had always been remarkable, so that his new musical development, allied to his facility in mechanical execution, simply added another dimension to his immaculate phrasing and charm of tone.

His repertoire included the concertos of the German masters and those of the French and Belgian schools. Lalo composed both his violin concerto and 'Symphonie Espagnole' for Sarasate. Saint-Saëns had written his concerto for him when he was only fifteen. Whilst on tour in Germany, Sarasate met the composer Max Bruch, known then as a pianist at the beginning of his career. They toured together with great success and Bruch dedicated both his second violin concerto and his 'Scottish Fantasy' to Sarasate.

Sarasate generally avoided the music of Paganini, partly because he had little taste for it, and also because he had very small hands and could not manage the long stretches that these compositions demanded.

In Leipzig, Sarasate caused a sensation. He quickly followed this with a series of tours in Germany, Austria, England and Belgium, which were not only financially rewarding but earned him a reputation as a virtuoso. It was Sarasate's début in Vienna in 1876 that won him celebrity at the age of thirty-two. Hanslick said:

'There are few violinists whose playing gives such unalloyed enjoyment as the performance of this Spaniard. His tone is incomparable — not powerfully or deeply affecting, but of enchanting sweetness.' Hanslick praises his 'infallible correctness' and purity of tone. 'He is distinguished, not because he plays great difficulties, but because he plays with them.'[2]

Sarasate had first appeared in London in 1861, when he was seventeen, at one of the series of Opera Concerts at the Crystal Palace, and also at the St James's Hall, but the press failed to comment. Even when thirteen years later, he appeared at a Philharmonic Society Concert, the critic of the *Musical Times* was singularly unimpressed. He played Lalo's violin concerto, but 'neither the composition nor the performer excited any special sensation'. The best they could muster was that he 'has an agreeable but thin tone and executes with neatness'.[3]

But in 1879, also at a Philharmonic Society Concert, it was quite another matter. This time he was 'positively overwhelmed with applause and thrice recalled'.[4] When in 1883, he played the Mendelssohn concerto with the same Society, the room was crowded to its limit. One critic remarked upon Sarasate's 'emotional style' and compared it to Joachim's 'highly refined and intellectual interpretation',[5] but agreed that two distinct readings of a great work may be permitted. One dissenting voice bemoaned the excessive speed at which he played the last movement — a criticism which, incidentally, was to be levelled at Sarasate for the rest of his performing life.

An interesting account of such an interpretation of the Mendelssohn comes from Archie Camden. When aged eleven in 1899, he was taken by friends to a concert given by the Hallé Orchestra in Manchester, with Sarasate playing the Mendelssohn concerto under Hans Richter. Master Camden's acute ear noticed some discrepancy between soloist and orchestra, and he claimed that they were playing at different speeds, an idea firmly put down by his parents. Many years later, discussing the matter with Arthur Catterall, who had been on one of the back desks in the violin section of the Hallé at the time, Mr Camden found that he had been right. Apparently a row had erupted because Sarasate claimed that he as the soloist could choose his own tempo and the orchestra should follow. Richter had insisted that, irrespective of his privilege as a soloist, it was still too fast. After much wrangling (which is recounted in amusing detail in Archie Camden's memoirs), they agreed on an alarming compromise. When performing the solo sections, the orchestra would play in his time: when it was the turn of the tutti, they would obey the conductor. Carl Flesch tells us, incidentally, that Sarasate was the only violinist whom he ever heard playing the flying, thrown staccato of this movement at the extreme point of the bow. Usually it is played on the frog end of the bow.

Flesch maintains that when Sarasate visited the USA he was literally 'a flop', but the American Henry Lahee writes: 'he won great favor, for his playing is of the kind which appeals to the fancy, graceful, vivacious, and pure toned, and he plays Spanish Dances in a manner never to be surpassed'. He was compared with some of the most eminent violinists: 'Vieuxtemps was an artist with an ardent mind, and a magnificent interpreter of Beethoven; Joachim towers aloft in the heights of serene poetry, upon the Olympic summits inaccessible to the tumults of passion; Sivori was a dazzling virtuoso; Sarasate is an incomparable charmer.'[6]

In appearance Sarasate was striking. Flesch tells us that he and his contempories held in awe the small, black-eyed Spaniard with the well-trimmed coal-black moustache and eyes; black, curly, over-carefully arranged hair: 'It was a unique experience to see this little man stride on to the platform, with genuine Spanish grandeza, superficially calm, even phlegmatic, to witness how, after some stereotyped movements, he began to play with unheard of sovereignty and, in a rapid climax, put his audience into astonishment, admiration and highest rapture.'[7]

The poet and critic Arthur Symons writes of that pallid 'strange, attractive, contradictory face... The eyes are passionate and stormy even when the jaded indifferent face breaks into a smile of unaffected pleasure as the enthusiasm of a whole audience mounts in applause.'[8]

Sarasate lived in the rue du Bac in Paris, not far from his friend Whistler, the artist. Whistler painted a magnificent portrait of the violinist. After seeing it, Symons wrote: 'The man who holds the violin in his hands is a child pleased to please; not a student or a diviner. And Whistler has rendered all this, superbly. Note how Sarasate dandles the violin. It is a child, a jewel. He is already thinking of the sound, the flawless tone, not of Beethoven. Whistler has caught him, poised him, posed him, another butterfly, and alive.'[9]

What Symons saw as a virtue, others considered a shortcoming.

Flesch describes Sarasate as intellectually in 'the lower income brackets',[10] and Busoni dismissed him as having 'neither brains nor temperament'.[11] But irrespective of his intellectual ability, he had a ready wit and could be disarmingly candid. When he was in Bucharest, the Queen of Rumania invited him to be the guest of honour at a party, for which she had ordered the finest Rumanian gipsy band to entertain them. When asked what he thought of the performance, Sarasate replied abruptly, 'It's pretty bad!'[12]

As a composer, Sarasate has contributed some of the most popular pieces in the violin repertoire, and when played by himself, they usually brought the house down. It is interesting to note that Flesch, even in the thirties, thought the 'Spanish Dances' were too little considered by virtuosos who preferred 'perfumed . . . pot-pourri-like arrangements'.[13] He prophesied with accuracy that Sarasate's compositions would dominate the virtuoso repertoire much longer than those of any of his more learned colleagues. Today, these pieces, along with the compositions of Kreisler, are finding renewed favour.

Whatever other criticism was levelled at Sarasate, there was never a whisper against his technique. Hanslick, Flesch, Sir Adrian Boult and Sir Robert Mayer, all of whom heard him in the flesh, bear witness to his incomparable tone, immaculate phrasing and incredible left-hand technique over which he had the most perfect command. Sarasate influenced his contempories for about twenty-five years by his example of absolute purity of intonation which resulted in considerable raising of standards of technique. It has been said that his influence was both good and harmful. Good, because those who heard him had living proof of his excellence, but bad because he attracted so many imperfect imitators. In the same way that everyone had tried to copy Paganini, they tried to do the same with Sarasate, with the result that everything was magnified and inevitably coarsened. What Flesch calls 'passionless, smooth, eely tone production' became very fashionable until Ysaÿe came along to set the course in quite another direction. But he considers Sarasate to be 'the ideal embodiment of the salon virtuoso of the greatest style'.[14]

Flesch has some interesting observations on Sarasate's technique which he was able to study at close quarters:

With the precise and effortless function of both his arms he represented a completely new type of violinist. The finger-tips of his left hand were quite smooth and ungrooved; they hit the finger-board in the normal fashion, without excessive raising or hammering. His *vibrato* was rather broader than had hitherto been customary. Following an absolutely correct if unconscious principle, he considered his bowing first and foremost a means of producing the kind of tone which he regarded as ideal and which was of a pleasant and elegant smoothness... The label of 'sweet' tone which hung round his neck all his life was not so much the result of an inner need as of a technical peculiarity.[15]

Flesch explains that Sarasate made his stroke on the strings exactly in the middle of the distance between the bridge and the fingerboard, and hardly ever played near the bridge, where the sound is more strident and oboe-like.

Sarasate never took pupils; he was essentially a performing artist in every sense of the word. He received very high fees for his services and was once called the highest-paid player in Germany where he was said to have received 3,000 marks for one concert. Even Joachim was paid only 1,000.

In his later years Sarasate's playing deteriorated and he was inclined to play sharp; his vibrato, too, was less secure. But the old magic never left him, and he could fill a concert hall without difficulty. His health had been failing for some time due to a chest complaint. He died suddenly in 1908 in Biarritz from a collapse of the lungs.

15

The Great Teachers

August Wilhelmj; Leopold Auer;
Otakar Ševčik; Jenö Hubay;
Carl Flesch

Two contemporaries of Sarasate greatly influenced the development of violin playing by the application of their individual gifts. They were the German, August Wilhelmj, and one of the greatest teachers of all time, the Hungarian, Leopold Auer.

With August Wilhelmj (1845–1908), we have one of the comparatively few great violinists born into a wealthy family. His father was a distinguished lawyer and owner of important vineyards on the Rhine, and his mother a pianist who had studied with Chopin. It was she who encouraged early signs of talent in her son. She sent him to the Court Konzertmeister, Conrad Fischer at Wiesbaden, with whom he made the usual swift progress of the prodigy. But when the boy showed signs of wanting to make it his career, he received little response from his father. It was only after Prince Emil von Wittgenstein had obtained the blessing of Liszt that he was allowed to train further. Liszt took the boy to Ferdinand David at Leipzig, and he was immediately taken on as a pupil at the Conservatoire.

Wilhelmj made his début at the Gewandhaus in November 1862 at the age of seventeen, playing Joachim's 'Hungarian Concerto', with great success. There is a story concerning Joachim, who happened to be passing through Leipzig late at night and called in on his old master. David was full of enthusiasm for his clever pupil, Wilhelmj, and told Joachim that he played his concerto so well he could play it in his sleep. Joachim said to David: 'Wake him up and let me hear him.'[1] It was two o'clock in the morning, but the sleepy student, clad in dressing gown and slippers, apparently gave a faultless performance of the work.

In later years, Joachim was less kindly disposed towards Wilhelmj. In many respects, Wilhelmj's powerful and beautiful tone and 'racy virtuosity',[2] combined with an outstanding technique, made him a serious rival to Joachim. But more important was Wilhelmj's early involvement, through Liszt at Weimar, in the neo-German Wagnerian movement. It was he who persuaded Wagner to come to London in 1877. Wilhelmj also made paraphrases of Wagner's music and 'arrangements' of many of the classics. The one for which Joachim never forgave him was the still popular 'Air' from the Bach Suite in D major, which he transposed to C major, and played on the G string only. Once, when the French violinist Lucien Capet played the 'Air on the G string', Joachim flew into a rage and reduced the Frenchman to tears. With typical arrogance he considered that Bach was his province and rejected such travesties of the master's work.

For some time Wilhelmj travelled widely as a virtuoso violinist in Europe, Russia, America, Australia and Asia. His American début was in New York in 1878, and although he achieved success for his playing in the grand manner, he did not appeal to the heart in the same way as had Ole Bull and Reményi before him.

In 1885 Wilhelmj was invited by the Sultan of Turkey to perform to the ladies of the harem, a unique privilege never previously granted to any other violinist. What the houris thought of him is not on record but the Sultan decorated him with the Medjidie Order of the second class, and presented him with a gift of diamonds.

On the concert platform Wilhelmj cut a splendid figure, like a Greek statue. He was 'tall, broad-shouldered, with a massive forehead surrounded by a mass of long wavy hair, the picture of dignified repose', writes E. van der Straeten, who remembered hearing him at the height of his powers; and, 'whether he played a simple air or a Paganini concerto, his quiet pose remained the same. His notes issued from his violin like clarion notes, scintillating with extraordinary brilliance, always beautiful, never forced and rarely equalled in purity of intonation.'[3] A well-known London violin dealer once said: 'He tried some violins [in my shop] — I think he could make a cigar box sound like a Cremona fiddle.'

At his peak, Wilhelmj was certainly one of the greatest players of the late nineteenth century, but as a performer he deteriorated early. He was only forty when he retired from the concert platform to devote himself to teaching. A variety of reasons are given for this decision; some say he suffered from ill-health, others that he was overfond of good Rhenish wine.

Nevertheless, his reputation as a teacher is without blemish. His equable temperament was eminently suited to teaching, and in 1894 he was appointed principal professor of violin at the Guild-hall School of Music, where he remained until his death in 1908. The English violinist, Dettmar Dressel, who studied with him, tells us that his methods were highly personal and that he had infinite patience. He may not have produced any world-famous violinists, but he trained a large number of first-class professionals and greatly raised standards of playing in Britain.

It was not until after the Revolution of 1917, when he founded an Academy of Violin Playing in New York, that the musical world became fully aware of the significance of Leopold Auer (1845–1930) as a teacher. He had been violin professor at the Imperial Conservatoire, St Petersburg, for forty-eight years before making his American début, at the age of seventy-two at the Carnegie Hall in March 1917. Kreisler and many of his pupils were in the audience. Richard Aldrich, then critic of the *New York Times*, found a 'fluent ease' in his playing of a programme of 'Old Masters' including Handel, Locatelli, Nardini, Vitali, unaccompanied Bach and 'his own arrangements of a Haydn Serenade . . . and a *vivace* that would have been a task for younger fingers'. And yet this was the violinist who, in 1878, when Tchaikovsky dedicated his violin concerto to him, refused to tackle it because it was too difficult. He later revised this opinion, but the first performance was eventually given in Vienna in 1881 by Adolph Brodsky, to whom Tchaikovsky re-dedicated the work. On hearing this first performance, Hanslick wrote: 'The violin is no longer played. It is yanked about, it is torn asunder, it is beaten black and blue . . .'

The son of a house-painter, Leopold Auer was born in the small town of Veszprem in Hungary. He played the violin from the age of six and took his first lessons as best he could with the local church organist and jack-of-all-music. When he was nine he entered the Budapest Conservatoire under Ridley Kohne, who was also Konzertmeister at the Budapest National Opera House. A curious coincidence was that Kohne's colleague at the first desk was Carl Huber, also on the Conservatoire staff. His son, Eugen, later became famous as Jenö Hubay, using a Magyarized form of his name.

At this time, Paris dominated the violin scene and it was the dream city of all aspiring performers. In his book *Violin Playing as I teach it*, Auer tells us that despite the importance of the Conservatoire at Leipzig, neither this nor the one at Vienna were well known outside the German-speaking countries. Auer's parents could not afford Paris, so he went to Vienna, where he studied with Jakob Dont at the Conservatoire. He completed his course in 1858, aged thirteen, having received the coveted medal and diploma which served him as a passport in the provincial towns in which he played. In 1862, he completed his studies with Joachim at Hanover. When Auer left that city he toured as a fully fledged virtuoso performer, playing at the Gewandhaus in Leipzig and leading concert halls in Germany, Holland, Scandinavia and England.

The training with Dont in Vienna is almost certainly a key factor in Auer's development. Dont, who had been taught by Böhm, was one of the most influential figures in the development of the Viennese school of violin playing which, through several generations of its representatives, made a significant contribution. The Auer pupils are the most obvious result: Mischa Elman, Efrem Zimbalist, Toscha Seidel, Isolde Menges, Nathan Milstein and Jascha Heifetz, to name half a dozen.

In 1868 Auer succeeded Wieniawski as professor of violin at St Petersburg under three Tsars, Alexanders II and III, and the ill-fated Nicholas II; he was knighted by the last-named in 1894. Whilst at the Conservatoire, he founded the famous St Petersburg Quartet.

Auer's influence in St Petersburg was immense. Carl Flesch, fellow Hungarian who first met Auer in Russia in 1910, contends that in the Russian ghetto he had the best possible choice of pupils, and compares his circumstances with those at the Berlin Hochschule, where out of forty students sitting for the entrance examination only about four were above average. Flesch also maintains, no doubt correctly, that in Russia the technical preparation for violin playing has always reached a high level.

Milstein, who studied with Auer at St Petersburg, says that he considers Auer's great strength was that he did not know too much. 'If you asked him a specific question about the playing of a certain passage, he would say, "Go away and think it out for yourself". In the long run it was the best way because you develop your own style and do not copy anyone else.'[4] And this is borne

out by the widely diverging performing style and personality of
his pupils.

There is no doubt that Auer succeeded in combining many of
the highly individual characteristics of Joachim, Wieniawski and
Sarasate, and his insistence upon sonorous tone and mental
approach to study brought violin playing into a new era. He
placed the greatest importance on purity of intonation and tone,
neatness of execution and good taste. It was the dynamic force of
his personality which inspired his pupils and thus enabled him to
wrest the best results from them. He disliked the excessive *vibrato*
which came into vogue in the last two decades of the nineteenth
century; he advised his students to use it sparingly, and then only
on sustained notes. Like Corelli, he was adamant about bow
technique and recommended the practice of bowing exercises for a
whole year before touching on the left-hand technique. He was
also against the use of either shoulder-pad or rest. He considered
that the presence of any extra body destroyed the vibrations of the
violin, and maintained that if the instrument is held properly, no
such support is necessary. Auer's most famous pupils have always
avoided shoulder-rests.

One of the best descriptions of the Auer 'sound' comes, as so
often, from Carl Flesch. It was the tone which interested Flesch
most; 'it seemed to possess a roundness and mellowness not easily
to be found elsewhere'.[5] Flesch made a particular study of bowing,
and perceived that the Russians placed the index finger approximately one centimetre higher on the stick towards the wrist than
was customary in the Franco-Belgian school. He admits that he
later adopted this manner of holding the bow; it can be seen,
described in much detail, in his *Art of Violin-Playing*, Vol I. It is the
way that many modern players hold their bows, but is still known
as the 'Russian' hold.

Carl Flesch cannot allow Auer to have it all his own way. He
believes that with him, musical considerations were subordinate
to the study of the technique of violin playing. He maintains that
the 'typical' Auer pupil values 'sensuous sonority' more than the
shaping of musical ideas as such. But he gives Auer the benefit of
the doubt. 'If Auer had attached as much importance to a strict
musical education as to the perfection of every aspect of violin
technique, he might have been the greatest teacher of all times.'[6]

The latter half of the 19th century was a vintage period for great

August Wilhelmj, as principal professor at the Guildhall School of Music, considerably raised British standards of playing at the turn of the century

Leopold Auer, the great teacher who refused to play Tchaikovsky's concerto, as a young man

Otakar Ševčik, the first to analyse the
fundamentals of violin playing, with his
French 'disciple' Andrée Alvin

Jenö Hubay, the autocratic teacher who
established a definitive Hungarian school

Carl Flesch, great teacher and pioneer of the modern master-class

teachers. Auer, the first important influence of his time, must be given the credit for the establishment of the fundamental principles of tone production. He was closely followed by two more Hungarians and a Czech — Jenö Hubay, Carl Flesch and Otakar Ševčik.

With Hubay's appointment at the Budapest Academy there came into being a specifically Hungarian school. Flesch's importance lies in the fact that he had been exposed to three important streams of violin playing: the Viennese, the Franco-Belgian and the Russian, and incorporated all three in his teaching. Ševčik was the first to analyse the fundamentals of violin technique and devise a system which would produce a Paganini-like facility with mathematical certainty.

When Ševčik was over eighty, he was asked how he managed to remain energetic throughout a day which began at five a.m. and ended at one a.m. the next morning. 'A vegetarian diet, no strong liquor and long walks'[7] was the instant response. Had he been less modest, he might have added that simplicity of nature, innate generosity and a love of work were also contributory factors. His enthusiasm was such that in order to attend a pupil's concert, he would travel third class for hours in the icy carriage of a branch line.

The son of a schoolmaster, Ševčik (1852–1934) was born in the hamlet of Horazdowiz in Bohemia and entered Prague Conservatoire at the age of fourteen, having twice failed the entrance examination. One learned adjudicator had rejected him as hopeless and entirely without talent. Fortunately, a rich patron intervened and he was placed with Anton Bennewitz, a pupil of Moritz Mildner who had studied with Pixis, whom we remember as Viotti's pupil when he was in exile in Germany.

Following the completion of his studies, Ševčik toured successfully as a soloist and held a number of leaderships in important orchestras including that of the Mozarteum at Salzburg. But it was while he was professor of violin at the Imperial School of Music at Kiev (1875–92) that he completed his work on the system that had occupied his thoughts for so many years previously. He left Russia to take up the post of principal professor at the Prague Conservatoire, and devoted himself to teaching for the rest of his life.

The loss of the sight of his left eye and increasing attacks of shyness on the concert platform merely confirmed his own belief that his true vocation lay in the pedagogic side of his art. He stayed for fourteen years at Prague where he put his system into practice, and had the twelve-year-old Jan Kubelik as one of his first pupils. Ševčik produced a generation of virtuosos who were living proof of the brilliance of his teaching, from the Russian Michael Zacharewitch (and later another Russian, Efrem Zimbalist) to the Viennese Erica Morini.

As Ševčik's fame spread abroad, he was invited to hold classes throughout Europe and in the USA. From 1909 to 1919 he was principal violin professor at the Vienna Music Academy, after which he returned to Prague. In 1933, at the Guildhall School of Music, he organised the first English Masters' School to be held in Britain. But it was at Pisek, a picturesque, sleepy little town in Southern Bohemia, that Ševčik founded his summer school, and established a centre to which violinists from all over the world made their pilgrimage. After the 1914–18 war, Ševčik resigned from his post in Prague in order to devote himself totally to his school. The total number of students over the years is thought to have been about five thousand.

Simplicity and austerity ruled Ševčik's personal life, and the room in which he taught in Prague reflected his personality. One student said it resembled a waiting room on a railway station, with neither carpets nor furniture, the only human element being the hundreds of photographs which adorned the drab walls. Lessons were held from seven in the morning to ten at night every day except Sunday. On Saturday evenings Ševčik would join his students in the little restaurant run by a Czech who had lived in New York and spoke English with a strong Bowery accent. Here he would converse on any given subject and in almost any language. He extorted high fees from those who could afford it, but his generosity to those who could not was well known. He gave free lessons to a number of poorer students, and if they ran short of money on the course, he would invite them to eat 'on the house', and invariably slipped them a little extra cash to help with the journey home.

Ševčik had endless patience with his students, but could not tolerate laziness. Highly critical of the slightest lapse in intonation, he had a phenomenal ear. In a *bravura* passage he would interrupt a pupil: 'Your 1st, 3rd, 9th and 15th notes were flat, your 8th and 12th were slightly sharp!'[8]

Ševčik's candour was sometimes acutely embarrassing. On one occasion, Kubelik, at the height of his fame, interrupted a world tour to visit Pisek. He had agreed to play the Beethoven and Paganini concertos with a students' orchestra (conducted by his son, the young Rafael Kubelik, then at the start of his career), in the old man's honour. The Paganini, executed with Kubelik's wonderful left-hand technique, held the audience spellbound. Then, halfway through the first movement of the Beethoven, Ševčik got up from his seat in the front row and left the room. The soloist gave no sign of having noticed, but as a student remarked: 'If Kubelik had not been as embarrassed as the audience, he must have been a great actor.'[9]

Ševčik's method is based on the semitone system. In his treatise, he writes: 'The semitones are produced on all the strings with the same fingers, thus giving rise to the same fingering on all the strings, so that the beginner experiences no difficulty in finding the intervals, because all the stoppings are the same on each string, and this materially helps him in acquiring pure intonation.'

Ševčik's guiding maxim was that 'Slow practice is the basis of technical perfection,'[10] and he allocated a greater part of each lesson to teaching his students 'how to practise'. He knew the disastrous results of parrot-like repetition of mistakes, and he was also aware that it is often the talented pupil who has the greatest difficulty with technical problems. Paradoxically, Ševčik's genius lay in the fact that he despised pure technique and yet devoted his life to the perfection of it. His favourite teaching works were those of Paganini, Ernst, Wieniawski and Vieuxtemps.

Ševčik's method has endured because it is based on scientific principles. He would say: 'Let us consider the universe which is ruled by the eternal laws. Symmetry, number and logic prevail everywhere and each phenomenon is subject to the universal rhythm.'[11] He maintained that the same cause and effect could be applied to learning the technique of a musical instrument. He once said: 'Whosoever carries within himself an ideal that he wishes to express, must have as his prerequisite, absolute mastery of his means of expression. Art must not tolerate any mediocrity and that is why technical perfection plays a prime role in matters of musical aesthetics.'[12]

Born in Budapest, Jenö Hubay (1858–1937) had his first lessons from his father, a professor of violin at the Budapest Conservatoire. Although he made his first highly successful public appearance at the age of eleven, it is much to his father's credit that he waited until his son was thirteen before sending him to study for five years with Joachim at the Hochschule in Berlin.

Hubay subsequently embarked upon a highly successful solo career. His own playing was a mixture of Magyar, German and Franco-Belgian elements, resulting in an individual and appealing style which even caused the highly critical Flesch to remark that, although he heard him only once, he considered him 'a noble violinist with outstanding technical and musical qualities'.[13]

In 1878 Hubay met Vieuxtemps in Paris, and for the remaining three years of the older man's life the two became close friends. The seventh violin concerto of Vieuxtemps is dedicated to Hubay, and it was also through his influence that Hubay was asked to take over as principal professor of violin at the Brussels Conservatoire in 1882. Hubay stayed four years in Brussels, and during this time decided that he had found his true vocation. When his father died in 1886, the Budapest Conservatoire offered him the vacant post. He accepted because like most Hungarians he had a fierce streak of patriotism, and saw the opportunity to consolidate his own teaching ideas in their natural, national setting.

Hubay did not have the large following of Ševčik or Flesch, but indisputably he raised the standards of violin playing in Hungary, and three of his star pupils later achieved phenomenal success on the concert platform: Franz von Veczey, Joseph Szigeti and Emil Telmanyi. Eugene Ormandy, conductor of the Philadelphia Symphony Orchestra, was also a pupil of Hubay in Budapest and started his performing life as a concert violinist.

Flesch tells us that the Hubay students could be relied upon to have a very well developed left-hand technique and that they had 'a natural feeling for tonal beauty', but he criticizes their *vibrato* which is too slow and too wide, and he bemoans a 'lack of dynamic differentiation'.[14]

Upon reflection, Joseph Szigeti realized with some amazement 'the lack of solid musical foundation and outlook' during his studies with Hubay. He played the Beethoven concerto 'but without awareness of its place in the microcosm that Beethoven's scores represent for us'. In the classroom 'there prevailed an atmosphere of... puerile technical rivalry' since all the students were completely absorbed in the externals of their craft. But Szigeti does not consider that this diminishes the effect of Hubay's teaching powers. He places the blame more on the parents, who 'generated such an unhealthy impatience'.[15] This was the era of the child prodigy and the Little Lord Fauntleroy velvet suit when ages were frequently 'doctored'.

A generation later, Nicholas Roth (b. 1903) was a pupil in Hubay's master class when he was seventeen, and took his place alongside half a dozen boys aged between twelve and fourteen. Hubay was called 'His Excellency' and his morning entrance competed with pontifical ritual. They would all stand to attention and Hubay would be at the head of a procession consisting of younger professors, one of whom would be carrying his violin case. He would solemnly remove the fiddle, tune it, and hand it ceremoniously to the master. In Roth's opinion Hubay was a marvellous violinist. He heard him when he was seventy-two playing the Bach Chaconne and the chords were just as articulate as if they had been played with the outcurved bow.

Born in Moson in Hungary, the son of a doctor, Carl Flesch (1873–1944) studied with Grün in Vienna from the age of seven, and later under Marsick at the Paris Conservatoire. Not only did Flesch admire his master's playing, but found an affinity with his perfectionist principles. 'It was he who taught me to think logically without endangering the spirit of the living world of art; and to him I owe the development of what later made me realize that teaching was the noblest of artistic activities.'[16]

Despite early struggles with chauvinism at the Conservatoire, Flesch carried off the first prize in 1894, and, after a period of orchestral playing, enjoyed a successful solo career. One of his most significant undertakings was a series of five concerts in Berlin in 1905, when he covered chronologically items representing the entire violin repertoire from Corelli to Reger.

Unlike Ševčik and Hubay, Flesch did not abandon concert-giving in favour of teaching; for him they were parallel developments. He played with most of the world's leading orchestras and under the greatest conductors. Nikisch, Hans Richter, Richard Strauss, Furtwängler, Mengelberg, Bruno Walter and Stokowski all conducted solo performances by Flesch, who had a built-in aversion to conductors as a breed — a fact he never tried to disguise. He also had a distinguished career in chamber music, most notably the many years of his association with the pianist Artur Schnabel with whom he gave hundreds of concerts throughout the world. He also formed a famous trio with Hugo Becker and, later, Gregor Piatigorsky.

His first teaching post in 1897 was in Rumania, when he became professor of violin at the Conservatoire in Bucharest. This period,

Flesch felt, had a decisive influence upon his 'human and artistic development'.[17] At this time he seldom made solo appearances, and when prevailed upon to do so, walked on to the platform with reluctance. He confesses to have brooded over his solo career and 'slid into the muddy channel of self-tormenting, hypochondriac fussiness'.[18] After Bucharest, Flesch's opinion of himself improved, and he taught or played in almost every musical centre of importance.

Flesch made his first highly successful visit to the USA in 1914, and ten years later was engaged as principal violin teacher at the newly-formed Curtis Institute in Philadelphia. From 1926 to 1935 he lived in Baden-Baden, and it was here in his own home that he established his school and attracted pupils who would become some of the greatest violinists of the day, including Henryk Szerying, the English leader, soloist and professor Thomas Matthews, the seven-year-old Ida Haendel, and Ginette Neveu.

Ida Haendel recalls that his method was, for the time, unconventional, but later developed into the master-class as we know it today. There was always a small audience of celebrated musicians, pupils and guests, as Flesch considered this made the transition from lesson to concert platform a less painful journey. He would always allow a pupil to play through without interruption, and when he or she had finished, he would 'slowly rise from the chair upon which he sat like a Caesar'[19] and read from the notes he had jotted on the score. First came the good points and then the onslaught from his merciless tongue. Although pupils cringed, they seldom bore resentment. Ida Haendel never personally feared Flesch, but liked and respected him: the 'head-washings'[20] as Flesch himself called them, were just as acceptable to her as the praise.

Flesch's book of studies was published in 1911, and the first of his two volumes of *The Art of Violin Playing* in 1923, the second following in 1928. Of these Professor Ševčik wrote to him: 'With your work you have provided violinists with a bible . . . nothing connected with the violin and violin playing has been left out of account, and to every question you have found a convincing answer.'[21]

Flesch encouraged the development of each pupil's individuality and established sure methods of overcoming technical problems. His treatment of bowing is of the greatest importance. Norbert Brainin, who studied with both Carl Flesch and Max Rostal (himself a pupil of Flesch), says: 'His own bowing was of the Franco-Belgian style, but he taught his pupils in the Russian manner. He believed that the Russian school of Leopold Auer was the most advantageous for good violin playing.'[22] In the first volume of his classic work, Flesch wrote: 'Personally, I am firmly convinced that just as today, after centuries of slavery, the theory of necessity for the unimpeded freedom of movement of the upper arm has been accepted, so the Russian manner of holding the bow will be exclusively taught in fifty years time, because of the energy saving and exceptional tonal qualities inherent in it.' This prediction was not far out. Although some use a combination of Russian and Franco-Belgian techniques, most great players today favour the Russian hold.

As a man, Flesch was highly complex. His posthumously published memoirs give an acutely observed and objective picture of his times. He reveals his own weaknesses with as much frankness as those of his friends. He is obviously something of a dual personality. There are instances of the dedicated teacher who spared no part of himself to reach a certain goal, and occasional glimpses of the frustrated virtuoso locked inside a pedagogic hair-shirt. When describing his early days in Paris, the exacting professor identifies himself with Bohemian Montmartre, and seems to have been as happy in the company of pimps and tarts as with musicians, painters and penniless aristocrats.

An interesting revelation concerns Ysaÿe, for whom Flesch had the greatest admiration. When Ysaÿe invited Flesch to Le Zoute he refused to go, because he feared that the great man's irresistible charm might endanger the independence of his own personality. But in retrospect he thought that perhaps Ysaÿe might after all have been able to help him to overcome certain inhibitions and thereby strengthen the more impulsive side of his personality.

The number of Flesch pupils is said to have been in the region of a thousand, and pupils of these pupils proliferate the world over. Flesch had boundless energy, and in spite of a heart condition taught up to within a few days of his death. His last physical action was to write several postcards to his pupils informing them of the dates of their next lesson. He died whilst the cards were in the post.

The Carl Flesch Medal 'for excellence in violin playing', instituted at the Guildhall School of Music in 1945, would seem a fitting memorial to a great man.

16

'As the birds sing'

Eugène Ysaÿe

Joachim and Sarasate emerge as the last representatives of the two opposing forces which dominated violin playing in the second half of the nineteenth century, Joachim representing classic seriousness, with depth of feeling paramount, and Sarasate, the wizardry of mellifluous tone and brilliance of technique. Inevitably, as the powers of these two poles of genius diminished, there arose a need for something new — a synthesis of the two styles which would unite technical perfection with intensity of feeling. In the last two decades of the nineteenth century the need was largely fulfilled by the Belgian Eugène Ysaÿe (1858–1931), who 'played the fiddle as the birds sing'[1] and whose personal magnetism was second only to Liszt or Paganini.

Ysaÿe's family had been humble nail-makers since the sixteenth century, but his father ignored tradition and became a tailor. A good amateur violinist, he was also musical director at the cathedral church of Liège. Although he had lessons on the violin from his father at the age of four, Eugène was no child prodigy. Ebullient and self-willed, he would have preferred the boisterous company of his friends to the interminable practice insisted upon by his parents. He entered Liège Conservatoire in 1865, when he was seven, won a second prize after his first year, but was expelled in 1869. The reasons for this drastic step are somewhat obscure, but it is more than likely to have been due to a disparity between his father's methods and those of the Conservatoire. They admitted he was 'talented' but complained that 'he did not work'. For the next few years, Ysaÿe accompanied his father in local musical activities, and an isolated attempt was made to apprentice him to an armourer. But he was soon sent packing, owing to his total lack of enthusiasm for the work.

One day in 1873 a chance encounter with Henri Vieuxtemps changed the direction of his life. The virtuoso was passing Ysaÿe's house, heard someone playing the Adagio from his own Fourth Concerto in D rather well, and knocked on the door to ask the name of the performer. The meeting was fortuitous for all concerned. Vieuxtemps became greatly attached to the boy, whom he was to regard as his spiritual successor, and Ysaÿe in turn remained devoted to his mentor and friend for the remaining years of the old man's life. When Vieuxtemps heard the story of Ysaÿe's dismissal from the Conservatoire, he had him reinstated, this time straight into Rodolphe Massart's master-class. His efforts were amply rewarded when Ysaÿe carried off both the first prize and the gold medal.

When Ysaÿe responded to Vieuxtemps' invitation to study with him at Brussels, he arrived to find the master had suffered a stroke and was stricken with paralysis of both hands. Nevertheless, he stayed on with Vieuxtemps, although he was never enrolled at the Conservatoire. When Vieuxtemps went to Algiers in search of a cure, Wieniawski, who succeeded him at the Conservatoire, was entrusted with his protégé for the next two years. Here there is an interesting dual link with Viotti, who had taught both Robberechts and Kreutzer, whose pupils, de Bériot and Massart, had been the teachers of Vieuxtemps and Wieniawski.

When Vieuxtemps returned to Paris, he sent for 'the young violinist with the marvellous E string',[2] and Ysaÿe, sponsored by a grant from the authorities at Liège, joined him for three years. During the summer vacation, the young student earned extra money as solo violin with the Kursaal Orchestra at Ostende. His beautiful 'line' attracted much attention, and it was here that the German conductor Bilse heard him and offered him the leadership of his own orchestra in Berlin. Ysaÿe held this post for two years, and again his outstanding playing aroused so much interest that eminent visiting musicians would attend concerts especially to hear him.

In 1881 Ysaÿe left Berlin for Paris, where he joined the coterie of young composers centred round Franck, Chausson and Debussy — all three of whom later dedicated works to him. It was from this date that Ysaÿe's solo career can be said to have started.

Although early recognized by musicians, Ysaÿe was in his

mid-twenties before he achieved anything like the public acclaim received by Joachim when still in a velvet suit. His first important concert was in Paris in 1883 under Colonne, when he played Lalo's 'Symphonie Espagnole' and Saint-Saëns' 'Introduction and Rondo Capriccioso'. A critic wrote : 'This was a triumph of execution, style and presentation.'[3]

Ysaÿe appeared in England for the first time in the spring of 1891, but did not win the hearts as easily as he had in Paris. George Bernard Shaw, then writing for *The World*, did not care for his playing, and, characteristically made no bones about it. Whilst admitting that his technical mastery made him Sarasate's only serious rival, Shaw abhorred 'his readiness to sacrifice higher artistic qualities to the speed of a dazzlingly impossible presto'.[4] When Ysaÿe played at a Philharmonic Society concert at St James's Hall in March, Shaw was scathing. He wrote: 'His determination to cap feats impossible to other violinists and his enormous self-assertiveness, really broke up and destroyed the Beethoven Concerto.' The cadenzas were Ysaÿe's own; Shaw castigated them as 'monstrous excrescences on the movements, nailed on, not grafted in', and maintains that they 'have no form, being merely examples of madly difficult ways of playing the themes that have been reasonably and beautifully presented by Beethoven. One comfort is that since Ysaÿe can hardly play them himself, nobody else is likely to be able to play them at all.' Shaw also found Ysaÿe's personality offensive. He accused him of titanically emphasising himself, 'elbowing aside the conductor, eclipsing the little handful of an orchestra... and all but showing Beethoven the door. The fact is he has created himself so recently that he is not yet tired of his consummated self.'[5] A few weeks later, however, Shaw reacted more favourably when he heard Ysaÿe at a recital. He was particularly impressed with his interpretation of chamber music. Later, in the eyes of English music lovers, Ysaÿe could do no wrong, and in 1901 he was awarded the Philharmonic Society's Gold Medal, an honour he shared only with Joachim.

Arthur Symons, in the *Saturday Review* (28 December 1907) wrote:

> You see the music in the great black figure [Ysaÿe stood over six feet four], that sways like a python: in the eyes that blink, and seem about to shed luxurious tears; the face like an actor's mask, enigmatic, quivering with emotion ... The lips suck up music voluptuously ...

the tones . . . are pleasure, not joy; the soul is not in them, but a luxury which becomes divine because it is an ecstasy, even if a carnal ecstasy. A marvellous passage of double-stopping in one of the cadenzas in Beethoven was played as if one's teeth met in a peach . . . He floats on the surface of a river of pure sound, and dreams; every note like drops of water . . . His technique, unclassical, romantic, though finished in perfection, is part of his unconscious revelation of himself.

Symons closes with some interesting discussion on the musician's approach to the 'sound' of each individual composer. 'Ysaÿe listens for that sound in the depths of Beethoven and on the heights of Mozart; it comes to him living and naked, and he clothes it with silken garments, as if it were a woman.'

If this description of Ysaÿe's playing and personal magnetism seems exaggerated, we have only to consult the hypercritical Flesch, who, although characteristically he cannot allow Ysaÿe to have unmitigated praise, certainly finds plenty of good things to say. He calls him 'the most outstanding and individual violinist I have ever heard in all my life'.[6] His tone, wrote Flesch, was 'big and noble' and capable of responding to his wishes like 'a horse to its rider'. His *vibrato* was 'the spontaneous expression of his feeling' and very far removed from the restrained quiver 'only on expressive notes' which had previously been accepted as correct. His left-hand agility and intonation was 'of Sarasate-like perfection', and 'there was no kind of bowing that did not show tonal perfection as well as musical feeling'. Flesch also extolled Ysaÿe's interpretation, 'the impulsive romantic . . . concerned not so much with the printed note values . . . as with the spirit that cannot be reproduced graphically'.[7] And as for his *rubato*, Flesch has nothing but admiration for his skill. Another endorsement comes from Josef Gingold, professor of violin at Indiana University, an ex-pupil of Ysaÿe: 'His *rubato* was indescribable. You could set a metronome and whatever happened in the duration of that bar, would come out, metronomically correct. He was on the beat every time.'[8]

Ysaÿe's first trip to the USA in 1894 was considerably more rewarding than his British début. When he arrived on the American continent he was a mature artist and the respected leader of the Belgian school; he was also founder and conductor of the Ysaÿe Orchestral Concerts in Brussels at which many famous artists appeared. He was principal professor at Brussels Conservatoire, a position he had held since 1886, and had had many decorations

bestowed upon him by the crowned heads of Europe. The
Americans were utterly charmed by him, and the women were
almost hysterical in their admiration. Critics claimed he was the
greatest violinist who had visited their country for many years.
Henry Lahee wrote: 'He plays with a bold and manly vigour, and
yet with exquisite delicacy . . . "he creeps up under your vest". He
disarms criticism, and he seems to be more completely part of his
violin and his violin of him than . . . any other player . . . He
combines Sarasate's tenderness of tone and showy technique with
more manliness and sincerity than Sarasate gives.'[9]

One of Ysaÿe's greatest triumphs was when he played the Bach
E major concerto under Nikisch in Berlin in 1899. The Berliners
had reservations about Belgians who played the classics, and again
like the British, were misty-eyed with adoration of their great
Joachim and his Hochschule activities. But Ysaÿe won them over.
The audience were deeply moved by the dignity and poetry of his
reading and recalled Ysaÿe fifteen times to acknowledge their
ovation.

During the 1914–18 war, all three of Ysaÿe's sons were fighting
at the front and he and his wife Louise (the daughter of a
high-ranking army officer whom he married in 1886), escaped to
England. They left behind all their possessions, with the exception
of Ysaÿe's violin — a beautiful Guarneri del Gesù, dated 1740
(now owned by Isaac Stern). They lived at 49 Rutland Gate in
Kensington where Ysaÿe was lionized by a great circle of pupils
and admirers. His soirées were major events in London musical
life, and he counted among his many English friends Elgar,
Vaughan Williams, Henry Wood, Beecham and many others. At
this time he also gave recitals with the young Artur Rubinstein,
Vladimir Pachmann, Frederic Lamond and Lionel Tertis.

Ysaÿe was no respector of persons. He once attended a dinner
party given by a famous London hostess, to which Queen
Alexandra and the Princess Napoleon had also been invited.
Ysaÿe, who liked his wine, was horrified when he saw the
magnificent food accompanied by plain water. The hostess made a
speech in halting French, saying that her husband, the colonel, had
gone to war, taking everything with him . . . 'her thoughts . . . her
heart'. Ysaÿe, in an audible aside to his companion, said, 'He's
taken the key of the wine cellar as well!'[10]

In 1918, Ysaÿe accepted the conductorship of the Cincinnati
Symphony Orchestra in Ohio. He also took the chair of music at

the Conservatory in that city, and produced the first generation of American performers to be guided by his principles. Here he promoted the works of contemporary Belgian and French composers, and we see yet another side of the many important aspects of Ysaÿe's influence: he was always a strong advocate for performances of modern music. He had given the first of many subsequent performances of the now famous sonata dedicated to him by César Franck, when that composer was completely unknown. A few days before Ysaÿe's wedding in September 1886, a celebration banquet was held in Luxembourg. Headed by Charles Bordes, the French scholar and composer, the Paris coterie had arrived in force. When the after-dinner speeches had been made, Bordes produced a manuscript and presented it to Ysaÿe with greetings from 'le père Franck' who had composed a sonata especially for his marriage. Overcome with emotion, Ysaÿe said he would like to perform it there and then. He asked Léontine Bordes-Pène, the distinguished pianist and sister-in-law of Charles, if she would consent to be his partner in this unique première. The two proceeded to sightread the sonata and moved the guests to tears. Madame Bordes-Pène also joined Ysaÿe in the first public performance in Brussels on 16 December the same year. Ironically, Ysaÿe receives little credit from Franck's biographers.

Ysaÿe returned to Belgium in 1922. His wife died in 1924 and four years later he married Jeannette Dincin, one of his American pupils who had come to study with him in Brussels. Ysaÿe was seventy and his bride twenty-four, but it would appear to have been one of those happy marriages for which elderly maestros seem to have the flair. Ysaÿe's health was a constant trouble to him but his young wife helped considerably in persuading him to maintain a strict diet to combat the diabetes from which he suffered for many years. He could never overcome the attacks of cramp and the tremors which affected his hands. Flesch typically attributes this trembling of his right hand to faulty bow technique, but Josef Gingold has assured the author that this tremor was ever-present: even if he tried to hold a glass of water, he often had to steady his right hand with his left.

Ysaÿe's teaching skill lay in his ability to demonstrate. He always taught with his fiddle in his hand. One of the great American teachers, Louis Persinger, first heard Ysaÿe at the Gewandhaus in Leipzig, and did not rest until he had the opportunity to study with him in Belgium in 1905. Josef Gingold gives us valuable first-hand evidence of Ysaÿe's skill as a teacher. He was auditioned at 'La Chanterelle' (literally 'E (top) string'), the magnificent summer home Ysaÿe built for himself at Le Zoute in Belgium.

> I had prepared the first movement of the Brahms concerto and arrived, full of enthusiasm. Ysaÿe said very calmly in that deep voice of his, 'Will you please play a G major, three-octave scale for me?' Momentarily I was stunned, but I did what he asked. This was followed by my having to play scales in every conceivable manner of bowing, and finally I was allowed to play the Brahms.[11]

Gingold was accepted as a pupil but with the proviso that he learned the French language. Ysaÿe declared that he would speak to him in English only for a few weeks.

The first technique that Ysaÿe corrected was Gingold's method of string crossing (moving the bow from one string to another without a break), by demonstrating the Franco-Belgian method of using the forearm stroke to develop a more powerful and sustained tone connecting one string with another. Ysaÿe worked for two months with Gingold before he was satisfied with his bow arm. Only then did they begin on repertoire, the first work being Vieuxtemps' fifth concerto.

Ysaÿe's dry sense of humour was an outstanding part of his personality. Once when Gingold was preparing the Beethoven concerto for his first important solo engagement in Antwerp, 'a big occasion for a boy of eighteen', he had some extra lessons. The closing bars of the solo part in the last movement are marked *pianissimo* on the score, with the final cadence from the full orchestra, contrasting, *fortissimo*.

> I played it and tried to observe the composer's intentions, but Ysaÿe shook his head, 'No, no, it's too soft. Play it like *this*' and he took up his own fiddle and what he gave was a good *forte*. Normally, I was a good student. I never argued with him, but this time I was a little worried. I knew that if Ysaÿe himself played it loud, everybody would say '*What* an innovation', but if I, an unknown, would do so they would say 'The boy can't read music!' So I ventured to say, 'Maître, do you not think that if one plays this passage softly and then when the orchestra comes in *fortissimo* it is rather a nice surprise?' He smiled and answered me slowly .... 'My boy, if you have not surprised them until then, it's too late!'[12]

Ysaÿe had a heart as large as his frame and his generosity extended to all kinds of people. Success brought him riches and distinction, but although he had a sense of grandeur which he could summon as the occasion demanded, he remained essentially an 'ordinary' man of the people. In fact, the artificial trappings of success occasionally disgusted him so much that he was prone to fits of melancholia, which were in sharp contrast to his normally ebullient disposition. At these times he took refuge in his magnificent library at 'La Chanterelle', for despite his initial lack of education, he had acquired a wide knowledge on a variety of subjects including fluency in several languages.

An inveterate pipe smoker, Ysaÿe would delight his students at the Conservatoire by lighting up right under the 'No Smoking' sign. Once when smoking whilst waiting to go on stage, the duty fireman approached him politely, 'Excuse me, Monsieur, there is no smoking here'. Ysaÿe continued to puff away and, between his teeth, calmly replied 'Don't be stupid. You can see perfectly well that there is.'[13]

A virtuoso in every sense of the word, Ysaÿe brought a magical individuality to every performance. His platform manner was easy, and he was singularly relaxed in his movements. Gingold recalls the most lasting memory of his artistry was in that of the *grande ligne*, the rendering of a long phrase. His memory was phenomenal. Chausson dedicated his famous 'Poème' to Ysaÿe, and when he played the work for the first time, he had simply run through it with a pianist and studied the score on the train. With only one orchestral rehearsal, he was able to memorize it for a perfect performance. As a composer, Ysaÿe contributed some of the most attractive and, for his time, the most advanced solo sonatas in the repertoire of the violin. They include almost every technique by the performer and are fiendishly difficult to play. In many ways, both as composer and performer, he was ahead of his time, although strangely enough he deferred playing the Brahms concerto until he was over forty. Joachim's equivocal comment on that occasion had been that he had 'never heard it played like *that* before'.[14]

Ysaÿe fought for many causes. He was an avid protagonist of the movement to bring about copyright laws for the composer. He was a staunch defender of Paganini and collected much evidence to disprove the legends of empty acrobatics. He maintained that without the technical invention of virtuosos, the development of symphonic works would have progressed more slowly. And Paganini provided a common store of richness from which others have drawn new effects. Ysaÿe would tell his students that compositions by virtuoso-performers are necessary to instrumental art because it is only by practical demonstration that the composer can be sure that a work is playable. Josef Gingold recalls that in the twenties when he was preparing for his first recital in Brussels he planned to perform the Paganini D major concerto in the Wilhelmj version, in which the first movement only is played — a fashionable showpiece of the time. But Ysaÿe insisted that he play the original and, furthermore, directed him to tune the violin up a semitone as Paganini did — in order to adhere to tradition.

When Ysaÿe was dying he was visited by the young violinist Philippe Newman who decided to play for him. He chose one of Ysaÿe's solo sonatas, the fourth, which he had dedicated to his great friend Fritz Kreisler — the barely conscious Ysaÿe thought at first that it was Kreisler playing. When the piece was finished, he managed to show that the old lion was still very much alive: 'Splendid . . . . but the finale . . . a little too fast.'[15] These were his last words.

17

Symbol of an Epoch

Fritz Kreisler

In the entire history of violin playing there is probably no performer who was more universally loved and admired than Fritz Kreisler. He was the first of the twentieth-century violinists to anticipate by instinct the growing need for emotional expression in playing. He appealed to the heart of his audience, not only by his virtuosity but by a quality that exuded a subtle vitality, humour, sweetness and pathos in an interfusion of tone, technique and communication.

The young Szigeti was 'bowled over' when he first heard Ysaÿe, Kreisler and Elman in 1905. Although there was disparity in their ages, and their roots were in three different schools, for him they formed an entity, 'the opening of a door'.[1] He maintains that the advent of these three, together with Thibaud and, later, Heifetz, brought together a group of distinctly individual violinists who nonetheless possessed a common denominator which represented twentieth-century playing. A new conception of beauty of playing was being formulated around this time and only those whose style reflected this development could survive. Kreisler not only survived, he was the high priest of the school.

Born in Vienna, that most musical of cities, in 1875, Kreisler could read music before he had learnt his alphabet. His father, a doctor of moderate means with a passion for string quartet playing, gave him his first lessons when he was four. Further instruction from Jacques Auber, Konzertmeister at the Ringtheater, brought him up to his first public performance at the age of seven, when he appeared as supporting artist to the singer, Carlotta Patti, sister of the better-known Adelina. His fee was a box of sweets.

The same year he was accepted as the youngest pupil ever at the Vienna Conservatoire, their normal age being ten. Under Joseph Hellmesberger for violin and Anton Bruckner for harmony, young Fritz carried off the gold medal at the age of ten.

Proceeding with a scholarship to the Paris Conservatoire, he entered Massart's class and was placed with the amiable but promiscuous Delibes for composition. This time, in the face of heavy competition from older students, he was awarded the *ne plus ultra*, the Prix de Rome, at the age of twelve. Two years later he toured the USA with the brilliant pianist Moritz Rosenthal. In a velvet suit with knee-breeches, 'Master Fritz Kreisler' took part in fifty concerts for which he was paid $50 a performance.

Despite the phenomenal success of the tour, he returned to Vienna, quietly finished his normal education, studied two years at medical school and completed his national service. In 1896, at the age of twenty-one, he decided that music was the only career for him.

But when Kreisler auditioned for a place at the second desk of the first violins in the Hofoper Orchestra, the Leader, Arnold Rosé, who later became internationally famous as leader of the Rosé Quartet, turned him down on the pretext that his sight reading was inadequate. Apart from being a gold medallist at two of the most important musical institutions in Europe, Kreisler had been composing since he was a child. He was also a self-taught but superb pianist. Maybe Rosé recognized a superior talent and felt threatened.

It took almost five years before Kreisler gained recognition, but the time spent in the Vienna cafés and the famous Tonkünstlerverein (Musicians' Club) afforded him the stimulus he needed through the company of fellow artists. Here he met Brahms, who became his idol and with whom he often played; and Joachim, with whom he could seldom agree but admired as a musician.

On 23 January 1898, Kreisler's Viennese début took place. With the Vienna Philharmonic Orchestra under Hans Richter, he played Max Bruch's second concerto, and critics were impressed with his 'brilliant virtuosity'[2] and 'the sweetness of his tone'.[3] But the opportunity which was to prove a decisive moment in his life came a year later on 1 December 1899, when Nikisch presented him as soloist at a Berlin Philharmonic Society concert, playing the Mendelssohn concerto. Ysaÿe happened to be present and rose to his feet applauding loudly. The inspired audience followed suit and Fritz Kreisler, virtuoso violinist, was a reality. These two great fiddlers later became close friends and Ysaÿe dedicated the fourth of his solo sonatas to Kreisler.

An amusing sequel to the Berlin triumph came in 1901 when Ysaÿe, engaged to play the Beethoven concerto with Nikisch and the Philharmonic, was taken ill after the morning rehearsal. Kreisler deputized at the last moment and, without rehearsal, played magnificently. Not only had he been unable to rehearse, but had to play with a borrowed fiddle, since his own had been pawned to pay for the extravagant tastes of 'Mimi', his current lady-love. Typically Viennese, the young Kreisler took life as it came and found pretty girls irresistible.

When Kreisler reappeared at the Carnegie Hall in New York on 7 December 1900, he achieved a tremendous success. His own orchestration of Tartini's 'Devil's Trill' Sonata, with a brilliant cadenza, inspired rave notices extolling his astonishing violinistic powers. He then completed a twelve-month coast to coast tour and audiences flocked in their thousands to hear him.

On board ship on his way back to Europe, Kreisler met the beautiful red-headed Harriet Woerz, whom he married the following year. Harriet has been described as bossy, powerful and overorganized, but she was also generous and quite without fear. No doubt she could be overpowering at times, but she certainly protected the vulnerable Fritz from over-zealous admirers and saw to it that he arrived on the platform in one piece. Kreisler never suffered from nerves on stage, but was very retiring in private life.

Harriet was also his business manager. Some say she prevented her husband from making his own decisions; others say that, since they were opposites, they complemented each other. Nevertheless, Kreisler adored her, was totally dependent upon her and miserable when they were apart. However, he seldom suffered this deprivation, for wherever Fritz went, so did Harriet. Even when he was called up to serve in the Austrian Army in the 1914–18 war, she became a nurse and placed herself strategically in a nearby field hospital.

Kreisler made his London début in 1902 with little success. The *Musical Times*, cool and inaccurate in describing him as 'yet another Hungarian', considered that 'although failing to give the impression of being a great executant, he played with intelligence, tenderness of expression, and skill which excited attention'.

But when Kreisler played at one of Henry Wood's concerts at

the Queen's Hall a few years later, it was quite another matter. Arthur Symons, in the *Saturday Review* on 4 May 1907, wrote of Kreisler's interpretation of the Beethoven concerto that he 'played it as if Beethoven had revealed it privately, over again, to him ... His soul seems to confide in his fiddle, and the fiddle tells us the secret ... His playing has that energy which comes to flower in grace, with a supple concealed agility, a skill which is never allowed to tell for itself, to mean anything apart from what it expresses.'

On 10 November 1910 came the historic world première of the Elgar violin concerto, dedicated to Kreisler. It was at the Queen's Hall in the opening concert of the ninety-ninth season of the Philharmonic Society, with Elgar conducting. The critics were unanimous in their praise for all concerned. The *Musical Observer* commented that 'the composer was determined that no ordinary violinist should attempt the work, for the solo part is of great difficulty'.

Late in 1914, Kreisler was invalided out of the Austrian Army, whereupon he went again to the USA. As soon as his health was restored, he resumed concert-giving. He was now a highly successful artist earning large fees and had also been receiving considerable royalties from his recordings since 1903. His generous nature prompted him to donate a large part of his income to Austrian war orphans and wounded in Europe. This gesture caused havoc with the Americans, and particularly enraged those Amazons, the 'Daughters of the Revolution'. He was criticized and castigated to such an extent that in 1917, when America entered the war, he withdrew from all public engagements at a loss of some $85,000 in broken contracts. Resourceful as ever, Kreisler spent the time composing an operetta called 'Apple Blossoms' which ran for over a year on Broadway.

In 1919 Kreisler returned to the concert platform at a charity concert at Carnegie Hall where socialites had paid $100 each for their boxes. He received a five-minute standing ovation before he played a note, and after the concert the audience became almost hysterical in their appreciation of this modest artist who, in the name of patriotism, had been forced off the platform two years earlier. This was not the end of hostility. A new militant organization, the 'American Legion', was on the rampage at every Kreisler appearance. At Cornell University they cut the electric light cables in the middle of a concert, but Kreisler, unperturbed as always, simply continued to play in the dark.

Kreisler made his comeback in Britain in May 1921 and his reception at the Queen's Hall was overwhelming. Melba presented him with a laurel wreath after the first concerto, and after the second, the great English violinist Albert Sammons presented him with another.

But Kreisler waited until the autumn of 1924 to make his reappearance in Paris. He was given a heart-warming reception and the audience 'cheered him for hours'.[4] It was a highly emotional experience for Kreisler. The French acknowledged him as the greatest of his time and two years later they made him an officer of the French Legion of Honour. Kreisler now had the world at his feet. He had toured China and Japan in 1923, Australia and New Zealand in 1925. His records were bestsellers on every continent, and his renewal contract in 1925 with the Victor Company of USA (HMV in UK) guaranteed him royalty earnings of $750,000 over a period of five years — the largest sum paid to any artist to date.

But he became weary of travelling. He was welcome everywhere but domiciled nowhere. Over the years he had amassed a valuable collection of violins, rare books, manuscripts and objets d'art from all over the globe, but had nowhere to keep them. In 1924 the Kreislers bought a property set in several acres of woodland in the quiet residential area of Grünewald in western Berlin. Harriet and Fritz settled there with all their treasures, and it was only in 1939 that they left for the USA. They had the good sense to transfer the book collection to safe keeping in England, which did not endear them to the Germans. During the course of the war the Grünewald house was bombed to the ground. When the news reached Kreisler, it was typical of the man that his first question was to ask if there had been any human casualties.

Kreisler was probably the most happy-go-lucky violinist of all time. His strong gambler's streak, which manifested itself at the tables whenever he had the chance, also permeated his attitude to the occupational hazards of a virtuoso's life. He never practised and seldom took up his violin between performances, insisting that to wash his hands in warm water before playing was sufficient to keep them flexible.

The double-bass player Horace Green recalls an incident from 1933 when Kreisler made his historic recording of the Brahms concerto with the London Symphony Orchestra under Barbirolli.

At the rehearsal, Kreisler opened his violin case only to find that his three top strings had gone. He sighed 'Oh dear' in a voice quite untouched by concern and proceeded to fit new ones. With no more than a few minutes' delay, the rehearsal began. The recording which finally emerged is positive proof that Kreisler could meet sudden emergency and still play superbly.

The rank and file musicians adored Kreisler. He had no side about him, and never tried to dramatize himself. He would sit and chat to the players as if he were one of them. Kreisler could count among his personal friends most of the great musicians of his time, but perhaps his closest was Rachmaninov, with whom he made some recordings. Those of the beautiful Duo in A major by Schubert and the Beethoven Sonata Op. 30 No. 3 in G major are two that to this day remain outstanding. They are proof of the extraordinary affinity that existed between the sombre Slav and the extrovert Viennese.

It is generally claimed that, owing to his own lack of practice which he could scarcely recommend to a pupil, Kreisler did no teaching. But like Paganini, he did have one pupil. David McCallum (1897–1972), for many years leader of the BBC Symphony Orchestra and a fine soloist in his own right, studied with him whenever he was in Britain. Although it is agreed that no violinist has ever succeeded in sounding exactly like Kreisler, David McCallum was considered by many to have been the nearest approach.

Kreisler died a few days before his eighty-seventh birthday in January 1962. All over the world, newspapers carried touching tributes to this great artist. In Britain, *The Times* and *The Guardian* perpetuated the error (still uncorrected in *Grove's Dictionary of Music*, fifth edition) that Kreisler was a pupil of Auer. Chronologically and geographically this would be impossible. Born in 1845, Auer took up his post in St Petersburg in 1868, seven years before Kreisler's birth, and stayed there until the Revolution of 1917. His only time in Vienna was when at the age of ten he studied with Dont.

The Times praised his 'sweetness of tone' but criticized him for taking 'the easy course marked out for him by his great popularity, choosing his programmes from attractive and musically trivial pieces, which delighted the audience, and playing them with an ease that became almost mechanical'. But there was no mention of his mastery of the bow. By 1962 all violinists had become

Eugène Ysaÿe, one of the most individual
violinists of the late nineteenth/early twentieth
centuries

Jan Kubelik, one of the many brilliant young
virtuosos who were overtaken by Heifetz

Fritz Kreisler, Georges Enesco and Jacques Thibaud together in the forties

obsessed with the technique of the left hand.

Kreisler played all the classic concertos. Before he was twenty, he composed cadenzas for the Beethoven concerto which Milstein described as 'epoch-making',[5] and the famous American critic Henry T. Finck as summing up 'the essence of Beethoven's music as a few drops of attar of rose do the fragrance of an acre of flowers'.[6] Kreisler played the Brahms concerto superbly. He not only knew Brahms personally, but later acquired (for $7,000) the original manuscript of the concerto, with all Brahms's own markings. Kreisler played chamber music, not only with Thibaud, Casals and Bauer to a cheering audience, but for pleasure: a luxury for which he never had enough time. He told the *Musical Courier* in 1910, 'I look forward to every summer, when Ysaÿe, Thibaud, Casals, Pugno and I meet in Paris. Ysaÿe and I alternate in playing viola, but the queer thing about it is that we all want to play second violin.'

No obituarist thought fit to mention the humane side of Kreisler. We have already learned of his generosity to the war orphans of the First World War. During the Second, he donated all royalties from his record sales in Britain to the British Red Cross Fund, and made similar gestures in the USA. In 1947 he put up his collection of rare books and manuscripts, representing forty years of acquisition, for auction because he felt it wrong to hold on to such possessions when people all over the world were in need. The sale realized $120,000. Kreisler donated the entire sum to charity.

The critics could never truly accept Kreisler's own charming salon pieces — the so-called 'trivia'. But these were the pieces with which he conquered the world. These were what audiences wanted to hear and this was the music that sold his recordings by the millions. And they are certainly far from trivial. Some are extremely difficult to play, and are little masterpieces in their own right. Today they are firmly established in the solo repertoire, but the wide variety of interpretation shows just how subtle these pieces are. They can be tender, musicianly and beautifully phrased, or ruined with excessive *vibrato* and sliding. 'Tambourin Chinois' was considered by Thibaud to be one of the greatest salon pieces ever composed. It is fiendishly difficult and full of traps for the performer who thinks Kreisler is 'light' or 'easy'.

Kreisler's greatest sin was the famous hoax for which the eminent critic Ernest Newman never forgave him. In his youth,

Kreisler had found the solo violin repertoire limited. When he needed more short pieces for his recitals, he wrote them in the style of composers completely unknown at the time — Vivaldi, Porpora, Pugnani, Dittersdorf, Stamitz and Couperin — and presented them as 'arrangements'. If he had announced then that these were his own compositions, he would not have been taken seriously. They were an instant success and the critics congratulated him on his researches. It so happened that Heifetz, Enesco and other close friends knew about the deception, and Kreisler himself had hinted at the truth many times but no one believed him. Eventually he decided to admit that these were originals and not transcriptions, and instructed his publishers to print an announcement to this effect in their next catalogue. Olin Downes, then chief music critic of the New York Times, wrote a very fair article accepting Kreisler's justification of what he had done. The critics were taken aback, but none quite so much as Ernest Newman. The battle which raged in the London Sunday Times became a cause célèbre as far as Newman was concerned. He took the view that anyone could, if they tried, write in the style of Handel or Vivaldi, so therefore Kreisler's achievement in that respect was nil. But it was the deception, what he saw as the unethical nature of the entire operation, that so incensed Newman.

In an excellent letter to the Sunday Times on 10 March 1935, Kreisler states that the critic's prestige is not endangered because that which has been pronounced good is found to be composed by someone else. 'The name changes, the value remains.' Kreisler goes on to say that many people suspected that they were in fact originals, and that even the 'Newmans of the day' were informed that the 'arrangements' were very free.

The last word in the argument came wittily from Olin Downes: 'Mr Kreisler has added to the gaiety of nations and the violinist's repertoire. Shall we begrudge him that? Should the man who kissed the wrong girl in the dark condemn the practice of kissing?'

An incident which took place in Antwerp before the First World War is typical of the esteem in which Kreisler was universally held. Browsing round an antique shop, he came across a nondescript fiddle and asked the price. The answer did not satisfy Kreisler so as a test, he took out his own priceless Guarneri and asked the dealer if he was interested in buying it. The old man caressed it with reverence and said he had an Amati at home which his customer might like to see. He then vanished and shortly returned somewhat flustered without the Amati, and accompanied by a policeman. 'That man is a thief; he's stolen Fritz Kreisler's violin', he shouted. 'Arrest him!'. Kreisler unfortunately could not prove his identity because his passport was back at the hotel. Suddenly he smiled, picked up the fiddle and played. The antique dealer beamed and then blushed with shame. 'Nobody else can play "Schön Rosmarin" like *that*.'[7]

Josef Gingold, in a speech given at the Kreisler Centennial Concert at Indiana University on 2 February 1975, summed up Kreisler by quoting Flesch. 'He will live not only as an artist whose genius stimulated and expanded the art, but also as a most valuable symbol of a whole epoch.'[8] The 'epoch' was that of the individualist.

Whether playing virtuoso or classical compositions, Kreisler's phrasing was never glib, his notes never just brilliant black and white. In his hands, every note had a meaning and was an integral part of the composition. He was an orator on the violin and could sway his audience, lay or professional, whichever way he wanted. He was imbued with the Italian-French influence via the Massart-Kreutzer-Viotti link. Through Hellmesberger-Böhm-Rode-Robberechts-Viotti, he had inherited something from each of the Viennese, Belgian and Italian schools of playing. Whatever he had drawn from these influences he transformed into a style of playing which combined a strength and sweetness distinctly his own. 'Even in his most brilliant technical feats there was never anything of the steely, machine-like perfection which has become common to-day,' wrote Martin Cooper in his obituary in the *Daily Telegraph*.

Kreisler's so-called 'continuous' *vibrato* was criticized by the purists — followers of Joachim who insisted upon no *vibrato* except in the most expressive passages. Yet Kreisler's *vibrato* was not 'continuous', neither was it the sentimental oscillation of the tea-shop fiddler. Kreisler was the first to use the *vibrato* in a more highly developed way. It was very fast, highly centralized with his fingers firmly on the string. It was this that produced the vibrant golden tone that every violinist tried — mostly without success — to imitate. Today violinists aim at a *vibrato* that is capable of modulation so that it can be applied to the varying moods of the music. Kreisler did this as naturally as breathing.

Gingold, who never missed a Kreisler concert, may be allowed the last word on this most loved of violinists.

When he made his stage entrance his majestic bearing demanded attention even before he played a single note. However, once he put his violin under his chin he was completely transformed. A certain modesty and humility were evidenced as he seemed to say 'I would love to play for you'. I felt that Kreisler played personally for each listener in the audience, so personable was his magnetism.'

18

The French Phenomenon

Jacques Thibaud

With a few notable exceptions such as Wieniawski, most of the top-rank violinists from the Belgian school were natives. With the French school it was exactly the reverse. Apart from Emil Sauret, it was almost a hundred years since the French had produced an outstanding violinist.

Then suddenly with Jacques Thibaud France produced her greatest violinist. His bewitching tone, his mastery of both left- and right-hand technique, his ebullient and individual style of playing, particularly suited to the characteristics of French music, gained him a reputation which never dimmed. His colourful personality endeared him to all who knew him, and his tall, slim figure and devastating good looks won an immediate response from his audiences.

Thibaud was born in Bordeaux in 1880, into a family where music was taken for granted. His father was a violinist and local music teacher: his two brothers played cello and piano and in later years they worked together as a professional piano trio.

Thibaud is a rarity among violinists in that he originally intended to be a pianist. In fact, he was so skilled on the keyboard that he made his first public appearance as a soloist at the age of five. Two years later he was taken to a concert where he heard the Beethoven violin concerto and was moved to tears. He gave his father no peace until he agreed to give him some lessons on that instrument. His progress was so remarkable that when Ysaÿe heard him at the age of nine, he predicted a bright future and encouraged him to take further study.

Thibaud entered the Conservatoire in Paris under Marsick

when he was thirteen, and three years later carried off the first prize. To supplement his modest allowance, Thibaud played in the band of the Café Rouge where he was spotted by Edouard Colonne — founder of the popular Concerts Colonne — who immediately took him into his orchestra. One day, when the leader was unwell, Thibaud took his place. His exquisite playing of the violin solo in the Prelude to Saint-Saëns' 'The Deluge' caused a sensation and soon he was so inundated with solo engagements that he was obliged to give up his orchestral job. He made his solo début in Angers in 1898 and subsequently appeared in over fifty concerts supported by the Colonne Orchestra.

In 1899, Thibaud made his first appearance in London at one of the 'Pop' concerts under Henry Wood. He was to return frequently to play in this same series and became a favourite of English audiences. In Berlin in 1901, barely twenty-one, he took the Germans by storm. As 'the long-awaited exponent of the French type of violin playing', Flesch tells us that 'above all, it was his tone which, though not big in itself, fascinated the listener by its sweet and seductive colour, literally unheard of at the time'.[1]

Americans heard Thibaud for the first time in 1903 with the Wetzler Symphony Orchestra at Carnegie Hall playing the Mozart E flat and the Saint-Saëns B minor concertos. Whilst the critics made no wild claims as to Thibaud's greatness, they fully appreciated that they were hearing something remarkable, although possibly the subtleties of Thibaud's Frenchness might not have made an immediate appeal to American audiences. The critic of the *New York Times* wrote that his temperament was 'poetic and gracious rather than impassioned and impetuous' and praised his warm, pure tone.

In 1905 Thibaud's love of chamber music led him to form the remarkable Cortot-Thibaud-Casals Trio, perhaps the greatest combination of talent ever seen in a musical ensemble. From their inception they were in constant demand and achieved universal acclaim. Fortunately for posterity, their recordings remain as evidence of their artistry. Their recording of the Beethoven 'Archduke' is one of the most memorable.

During the Great War, Thibaud served in the French Army. Although he saw active service at many of the historic battles — Ypres, Marne, Aisne, Arras, Verdun — he was only slightly wounded and was discharged before the end of the war.

It was during the period between the two wars that Thibaud

travelled the world and established a reputation for his unique interpretations of French music. His playing of the concertos of Bach, Mozart and Beethoven was always well received but it was in the music of Lalo, Chausson, Saint-Saëns and Franck that he excelled. His travels brought him into close contact with many diplomats and others in high places, many of whom became his personal friends. This had a sequel in the Second World War when Thibaud retired, ostensibly to write his memoirs. In reality he was a valuable member of the French Intelligence, working surreptitiously with many of the world's military leaders.

According to Flesch 'it is always an artist's character that provides the master key to an understanding of his art'.[2] In Thibaud's case it was simple. He was French, he loved life and he loved women: for him the eternal feminine was an absolute necessity. His playing 'was imbued with his yearning for sensual pleasure, with an unchastity that was all the more seductive for its refinement'.[3] Thibaud was never guilty of vulgarity or over-expressive display, yet his playing was always virile. The caressing quality which was uniquely Thibaud could convincingly be equated with a lover wooing his mistress. One of his main influences on violin playing was the introduction of a levelling up of a flat intonation on sustained or expressive notes. An integral part of his playing, it never failed to come off. Unfortunately, when it was copied by less accomplished performers the result was disastrous.

Thibaud was a close friend of both Kreisler and Ysaÿe. At one time he studied with the great Belgian and his playing showed a great deal of the master's influence. Although he did not actually suffer from platform 'nerves' as such, Thibaud was a temperamental artist who could be disturbed by the slightest distraction. For this reason he always tried to concentrate in silence on the music for fifteen minutes before going on to the concert platform.

The social value of music was very important to Thibaud. He considered that music had a special mission to take people's minds off the pressures of everyday life. He was impatient with those who insisted that the main purpose of modern music is to depict the realism and ugliness of the present. 'People do not want to have their miseries and worries reflected in music; they want to get away from them.'[4]

Thibaud was opposed to those who go to a concert simply to find fault. He maintained that no artist can be free of imperfections. Nicholas Roth, a former musical director of the Hague radio station, heard him many times in Holland, and also at a Wigmore Hall recital in London when he was over seventy. Roth says: 'There was a wonderful French charm in everything he did. I heard him play the "Introduction and Rondo Capriccioso" [by Saint-Saëns] and he made mistakes; he was out of tune and he scratched. But the audience gave him a standing ovation and the mistakes were washed out as soon as they were made.'[5]

Thibaud was still performing all over the world at the age of seventy-three. On 1 September 1953, the plane in which he was travelling crashed into one of the highest mountain peaks in France. There were no survivors.

19

To Dance in Chains

Georges Enesco;
Jan Kubelik

'I am a son of the soil, born in a land of legends. My whole life has been spent under the eyes of my childhood deities',[1] wrote the Rumanian Georges Enesco (1881–1955), one of the last of the great teachers born in the nineteenth century.

As Menuhin points out in his autobiography, *Unfinished Journey*, Enesco never lost contact with the soil, although his 'childhood deities' sent him far afield, and by the turn of the century he was a highly successful virtuoso, always on the move. He made his home in Paris but also had a country retreat in Rumania appropriately called 'Villa Luminisch' (House of Light).

Enesco was born in Dorohoiû, a village in Moldavia where the inhabitants were of mixed Turkish, Greek, Magyar and Ukranian blood. He was admitted to the Vienna Conservatoire under Hellmesberger at the age of seven. Two years later he was taken into the adult class and graduated, carrying off the highest award for violin playing, at the age of twelve. Composition was already of the greatest importance to the young Enesco; he had written his first four-voice fugue at the age of ten. It was Hellmesberger — then leader of the Vienna Opera Orchestra — who gave him the opportunity to learn how to orchestrate. Whilst at the Conservatoire he lived in his master's house and night after night Hellmesberger would smuggle him into the opera house and hide him behind the drums. Here he would sit absorbing the variety of sounds and colours, so learning the capabilities of each instrument first-hand. After his first Wagner opera Enesco came away intoxicated. He later said of the experience: 'I didn't want to look at the sky because I had seen all the stars there were in Wagner's music.'[2]

From Vienna Enesco went to Paris where he entered the Conservatoire as a pupil of Marsick and studied harmony and composition with Gedalge and Fauré. Again, in 1899, he took away first prize. But his was success with a difference. He had no desire to be a virtuoso — he did not even want to be a violinist. He much preferred the piano, which he played superbly, and nursed an even greater ambition to be a composer. Having had his first work 'Poéme Roumain' performed by the Colonne Orchestra in Paris while he was still a student would have seemed a good start. He also played the cello and mastered eight languages with equal fluency.

While still a young man, Enesco decided that he would play the violin solely to make himself enough money to buy a piece of land in Rumania. He planned to retire early and compose to his dying day.

Mad about composing, I grudged every minute I had to give to my violin, and although I had no delusions about what I was writing, I very much preferred my own humble attempts [at composition] to the persistent study of an instrument that gave me so little satisfaction in return for all my efforts. I have so often looked at my fiddle in its case and said to myself: You are too small, my friend, much too small.[3]

His view was an isolated one. The *New York Times* critic wrote on 23 January 1923: 'He is first and last a musician and an interpreter, devoted solely to expounding music and not at all to the display of his technical powers. These are indeed remarkable but they are employed entirely as a means to an end . . . his playing is notable for its exquisite purity of intonation, especially in double-stoppings.' He was also commended for choosing to play the entire Bach Partita in D minor instead of selecting, as most violinists do, only the Chaconne, the execution of which was described by the critic as 'delivered . . . with a remarkable repose and apparent freedom from effort'.

The 'apparent freedom from effort' was helped, no doubt, by an intensive study and love of Bach from early childhood. When Enesco was in Paris, he would return to Rumania for his summer holidays, and it was then that Queen Carmen Silva presented him with the complete set of the Bach Gesellschaft edition. This became a source of study and joy for the rest of his life. Many of Enesco's pupils have confirmed that he knew at least 120 of the cantatas from memory.

He often pointed out to pupils that the bulk of Bach's music was written (or set) to *words*, only a small portion being written solely for instruments. He suggested that they took the time to study a few of the cantatas, so that they could begin to feel the 'pull' of the harmonic structure in relation to the words. This close emotional relation between words and music was for Enesco the key to the performance of the instrumental works. The American Helen Dowling, a close associate of Enesco who studied with him for four years, said: 'It was a revelation to study Bach with Enesco. Gradually the music began to speak to you, and you in turn had to find the way of communicating this to your audience.'[4]

Enesco held master classes every summer in Paris. He hardly ever concerned himself with technique since he felt that was the job of the regular teacher. He tried to give his pupils a newer and deeper understanding of music. He never insisted that they should play his way, but he gave them a general musical concept from which they could begin to find their own way. He said:

> 'You must learn to dance in chains' by which he meant that one should learn to move freely and yet remain within the framework set by the composer ... His universe was music, and he felt himself its very humble servant. Nothing else in life mattered. It was this single-minded devotion to music that left its mark on all those who came within his orbit![5]

Flesch describes Enesco as towering 'above his musical compatriots like a solitary rock in a sea of mediocrity'.[6] He says that it is impossible to know which of this versatile musician's gifts were the greatest: he seemed to be equally accomplished as teacher, composer, conductor, violinist and pianist. Today Enesco's compositions are seldom played. Boult wrote of his famous Rhapsody that 'however impossible, musically, [it] showed off finely the virtuosity of the orchestra'.[7]

An earlier encounter reveals a great deal about both parties concerned. When Enesco was only fifteen he played for Joachim in Berlin. The great teacher was suitably encouraging with regard to his talent and his playing. Enesco then produced his own Sonata No. 1 written when he was in his early teens, and timidly asked permission to play it. Enesco played the piano and Joachim read the violin part. When they had finished, the old man looked horrified. 'Why,' he retorted, 'it is even more modern than César Franck!'[8]

Today it is as a teacher that Enesco is remembered best. Ida Haendel, then a child but already a virtuoso performer, had been temporarily rejected by Flesch in one of his bursts of anger. She had always wanted to study with Enesco, and was taken to Paris by her father to have a few extra lessons. Though still so young she knew she found herself in the presence of 'the most inspired and uplifted of human beings. The shortness of his stature, his rounded spine [in later years Enesco suffered from a terrible crippling disease], indifferent attire, seemed almost to enhance his greatness and spiritual quality'.[9] Again it was in a lesson on Bach that she found Enesco 'firm and uncompromising, he removed all the frills ... so allowing the true form and anatomy to be exposed'. When the music had been freed of all embellishments it sounded strange but she realized that his emphasis on purity of line served to show the real grandeur of its structure. 'I seemed to hear Bach the giant for the first time.'[10]

Much later in her career, Ida Haendel visited Enesco in Paris and played him the Chaconne from the Bach Partita, although she had never actually studied the piece with him. It was also Enesco's birthday and she had brought him a cake. When she had finished playing, Enesco asked 'Have you studied the Chaconne with me?' 'No, maître, but I heard you play it in New York.' She waited for the verdict. 'By playing the Chaconne the way you did, you brought me a much bigger present than the cake.'[11]

Ida Haendel draws an interesting comparison between Flesch and Enesco. The latter never tried to impose his ideas on a pupil; his remarks were more like suggestions than advice. Flesch's approach was more methodical and clinical. With Enesco a pupil seldom had the chance to perform a work without interruption, and he very rarely demonstrated a point on his violin. He would work verbally from the piano.

Menuhin also studied with Enesco in extreme youth, and remembers today the infinite value of that encounter. He writes:

A lesson was an inspiration, not a stage reached in a course of instruction. It was the making of music much as if I were his orchestra ... for while he accompanied me at the piano he also sang the different voices of the score ... What I received from him — by compelling example ... was the note transformed into vital message, the phrase given shape and meaning, the structure of music made vivid ... Music was hardly dead for me; it was a fierce passion, but I had never known it to have such clear and vital form before.[12]

In complete contrast, Enesco's contemporary Jan Kubelik (1880 –1940) was without doubt one of the most outstanding technicians of his time. As Ševčik's best-known pupil, it was through his example that his master's 'Method' was universally introduced to the musical world. The main characteristics of his playing were firmly rooted in technical mastery and although he included most of the classic concertos in his repertoire, he was happiest when exhibiting the bravura gymnastics of the more virtuosic spellbinders.

Throughout his career the critics remained unmoved, although greatly impressed by his brilliance. In 1907, Richard Aldrich of the *New York Times* explained: 'There is something aloof in him as he plays ... yet few have the power of so ravishing the senses with the sheer beauty of his tone, the charm of his cantilena, the elegance and ease with which he masters all the technical difficulties.' On another occasion Aldrich admitted that in a performance of the Mozart Concerto in D major 'he showed a style of unaffected sincerity and strength ... Yet there was a certain sort of constraint in it which immediately dropped from him when he began Wieniawski's more brilliant work [Concerto in D minor]. Here he was more at home.'

Kubelik was born at Michle, a small town on the outskirts of Prague. His father was a market gardener and a good violinist who also conducted a local band. In his latter days, when living in Beverly Hills, Hollywood, Kubelik reversed the process by becoming a keen amateur gardener.

Having received his first instruction from his father, Kubelik had some lessons with Karel Ondřicek, and then entered the Prague Conservatoire under Ševčik at the age of twelve. He studied with Ševčik for six years and left the Conservatoire a proclaimed virtuoso after a performance of Paganini's D major concerto.

His Vienna début in 1898 was equally successful and he continued to astound his audiences throughout Europe. In 1900 he appeared for the first time at a Richter concert at the St James' Hall in London. The *Musical Times* critic wrote: 'Fine orchestral playing and superb interpretations of the classics are very well in their way, but what can they avail with a London audience against a fiddler with a phenomenally developed technique, a dead-sure intonation, a beautiful tone, and an uncanny way of playing the most wonderful difficulties?' The critic goes on to say that he does not blame Kubelik for not playing one of the four classical 'test' concertos by Beethoven, Mendelssohn, Bruch or Brahms, but that 'at present he revels in surmounting seemingly impossible technical difficulties. As he grows older he may ... revel equally in unravelling the beauties and depths that lie hidden in the aforesaid masters' works.'

Kubelik crossed the Atlantic in 1902 and here, as elsewhere, his audiences were bowled over by his facility, although, as we have seen, the critics described him as lacking depth of feeling. Nonetheless, by giving the public what they wanted, Kubelik amassed a fortune. His meteoric rise to fame as a prodigy meant that before the age of twenty he became a very rich man. As early as 1904, he purchased an estate, complete with baronial castle, for $160,000 — netted from his first American tour. He was also recording with the Victor Company and received substantial royalties. When Melba made her historic recording of Gounod's 'Ave Maria', it was Kubelik who supplied the violin obbligato.

In 1903 Kubelik married a Hungarian countess, and the youngest of their seven children is the conductor Rafael Kubelik. In the USA there were many critics of the violinist's public image. The press constantly exploited stories of his castles, aristocratic connections and his 'highly valued fingers'[13] which appeared more important than good taste in musical performance. Certainly he managed to achieve much publicity that was not strictly concerned with music. In 1902 he had to live down allegations that he was under the influence of a Svengali-like secretary, who directed him mechanically and pocketed the gain. Once, when travelling in an elevator in a Chicago hotel, he noticed a picture of Paderewski, the great pianist, on the wall. He tore down the poster, exclaiming: 'That's what you do for another artist, when *I'm* the man who made your hotel famous!'[14]

In the early thirties Kubelik suffered many misfortunes. The depression drove him out of Europe, where his speculations had extended to five manorial estates in Bohemia and Hungary. At this time he also owned sixteen valuable violins, including his famous 'Emperor' Stradivari (dated 1715) and his Guarneri del Gesù of 1735. In 1932 he was forced to sell many of his treasures, including the del Gesù (which is now owned by Kyung-Wha Chung), but he never parted with his 'Emperor'.

Although he returned to Europe and died in Prague in 1940, Kubelik settled for some time in California, where he retreated to a modest cottage high up in the Beverly Hills. Surrounded by orchards and high hedges of red poinsettia bushes, he devoted himself to composition, writing several concertos and small pieces for the violin. He told a reporter in 1938, 'I pay the film world its due by writing them scenarios . . . my son is to star in one shortly for a Vienna concern . . . I may play my fiddle in it.'[15] It is unlikely that this ever materialized.

Kubelik did not play much in his later years, his hearing becoming so impaired that his intonation was affected. He was one of those whose place in the top echelon of violinists was threatened and finally overtaken by Jascha Heifetz, who comes later in this story.

20

The Unbridled Individualist

Bronislav Huberman

When Ida Haendel was a small child, she played for Huberman (1882–1947) at a banquet in Warsaw. Recalling the incident some forty years later, she said:

> I looked at him, the idol of thousands, and I could hardly believe it. He smiled at me gently and he was beautiful to me. I saw none of his defects — the famous cross-eyes, the protruding lower lip and the over-large head. All I saw was a great spirit shining in that powerful, determined face, which for a moment made me think of Beethoven.'[1]

This perceptive child was near to the truth. Huberman felt an affinity with Beethoven which went further than the music itself. He shared the composer's love of mankind and firmly believed that a united Europe was the only solution to world peace. As one of the leading musical personalities of the era, he was able to influence the furtherance of the Pan-European Movement to which he gave much time and money. Like Beethoven, he saw music as a unifying force, 'a lofty reconciling spirit . . . seeking to unite all listeners'.[2]

Huberman refused to play in Nazi Germany, even though the conductor Furtwängler wrote begging him to change his mind. A decree had been drawn up to allow any artist 'no matter what his race or nation' to perform. Furtwängler pleaded: 'Someone must make the first move to break down the barrier.' Although Huberman appreciated Furtwängler's efforts to overcome the difficulties, he could not excuse 'the menaced destruction by racial purgers'[3] and the deposition of Mendelssohn, Rubinstein and Joachim because they were Jews. He held to his decision and never appeared in Hitler's Germany. There were others who also took this view. Toscanini refused to go to Bayreuth, and Thibaud, a non-Jew, also declined Furtwängler's invitation.

Bronislav Huberman was born in the small Polish town of Czenstochaus, the son of a barrister who gave him every encouragement when he showed early talent on the violin. He studied at first with Michalowicz, a pupil of Auer and teacher at the School of Music in Warsaw, and then with Lotto, who had studied with Massart. At the age of seven, the child performed Spohr's second violin concerto at a public concert and followed this by taking the part of leader in a quartet by Rode.

When the chance came for Huberman to study with Joachim in Berlin, he was ten years old, but he stayed with him only nine months. At the time it was not understood why he threw away the opportunity to study with one of the great teachers. In later years he revealed that not only was he more often taught by Joachim's pupil, Markees, than by the master himself, but it was also the atmosphere of pedantic academicism then infecting Berlin which he found so stifling. The individualism that was the hallmark of his personality was already manifest: so he sought tuition elsewhere.

After short spells with Heermann in Frankfurt and Marsick in Paris, Huberman received no further training, and embarked upon his solo career at eleven years of age. He toured the main cities in Europe — Amsterdam, Brussels, Paris and, a year later, London, where he was heard by the singer Adelina Patti. The *prima donna* took him to Vienna and presented him at her farewell concert in 1895; his future was assured.

In 1896, Huberman played the Brahms concerto for the first time. Many famous musicians, including the composer himself, sat in the management box waiting to hear what this child could make of a work which had frightened off so many leading violinists, even in their riper years. The result was phenomenal. Brahms's biographer Max Kalbeck tells us that from the first stroke of the bow he was astonished, 'and when the Adagio was reached his eyes moistened. At the end of the Finale, he embraced the young boy whose musical genius had found the exact mode of interpretation of the concerto.'[4]

From this time Huberman's European reputation went from strength to strength. In Poland he was treated as a god. Strangely enough he was never truly appreciated in England. Menuhin offers the explanation that 'Such artists reflect a certain culture, temperament, mixture of races, and they thrive most happily in home soil.'⁵ When he first appeared as an adult performer in the USA (he had given concerts as a child prodigy in New York in 1897) Huberman was not an unqualified success. Richard Aldrich of the *New York Times* considered that his 'talent is manifested with a certain crudeness'. He admits he is unpretentious and that his mind is apparently more on the music itself than on the effect he is making as a player. On this occasion, Aldrich is disturbed by Huberman's 'back-bending' and straining to produce certain effects. His tone is 'powerful, but it is not notable for warmth or appealing quality.' However, in 1936, *The Strad*'s correspondent in Alexandria, Alexander Ruppa, found Huberman to be 'endowed with the rare power of portraying the whole gamut of human emotions from the most exquisite tenderness to the most brutal violence.'

Huberman would seem to have been one of the first of the modern violinists to sense the links between psychology and music. Thibaud had recognized the effects of music as an anodyne or escape, but his approach was both a more conscious and a more emotional one. For Huberman, Beethoven was the supreme example of what he most admired in music, and he placed Brahms next as speaking to him with the greatest intimacy. He saw Brahms as a synthesis of the human and transfigured sensual, as revealing a conscious renunciation of impulsive longings, not so much rejection as resignation, expiation and forgiveness.

Huberman had strong views on the role played by the interpretative artist. He did not see him as a passive mediator. He felt there were two important aspects that determined the approach to performance. First, in the reproduction of a work, the interpretative artist must make the listener feel his personal experience of the moment. Secondly, 'he must make the listener aware of the inner storms and birth-pangs which buffeted the composer in the act of creation',⁶ and to bring this about is obliged to study every minute detail of tempo, dynamics, harmonization and orchestration. Huberman was adamant in his view that the composer's intentions must always be observed. He often took a long time to learn a work. 'I must live the piece before I can play it beautifully. That moment may come when I am playing it upon the stage for the first, the fifth or the tenth time: But if it does not come, I discard the composition, no matter what pains its mastery may have cost.'⁷

One of Huberman's most severe critics was Carl Flesch. He deplored his lack of training, his *vibrato*, his holding of the bow in an outmoded style, his self-willed personality and his habit of adjusting the 'tone of the work to the pitch of his own ego'. In Flesch's opinion, he will survive only 'as the most remarkable representative of unbridled individualism, a fascinating outsider'.[8] Hans Keller, editor of the Carl Flesch *Memoirs*, takes another view. 'Huberman was one of the greatest musicians I have ever come across . . . a long line of artists has testified to his towering stature as an artist, violinist and man.' He concedes that his technique was always individual and depended greatly upon the prevailing mood, but 'When he was "on form", both hands evinced a virtuoso technique of the utmost brilliance and an almost uncanny verve.' Hans Keller rebuts all Flesch's accusations regarding his *vibrato* and manner of holding the bow. As for his intonation, Keller does not know 'of another violinist who adjusted his intonation so consistently to harmonic and melodic requirements'.[9]

Perhaps Huberman's most enduring achievement is his musical pioneering in Palestine. In 1936, assisted by Toscanini and other leading musicians, he founded the Palestine Philharmonic Orchestra, which later became the Israel Philharmonic. It was the displacement of Jews through the growing menace of Nazi Germany that prompted Huberman to establish, in the land where so many sought refuge, a firm musical basis upon which they could build. In Israel today the results are self-evident.

Bronislav Huberman, founder
of the orchestra that later
became the Israel
Philharmonic

Albert Sammons, the first
British violinist to achieve
international fame

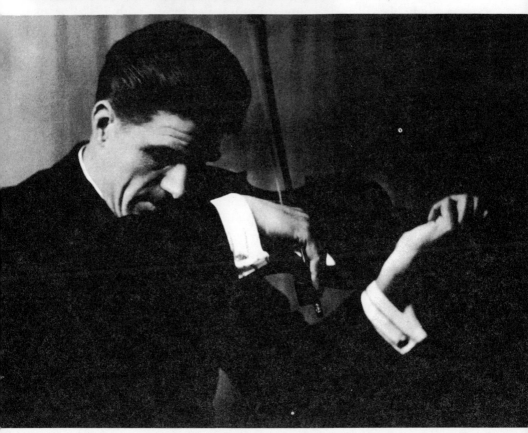

21

'Our Own Albert'

Albert Sammons

For well over two hundred years extending until the 1930s, Britain was dominated by foreign musicians. The public fancied the British lacked the charisma that surrounded the imported artist. Violinists were the breed most affected by this prejudice. Spohr, Paganini, Ysaÿe and Kreisler were all names with magical connotations. The only alternative open to the British artist was to study abroad for a couple of years, and return with a 'ski' or an 'ini' added to his name.

One of the artists who, by his own example, did much to elevate the status of the British performer was the London born Albert Sammons (1886–1957) — 'Our own Albert', to his colleagues. Sammons was born into a musical family. His father, a good amateur musician, gave him his first lessons on the fiddle. As a boy of eleven he attended school by day and spent his evenings playing in the orchestra of a Piccadilly restaurant. When he left school, a year later, his experience in playing the light classics enabled him to become a freelance professional — at the palm court of a Harrogate hotel or a hunt ball in the Shires, often required to dress up for a particular function. The authentic 'Hungarian band'[1] with whom he frequently played were ordered to keep a trappist silence, lest it should be discovered that their only language was, for the most part, broad Cockney.

Sammons's first great breakthrough came in 1908, when he was leading a small orchestra at the Waldorf Hotel in London. Thomas Beecham had heard that they had a violinist of uncommon dexterity and had dined there in order to hear him. Beecham put in a request for a solo and was rewarded with the finale of the

Mendelssohn concerto, played at a speed which flabbergasted the conductor who had a reputation for some fairly rapid tempi himself. He scribbled on a card 'Splendid, but the right tempo is so and so',[2] indicating by a metronome mark what he thought it should be. Sammons's response was to play it again — at the requested tempo.

Beecham immediately offered Sammons a place in his own orchestra. A few months later he became leader, and held the position for five years. Beecham never flagged in his enthusiasm for Sammons. In his memoirs, *A Mingled Chime*, he wrote: 'This gifted and resourceful youth developed into the best all-round concert-master I have ever met anywhere, uniting in himself a technical facility equal to any demand made upon it, a full, warm tone, a faultless rhythmic sense, and a brain that remained cool in the face of any untoward happening.'

Sammons had a few isolated lessons from John Saunders and Frederick Weist-Hill (a pupil of Ysaÿe) but, like his eminent predecessors Paganini and Ole Bull, was largely self-trained. Nonetheless, his technique lacked nothing. By assiduous application to the study of all the important aspects of technique he acquired a mastery of the instrument which led him to become outstanding both as soloist and teacher.

In 1909, Sammons's love for chamber music prompted him to form the quartet which later became famous as the London Quartet. Their association lasted until 1919, when Sammons regretfully gave it up in order to devote himself to solo work.

Sammons's career as a virtuoso began with an outstanding performance of Bruch's G minor concerto under Stanford at a concert at the Queen's Hall in 1911. A few days later a letter arrived from Sir Landon Ronald, saying he had never heard a finer performance and could Sammons play for him at the Albert Hall. That same year, Sammons was appointed Musician in Ordinary to King George V, and in 1912 was chosen to play the Saint-Saëns B minor concerto in the presence of King George V, Queen Mary and the aging composer, at the Queen's Hall.

By 1913 Sammons's fame had spread abroad, and he was invited to lead the Dieppe Symphony Orchestra under Pierre Monteux; but when war broke out the following year, he returned to his own country.

It was during the war, when so many of the imported virtuosos were not readily available, that the British musical public began to

realize they had a remarkable native talent in Albert Sammons.
When Ysaÿe heard him play for the first time, he exclaimed: 'At
last, England has found herself a great violinist!'[3]

Perhaps the work with which Sammons was most closely
associated is the Elgar concerto. It had been sadly neglected since
its first performance in 1910 by Kreisler. Sammons played the
Elgar for the first time on 23 November 1914, at the Queen's Hall
with Vassily Safonov conducting the London Symphony Orchestra. At the time, Sammons was one of the very few violinists
capable of tackling the work, and he devoted to it a considerable
period of his study. After this performance, the critic of *The Star*
wrote:

> It has for some time been clear to musicians that Mr Albert Sammons
> is a violinist of quite uncommon gifts, who only needed a few chances
> to convince the public at large of his powers; but the chance never
> came. It apparently needed a European war to give it to him. He had it
> last night, and made splendid use of it. His performance of the difficult
> solo part put him in the front rank of violinists, and the public cheered
> him with as much enthusiasm as if he had had a foreign name.

Later, through countless performances, Sammons became one
of the world's greatest exponents of the work. Elgar himself
admitted that no-one seemed to get to the heart of the piece as
Sammons did. John Barbirolli, after a performance with the Hallé,
wrote to the violinist: 'We felt privileged to be associated with you
in the performing of the Elgar, which will live long in our
memories.' It has often been said that it was the 'Englishness' of
Sammons's playing which made him such a sensitive interpreter
of national composers.

Another fine English concerto, apt to be overshadowed by the
Elgar, is the Delius, dedicated by the composer to Sammons. It is
an elusive work which even today tends to be neglected. Sammons made a careful study of it when it came to him fresh from
the composer's pen, and found that much of it needed amending.
Despite the fact that Delius played the fiddle, some passages were
violinistically impossible. Grateful for Sammons's suggestions,
Delius prepared a revised version. It received its first performance
on 30 January 1919 in a Philharmonic Society concert at the
Queen's Hall conducted by Adrian Boult. Next day *The Times*
critic wrote: 'The work has two moods rather than sections, one
of agitated inquiry followed by one of happy trover. It was the

latter that suited Mr Sammons, as if written for him: he can play poetical, throbbing cantilena like practically no-one else.' Delius was much moved by the performance. He considered there were only three musicians who could properly interpret his music: Beecham, Eugène Goossens and Sammons.

However, there was a background drama to this first performance that almost resulted in a cancellation. At the time Sammons was serving as a private in the Grenadier Guards. He was leading the string section of the orchestra and doubling on the clarinet in the military band: he had never learned this instrument but was forced to double out of necessity. At the last moment he found himself ordered to play at a grand ball at the Albert Hall on the night before the final rehearsal and concert. Knowing how difficult it would be to do justice to a new work after a late night of continuous dance-music, he asked for leave of absence from the ball. His bandmaster refused his request. Thereupon two panic-stricken directors from the Royal Philharmonic Society rushed to Wellington Barracks to plead with the Colonel and the Adjutant of the Grenadier Guards. The officers were sympathetic and overruled the bandmaster's decision, so the situation was saved. It was not long before Sammons secured his discharge from the army — much to the satisfaction of everyone except the bandmaster.

Sammons's interpretation of the Brahms concerto was said by critics to rank with the best from abroad, and he played the Beethoven over a hundred times, seventy of them during the Second World War. He considered the Mendelssohn, which he loved, a difficult work to play well, and most violinists today still hold that view. He had some reservations about the Bartók concerto. Although he thought it was fine music, in Sammons's opinion it was not successful as a violin concerto per se, for Bartók misjudged the size of the violin's tone in contrast with that of the full orchestra. He drew a comparison with the Bloch, which he considered entirely suitable in this respect.

As a man Sammons remained simple and unassuming. 'Our own Albert' had no use for the snobbish upper echelons of the musical world. He was adored by the orchestral players, with whom he would often sit down and chat after a rehearsal. More often than not their conversation revolved around sport rather than the latest piece of musical gossip. His great hobby was golf, and in his prime he was a match for anyone. On one occasion,

Sammons won a championship at Bognor and gave a recital there the same evening. A reporter asked if his golf interfered with his fiddle playing. Sammons chortled: 'No! On the contrary, my fiddle playing is apt to interfere with my golf!'[4]

A connoisseur of master violins, Sammons owned a number of beautiful instruments by celebrated makers. For many years he used a Guadagnini and later a Stradivari, but his favourite fiddle, and one he used to the end of his performing life, was a superb Matteo Gofriller dated 1696. Once, in the Cobbett competition for violin makers, he played behind a screen a violin made by the English Alfred Vincent and one by Stradivari. The majority of the judges were in favour of the sound of the modern instrument and Sammons himself used it for many years.

As a soloist the outstanding feature of his playing was a searching power and depth of tone that enriched every phrase — light and lilting, or intense and emotional. Hugh Bean, for many years leader of the Philharmonia Orchestra, says: 'Sammons made a very warm, rich sound. His great sincerity and dignity as a man came over in his playing.'[5] Bean feels that his recordings do not do him justice. Even the reissue on LP of the 1944 Delius recording had to be taken from a good set of 78 r.p.m. discs because the matrices of the original recordings were destroyed in an air-raid.

Composition was yet another of Sammons's accomplishments. In addition to a number of attractive solo works for the violin, he published three volumes of a concentrated form of exercises entitled *Secrets of Technique*. This project was the result of many years diligent research into the technical aspects of the instrument, and the studies illustrate his novel approach, especially with regard to the way to practise. Hugh Bean was reared on these exercises and considers them of vital importance:

> Sammons worked out what matters most and put it down in a concise and logical way. He taught me precisely how to use ten minutes in the best possible way. For example — you arrive late for a concert because the train is late. The hall is cold and there is no hot water. You have ten minutes to prepare yourself. He taught me how to overcome these hazards and it is all there in these little books.[6]

These exercises are at present out of print and the publishers cannot be persuaded to reissue them, despite the fact that many teachers use their own tattered copies and swear by them.

Sammons was a painstaking and flexible teacher. Not affiliated to any school, he had gained his experience by many years as an orchestral player. This brought home to him the realization that a musician never stopped learning. Such humility stood him in good stead with his pupils. He was professor of violin at the Royal College of Music from 1939 to 1956, and among his many pupils who have achieved outstanding success are Thomas Matthews, Alan Loveday and Hugh Bean, who studied with Sammons from the age of nine for a period of some twenty years. Bean recalls Sammons's ability as a teacher:

> His wonderful directness and simplicity of character enabled him to communicate with his pupils. Since he was virtually self-taught himself his problems had to be worked out in a matter-of-fact, thoroughly down-to-earth manner. He was not one for sophisticated phrases. He would either describe what he wanted in a straightforward way that everybody could understand, or demonstrate — not to show how brilliant he was, but how the problem could be analysed in a way that would be relevant to the particular pupil. But he was very suspicious of any slick way of solving a technical problem. It had to be founded on rock-like foundations. Anything that resembled a gimmick or streamlining for effect would be absolutely alien to him. But even then if he saw that such a course came naturally under a student's fingers and that it worked for him, then he would not oppose him.[7]

For all his students Sammons had one unbreakable rule: 'Concentrate upon perfect intonation. You will never distinguish yourself until your intonation is perfect, for it is this and artistic interpretation that marks the difference between the work of the great violinist and the mediocre.'[8]

22

The Russian Vanguard

Efrem Zimbalist; Mischa Elman

Two of the first important violinists to emerge from the Auer School were the Russians Efrem Zimbalist and Mischa Elman. Regarded as competitors for many years, there was a time when Zimbalist achieved even higher public acclaim than his distinguished rival.

Zimbalist was born at Rostov-on-Don in 1889, the son of a professional conductor, and naturally received a first class grounding in music from his father. He was leading the orchestra at the opera house in Rostov at the age of nine. He was thirteen when he entered Auer's class in St Petersburg, and three years later left that establishment having won the gold medal and the Rubinstein scholarship, worth 1,200 roubles.

The next few years brought the young Zimbalist success on every side. The year of his début at eighteen with the Brahms concerto, in Berlin, he thrilled London audiences with his brilliant interpretation of the Tchaikovsky concerto and the Lalo 'Symphonie Espagnole' a work for which he had an uncanny inner feeling and in the performance of which he was later said to have no peer since Sarasate. As a fully fledged virtuoso he toured Europe receiving rave notices everywhere, and he was the first violinist invited by the Leipzig Gewandhaus to play on New Year's Day, continuing the Joachim tradition, unbroken for fifty years.

In 1911, Zimbalist crossed the Atlantic. When he played the Glazunov concerto with the New York Philharmonic Orchestra conducted by Josef Stransky at the Carnegie Hall, the *New York Times* critic wrote: 'He is already a virtuoso in the best sense of the word, of the first rank, a mature artist who can stir feelings that it is not given to many to touch.' In the more decorative and brilliant passages the critic praised not only a 'technique of perfect security, but his power of transmuting a perfunctory work into something more noble than it merits. Few artists are more unassuming than Mr Zimbalist, more absorbed in the music they are playing.'

In a recital at the same hall a few days later, Zimbalist again compelled admiration as 'an artist of truly remarkable powers'.[1] It is interesting that in a programme of music by Brahms, Paganini and Tchaikovsky, he also included pieces by York Bowen and Cyril Scott, two comparatively unknown English composers.

Zimbalist reached the highest point of his achievement in the prelude and fugue from the solo sonata in G minor by Bach, which 'he interpreted with magnificent breadth and dignity of style, and with that tone which, the oftener it is heard, seems more astonishing in its power, virility and beauty'.[2]

Zimbalist composed a considerable amount of music for his instrument, although none has found its way into the regular repertoire. But he will be remembered for his painstaking researches into the resuscitation of early music for the violin at a time when the works of composers such as Torelli, Uccelini and Bassani were largely unknown to violinists.

Zimbalist was a genial and modest man much admired by his fellow musicians. An avid collector of books and rare manuscripts, he was also a connoisseur of vintage wines and cigars. He loved social life, and an invitation to one of his dinner parties promised a varied evening of entertainment. A sumptuous meal would be followed by some string quartet playing, but that was not all. Donald Brook writes in 1948: 'He is always most generous and consequently there is something of a fifty thousand dollars a year atmosphere about the place by the end of the evening . . . . An evening with Zimbalist generally concludes with bridge or poker, but unless you are an exceptionally good player it is better to think of some ingenious excuse for an early departure.'[3]

At the Royal Festival Hall in October 1961, a short-legged, portly, bald-headed little man played both the Brahms and the Mendelssohn concertos to a rapt audience who gave him a standing ovation. Next morning the press was also unanimous in praise of this great artist who had first appeared in an ill-fitting suit before a British audience fifty-six years previously. The violinist was Mischa Elman and the concert took place nine months after his seventieth birthday.

The first of Auer's pupils to gain world-wide reputations: Efrem Zimbalist *(left)*, and Mischa Elman*(below)*, at the age when he took the world by storm

Pianists and conductors would appear to be indestructible. Some singers are often capable of giving good performances well into their later years. Elisabeth Schumann was still singing beautifully at sixty-four and recordings made by Melba well into her sixties are proof of that lady's evergreen reputation. But throughout the history of violin playing, there are few soloists who have carried perfect accuracy into old age. Ysaÿe, Thibaud and Kreisler all declined towards the end of their performing years, but Mischa Elman (1891–1967) retained his glorious tone and perfect intonation until the close of his career. In fact, he died in action at the age of seventy-six. He had been practising for a forthcoming concert when his heart failed.

Elman was born in Tolna, a village near Kiev, the son of a Jewish schoolmaster who played the violin. When Mischa was four he received some preliminary instruction from his father. His phenomenal progress prompted his parents to send him to the Imperial School of Music at Odessa, where he studied with Alexander Fidelmann. One day, Leopold Auer was visiting the school and heard young Mischa play; he was so taken with the boy's talent that he immediately offered him a place at the Conservatoire at St Petersburg. Since it was not possible for a Jew to attend a school outside his own domicile, the authorities raised objections. But Auer even threatened to resign his post if permission was not granted for this, the most talented boy he had ever encountered. Eventually Auer won the battle and the entire Elman family moved to St Petersburg.

From the onset, he became Auer's favourite pupil, and so astounding was his progress that in 1904 Auer presented him before a critical Berlin audience where he was given a stupendous reception. He was immediately offered a number of further engagements to appear again in Berlin and other German cities.

Elman's St Petersburg début came about as the result of a ruse. Auer himself had been invited to play the Paganini 'Moto Perpetuo' and the Mendelssohn concerto, but at the last moment he feigned illness and pushed his prodigy on to the stage. Everyone was astonished at his exquisite playing and would not let him go until he had given half a dozen encores.

Elman was thirteen when he made his triumphal British début at the Queen's Hall on 21 March 1905. *The Strad* critic wrote:

> From the moment he stepped on to the platform until he had played his last encore at 11.20 p.m. (and even then the public seemed to want

some more) his success in this country was an assured thing. He tackled the terrific difficulties of Tchaikovsky's D major Concerto as though they were a mere bagatelle ... [Auer, it will be remembered, thought this work unplayable] this little fellow literally 'waltzed round it', made light of its technical pitfalls, and gave a rendering of it so thoroughly in accord with the spirit in which it was written, that the audience literally rose to him ...

A year later Elman gave his first performance of the Brahms concerto with the London Symphony Orchestra. The *Musical Times* of July 1906 considered that he interpreted 'the solo part with astonishing depth of expression and technical mastery'. This was one of the works that many of his eminent predecessors had tackled only in their adult prime, and some had avoided it altogether.

An interesting article by Harold E. Gorst, on the merits and drawbacks of infant prodigies in general, appeared in the *Saturday Review* in June 1906. Of Elman, he writes:

His genius is as robust as that of a musician who has developed and matured slowly by natural stages ... I found in him not a young boy precociously proficient on the violin, but a musical giant, standing head and shoulders above most of his contemporaries ... The dryest technical passages are phrased with such masterly conception that everything he plays is galvanized into life, and is made to convey some meaning, in the form of musical ideas, to the listener ...

Gorst's summing up is revealing. 'Mischa Elman has survived the ordeal of the infant prodigy stage because his genius is spontaneous, not the imitative cleverness of a precocious child.'

Elman was seventeen when he made his first American appearance in New York on 10 December 1908 playing the Tchaikovsky concerto with the Russian Symphony Orchestra. 'United to an amazing technical precision there is a still more amazing emotional temperament, all dominated by a powerful musical and mental intellect that is uncanny,'[4] wrote James Gibbons Huneker.

It was at his first New York Recital at the Carnegie Hall, a week after his first concert appearance, that the *New York Times* considered an aspect of Elman's playing which was to be seized on by critics throughout his career, but about which his admirers totally disagreed. There were said to be 'serious defects in his playing ... he has in abundance what is known as "temperament"; and his playing suffers from its lack of poise and restraint'.

What this and other critics blamed him for was his tendency to force the note of pathos and sentiment which caused a lack of breadth and simplicity in his playing. Elman's own response was simply 'I play how I feel'.

But the critical voices were in the minority and Elman continued to pack the concert halls on both sides of the Atlantic. He returned to Britain soon after his American success, having decided some years before that he preferred to live in that country. The only place large enough to accommodate his audiences was the Albert Hall, and Londoners flocked in their thousands to hear him. His presence was commanded at Buckingham Palace on several occasions for Queen Alexandra was especially fond of his playing.

On one occasion, when playing to the Royal family, Elman appeared with two distinguished fellow artists, Melba and Caruso. The friendship which developed between the great tenor and Elman stemmed from this meeting. When he lived for a couple of years at the Knickerbocker Hotel in New York, where Caruso also had a suite, the two would often meet to make music together. They also made a number of recordings, which were naturally bestsellers. Elman had a substantial royalty income from his recordings, which reached sales of over two million by 1948.

When the 1914 war broke out Elman received a message from Nicholas II granting him dispensation from military service, on account of his great value as an artist, and saying that 'Russia would not wish harm to come to one of her great geniuses'.[5] Elman never returned to his native country, but like all Slavonic expatriots became misty-eyed when talking about it. When the Russians began the restoration of the Tchaikovsky Museum at Klin, he lost no time in making his contribution by way of a complete set of his recordings of the composer's music.

Elman went to America in 1914 and in 1923 he took out US citizenship. Two years later he married an American, Helen Katten. His wife's wedding gift was the superb Madame Récamier Stradivari dated 1717, said to have been presented to the famous beauty by Napoleon. It was purchased in Paris whilst on their honeymoon, and said to be worth £10,000, an extremely high price for the time.

Elman's long career experienced several ups and downs, but his tremendous resilience stood him in good stead. A world celebrity at sixteen, at twenty-five he had to compete with the phenomenal

Kreisler, who stole much of the limelight on the American concert platform. At the same time, Heifetz was emerging as the most formidable rival of all. Ten years later the twelve-year-old Menuhin took the world by storm. There was also the young Nathan Milstein from the Auer School, and by the 1930s, another Russian, David Oistrakh, had joined the galaxy.

Elman's survival through all this fierce competition was largely due to his innate sense of purpose and a stability which many other artists lacked. Auer tells a story about this quality which he already exhibited as a boy. Auer had a theory that a pupil with great talent and unusual physical advantages will rise above the general level if he is set a task well beyond his power. He decided to experiment with Elman when he was only twelve years old, and set him the first movement of the Tchaikovsky concerto at a public examination. At a rehearsal the boy was struggling with a passage in thirds in the cadenza. Having told him to repeat the passage several times, Auer said it was obvious he could not play the Tchaikovsky and he should therefore prepare another piece. 'With eyes filled with tears, and a voice full of determination, he assured me that at the examination the passage would go well.'[6] Auer insisted that he doubted it, and he should find an alternative, but that he should also perfect the concerto. When the dress rehearsal came round, Elman played the Tchaikovsky faultlessly.

Perhaps as an insurance against the abundance of talent on the solo side, Elman founded the Elman Quartet in 1924, and achieved success despite the virtuoso element in his playing. The performance of the Mozart B flat quartet at their first concert was spoken of as being 'positively thrilling',[7] and the recording they made of the Andante Cantabile from the Quartet in D major, Op. II No. 1 by Tchaikovsky was a bestseller on both sides of the Atlantic.

Then suddenly, when he was over fifty, Elman returned to the solo arena. Although at first almost unnoticed, he soon reestablished himself among the top rank of players. And he maintained that position until the end of his days.

Like Kreisler, Elman was equable in temperament and not given to rages if things went wrong; he beamed with good humour. There is a story of the boy who reappeared regularly after a number of concerts, always to collect his autograph. Elman asked him why so many. Nonchalantly the boy replied: 'Oh, I'm trading my pal five Elmans for one Kreisler'.[8] Elman took it all in good part and would tell the story on himself.

But there were things Elman felt strongly about. He was highly critical of the mania for speed which was beginning to develop in his lifetime. He considered there was something radically wrong with teaching methods which allowed talented students to become obsessed with the idea that speed was the most important element. He also regretted the trend to place too much importance on sheer mechanics. Sam Applebaum discussed this problem with Elman, and in his book *With the Artists* reports him as saying: 'Students are prone to lose sight of the nature of their instrument as a medium second only to the human voice as expressive of tonal beauty. I would place strong stress on impressing pupils with the fact that the violin is a singing instrument — appreciation of its musical function should be cultivated and they should not be carried away by dazzling technical display.'

Elman was the first of Auer's pupils to spread his master's fame abroad, and it was through him that the 'Russian' grip of the bow was made known. Flesch describes it thus: 'The index finger touches the stick at the line separating the second from the third joint, and in addition embraces it with its first and second joint.'[9] When this hold is correctly employed the index finger guides the bow and the little finger only touches it at the lower half while playing. David Oistrakh was a perfect example of a player who used the Russian grip in its 'classic' form.

What Elman will be remembered for is his superb dark, mellow tone, individual and unmistakable as that of Kreisler or Heifetz. Flesch described it as 'overflowing ... with a sensuous mellifluence, an Italian *bel canto* in oriental dress ... His intonation, which is as clear as a bell, further enhances the charm of his tone.'[10] And yet Elman's hands were small and his fingers short and thick. Like Sarasate, he was unable to play certain works by Paganini.

His repertoire was extensive. Although he played Handel and unaccompanied Bach superbly, he could turn to the Lalo 'Symphonie Espagnole' and touch quite another mood. The salon pieces of Wieniawski, Massenet and Saint-Saëns were all masterpieces in his hands. But above all, he made the Tchaikovsky concerto his own. Many consider Elman's performance the best of his time, and his recording on HMV 78 r.p.m. (now also on LP) is proof of it.

Donald Brook aptly sums up the phenomenon that was Elman. 'The outstanding feature of his playing is not the technical mastery of his instrument . . . nor yet the satisfying breadth of tone, but that spiritual Hebraic quality that artists of Jewish ancestry seem to be able to put into music of a sombre mood.'[11]

23

The Scholarly Virtuoso

Josef Szigeti

When Josef Szigeti's *With Strings Attached* was published in 1947, a reviewer commented: 'as a writer of personal reminiscences he has one serious fault; he dislikes talking about himself. He does not seem . . . to have the virtuoso soloist temperament at all.' Szigeti appears to be 'more interested in other people and in music as an art than he is in his own personality'.[1] The same writer also draws attention to the time and energy that this remarkable man spends on the promotion of new music. Szigeti (1892–1973) probably holds the record for first performances of new works by living composers, many of which were dedicated to him.

Szigeti was born in Budapest, where the gipsy fiddler was an integral part of everyday life; he could not recall a time when music was not present in his consciousness. His father, who gave him his first lessons, was the leader in a café orchestra and all the rest of his family played a stringed instrument; his uncle, who stood six feet four inches, was appropriately put to the double bass.

Szigeti's mother had died soon after his birth, so his childhood was divided between Budapest and the home of his grandparents in a little village in the Carpathians called Maramaros-Sziget — hence the name Szigeti. His real name was Joska Singer.

Joska was taken at an early age to study at a private preparatory conservatoire in Budapest. His tutor, a rank and file member of the opera orchestra, was kindly but inadequate as a teacher. Nonetheless, when later taken to play for Hubay at the Music Academy, Joska was taken straightaway into his master-class.

Szigeti always remained grateful for his studies with Hubay, but nevertheless was aware that there were certain aspects of the Hungarian school that attracted criticism. In the chapter concerning Hubay himself it was mentioned that the opportunities for hearing music outside the traditional repertoire were limited at the Budapest Conservatoire. Hubay, epitome of the establishment, did not care for the music of either Bartók or Kodály and was surprised when his young pupil showed enthusiasm for it. Although Hubay was an excellent teacher and a fine musician, as a pupil of Joachim he was in many ways still under the spell of his master's high ideals. At the same time he was pulled in quite another direction by the insatiable demands of parents to turn their children into prodigies. Szigeti's formative years must have been influenced by this situation, especially when the violin playing world was being inundated with a host of brilliant players like Elman and Zimbalist from the Russian school of Auer with an entirely new concept of sensuous sound and emotional projection. As if this were not enough, the young Szigeti had also to compete with Kreisler.

After Szigeti's début in Budapest, playing the Viotti A minor concerto, there are none of the instant success stories associated with so many of his contemporaries. At this time, Budapest was one of the favourite places in Europe for discovering international talent. Szigeti remembers the 'cigar-chewing, fur-coat-sporting' impresarios hovering around their prodigies Vecsey and Kubelik. They were frequently photographed with their 'wards' as if to show that they had a share in the 'almost occult hair-raising accomplishments of those they promoted'.[2] It was the observance at close quarters of these agents that influenced Szigeti's future decision that it was better to avoid such offers of 'management'.

Szigeti's Berlin début took place in 1905 when he was thirteen. It was at the small Bechstein Saal and for economic reasons took place in the morning. Despite a programme which included Bach's Chaconne, Ernst's F sharp minor concerto and Paganini's 'Witches' Dance', the only response from the press was an honourable mention in the Berliner Tageblatt of 10 December, by way of a photograph captioned 'A musical Prodigy, Josef Szigeti'.

The thirteen-year-old soloist spent the next few months with a fourth-rate summer theatre company in a small resort in Hungary where he made solo appearances between acts of Hungarian folk operetta. All the music had to be orchestrated by the pianist conductor to suit the seven- or eight-piece ensemble. This experience did little to further Szigeti's musical education but it taught him a great deal about the facts of life.

An even more unlikely engagement for the violinist who was to become known as 'the Scholarly Virtuoso' was a few months' employment at the Zirkus Albert Schumann Theatre in Frankfurt-am-Main. At first Szigeti's father refused, but when a large fee was proffered he agreed on condition that his son should take a *nom de plume*. As 'Szulagi' Szigeti made his début in the music halls, appearing with acrobats, a trained dog act and Abbie Mitchell, an American negro singer, with her group of 'shuffle-dancing, spiritual singing, banjo-playing young negroes' called the 'Tennessee Students'.[3] In later years, when Abbie Mitchell was asked what she remembered of the young boy who played the Mendelssohn concerto so beautifully in between the circus acts, she said he was intensely serious and isolated, but when he played his face lit up and a complete metamorphosis took place. His father, always watching from the wings, hovered over him 'like a mothering hen'.[4]

In the winter of 1906, Szigeti made his London début at the Bechstein (now the Wigmore) Hall. Owing to a rather unorthodox dual management consisting of a former music critic and a backer of stage plays, he appeared alternating with a pianist for the salon pieces and a small orchestra for the Ernst and Mendelssohn concertos. Szigeti remembers his embarrassment at being ordered to wear an alpaca sailor suit with short trousers, which necessitated having his legs shaved.

However, the experience was successful enough to bring in engagements to play throughout the country, especially the seaside resorts. These concerts were sponsored by the National Sunday League in an effort to brighten the gloom of the Victorian Sabbath. Ostensibly they were confined to religious music only, but naturally secular items were slipped into the programmes whenever possible. Szigeti recalls in his memoirs that the Salvation Army and other religious organizations were on the rampage, trying to block all Sunday performances. On one occasion he remembers the Army setting up a brass band at full blast outside the hall in protest whilst he attempted to convey the sensuous charm of the Wieniawski concerto within.

When Szigeti was fourteen, Hubay took him to play for Joachim in Berlin. The gout-crippled master was sufficiently impressed to suggest he should finish his repertoire studies with him. Szigeti and his father were invited to attend one of Joachim's classes at the Hochschule, where the old man sat on a small platform in the middle of the room. Although he listened to his students and criticized verbally, Joachim had no violin in his hand. Young as he was, Szigeti felt that this distance symbolized the absence of rapport between the two. Szigeti declined Joachim's offer, not only because of his negative impressions but also because he felt a loyalty to Hubay, with whom he had promised to study at his summer school in Ostende.

For the next six years Szigeti made his home in England, having been adopted by a musical family who lived in Surrey. Besides fulfilling engagements all over the country, he gave in 1908 the first performance of Hamilton Harty's violin concerto, which the composer dedicated to 'Joska Szigeti, in Friendship'.

It was also during this time that Szigeti toured with the legendary Melba and the twenty-five-year-old John McCormack. With either Busoni or Backhaus as 'assisting' pianist, and Philip Gaubert, the French virtuoso flautist, to provide obbligatos to some of the *prima donna*'s *coloratura* arias, they formed an interesting and diverse company.

In 1913 Szigeti had his first serious setback when it was discovered he was suffering from tuberculosis. He spent the next three years in Davos undergoing treatment, after which the cure was fortunately complete, enabling him to resume his solo career in 1917. That same year he succeeded Henri Marteau as professor of violin at the Conservatoire in Geneva, a post he held for seven years. During this time he appeared in all the principal cities of Europe under leading conductors, and was a great favourite with Nikisch for his concerts in Berlin.

A chance meeting with Leopold Stokowski in Geneva in 1925 brought Szigeti his first invitation to play in the USA. Stokowski was then conductor of the Philadelphia Symphony Orchestra and he engaged the young violinist to play the Beethoven concerto in December of that year. Szigeti recalled the first rehearsal as he stood waiting for the entry of the solo violin, getting weaker and weaker at the knees 'as the silken sheen of that orchestral introduction enveloped me'.[5] The performance was praised for his musicianly interpretation, but it did not attract the hysterical acclaim other artists received. And when Szigeti gave his first recital in New York on 19 December the popular journalists did no better. However, Olin Downes, music critic of the *New York Times*, wrote:

Mr Szigeti appears to be most himself, and to show most effectively the different phases of his artistic personality when he can get close to his audience and discourse the music of different composers. He played last night Tartini, Bach, Mozart, Bloch, Prokofiev, Veracini, Dvořák, Kreisler and Paganini.

There was lightning change from the radiant Mozart to the savage rhapsodic orientalism of Ernest Bloch. His two pieces 'Vidui' and 'Nigun' are masterly in their brevity and intensification of mood . . . Hebraic in the emotional force and the jagged contour of the melodies. They were given their true character, their utmost significance by Mr Szigeti . . .

Apart from Carnegie Hall recitals, where the programmes favoured the 'classics', the musical hotch-potch presented in other places caused Szigeti much concern. Programmes composed entirely of salon pieces were lapped up by the public. Once, during a heated argument on the subject with an executive of one of the country's leading concert circuits, the promoter retorted: 'Well let me tell you, Mr Dzigedy — and *I* know what I'm talking about — your Krewtser sonata bores the pants off my audiences!'[6]

Another zealous impresario was known to crouch camouflaged by the potted palms on the platform and train opera glasses on the audience to note their reaction. The measure of their approval was not rapt silence but the variety of nods and nudges conveyed to their companions.

Despite the demands of such commercial-orientated promoters, Szigeti built up his reputation painstakingly as a scholarly interpreter of the great composers, so that by the early 1930s he had achieved world fame. His concert tours took him twice round the world and it is almost impossible to name a country in which he did not play. He made many visits to the Soviet Union and regarded the audiences in that country as some of the most cultured in the world. He tells in his reminiscences of the strange way in which an unknown performer can fill a hall which may have been half empty when he started. When an artist shows himself to be out of the ordinary, the enthusiasts will slip out one by one and telephone their friends. The news is passed on and gradually the newcomers arrive. When the concert is over, the hitherto unknown player finds he has a packed house, all loudly applauding his performance. Conversely, a bad performance can achieve the opposite effect.

It was Szigeti's polish and style that appealed to the discriminating music lover. Alexander Ruppa, *The Strad*'s critic in Egypt, writing about a concert at the Alhambra Theatre in Alexandria on 21 March 1935, said: 'Szigeti has the technical equipment of Heifetz plus musicality.' Ruppa describes his tone as 'satisfyingly full, woody, elastic, and extraordinarily equal on all four strings'. He praises Szigeti's varied choice of programme and above all his Mozart: ' . . . his crowning feat was decidedly the exquisite D major Mozart Concerto which became a scintillating jewel in his hands. All the refined grace and musicality . . . were delicately brought out by Szigeti with amazing skill . . . ' It is interesting that this entire recital was accompanied on the piano — and by no less a personage than the Prince Nikita de Magaloff 'with the utmost competence and restraint', and all without a score.

Carl Flesch admired Szigeti both as man and musician, although he criticized what he called his 'archaic' bowing technique. Certainly Szigeti held his arm closer to the body than any other violinist — a position condemned by others besides Flesch. Nonetheless, the result was a wonderful elasticity of bowing. One critic declared that 'he had the most elegant right arm of living violinists'.[7]

Flesch was probably nearer the truth when he said that Szigeti's real significance was his feeling for contemporary music and progressive programme building, rather than in purely violinistic fields. In the latter respect he compares him to Joachim in the nineteenth century. And like his eminent predecessor, in this art Szigeti had few rivals. He would spend much time organizing his pieces, not only in chronological order but with special consideration for their 'mood and density'.[8] He believed that the order in which pieces are played can be just as important as the way an artist displays paintings on a wall.

Szigeti's repertoire was enormous. When Ernest Bloch wrote his violin concerto, first performed by Szigeti under Beecham in 1939, he dedicated the work to Szigeti because he felt that in his hands it would receive sympathetic treatment. Much earlier in his career, Szigeti had been closely associated with Busoni and given the first performance of his concerto in Berlin in 1912 with the composer conducting.

Prokofiev always regarded Szigeti as one of his finest interpreters and dedicated his first violin concerto to him. Bartók, with whom Szigeti enjoyed a close friendship, also spoke highly of his readings; in 1939, Szigeti, Benny Goodman and Endre Petri gave the first performance in New York of his 'Rhapsody' for clarinet, violin and piano, which Bartók dedicated to Szigeti and Goodman. The following year it was performed in its final three-movement version, re-named 'Contrasts' with Bartók at the piano.

Szigeti came late on the recording scene, and techniques had vastly improved by the time he was making regular recordings. The number he made from the end of the First World War (there were recordings of his as early as 1908) is considerable and range from Bach, Brahms and Mozart to Bartók (many with the composer at the piano), Berg and Ives. His recording of the ten Beethoven sonatas (complete) with Claudio Arrau is particularly memorable. Flesch used to say that Szigeti was better '"canned" than live'.[9] The English violist Frederick Riddle was a member of the orchestra when Flesch and Szigeti made their famous recording in 1937 of the Bach double concerto conducted by Walter Goehr. Before the rehearsal the two artists were feverishly practising virtuoso exercises, each trying to outdo the other. When the actual recording took place 'it was more like a competition than a concerto'.[10] Flesch was difficult as always, and it would seem that Szigeti also for once abandoned his cool approach, with the result that in the Vivace the homogeneous spirit of the music was lost. This comes over clearly in the recording; there is a strange 'distance' between the two soloists. But in the slow movement Bach becomes the mediator, and all sense of rivalry is dissolved.

Apart from such isolated incidents, Szigeti was popular with his fellow musicians and greatly respected for his interests outside music. He was a voracious reader and a witty and lively conversationalist who could tackle any subject ranging from science, art and literature to sport — cricket being one of his passions. He held the view that sport allied to a good background of general culture was indispensable to any musician, and he frequently deplored the one-track mind of so many of his colleagues.

On Szigeti's eightieth birthday, the American critic Henry Roth wrote a general appreciation in *The Strad*:

'Szigeti offered new vistas of imagination, breadth of vision, grandeur of spirit, sincerity of purpose, ineffable sensitivity and the exhilaration which accompanies daring new musical explorations. And he played with an intense visceral power which somehow always radiated his own humanism.[11]

Sixty-six years earlier, in 1906, the fourteen-year-old Szigeti had received an autograph from one of the great figures of the day which read:

My wish is:
May your art satisfy you — others will then
rejoice in it,
but the former is the more important.

Ferruccio Busoni[12]

It was advice that Szigeti heeded throughout his life.

24

'King of Violinists'

Jascha Heifetz

When Heifetz made his London début in 1920, George Bernard Shaw was sitting in the audience. In his own days of music criticism, Shaw had been an astute judge of musical sheep and goats, and many of his prophecies came to pass. He was very touched by the performance of the nineteen-year-old and wrote to him making a forecast which has an uncanny veracity about it:

> My dear Heifetz,
> Your recital has filled me and my wife with anxiety. If you provoke a jealous God by playing with such superhuman perfection, you will die young. I earnestly advise you to play something badly every night before going to bed, instead of saying your prayers. No mortal should presume to play so faultlessly.
>
> G. Bernard Shaw[1]

In an article in *Time* magazine of 31 October 1969, Roger Kahn takes up this idea in a moving and perceptive article that suggests that Shaw was right in that Heifetz 'presumed' and has 'paid for his genius with his humanity'. The significance of Heifetz's influence upon violin playing throughout the world is tremendous. Three generations of players have murmured his name with reverence and he remains their model, still unsurpassed. The American writer-violinist Henry Roth summed up the situation perfectly: 'Had Heifetz never lived, violin playing might never have attained the pinnacle of perfection on the instrumental level that it enjoys today — a fact freely admitted by his colleagues everywhere!'² But the most famous violinist in the world today never plays in public, and lives alone in a large luxurious house in Beverly Hills, California, separated from the outside world by four acres of ground and an electrified gate.

Jascha Heifetz was born in Wilna, Lithuania, in 1901, son of the leader of the Wilna Symphony Orchestra. From infancy Jascha responded to music and at the age of three was given a quarter-size fiddle, which he mastered within a week. He received his first lessons from his father but soon surpassed his knowledge and entered the Imperial School of Music at Wilna. He was not quite five when he made his first appearance in public, in the crowded auditorium of the Music School. A year later he played the Mendelssohn concerto to an audience of over a thousand.

Heifetz graduated from the Music School at the age of seven and was taken to St Petersburg to play for Auer. Heifetz was not accepted immediately into his master-class, as is generally believed. He had to wait until he was nine before Auer took him on as his personal student, but he was still the youngest-ever to have been admitted to the St Petersburg Conservatoire.

According to Heifetz, 'Auer was a wonderful and incomparable teacher. I do not believe that there is any teacher in the world who could possibly approach him. Don't ask me how he did it, for I would not know how to tell you, for he is completely different with each student.'³ Heifetz studied with Auer for about six years, both privately and in his class. But he never played exercises or technical works of any kind, and apart from concertos and sonatas, the professor allowed him freedom of choice as to repertoire.

Although Auer's pupils were supposed to be sufficiently advanced in technique for Auer to concentrate on interpretation: 'Yet there were all sorts of technical finesses which he always had up his sleeve; any number of fine subtle points in playing, as well as in interpretation, which he would disclose to his students as it became necessary.'⁴ Auer's maxim appeared to be that the more interest and ability a student showed, the more he gave of himself. A glimpse of the inside workings of the Auer school is furnished by the American violinist Albert Spalding, who attended an Auer class in 1913 when on a concert tour of Russia. He says that 'the other "star" pupils were eclipsed by this miniature wizard in his early teens', and describes Heifetz's rendering of the difficult Ernst concerto: 'The first flush of fingered octaves was attacked with a kind of nonchalant aplomb. The tone was firm, flowing and edgeless, the intonation of fleckless purity. A kind of inner grace made itself felt in the shaping of the phrase.' Auer strode nervously up and down, casting a periodic glance in Spalding's direction to note his reactions. 'His dark, restless eyes danced with delight as the wonder boy threaded his effortless way through the tortuous technical problems ... he would turn away with a helpless shrug of the shoulders as if to say, "Was there ever anything like it?" '[5]

Even whilst at the Conservatoire, young Jascha was giving public recitals in St Petersburg and many other Russian cities. He once played at an open air concert at Odessa where 25,000 people gave him a standing ovation. Reports began to circulate throughout Europe long before he set foot outside his native country. He was only eleven when he made his Berlin début under Nikisch, playing the Tchaikovsky concerto. Nikisch was one of the few conductors who had originally trained as a violinist and he admitted he had never heard anything to equal the playing of this child. Heifetz subsequently performed under Nikisch in Vienna and Leipzig, where he took the audiences by storm. When he played Bruch's G minor concerto at the Gewandhaus in Leipzig in 1913, he was told that Joachim was the only other violinist as young as himself to have appeared as soloist with the orchestra. It was at this particular concert that Kreisler first heard him and made the legendary remark to Zimbalist: 'You and I might as well take our fiddles and break them across our knees.'[6]

The jest was not far off the truth. Although Kreisler never suffered personally, there were many established violinists who were overshadowed by this rising star. We know that Kubelik was one of the casualties whose career was damaged by the young Heifetz. According to Flesch, violinists tended at the turn of the century to copy Kubelik's way of playing rapid passages; clearly, but not too fast. After Heifetz appeared on the scene, 'young fiddlers are possessed by the devil of speed and are trying to establish records'.[7]

The outbreak of the 1914–18 war brought international concert-giving to a halt, and when strong rumours of the impending revolution in Russia presented an additional hazard, Heifetz's father decided to risk a war-time crossing of the Atlantic for his son to make his American début. This took place at the Carnegie Hall in New York on 27 October 1917. Heifetz was sixteen years

Joseph Szigeti, who
revolutionized
programme planning
in the twentieth
century

Jascha Heifetz, the
greatest single
influence since
Paganini

old, slim, blue-eyed with fair curly hair. He astonished his audience, which included all the top string players in the city, not only by his brilliant playing but by his cool platform manner. His programme included the Wieniawski D minor concerto, Paganini's twenty-fourth caprice and Tartini's variations on a theme by Corelli. The *New York Times* critic said that there was

> never a more unassuming player ... Mr Heifetz produces tone of remarkable beauty and purity; a tone of power, smoothness and roundness ... His bowing is of rare elasticity and vigour, excellent in many details as is his left-hand execution, which is accurate in all sorts of difficulties.

There then followed the understatement of the century:

> In his technical equipment, Mr Heifetz is unusual.[8]

The musicians who had witnessed this miracle were all members of 'The Bohemians', the New York Musicians' Club whose membership consists of some of the most celebrated artistic personalities in the world. They decided unanimously to give a dinner in Heifetz's honour on Saturday, 29 December 1917 at the Biltmore Hotel. Everybody who was anybody was there, including Kreisler, Zimbalist, Franz Kneisel (of the Kneisel Quartet) and a host of others. It was the Bohemians' recognition that placed Heifetz firmly on this throne as 'King of Violinists', although with such a talent he would probably have risen to the top regardless. He has remained a member of this exclusive club ever since, and reciprocated by playing at a concert at the Bohemians in honour of Fritz Kreisler's birthday in 1940. Curiously enough, Heifetz and Kreisler share the same birthday, 2 February.

As Heifetz's fame spread, his earnings soared. In the USA in December 1919 he received a fee of $2,250 for each concert, the highest ever paid at that time to a classical artist. In November of that year, Kreisler collected only $2,000, and he was already considered to be highly paid.

Heifetz's London début took place on 5 May 1920 at the Queen's Hall. Through the phenomenal success of his gramophone records (70,000 of which had already been sold in Britain before he set a foot on British soil), the hall sold out well before the day of the concert. The *Musical Times* described him as 'the greatest sensation of the musical world so far'.[9] Heifetz was offered engagement upon engagement, playing always to packed houses. He repeated this success all over the world and his name became known on every continent.

Eventually, Heifetz was so busy that he fulfilled some two hundred engagements a year. For the most part he received rave notices for every concert. They praised his impeccable playing, his superb left hand, his wonderful bowing arm, his phrasing, his musicianship. There were no words which could rightly proclaim his genius. After a recital at the Queen's Hall in London in 1930, a critic wrote of Heifetz winding up his programme with the 'Moto Perpetuo' of Paganini at an impossible speed. Turning to his neighbour, he exclaimed ' "Good Heavens, he'll never keep up that speed!" He did; and each note shone like a glittering diamond. What execution. The audience literally rose to its feet and shouted its approval.'[10]

But Heifetz has also been accused of gimmickry — such as in the Bach double concerto, playing both parts himself. But is it gimmickry that disturbs his critics? Is it perhaps their inability to believe that one virtuoso can play two parts with such artistry and expression? Do they not echo Shaw's concern? The slow movement of this recording is not only ravishing in tone but profound in its depth of feeling.

Nonetheless, there have also been critics who persistently accused Heifetz of coldness. 'How frigid is this dazzling playing',[11] wrote Henri Prunières after a recital at the Paris Opéra. Another asked: 'His command of the mechanics of the fiddle is still what it was, well-nigh impeccable. But is he broadening and developing in other respects?' That particular critic found that during the course of the years Heifetz was 'beginning to appeal to the emotional as well as to the intellectual'.[12]

But perhaps a remark made by an old lady overheard as she left a concert in 1922 holds the most significance: 'That young man only needs some great sorrow, some terrible disappointment to make him really wonderful, because he will then be more human. Today he suggests a disembodied spirit.'[13]

Flesch considers that Heifetz 'represents a culmination in the contemporary development of our art'. He likens his finger and bow functions to a machine that runs at maximum capacity as soon as the button is pressed. 'His tone has a noble substance and is of a magical beauty, and there is not the smallest flaw in his technical equipment.' However, Flesch cannot allow this perfection to go unsullied and maintains that Heifetz takes the Russian grip of the bow to 'its utter extremes, exaggerating it, in fact, in a way that would render it useless for ordinary mortals'. He also criticizes his bad dynamic habit which 'he shares with most Auer pupils'[14] of a decrescendo on the down-bow and forte on the ascending passage (up-bow).

Flesch wrote his memoirs in 1940, when Heifetz was approaching forty and at the height of his career, but the enigma was already present. Flesch puts forth the argument that Heifetz, like Mozart, was born with gifts from heaven. He never had to struggle to perfect his technique — it just happened. He was therefore led towards neglecting his personality and fell into the habit of playing with his hands and allowing his mind to rest. Flesch cites as the exception the superb Heifetz recording of the Sibelius concerto, whose transcendental qualities bear witness to a different mood. Flesch could be right when he says that the infallibility of Heifetz's technical approach is his worst enemy. 'He is a living example of the relativity of a virtue which, when it overshadows something more essential, may come to be felt as a defect.'[15]

Heifetz is often described as being a man with a mask. His flat, tartar features wear a supercilious expression when he is displeased. But his friends of earlier years tell stories of his great sense of humour and the wicked mimicry he exhibited at parties. In his day a great raconteur, he would also tell jokes on himself with gusto. There was the time when he took a rather good-looking negro valet with him on a European tour. They were passing through Switzerland early in the morning, and Heifetz was still asleep when the porter knocked and asked 'At what hour does His Highness wish breakfast?'[16] Heifetz thought that he had been mistaken for a nobleman travelling incognito, but it transpired that the entire train staff were under the impression that his valet was a Maharajah and Heifetz a member of his entourage.

Heifetz always had a wide range of interests. As a young man he was 'camera crazy' and took pictures of everything. He used to play an excellent game of tennis and is known for his skill at ping-pong. He is an avid collector of rare books and will occasionally take a special guest on a conducted tour of his massive library. Here, Heifetz's voice softens and his expression relaxes as he fondles his first edition Dickens and his Kelmscott Chaucer. He apologizes for having only a fourth folio Shakespeare.[17]

Heifetz made the last of his rare public appearances on 27

October 1972 in Los Angeles. He occasionally plays chamber music with a select group of friends. His self-imposed, hermit-like existence is open to much debate. Some say that Heifetz has had everything in life — wealth, success and the adulation of millions, and that he is now bored and cannot take the trouble to perform in public. Yet he still practises diligently for concerts that do not take place.

Another side to Heifetz — as a teacher — comes from one of his 'star' pupils, Eugene Fodor, who was awarded a scholarship to study with him for a year in 1968. In 1974, Fodor was the first American since Van Cliburn to win one of the top prizes in the Tchaikovsky Competition in Moscow. He is one of an increasing number of virtuosos who play modern violins made by Sergio Peresson, an Italian-American living in New Jersey.

At Fodor's audition, Heifetz was charming. 'It was a really enjoyable meeting. He was kind and helpful in every way. After he had heard me he put his palm against mine and told me that I had the perfect hand for playing the violin. He even said that I was luckier than he because my fourth finger is almost as long as my third. It was a thrilling experience.'[18] It has been suggested that Heifetz has an unusual hand formation: his index finger is abnormally long and his little finger 'falls exactly in the right place so that he never plays octaves or tenths out of tune'.[19]

In a room at the University of Southern California, the class of four students met twice weekly for seven hours, which meant that each individual had two to three hours with Heifetz each week. Fodor confesses he never worked harder. 'Working with a man like that for a year was like having a ten-year course — one learned so much', says Fodor. He gave as an instance Heifetz's method of teaching staccatos. Heifetz would make him play staccatos for fifteen minutes, during which time Heifetz would slowly encircle him watching his technique for down-bow staccato. In the Wieniawski concerto Heifetz insisted that Fodor should play the same cadenza from which he had learned staccato from Auer. Fodor is now famous for his up-bow and down-bow staccato. Of his teacher Fodor concludes; 'He isn't a pedagogue in the accepted sense of the word, but he shares his philosophy on his approach to the concert stage, and to performing in a way that is unique. It is impossible to describe because it's something that can't be taught. It has to be felt.'[20]

There were also less elusive influences, such as an insistence

upon seven hours practice each day and restrictions on his pupils'
outside activities. Heifetz not only stopped Fodor from riding
around the Southern California hills on a Triumph 650 motor-
cycle; he made him sell it!

Overall, Fodor is convinced that the most important single
thing that he learned from Heifetz was how to store nervous
energy and release it whilst playing. This is something that Heifetz
has certainly maintained and practised all his life. Public performing requires a stupendous effort both psychologically and physic-
ally, and an artist must have reserves to deal with emergencies.
The twentieth-century performer must also face the extra hazards
of progress: sudden changes of climate, bad acoustics and jet-lag.
Fodor says: 'All this has to be taken into consideration. Under
adverse conditions one has to prepare more than a hundred per
cent. Heifetz taught me to do this.'

Fodor is of the opinion that the public is misled by the stark,
bland, sphinx-like expression that Heifetz maintained throughout
his performances.

> To me it is refreshing. All the emotions are in the music. He doesn't
> allow himself the luxury of grimacing or moving around — maybe to
> distract from something that is not quite perfect going on in the
> hands. He taught me always to have my head facing my hands when I
> perform. That way it is very difficult to move about. The mechanism
> of a musician who is highly trained is beautiful to watch: the pure
> execution is much more gratifying than superfluous emotion.[21]

Heifetz's formidable but effortless execution, his tone, his
accuracy of intonation and his ability to bring an infinite variety of
nuance into his bowing were unique. On the interpretative side,
he had a sensuality of expression that never spilled over into
sentimentality. Here again, he was unique.

As a man Heifetz remains an enigma — by choice. As a violinist
his influence will reverberate for centuries to come.

25

Child of the Revolution

Nathan Milstein

When Szigeti was on a concert tour of Russia in 1924, Auer's daughter, Nadine, invited him to her house to hear a young up-and-coming violinist, 'a fabulously gifted young man who seemed diffident about his impending trip across the borders to Berlin'.[1] Szigeti reassured him that Europe was waiting for such artists with enthusiasm. His forecast was perceptive. The budding virtuoso was Nathan Milstein.

Born in Odessa in 1904 into a family who loved music but had no previous history of professional musicians, Nathan was the middle child in a family of five boys and two girls. He confesses that he was by far the most aggressive. 'I think my mother wanted me to play the violin because she hoped it might stop me from doing grievous bodily harm to my brothers and my friends.'[2] His first lessons from a local teacher ended abruptly when wrong notes were met by physical punishment. At the age of seven Nathan went to the Music School in Odessa under Stolyarsky, whose methods were more conventional, and was finally accepted into Auer's class at St Petersburg when he was twelve.

Milstein has remained grateful to Auer because he allowed his pupils to develop within their own personalities. Certainly out of the dozen or so internationally famous violinists that Auer produced, all are completely different, not only as human beings but as violinists. Milstein says: 'I knew others who were better musicians than Auer, who knew much more. But this is not always a good thing. They dictate every point of technique and impose their own style upon their pupils, with the result that they've not produced a single soloist at international level.' And 'at a certain stage it is not enough just to practise. You must develop your technique, of course, but violin playing is what you *do* with your technique — if you have a teacher who knows too much you will never find your own way. When you are concertizing on your own, you must know yourself where you are going.'[3]

When the Revolution broke out in Russia, and Auer fled the country, the thirteen-year-old Milstein had the opportunity to put these ideas into practice. Despite the chaotic social and political upheaval, he was engaged for concerts arranged by the Ministry of Education in and around Odessa. The hybrid population of this city consisted of Greeks, Turks, Italians, Jews and Russians, all of whom loved music; consequently the city had several excellent musical institutions, two symphony orchestras, many repertory theatres and a good opera.

In 1922 Milstein met the young pianist Vladimir Horowitz, fresh from the Conservatoire at Kiev. As solo artists they gave a series of highly successful concert tours in Russia, eventually appearing in Moscow. The respected and cultured Lunacharsky was at this time Commissar of Fine Arts and Education. Following one of the young players' concerts he wrote a review in a Moscow newspaper and headed it 'Children of the Soviet Revolution'. It provided excellent publicity and brought the two many further engagements. 'We made a great deal of money but there was nothing to spend it on so we gave it to the beggars who sat on every corner. They soon got to know us and waited for their money.'[4]

It was probably on account of Lunacharsky's review that the young musicians were allowed to leave Russia to undertake a European tour. Milstein recalls the occasion as a landmark in his life. 'It was on Christmas Eve, 1925, that I left. It was a wonderful feeling. I didn't know then that I would never go back: there was something in the back of my mind. But I didn't run away. I left officially with a Soviet passport. It was just that I never returned.' Their first call was at the Russian Embassy in Paris. When they asked when they would return to Moscow, the Cultural Attaché told them; 'Stay as long as you like. Look around and learn, and let the capitalists see what gifted young performers we have in our country.'[5]

The two took his suggestion to the letter. Although their concerts in Paris and elsewhere were well received, it was in Spain that they achieved their first triumph. After a highly successful trial concert in Madrid, a further fifteen engagements were immediately booked for them, followed by a tour of South America, where they gave some fifty-six concerts performing every two days. Milstein reflected: 'It was a very good life. In the late afternoon we would play bridge and sometimes spend a whole day in the mountains, returning to the hotel half an hour before the concert. We never worried about performances. Today I can't even eat *lunch* if I have to play in the evening.'[6]

Within two years Milstein had earned himself an international reputation which was further enhanced when he made his American début. He had had the good fortune to meet Stokowski, who seems to have been the fairy godfather of so many young violinists; it was he who gave Milstein his first opportunity to play with a great American orchestra. Milstein's début in Philadelphia took place on 28 October 1929, when he played the Glazunov Concerto in A minor. The *Evening Bulletin* critic wrote that the soloist was 'a young, dark, vibrant Russian capable of magical things upon a violin', and that 'above and beyond his prodigious technical equipment is a brilliant mind moulding the music into a coherent and symmetrical whole'. For the next ten years Milstein toured the USA and Canada, repeating his successes up and down the country, and in 1943 he took US citizenship.

When Milstein appeared for the first time in January 1935 in Egypt, Ruppa, *The Strad*'s critic in Alexandria, called him 'a star of the first magnitude' and praised his wonderful bowing technique, especially his 'scintillating *spiccato* at all speeds; which he calls *une cascade de perles*'. As for his left hand, 'its dexterity and precision are amazing, even in the most rapid and exacting passages, the intonation remaining throughout of a crystalline purity'. But Ruppa warns: 'As a violinist you will be dazzled. As a musician you will be disappointed.' He considered that Milstein's temperamental fervour lacked conviction and that he 'fails to emotionally grip his audience'. Ruppa also considered that Milstein was far better suited to the music of Ernst, Wieniawski and Paganini than to that of Corelli, Bach and Beethoven.

Milstein made his first appearance before a British audience at the Queen's Hall on 14 November 1932, playing the Brahms and Tchaikovsky concertos conducted by Sargent. Next morning *The Times* correspondent considered that he had 'missed none of the more obvious performer's points in the Brahms concerto ... His clear cantilena, his organ-like double-stopping, his impeccable

Nathan Milstein, 'Child of the Revolution'

Alfredo Campoli, successful virtuoso in both light and classical fields

octaves in the finale . . . proclaimed him to be a violinist of a high order; but in the end we found we had listened more to Milstein than to Brahms, and while he was playing his cadenza we wondered whether he had forgotten all about Brahms'.

Four years later, after a recital at the Wigmore Hall in London on 22 October 1936, the *Musical Times* critic wrote that: 'He gave Vivaldi's sonata in A major with a fire and precision that fairly caught one's breath, just because it breathed life into music that until now had seemed to be dry bones. This was the Vivaldi whom Bach admired: not the pedagogue in whose likeness most people present the old Venetian.' But this critic seemed less happy with his Beethoven (Sonata in G major for violin and piano, Op. 30), not because his execution left anything to be desired, but because 'some of Beethoven's thoughts . . . are still to Milstein a closed book.' This is an interesting observation of the man who was to become accepted the world over as one of the great interpreters of Beethoven's violin concerto.

Some forty-two years later Milstein is still playing superbly. If there ever was any substance in these criticisms of his artistic ability, he long ago transcended them. Today he has a reputation for performances that are the very antithesis of such an approach, although his playing has always been spirited and vigorous. His recording of the Goldmark concerto is one of the many living examples of his integrity in playing that is stylish yet scrupulous in attention to detail. Immaculate phrasing, perfect intonation: with Milstein there are no gimmicks, no tricks, and yet the music becomes exceptional on account of his innate musicianship and honest playing. It is the music which predominates, not the personality of Milstein.

He never plays a work in quite the same way twice. A good example is his recent recording of the Brahms concerto under Jochum with the Vienna Philharmonic Orchestra. In his personal opinion this is a more romantic interpretation than his previous recordings. He maintains that one develops in the direction that the music requires and this is the way he now feels about the Brahms.

He also feels that his Bach has changed. 'I played the Bach sonatas twenty years ago . . . but the approach was less improvisational, more playing. Bach is always improvisational.' Milstein holds that it is of vital importance to try to build some sort of contact with the composer before attempting to stand up and play the work. Here, then, is the heart of Milstein who passes on to his pupils the advice that Auer gave to him: 'Don't practise with your fingers — practise with your head!'[7]

As a player Milstein remains vigorous and exciting, and has several new recordings in mind — Brahms, Beethoven, César Franck. He recently published a new cadenza for the Beethoven concerto. Dividing his time between his homes in Paris and London, he holds master-classes in Switzerland. He is unbelievably sprightly in his seventies.

Milstein has firm views on the past and its relation to our musical present. In his opinion London is not, as so often quoted, 'the most active music centre in the world', but 'like New York it is an enormous musical supermarket.' He feels that too many people participate so that music and art are no longer 'special', and suffer in consequence. 'Not everyone who goes to concerts is so devoted to the music. It is often more of a social occasion. In the eighteenth and nineteenth centuries they listened to music because they loved and understood it.' He quotes Beethoven as an example:

> He went to people's houses to play quartets — which is how the music came to be written. When you had an élite, you had an example for the people who looked up to those who provided the works of art. All the artistic treasures we admire today were brought about by these people; the popes and the Medicis. If it were not for them we would have no idea of what happened in the past. In order to recapture this love of music and the need for great artists, we must bring back the kings and princes. We must have an élite. Today we have no group whom we can respect spiritually, and we are losing ground all the time.[8]

26

The *Bel Canto* Virtuoso

Alfredo Campoli

Alfredo Campoli is probably unique among British virtuoso-violinists in that he has successfully walked the tightrope between the light and classical fields of music and achieved a consummate balance. Today he is still before the public and his playing has lost none of its elegance or style. In an age when an almost uniform virtuosity abounds, the sweet purity of his cantilena is immediately identifiable.

Alfredo Campoli was born in Rome in 1906, the son of a professor of violin at the Accademia di Santa Cecilia and leader of the orchestra at the Teatro Massima. His mother, Elvira Celi, was a well-known dramatic soprano who toured with Caruso and Antonio Scotti and sang many times at La Scala. In 1911, when she was engaged for a season at Covent Garden, the Campoli family came to England. They never returned to live in Italy.

Alfredo had shown interest in the violin from the age of four, and received his first lessons from his father, who remained his sole instructor. He made such rapid progress that he was already giving public performances in his adopted country before he was ten. Campoli recalls being dressed in a sailor suit and playing to troops and wounded soldiers during the First World War.

By his twelfth birthday Alfredo had won several first prizes, two gold medals and a silver cup in music competitions. In fairness to the other candidates the authorities asked him to abstain from entering further competitions. However, he was allowed to enter the London Music Festival at the Central Hall, Westminster in 1919, and carried off the gold medal for his performance of the first movement of the Mendelssohn concerto.

When the sixteen-year-old Alfredo Campoli made his Wigmore Hall début on 18 May 1923, a footnote inserted in the programme read: 'Birth certificate can be verified in the vestibule.'[1] Even as a boy he was heavily-built, and looked older than his years. Certainly the programme, which included concertos by Bruch and Wieniawski and the Nardini sonata in D major, might have been chosen by a veteran. The *Morning Post* declared that he played 'not as a prodigy but as a mature artist'.[2] Others mentioned his brilliant execution and 'breadth of style'.[3] Perhaps the most significant comment was that 'his talents seem to be of an enduring kind'.[4]

All seemed set fair for a distinguished solo career when the effects of the mid-twenties slump began to pervade music and the other arts. In spite of the economic depression, however, the gramophone business was booming, and radio broadcasting was continually developing new techniques that increased its popularity. The cumulative effect of these competitive elements made concert-going a luxury. Halls everywhere had to close down, and even Kreisler and Heifetz were hard put to draw capacity audiences. Some musicians opted out of the profession altogether. There is no doubt that at this time the musical world suffered a loss which can never truly be assessed.

Campoli was fortunate in being engaged for a series of celebrity concerts touring with Melba and Clara Butt, and assisted his father with his teaching. Then in 1926 Edward Lewis asked Campoli to form a small orchestra to record a few popular classics for Decca. 'We recorded a piece called "Serenade" by Heykins and sold half a million copies in a few months.'[5] Within two years Campoli and his Salon Orchestra became known throughout Britain. He also had a trio, and worked for at least half a dozen ensembles for film studios and light entertainment in general. When the Dorchester Hotel opened in 1931, Campoli and his Salon Orchestra moved in to provide the musical entertainment. He proved himself an excellent conductor as well as a superb violinist. He says: 'I always tried to make the orchestra sing.'[6] But it was also the warmth of his personality that drew the crowds to hear him play.

Campoli's father was unimpressed by his son's success. He thought he had made the wrong decision. Nonetheless, Campoli has no regrets: 'I am not ashamed of having worked in light music. I think I am a better musician *because* of it.'[7]

Despite his phenomenal following in the lighter field, Campoli never relaxed his hold on his original ambitions. He continually practised the classic repertoire and appeared concurrently in recitals and as soloist with orchestra. In 1938 he played the Paganini Concerto No. 1 in his first Promenade Concert under Sir Henry Wood.

The Second World War brought additional hazards for Campoli, who narrowly missed being interned. Professor Campoli had never taken British naturalization: 'He had the idea that it was almost immoral to sign away your birthright.'[8] But unknown to his father, his son had applied for British citizenship, which was due to be legalized a few weeks after the Italians entered the war on the German side. Campoli had to surrender both his car and his radio — forbidden possessions of an 'enemy alien'. The problem was resolved when invitations came to tour the country giving concerts for the troops and in factories. Campoli was then able to own a car once more and his radio was returned.

After the war, Campoli returned full-time to the classical field and quickly achieved an international reputation. He made his American début in 1953 with the New York Philharmonic Orchestra under Georg Szell, playing the Lalo 'Symphonie Espagnole' at the beginning of a tour of the USA and Canada. Since then, Campoli has performed in almost every country in the world. He has made many tours of Canada, Australia and New Zealand and has twice visited Russia and Japan where he has also made some recordings. He gave the first performance in Moscow of the concerto that Sir Arthur Bliss dedicated to him, and was given a warm reception by one of the most discriminating audiences in the world. David Oistrakh attended several of his concerts and went backstage to offer his congratulations.

Campoli's repertoire is extensive but is limited where contemporary music is concerned. He says: 'I am very fond of the Walton and have played it many times. But I refuse to go further than this concerto. Atonal music is not for me. In my opinion it is not really music for the violin.'[9]

An unashamed lover of music of the baroque, Classical and Romantic periods, Campoli thinks he must have played the Mendelssohn concerto almost nine hundred times. He regards the violin as a singing instrument, and this influence stems from his childhood lessons with his father. He says: 'From the very beginning I was taught the *bel canto* singing style of playing. My father believed that the violin is the finest man-made instrument because it is nearest to the human voice.'[10] Professor Campoli would illustrate by playing recordings made by the leading singers of the day; the voices of Battistini, de Lucia, Volpi and Gigli rang in Alfredo's ear when he was making his own first attempts at 'singing' tone.

Campoli explained in an interview with the author how this has affected his own playing in a positive way: 'You must learn how to control your sliding so that each phrase has a natural sense of breathing — just like a singer.' As an example he took the octave leap: 'You have to imagine yourself singing. You wouldn't then make the jump in a jerky staccato manner. You must take the slur smoothly. When you come down again you make up your mind as to whether the up-bow or the down-bow is the correct one.' He further illustrated the point by saying that Toscanini 'could make a whole orchestra sing'. Campoli bemoans the fact that the British know so little about *bel canto*. 'English composers never write in this style. You have Vaughan Williams using the great effects of English choral music, but not quite *bel canto*. It is the Latin element in every Italian that comes naturally to him long before he has had a single lesson.'[11]

Campoli has strong views on the use of a shoulder-rest. He maintains emphatically that any form of pad or rest ruins the vibrations of the violin, an opinion he shares with Erica Morini, Milstein and Heifetz. On the platform, Campoli is an undemonstrative player. A critic once commented: 'Unlike other violinists Mr Campoli played the fast and furious finale [of the Tchaikovsky] in a standing position instead of on all fours.'[12] He holds the violin high and well to the left. He considers that in this position the player can move freely and rapidly into the high positions without muscular strain. Certainly Campoli gives the impression that he is at one with his instrument. His shimmering, singing tone and an elegant and relaxed bow arm are hall-marks of his playing. It is not difficult to understand why when asked whom he most admires, he replies 'Kreisler, Szigeti and Grumiaux'.[13]

Many of Campoli's old recordings have recently been reissued, including the Elgar, Saint-Saëns No. 3 and Beethoven concertos and the Brahms double concerto. New recordings too are still being made. In 1976 he recorded all the 'Spanish Dances' by Sarasate and was joined by his pupil, the young New Zealander, Belinda Bunt, in a dazzling performance of Sarasate's 'Navarra'.

At a recital at the Wigmore Hall in 1978, Campoli opened his programme with Tartini's 'Devil's Trill' sonata — with his own cadenza — and followed it with the Bach Chaconne for unaccompanied violin. He was then joined by Belinda Bunt for what was probably the first performance in Britain of the Theme and Variations on 'La Folia' for two violins, cello and continuo by Vivaldi, a colourful piece of writing with the Venetian at his virtuoso best. Then Campoli and his pupil gave the audience 'Navarra' as an encore. The concert took place only a few weeks short of Campoli's seventy-second birthday.

In a long and distinguished career, Campoli has shown that whether the music is light or serious, the singing tone so beloved of Viotti and Spohr and their followers is the quality most admired by the public. From the beginning of the history of the violin, it has been the beautiful sound that has remained in the memory.

27

The Entertainers

Albert Sandler; Tom Jenkins; Max Jaffa; Reginald Leopold; John Georgiadis

In considering 'great' violinists, it is important not to underrate the performers who have attracted millions of music lovers to the violin not by playing unaccompanied Bach but by the popular classics well played.

Much of the serious violin repertoire is fiendishly difficult, but so are most of the entertainers' show pieces. Sarasate's 'Zigeunerweisen' or Bazzini's 'Ronde des Lutins' are prime examples. These, and dozens more, all have to be memorized by the violinist, who must be ready to perform at a moment's notice. In the Palm Court Trio and similar ensembles, unusual requests are regular occupational hazards. If asked for Paganini's 'Moto Perpetuo' or a Liszt transcription, the player can scarcely protest that he must go home and work out the fingering.

Campoli went into entertainment purely for financial reasons. One of the great violinists who intentionally followed the lighter field was the London-born Albert Sandler (1906–48), a contemporary of Campoli's, who died tragically at the age of forty-two from a liver disease. Robert Lewin wrote of him:

> He loved what we call light music and hardly ever in his whole life attempted the serious classics. He was a natural for light popular music and with a violinistic equipment almost the equal of any virtuoso could handle a large repertory of pieces, from Sarasate to the operatic excerpts the public knew and liked. With his limpid tone and happy phrasing he went straight to the hearts of millions.[1]

Although Sandler's family loved music, no professional musicians had existed until Albert's generation, when there were suddenly three: Albert, his elder brother and sister. Albert was given his first lessons by his brother, punctuated by a sharp box on the ears for every mistake. His progress soon merited his being placed with the Viennese Hans Wessely, a pupil of Hellmesberger at the Vienna Academy and private pupil of Grün. But Sandler considered that his most important teacher was another of Grün's pupils, Kalman Ronay, a nephew of Auer, who later studied with Joachim at the Hochschule in Berlin.

On leaving school Sandler worked as a cinema violinist for five shillings a week, but was soon elevated to the post of leader. At sixteen he was engaged to lead an orchestra in one of the Lyon's Corner Houses. These were extensions of the Lyon's tea shops, to cater for shoppers and theatregoers, and were at strategic points in the West End of London: Oxford Street, Tottenham Court Road, Marble Arch, and the Strand; the largest was in Coventry Street, off Leicester Square. There were four floors, with a variety of restaurants to suit every taste, each one possessing its own orchestra. The most popular was that on the first floor, where the players wore evening dress and the patrons could listen for a whole enchanted evening to Albert Sandler and his band for the price of a cup of tea and a slice of Dundee cake.

From the Corner House, Sandler was promoted to the Grill Room at the Trocadero, Lyon's star restaurant. But his greatest opportunity came in 1925, when Arthur Beckwith, musical director of the Grand Hotel in Eastbourne, left to tour the USA with the London String Quartet, the leader having suddenly been taken ill. Beckwith was offered the leadership of the Cleveland State Orchestra and stayed in the USA. Sandler took over his job at Eastbourne just as the BBC were trying out a Sunday evening broadcast from the hotel. It was highly successful, and 'Grand Hotel' became one of the most famous traditions in British broadcasting, lasting nearly half a century.

A year later the BBC decided to send the programme out live. It turned out to be one of the most popular in the history of broadcasting and Sandler became a household name. In 1928 he took on an extra appointment, that of musical director at the Park Lane Hotel, where he led an ensemble of seven first-class musicians. Later he toured the music halls with his Albert Sandler Trio, and became 'Top of the Pops', 1930s style. The millions who knew Sandler from the radio flocked to see him in the flesh and were not disappointed. A critic wrote: 'Mr Sandler's playing is remarkable because of his marvellous technical dexterity and sensitive feeling ... sonority, smoothness and excellent style ... they [the trio] held a large audience enthralled.'[2]

Although Sandler was a powerfully-built man with large, fleshy hands, somewhat like Ysaÿe's, he was a very light player. He disliked having to tear at a fiddle to produce tone, and played on a beautiful Stradivari dated 1701.

Despite his acknowledged preference for light music, Sandler never forced his tone or overdid his *portamento* or *vibrato*. He phrased beautifully and disliked 'tricks', a view shared by Campoli, who also contends that, 'if you are good enough as a fiddler you play the virtuoso pieces "straight" and they have more effect.'[3] Sandler never used harmonics because he thought them unsuitable in large restaurants and cinemas. He contended that passages played in the higher positions carry better without loss of tone quality. Sandler did not play more loudly when he wanted to be heard; he simply played an octave higher on the E string. His superb playing could usually surmount any amount of extraneous sound.

Sandler had no illusions about his work and admitted that many of the pieces he played were trifling by necessity, but he claimed that whatever a piece lacked in intrinsic merit he played it with as much care and preparation as if it were a masterpiece. He would say 'there is beauty in the simplest thing well done'.[4] Tokens of gratitude reached him by every post and many of the letters were highly amusing. One lady sent him a gift of some tiny marzipan violins decorated with pink ribbons.

If he was free, Sandler never missed a concert by Heifetz or Kreisler. He was a master interpreter of the latter's pieces and appeared to have reserves of technical dexterity that he hardly needed to draw upon. The essence of Sandler was that he, like Kreisler, infused his love for his music into every piece, however simple. By some uncanny insight, what he played was always what the listener most wanted to hear.

The violinist who took over as leader of the orchestra at the Grand Hotel Eastbourne in 1937 (Tom Jones and Leslie Jefferies had followed Sandler), was the twenty-seven-year-old Tom Jenkins (1910–57), another whose name became known throughout the British Isles until he too died an untimely death at the age of forty-seven. Born in Leeds of Welsh stock, he learned the fiddle when he was eight. He won first prizes at countless music festivals and appeared in his first concert at the age of twelve. At fourteen, he was already building a reputation as a soloist and had made his first broadcast. Like Sandler, he worked for a short period as a cinema violinist, and found the sight reading experience invaluable. In 1927 he became leader of the Municipal Orchestra at Harrogate.

At twenty-one, Tom Jenkins was invited by Julius Harrison to join Hastings Municipal Orchestra. During this time he performed as soloist, playing both the Bruch and Brahms concertos with the orchestra. A critic wrote: 'The technique was uniformly sure, and, best of all, the soloist gave us the spirit as well as the letter of this wonderful music. Never was there a trace of a false sentiment, though he realized to the full the romantic beauty underlying the work.'[5]

A year later Jenkins also appeared as soloist with the London Symphony Orchestra under Sargent at the Queen's Hall, playing the Brahms concerto. In 1936 he studied for a year with Carl Flesch in London and valued the experience very highly. This period of learning caused no break in Jenkins's playing, as so often occurs when a great teacher takes over a mature performer for the first time. In 1950, Jenkins also took some lessons with Sascha Lasserson, for whom he had such admiration. It was during this period that *The Times* reported on 'a dazzling Ravel's "Tzigane"'.

The appointment at Eastbourne came the following year. Almost all broadcasts of 'Grand Hotel' from this time onwards contained two contrasting violin solos, many of great technical difficulty, such as pieces by Wieniawski and 'Hora Staccato', or very simple, like MacDowell's 'To a Wild Rose'. Professors at music colleges would tell their students to listen to him — records not being as plentiful as they are now. When Jenkins heard this, it made him pay meticulous attention to every detail.

During the war, Jenkins left 'Grand Hotel' and served in the Indian Army until his demobilization in 1946. Two years later he acquired his Stradivari violin, dated 1667, and found it to be everything he could wish for in a fiddle. The 'Grand Hotel' programme had been resumed during the war by Sandler but was broadcast as a regular programme from the BBC studios. When Sandler died, Tom Jenkins was asked to deputize and 'wore the mantle of Sandler with taste and distinction'.[6] Finally, he made it very much his own programme until the mid-fifties, when he left to start his own orchestra at Scarborough.

A quiet, modest man, Jenkins was always rather surprised that he should be considered of any importance. He just loved to play the violin, and it made him happy that people wanted to listen. His press cuttings abound in all the superlatives possible. One critic wrote: 'His cantilena is so vocal'[7], a perceptive comment, for Jenkins, like Campoli, listened a great deal to singers and firmly believed that the violin is essentially a singing instrument.

His life's work proved to be the solo pieces in the violin repertoire, and he played them exquisitely and with superb musicianship. It was this quality that caused so many people to say that they felt they had met him when they had not, to write him long and touching letters and compose verses. There were two ladies who sent him beautifully illustrated poems over a number of years but who never revealed their identity. Tom Jenkins was yet another virtuoso violinist who proved himself capable of the highest standards of playing in the solo field, but who will be remembered as 'an entertainer'.

For a short spell in the mid-fifties the leadership of 'Grand Hotel' was in the hands of another first-class musician, Max Jaffa. His friendship with the pianist Jack Byfield and cellist Reg Kilby, whilst playing in the BBC's London Studio Players, led to the formation of the Max Jaffa Trio. This later became known throughout Britain. In 1979 Max Jaffa celebrated his twentieth year of leading and conducting the orchestra in the Grand Hall, Scarborough. Here in a non-stop season of seventeen weeks, they make it a rule not to repeat any piece of music in their programmes for at least three weeks in order to please the hundreds of patrons who buy season tickets.

London-born Max Jaffa was presented with a fiddle by his father when he was six, with the command 'You are going to be a violinist!'[8] After training at the Guildhall School of Music, where he was awarded the gold medal, he became leader of the Scottish Symphony Orchestra. Here he played under Weingartner, Barbirolli and many other leading conductors.

Jaffa later studied with Sascha Lasserson, yet another pupil of Auer. He was one of the many famous musicians who played at Lasserson's Memorial concert at the Wigmore Hall in 1978.

By inclination Max Jaffa is an interpreter of the 'classical' repertoire. But his stars have led him into a much wider field. He has appeared in films and on television: he has toured the USA, Canada, South Africa and Rhodesia. For the last three

Albert Sandler, first
leader of BBC's 'Grand
Hotel'

Reginald Leopold,
leader of 'Grand Hotel'
for eighteen years and
last in the line

years, with his wife, the contralto Jean Grayston, and his accompanist, Vincent Billington, he has spent six weeks aboard luxury liners on winter world cruises.

Jaffa's attitude to life and music was confirmed by an incident that happened when he was seventeen. In order to pay for his studies Jaffa was leading the orchestra in a London hotel. One day Kreisler walked into the lounge. Jaffa was panic-stricken at the thought of playing in front of the great violinist. He did his best and in the interval a waiter came to tell him that Kreisler had invited him to join him for a drink. Jaffa immediately apologized for the kind of music he had been playing. Kreisler rebuked him: 'Now look here, you must never apologize for playing music — whatever sort of music it may be. I, too, have played in cafés.'

After having made some complimentary remarks about the young man's playing, Kreisler continued: 'If I may offer you a little advice — it's this — and remember it throughout your professional career. No matter what you play, or where you play it, if you give a good performance, no matter how bad the piece is — then your own playing will never suffer and the value of the music itself will be enhanced by your performance.'[9] Jaffa has never neglected to heed that advice.

Reginald Leopold was last in the line of leaders of 'Grand Hotel', and served for over eighteen years in the longest-running programme in the history of the BBC. Reg Leopold was born in London, the youngest of eight children, all of whom played an instrument. At fourteen he won a scholarship to the Trinity College of Music; here he was placed under the Hungarian-born Louis Pecskai, who had studied with Hubay at the Budapest Conservatoire. However, Reg Leopold considers that the greatest influence upon him at this time was Ludwig Lebel, the head of ensemble playing, a pupil of David Popper, the German cellist. Reg Leopold is convinced that this thorough training, at the right age, in chamber music, especially string quartet playing, laid a foundation that has served him well in every kind of music. 'I happen to have specialized in ensemble work, but whatever you do in music you must have a solid foundation. You can then build on it whatever way you choose and the way it suits you.'[10]

Over the years, Reg Leopold has worked in a number of famous orchestras; he was at the Trocadero and played for many years in the Savoy Orpheans under Carroll Gibbons. Alongside him in the string section were names which have since become known in quite different fields: Eugene Pini, George Melachrino, who later formed his own orchestra, and Hugo Rignold, who has led several great British orchestras and eventually became conductor of both the Royal Liverpool Philharmonic and Birmingham Symphony Orchestras.

In 1934, Reg Leopold met Fred Hartley — 'The man who brought light music right up to date'.[11] Hartley had been at the Royal Academy of Music with Hugo Rignold and when he started the Fred Hartley Sextet, he appointed Rignold as his first leader, who in turn brought Leopold into the group. 'Hartley had a way of rehearsing that was absolute perfection. His precision was something you could not better in the finest string quartet in the world.'[12] There were other well-known musicians in that group, some of whom were professors from the Academy. The popularity of the sextet often attracted photographers, but as soon as the camera was poised for action, the more eminent members would vanish. It was more than their job was worth to be seen playing light music.

The opportunity for Reg Leopold to lead 'Grand Hotel' came in 1956. With its potted palms much in evidence, the programme was broadcast before an invited studio audience at the Concert Hall, Broadcasting House, and full dress was *de rigueur* for the instrumentalists. Leading this group for eighteen years was a responsibility, and at times a strain, since the programme went out live every Sunday evening.

Today Reg Leopold leads the London Studio Strings at the BBC and as a freelance plays in sessions which can be anything from jazz to pop or film music. His recordings of salon music are bestsellers, and he has recently formed his own Grand Hotel Trio, in response to the constant demand from a public, who felt they were cheated when such a popular programme disappeared.

Few members of the younger generation of players have explored the lighter side of classical music. If they move away from the classical field they tend to leap from serious to folk, pop or rock music. One who has reached the top of the orchestral world and turned successfully to the 'virtuoso and gypsy' repertoire is John Georgiadis.

Born in London in 1939 of a second-generation immigrant Greek and with a Welsh grandmother, Georgiadis knows of no previous history of any professional musicians in his family. He says: 'My father loved the violin. As a boy he used to sit on the steps of the platform at the Albert Hall listening to Kreisler and Menuhin. When I was six he asked me if I would like a violin for my birthday. I said "yes" thinking it was just another toy.'[13]

Georgiadis admits today that had he then known of the torment he would undergo for the next four years whilst his father dragooned him into practising each day, he might have declined the offer. He explained: 'I was no child prodigy, but I was quite good. I had a fairly sound basic technique from an early age and this was almost entirely due to my father's persistence. It was he who helped me to raise my playing to the standards required for a professional career.'[14]

As a small boy, John learnt from a local teacher Vanna Brown, and was already winning prizes in music festivals by the age of nine. At twelve he won a Junior Scholarship to the Royal Academy of Music, where he studied with Joan Rochford-Davies and Frederick Grinke. In 1960 he went to Paris for 'a not very successful year with René Benedetti'.[15]

Georgiadis's first professional engagement was two months as a rank-and-file player with the Hallé Orchestra under Barbirolli which was 'An exciting experience. I learned a great deal in a short time'. Then came 'extra' work with various orchestras, including the London Symphony, followed by 'number three' positions with the London Philharmonic and the BBC Symphony. Georgiadis was only twenty-three when he was appointed leader of the City of Birmingham Symphony Orchestra in 1963, moving two years later to the leader's seat of the London Symphony Orchestra. Serving under most of the world's greatest conductors, he fulfilled this post until his resignation in 1979, except for a break of three years between 1973 and 1976 when he left to pursue a solo career.

It was at this time that Georgiadis was drawn into the lighter field. With his wife as his accompanist he gave two recitals of virtuoso and gypsy music: one at a local church and another in Wales. 'These were the pieces my father and I both loved. I had been brought up on this kind of music. We also had to choose music with easy accompaniments as my wife was principally a viola player — piano was her second study. Fortunately the nineteenth-century virtuoso music tends to have relatively uncomplicated piano parts.' Their first two recitals were so successful that in a short while they were being offered engagements all over the country. 'We had thirty in our first year. In four to five years we gave some 250 'Virtuoso and Gypsy Music' recitals. The audiences loved the music. And I think there is a place for it. People enjoy this type of programme, either because it brings back memories or because they have the chance to hear pieces that are seldom performed.'[16]

It was inevitable that Georgiadis would eventually feel the need to expand. He now works with a new pianist, the Mexican-born Pilar Fernandez. He says: 'At our recitals we can now tackle anything from sonatas by Brahms or Beethoven to Ravel's "Tzigane". But apart from the straight sonata programme we place the emphasis more on the virtuoso than on the gipsy element.'

The virtuoso salon pieces virtually disappeared from the solo repertoire during the 1950s and 60s and were superseded by the sonata. In the thirties, Carl Flesch made an accurate forecast that the much-neglected music of Sarasate, especially the 'Spanish Dances', would one day achieve the popularity it deserved. Today there is a tremendous revival of interest in these and other salon pieces. Georgiadis says: 'Sarasate is probably my favourite composer from the period for that style of music. He understood the capabilities of the instrument so well and therefore he wrote almost better than anyone else for the violin. His accompaniments are straightforward but always in good taste.'

In Georgiadis's opinion there are no secrets in performing virtuoso music. 'It is a question of achieving a good technical facility and then taking the music seriously. For example: the art of playing Paganini is to make music out of it. I've heard many people *not* making music out of *Brahms*. You only have to listen to Heifetz playing all these virtuoso pieces and they are perfect.'

Georgiadis has tried to follow Heifetz's example by using gut A and D strings. He maintains they produce 'an enormous beauty of sound. Sarasate certainly used them'. However, one disadvantage in using all-gut strings is that they do not last as long as steel-covered gut, and in deference to the 'convenience' age in which we live, Georgiadis did not persevere: a decision he regrets.

Like Campoli, Georgiadis is not ashamed of performing light music. He has researched into ways of presenting the programmes so that the audience may appreciate different features of the music. He says: 'Since I have a Mexican pianist I get her to dance a few steps of the Zapateado before we start to play: we do the same thing with Falla's "Spanish Dance". The audience love it, and I think it gives them an extra dimension to aid their enjoyment of the pieces.'[17]

28

The Violin 'Hot'

George Morrison; Eddie South; Stuff Smith;
Joe Venuti; Stephane Grappelli

Throughout the history of the violin the Italian influence constantly resurges in some aspect of its development. Perhaps the most
unexpected is in the field of jazz. Black America produced not
only jazz but two outstanding violinists in Eddie South and Stuff
Smith. It took two musicians of Italian origin to popularize the
technique throughout the world: Joe Venuti and Stephane Grappelli.

An interesting insight into the difficulties that faced the black
musician in the early days of jazz can be gained from an interview
by Gunther Schüller with the veteran violinist and band leader
George Morrison, published in 1968.[1]

George Morrison (b. 1891) came from Fayette, Missouri, from
a family which had produced many generations of fiddlers. They
played by ear with a natural talent, and all the music they knew
was square dancing.

As a child of five George made himself a violin from a
hollowed-out corn stalk, a piece of wood and some string. He
used charcoal for rosin and his bow was a branch of pussy willow.
When he grew older he made his fiddles out of cigar boxes. At ten
he bought his first real violin with the money he earned shining
shoes in a barber's shop in Boulder, Colorado. He had his first
music lessons from a local teacher, and each day he would sit in
the alley behind the shop practising his Kreutzer studies, the music
propped upon a lump of coal. His progress was so exceptional that
he was subsequently accepted as a private pupil of Professor
Howard Reynolds, a teacher of considerable reputation.

George Morrison studied with Reynolds for twelve years, and

in 1911 his teacher put him in for a competition for all his pupils —
forty-two in all with George as the only black. He won the first
prize — a place at the New England Conservatory. But he never
took up the scholarship. That same year he married and moved to
Denver, Colorado where he played both violin and guitar in the
'parlor houses' for Mattie Silks, one of the famous madams.

About this time George had his first encounter with jazz and
could recall having heard violinists improvise, one of the most
outstanding being Benny Goodman — not the famous clarinettist,
but a violinist who had his own band. It was Goodman who first
inspired George to jazz up popular tunes by improvisation.

Jazz was in fact the only field in which a black musician could
hope to succeed. Although George Morrison studied theory and
composition with Horace Tureman, conductor of the Denver
Symphony Orchestra, and reached a high standard of musicianship, he could never have been considered for a place in the
orchestra. Tureman often told him that he would have taken him
as his leader had he been white.

Morrison completed his musical education at the Chicago
Conservatory under Professor Carl Becker, and subsequently
found his way to New York and modest fame. It was when he
was leading the band at the Carlton Terrace Hotel in New York in
1920 that he had an experience that he remembered for the rest of
his life. He was expected to play some violin solos each evening
and on one occasion had just played Kreisler's 'Tambourin
Chinois' when a man came up to him and said, 'Young man, you
are a very, very talented musician. ... Would you accept my
card?' Morrison was delighted but he nearly dropped his violin
when he read the name 'Fritz Kreisler'. There was an unusual
sequel to this meeting. Having invited Morrison to his home,
Kreisler, the man who never took pupils, gave him six lessons free
of charge. Morrison recalled: 'He gave me some help on my flying
staccato in the Mendelssohn and showed me how to get a beautiful
clean-cut pizzicato.'[2]

Morrison poses the question as to what might have happened if
Heifetz, Milstein or Menuhin had paid as much attention to
mastering the swing of popular music as they did to the classical.
Morrison quotes the example of Eddie South, a fellow student of
his at the Columbia Conservatory of Music. 'He was a trained
musician, and one of the best in the popular field ... Terrific in
jazz.'[3] In Morrison's opinion Eddie South was outstanding because

he had technique, and when he went over to jazz and popular music, 'he could just turn it upside down'.

Born in Louisiana, Eddie South (1904–62) was brought up in Chicago. He had his first violin lessons at the age of ten and later studied at the Chicago School of Music. He was inspired to turn to jazz by Daniel Howard, the New Orleans jazz clarinettist who also played violin in many of the groups in which South performed. Known as 'the Dark Angel of the Violin', South was soon considered one of the most brilliant of all jazz violinists. In addition to his superb technique, his playing was imbued with great depth of feeling. His phrasing and remarkable beauty of tone were said to be comparable with those of the great classical violinists.

During the twenties in Chicago and New York, South played with many groups including those of Charlie Elgar, Erskine Tate and Jimmy Wade. Be it jazz or exotic music of all kinds — gypsy, samba, rhumba, bolero, tango or European — to Eddie South it was as natural as breathing. From 1928 up to the forties he led his own group.

Although the connoisseurs regard him as one of the major jazz soloists, Eddie South never became particularly famous. If he had not spent time in Europe in the thirties and made recordings, it is quite likely that his name might have been forgotten altogether. The recordings he made with Stephane Grappelli of 'Dinah' and 'Fiddle Blues' are fine examples of his art, as are two interpretations of a section from the first movement of Bach's Double Concerto in D minor, in which the violinists first play the music straight and then improvise upon the same passage. On the same record Eddie South is accompanied by Django Reinhardt in 'Eddie's Blues', a performance that has been described as 'the greatest example of violin playing in jazz'.[4]

Hezekiah Leroy Gordon Smith (1909–65) — better known as 'Stuff' Smith — is the other great black jazz violinist who also never attained the success he deserved. Born in Portsmouth, Ohio, he had his first somewhat unorthodox violin lessons from his father. When he was fifteen he joined a music hall troupe where he danced and played violin. He subsequently played in various bands and in 1929 formed one of his own. In the years just before the Second World War he led a lively three-piece band at the Onyx Club in New York and, wearing a battered top hat, and sometimes with a monkey on his shoulder, he would deliver

Joe Venuti, first to achieve success in 'hot' violin playing

Stephane Grappelli, who with Django Reinhardt founded the Quintet of the Hot Club of France

comedy patter as an accompaniment to his virtuoso improvisation. But his talent as a comedian proved a dubious asset since many critics refused to take him seriously.

Smith was one of the first to use an electric amplifier on the violin and it gave his playing a penetrating, forceful quality. His vibrant, singing tone and swinging rhythm combined to give some of the 'most dazzling violin playing ever heard in jazz'.[5] His improvisations were audacious in the extreme; Milton Mezzrow called him the 'mad genius of the violin'. His recordings highlight his originality, not only in his improvisation on the violin but also as an all-round entertainer. His vocalizing is reminiscent of Fats Waller, whose group he took over for some time in 1942. Smith has also recorded with Herb Ellis and Dizzy Gillespie, and provided the backing for Nat King Cole in 'After Midnight'.

Joe Venuti (c.1890–1978), born Giuseppe Venuti in Lecco on Lake Como, taught himself to play the violin when he was four and soon began taking regular lessons. When he was still a child his parents emigrated to the USA and settled in Philadelphia. One of his playmates in this city was another Mediterranean émigré, Salvatore Massaro, who played the guitar. He later became world-famous as Eddie Lang.

The two youngsters teamed up together and took lessons on their respective instruments, but so great were their individual talents that they frequently exchanged instruments without difficulty. Both were born improvisers. They moved to New York and found work in the rapidly expanding recording business. By the mid-twenties they had achieved fame throughout the Western world. Their 'Blue Grass' series dating from this time is a prime example of the richness of their individual skills and the depth of their musical understanding. Both were equally at home in larger ensembles as they proved in their superb version of 'Beale Street Blues' that they recorded in 1931 with Benny Goodman and the Teagarden brothers. When Venuti died in 1978, Sinclair Traill wrote: 'Together, in terms of jazz, they brought out all the best qualities and powers of violin and guitar. Rhythmically they mated with consummate understanding, attack and tone, the music they made being perfectly balanced and always in the best of taste.'[6]

Venuti and Lang both worked for the two most prominent white band leaders of the 1920s, Jean Goldkette and Paul Whiteman. It was during his time with the latter that Joe's genius for practical joking caused him trouble. Whilst filming *The King of Jazz*, Whiteman told the band they were behind schedule and asked for their maximum cooperation in the last hurried extra sessions required. Venuti's response was to fill the bell of the sousaphone with five pounds of flour. The flour-storm that ensued lost them a morning's shooting. Joe was sacked and remained out of work for six months.

After leaving Whiteman, Venuti led his own bands for many years with much success. He appeared frequently on radio shows, many of which featured his life-long friend, Bing Crosby. He worked consistently throughout the forties and fifties in an unspectacular way, then in the sixties there was a revival of interest in his playing and he resumed international touring, visiting Britain in 1969 after an interval of thirty-five years. He was often to be seen at jazz festivals during the seventies and his participation in 'jam' sessions was always catalytic.

Venuti retained a pride in his own playing to the end of his days. He maintained that growing old did nothing to diminish his musical imagination, he just had to practise harder to keep his reflexes sharp. Venuti once described his earliest encounters with jazz: 'My people were mountain people, and they loved the pulse of the mountain music. When I first heard jazz it seemed to have a very similar beat. It came easy to me.' It was this 'ease' that made Joe Venuti such a remarkable innovator, and since he was the first in the field, his work will always remain important in its influence. His recorded solos show that he had an ability to improvise which has seldom been surpassed.

Stephane Grappelli was born in Paris in 1908, the son of an Italian teacher of philosophy who loved music. His mother, who was French, died when he was three and he was placed in a poor Catholic orphanage. At six he was picked to play the part of an angel in one of Isadora Duncan's dance performances at her school at Bellevue near Paris. Grappelli says: 'I was not a good dancer but I looked cherubic. When you are *not* an angel it is *difficile*.'[7]

It was here that Stephane heard the Colonne Orchestra play Debussy's *Prélude à l'après-midi d'un faune*. It was his first encounter with live music and it made a lasting impression on him. But this was July 1914, and a few weeks later war led to the closure of the school. Stephane's father was conscripted into the army. For the child who had had such a brief glimpse into another world, it was back to yet another orphanage where conditions were appalling.

The children slept on the floor and suffered from malnutrition. Stephane duly absconded and wandered the streets until his father returned from the war.

When father and son were reunited the one room they could afford was paradise. Stephane's father took him to concerts and his musical taste began to develop. Soon he wanted to play an instrument himself and they purchased a cheap three-quarter-size violin. Grappelli still has that small fiddle intact in his desk in Paris. 'I love it very much: I remember hugging it all the way home: it's a wonder it didn't break.'⁸

The twelve-year-old child mastered the instrument in a few weeks — by ear. Then his father decided they should learn to read music. He borrowed a book from the library and together they gained a rough knowledge of the elements of solfeggio. Stephane subsequently tried out his skill by joining some street musicians and found he could earn some money. He says: 'My father was a wonderful scholar — but a dreamer. You do not get money that way — so I see what I can do myself.'⁹

At fifteen, Stephane joined a pit band in a cinema playing accompaniments to silent films. He says: 'It was here that I really learned to read music properly. I was there for a year and we played for three hours twice a day — you have a lot of reading in this time and it can be all kinds of music from Mozart to popular songs.'¹⁰

A year later Stephane began playing in clubs. He not only earned more money than in the cinema but found that he could play the music he liked — George Gershwin, Cole Porter and Irving Berlin. 'I also began to hear jazz about this time and it made a great impression on me. I heard Louis Armstrong and that changed my destiny. I decided I would try it on my violin. At first it worked slowly because it was something new, but gradually it developed; like improvisation — it just happened.'¹¹

Meanwhile the Grappellis had acquired a cheap piano and Stephane proceeded to teach himself to play that instrument, as he has 'cooking and most other things: from books and by watching others'.¹² Soon he was as nimble fingered on the piano as on the violin. He later added saxophone and accordion to his accomplishments.

With the discovery that he preferred the harmonic capabilities of the piano, Stephane put away his violin for four years. He made a living from playing at parties and at the Ambassadeurs in Paris where 'five hundred women covered with diamonds'[13] dined every night with their wealthy escorts.

It was when Grappelli was working in a club in Montparnasse in 1930 that he first met the gipsy guitarist, Django Reinhardt. But not until four years later, when they were both playing in an orchestra for tea dances at the Hotel Claridge in Paris, did they think of a partnership. One day, after replacing a string, Grappelli began to play 'Dinah'. Django joined in. From then on they would improvise in their breaks. At first they played free jazz together. Then later they were joined by the bassist Louis Vola and Django's brother Joseph, on guitar. Finally, Roger Chaput provided the third guitar. Thus was born the first modern all-string jazz ensemble, one of the greatest groups of the thirties, the Quintet of the Hot Club of France. Their success was phenomenal and everyone flocked to Paris to hear them. Many of the hundreds of 78 r.p.m. records they made are still selling in reissues on LP.

During the war Grappelli found himself in Britain, separated from the other members of the Quintet. After the war he teamed up again with Reinhardt for a time but they had lost the closeness of the Hot Club association. The group as such had disintegrated. When Reinhardt died of a stroke in 1953 at the age of forty-two, Grappelli faded from the limelight.

For the next twenty years, Grappelli played and recorded with some of the most famous jazz instrumentalists in the world, including Duke Ellington, Oscar Peterson and George Shearing. But none of these was a guitarist. In 1973 he formed an all-string ensemble with the Canadian Diz Disley and his Trio — Diz Disley and John Etheridge, guitars, and Brian Torff, string bass. 'We leave the fifth chair empty — for Django.'[14] This latest ensemble has brought Grappelli before a new generation of younger listeners who respond with unexpected enthusiasm to his style. To the older generation he represents a nostalgic visit to an enchanted past. But Grappelli has the rare gift of making that past contemporary. He is great not only because he is a great jazz violinist, but because he is a great musician.

The partnership that best illustrates this point is Grappelli's association with Yehudi Menuhin. Their recording of 'Tea for Two' topped the charts in 1978. It was Michael Parkinson who brought them together to perform on television. The two artists — from such widely differing fields — work together with a compatibility that is difficult to comprehend. Grappelli himself gives a Gallic shrug and says: 'I tell you frankly, I have no technique at all. Instinctively I think I have a good hold for the bow. But when I play with Yehudi I see how much I can learn. I watch him for the perfect position for his fingers: *alors!* — this I cannot do because I have never studied it. Now it is too late for me to learn. But we *enjoy* to play together.' Grappelli confesses that the only experience which makes him nervous is when he appears with a string backing: 'Because I know they play better violin than me.'[15] Nevertheless, there is another side to the coin. Once when he and Menuhin were rehearsing, the latter looked at him in amazement, and said: 'Stephane! What you are doing is *impossible* on the violin!'[16]

These 'impossibilities' remain inexplicable. Grappelli says: 'My improvisation is always different. When I walk on to a stage I do not know what will happen until it happens. When I improvise and I'm in good form, I'm like somebody half sleeping. I even forget there are people in front of me.'[17]

In December 1978 Grappelli celebrated his seventieth birthday by making his début at the Royal Albert Hall, with George Shearing, Julian Bream, and the young French rock violinist Didier Lockwood. As always Grappelli's performance was elegant and stylish. Young and old alike were bewitched by his playing. At seventy he is at the height of his powers on the one instrument that tends to leave its devotees deaf or crippled in their advancing years.

29

More Ladies of the Bow

Marie Hall; Maud Powell;
Erica Morini; Gioconda de Vito

'We do not think the violin a lady's instrument. Better endeavour to excel on the piano or harp,' wrote the magazine *Choir* of 12 September 1863 in answer to a query. Women players were rare at the time, and the few who managed to surmount prevailing prejudice were probably influenced by the example of Lady Hallé (1839–1911), who did much to encourage women to take up the instrument.

Musical institutions were slow to accept women violin students. During its first half century the Royal Academy of Music, London, for example — founded in 1822 — could not boast a single female studying the instrument. By 1872 it had one. At the turn of the century there were rather more. What happened to the graduates is uncertain. In the orchestras there was fierce opposition to the employment of women, one reason put forward being that the conductor would not feel free to swear in front of the ladies. One who broke through in the 1880s was the Cheltenham-born Emily Shinner, a pupil of Joachim in Berlin. She maintained a highly successful career as soloist and quartet player, and was greatly praised in Britain. In 1887 she was the first to found her own all-female string quartet.

Marie Hall (1884–1956), the first British female violinist to achieve an international reputation, was born in Newcastle-upon-Tyne and as a child played in the streets, accompanied by her father on the harp. At the age of ten she attracted the attention of Elgar, who gave her some preliminary instruction. She subsequently received lessons from Wilhelmj, Max Mossel and Johann Kruse, a member of the Joachim Quartet. In 1899 she won an

Exhibition to the Royal Academy of Music against forty competitors but could not afford to take it up. A year later, Kubelik heard her play and, acting upon his advice, she went to Prague to study under Ševčik, who said that he had seldom, if ever, instructed a pupil with a talent equal to hers. When she played with Henry Wood and the Queen's Hall Orchestra in 1903, the *Musical Times* tells us that 'she was recalled six times after the Tchaikovsky concerto, and at the conclusion of Wieniawski's "Faust" Fantasia, she had to return no less than nine times to the platform'.

By 1902 Marie Hall was ranked as one of the leading virtuoso performers in Europe. She subsequently undertook world-wide tours and was received like a queen everywhere. She was also not afraid to play either contemporary music or works by lesser-known composers. She introduced Vaughan Williams's *Lark Ascending* with much success. In 1911 she married her impresario, and was gradually seen less on the concert platform. But her name remains among the great ladies of the bow.

The first American woman to earn an international reputation was Maud Powell (1868–1920). Born in Peru, Illinois, of an American father and German mother, she was given instruction on the piano at the age of four, and at eight took violin lessons from William Lewis of Chicago. Five years later she was taken to Germany to study with Henry Schradieck at the Leipzig Conservatoire. After receiving her diploma within a year, she was selected from eighty applicants for a place at the Paris Conservatoire. Here she became a pupil of Dancla, and completed her studies under Joachim at the Hochschule in Berlin.

Quickly achieving an international reputation, Maud Powell toured Europe and America and was hailed by the critics as one of the most outstanding violinists of her day. She made her British début in 1882 and two years later appeared in New York for the first time, giving the first performance of Dvořák's violin concerto at one of the Philharmonic Society's concerts. She subsequently toured Germany and Austria and on her return to New York in 1892, she became the first American woman to found her own string quartet. In later years she returned many times to Europe and became known for her immense repertoire. In her will she bequeathed her beautiful Guadagnini violin to 'the next great woman violinist'. It was presented in 1921 to the sixteen-year-old Viennese Erica Morini after her début at the Carnegie Hall. She proudly received the violin, but it was too large for her small hands. That girl is today an elegant lady in her early seventies, who in 1976, after an absence of ten years, returned to captivate her audience at a recital to celebrate her 55 years on the concert platform.

Of Italian extraction, Erica Morini was born in Vienna in 1905. She received her first lessons from her father, who ran a private music school in that city. At three she had perfect pitch and would hide behind the large stove in the studio and call out 'wrong' when one of the students played or sang off pitch. Her father then sat her at the piano, where she would pick out the right note with one tiny finger.

At a surprise party for the Austrian Emperor Karl Josef, she was placed behind a screen to perform. When she emerged he was dumbfounded to see that a five-year-old child had been playing like a mature artist. He lifted her on to his lap and asked what she would like as a reward. She told him, 'A doll with eyes that move'.[1] The request was granted.

Erica's development was phenomenal. In 1913, when she was eight, she was admitted into Ševčik's master-class in Vienna — the only child of that age. She recalled his unique approach to the technique of the left hand. 'When his pupils had a particularly difficult run he would make them learn it backwards first and it became much easier to play correctly.'[2]

That same year Erica brought off a dual triumph in Vienna by making her first appearance at a public concert and taking part in the Beethoven Festival. This was closely followed by her German début under Nikisch with the Gewandhaus Orchestra in Leipzig. 'It was the most important experience in my life. I was the only child allowed to play there.' After the performance Nikisch said 'She is not a wonder-child: she is a wonder and a child.'[3]

During the First World War Erica's concert activities were limited to Central Europe: Germany, Austria, Hungary, Czechoslovakia all welcomed her. When she appeared for the first time in Bucharest, she was unknown and only about twenty seats were occupied. She was well received and hoped for a better audience at a concert planned for the following day. The news had travelled fast. The Prefect of the city had issued an order that only two tickets should be sold to each person so that all would have an equal chance to hear her. And he stationed himself at the door to make sure his orders were carried out.

In 1917 the effects of the Great War were beginning to change

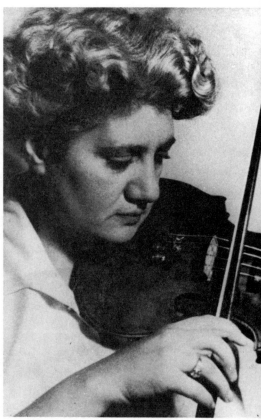

Above left: The American Maud Powell, one of the most outstanding violinists of her day

Above: Gioconda de Vito, who refused to play modern music

Erica Morini, a child prodigy and Ševčik's youngest pupil

the face of Europe, so Oscar Morini took his wife and six children to the USA. Although she toured the country with success, it was not until 1921 that Erica made her New York début. With Artur Bodanski conducting the New York Philharmonic Orchestra, she played concertos by Mendelssohn, Vieuxtemps and Mozart, and evoked an enthusiastic response from the press. It was on this occasion that she was presented with the 'Maud Powell' Guadagnini.

Erica Morini subsequently appeared with all the great symphony orchestras the world over. Something of her appeal is captured by a critic writing of her playing at a recital at Hunter College, New York in 1931. 'The violinist kept the mechanics of violin playing unobtrusive. Her inward, withdrawn style often gave one the feeling that she was performing for herself and letting us listen.'[4] In 1968, on her last visit to Israel, she gave twelve concerts with the Israel Philharmonic Orchestra to capacity audiences. The demand for tickets was so great that two extra concerts were sandwiched in and appropriately dedicated to the late Bronislav Huberman. Only two hours after the announcement was made, the three thousand seat auditorium in Tel Aviv was sold out. This was indeed a triumph in a land where the people have an insatiable appetite for violin playing and at least one in five has some training on the instrument.

As a violinist Morini has always been praised for her 'soaring lyricism' as well as her dazzling technique. She says: 'Through my father I was lucky to have the benefit of his knowledge of the Grün and Joachim method for the right hand and Ševčík for the left.'[5] When she played the Mendelssohn concerto under Georg Szell, Louis Biancolli of the *New York Telegram and Sun* said: 'This was Mendelssohn, the poet and singer ... It is as new as last night's performance. Morini treasures this experience: 'Working with Georg Szell was an unforgettable joy in my life.'

Her repertoire contained many of the much neglected classics. She is of the opinion that too many violinists rush to play new works and overlook the beauties of the older music. She gives the example of Spohr's 'Gesangsscene', which runs the entire gamut of technique. There is *spiccato*, staccato, with plenty of opportunity for left-hand brilliance, and marvellous passages to show phrasing and style to advantage. Morini has played all the Spohr concertos and advises violinists to include them in their repertoire. She has also played the Viotti Concertos Nos 22 and 23 and is sad that this composer's work is also unjustifiably neglected.

Erica Morini, like Lady Hallé, is one of the few women who prefers to play without a shoulder-rest or pad. She says: 'I have my own way of supporting the instrument with my neck. Without a shoulder pad you are much more at one with the instrument.'[6] Erica Morini has convinced many violinists to follow suit. In 1930, when she was coaching a few members of the Vienna Philharmonic Orchestra, she eventually persuaded the entire section to abandon their shoulder-rests.

Living today in New York with her Italian -American husband, Erica Morini is surrounded by treasures collected from all over the world. Hanging on the wall in her sitting-room is an embroidered linen handkerchief in a frame. Presented to Erica Morini by the Music Society of Madrid, it is the handkerchief which Sarasate wore in his breast pocket every time he played. He bequeathed it to 'the finest exponent of my Spanish Dances.'[7] It is no wonder that when Erica Morini was asked when she first became interested in music, she replied: 'I was born with music; it is like breathing.'[8]

In the 1950s, one name among women violinists predominated, that of Gioconda de Vito (b. 1907), whose interpretations of the Classical and Romantic repertoire earned her an almost unrivalled reputation throughout Europe. She never went to America despite invitations from Toscanini and Charles Munch. In 1961, at the age of fifty-four, she retired from the concert platform because in her own estimation she had 'reached the apogee of her abilities'.[9]

Gioconda de Vito was born into a cultured and musical family in the little town of Martina Franca in southern Italy. As a small child her first instrument was the mandolin, but at eight she taught herself to play the violin. Within six months she could play de Bériot's ninth concerto. She had her first violin lessons from her uncle — a professional violinist — and in theory from the conductor of the municipal band. At the age of eleven she entered the Conservatoire at Pesaro. Here she was a pupil of Remy Principe and obtained her diploma within two years. Her orchestral début took place in Rome when she was sixteen; she played the Tchaikovsky concerto.

In the Vienna International Competition of 1932 de Vito won first prize. Two years later she succeeded Teresa Tua as professor of violin at the Accademia di Santa Cecília in Rome. By the late thirties she was in constant demand as a soloist, but her main problem was to find time to fulfil all the engagements that came her way. Only thirty days annually were allowed by the authorities for concert-giving outside the Accademia and these were fully taken up by her tours of Germany. The war intervened and Britain had to wait almost ten years for her promised visit.

De Vito finally came to London in 1948, making her début at the Royal Albert Hall playing the Brahms concerto. The audience loved the warmth and vibrancy of her playing and critics praised her exquisite phrasing and musicality. She was inundated with offers to play all over the country, and she appeared at the Edinburgh Festival with Menuhin and Stern in 'The Festival of the Violin'.

During her entire career de Vito steadfastly refused to play works by modern composers. She made two concessions — a work by Castelnuovo-Tedesco which had been compulsory in the Vienna International Competition, and a concerto by Pizzetti. The latter work was written for her in a deliberately archaic and unabrasive style. The mere mention of Schoenberg, Bartók, Berg or Stravinsky had her raising her hands in horror, and even the concertos by Elgar and Sibelius never appealed to her as being suitable for her own style of playing. She stresses the importance of the Italian classical repertoire, and considers the Paganini Caprices 'musically beautiful'. But her favourite composer is Bach. She would always play some Bach to warm up in the artists' room before a concert.

De Vito's favourite concerto is the Brahms — her recording with Rudolf Schwarz and the Philharmonic Orchestra remains one of the most compelling performances in or out of the catalogue. However, despite the success of this and other recordings, de Vito does not feel that she was ever temperamentally suited to this medium. She was an expressive violinist who moved about whilst playing, and as this affected the microphone, she felt restricted in her performance.

She had individual ideas that were sometimes startling, such as her habit of commencing the solo entry of the Brahms concerto with an up-bow — to produce greater sonority. Her superlative readings of the concertos by Bach, Beethoven and Brahms are landmarks in the history of violin playing. In 1954 Eric Blom wrote: 'Her way of holding the balance between the outward appearance of a serene graciousness and a vibrant inner passion that is always felt in her playing without ever breaking through boundlessly is, if not unique, at any rate very difficult to discover in any other violinist of today.'[10]

30

The Enkindling Spirit

David Oistrakh

In one of their many heart-to-heart talks Yehudi Menuhin once asked David Oistrakh if he would ever consider living in the West. The reply was characteristically honest: 'I owe the state everything. They are responsible for my upbringing and have seen to it that I have had the best musical education and training. My family are there. It would be disloyal of me to live elsewhere.'[1] Oistrakh paid a price for that loyalty when, as a sick man, he undertook far too much work in his last years. No-one in power ever suggested that he should rest more and play less. His relentless travelling schedule was finally broken when he died in Amsterdam in 1974 at the age of sixty-six.

David Fydorovich Oistrakh was born in Odessa in 1908, into a musical family. His father, a poor book-keeper, played the violin and trained the chorus of the local operatic society. His mother was a singer and actress.

It is, therefore, not surprising that Oistrakh once said: 'I cannot think of my childhood without music. My father gave me a toy violin when I was about three-and-a-half and I remember trying to join a party of street musicians.' His enthusiasm was rewarded by the presentation of a real eighth-size fiddle at the age of five. He recalled his first audience. 'I can see myself standing in a courtyard surrounded by other children. I had some sort of music in front of me which I pretended to read but did not understand as I eagerly scratched away on that canary-yellow instrument. But the notes I drew from it sounded heavenly to me at the time.'[2]

That same year, David was accepted as a pupil of Pyotr Stolyarsky at the Music School of Odessa. His lessons were irregular, but free. Stolyarsky never turned away a pupil who could not afford to pay. Oistrakh once said: 'From the very beginning he instilled in us the need for perseverance and showed us how to enjoy the pleasures of the creative side of music.' Renowned for his special gift for instructing young children, Stolyarsky worked from seven in the morning until late at night. 'His incredible enthusiasm was contagious and we were all affected by it.'[3]

Even as a child, Oistrakh had an excellent musical memory and a marked perception of form and rhythm. Most remarkable of all was his highly developed musical imagination — rare in one so young. Nevertheless, he was not a child prodigy and Stolyarsky was wise enough to allow his talent to ripen slowly. At the age of fifteen he was admitted into Stolyarsky's master-class at the Conservatoire in Odessa, but his first position in the orchestra was as a rank-and-file viola player. He was soon appointed leader and within a few months appeared as soloist, playing Bach's A minor concerto. A year later he made his début at a solo recital in Odessa, and followed this with a tour of the Ukraine.

Oistrakh had no more tuition after the age of eighteen and spent the next two years touring the Soviet Union. In that country news of an outstanding violinist travels fast, and he found himself playing to capacity audiences everywhere. When he made his Leningrad début in 1928 playing the Tchaikovsky concerto with Nikolai Malko conducting, he was acknowledged as a master and given a standing ovation. A year later he repeated this success in Moscow.

In 1930 Oistrakh was married to Tamara, a professional pianist who gave up her own career to devote herself to her husband. In later years when he spent most of his time travelling abroad, she was always at his side. Their only son, Igor — later to become a virtuoso violinist in his own right — was born on 27 April 1931.

Oistrakh now added teaching to his accomplishments. In 1934 he was given a lectureship at the Tchaikovsky Conservatoire in Moscow and he and his family left Odessa to move into a three-roomed apartment in the capital — a great privilege in a land where creature comforts were few.

Two years later Oistrakh came second in the Wieniawski Competition in Warsaw. The first prize was awarded to the fifteen-year-old Ginette Neveu. Ida Haendel, then aged seven, took the first Polish Prize at the same competition. She was 'captivated by his [Oistrakh's] beautiful tone and brilliant technique'.[4]

It was in Brussels in 1937 that David Oistrakh surmounted the first hurdle in the international field by winning the Queen's Prize in the first Ysaÿe Contest, held to commemorate the work of the Belgian virtuoso. During his lifetime Ysaÿe had continuously hankered after the idea of holding a competition. He had always favoured freedom both in ideas and in the music itself. By the provision of extra funds, he wanted to give young people the opportunity to explore this freedom for themselves. But it was only after his death that Queen Elisabeth, a friend and devoted pupil of Ysaÿe, brought these plans to fulfilment.

Lionel Giraud-Mangin, the then director of the Beaux-Arts, recalled the touching scene when this unknown Russian received the jury's unanimous approval and a standing ovation. 'The Queen called the young man into her box and personally presented him to the audience for a round of further applause.'[5] When the Ysaÿe Foundation was founded in 1961 Oistrakh became its first president. The competition was held in Ysaÿe's name for only two years and was renamed the Concours Musical International Reine Elisabeth.

Oistrakh's success in Brussels prompted many offers to play abroad. Thibaud, one of the most enthusiastic members of the jury, pressed him to come to Paris at the first opportunity. But at this time the Soviet Union was slow to allow artistic freedom, and before any plans could be discussed Europe was plunged into war.

Now elevated to the appointment of violin professor at the Moscow conservatoire, Oistrakh continued to teach and to play in his own country. When Hitler's armies invaded the Soviet Union in 1941, he travelled to the front, giving concerts to the troops and to workers in the factories. The conditions were sometimes unbearable. During the occupation of Leningrad he gave a memorable performance of the Tchaikovsky concerto in an unheated hall with the temperature well below zero. Against an unsolicited background accompaniment of intermittent gunfire and fire-alarms, Oistrakh — typically — remained unshaken throughout.

When the war ended Oistrakh was at the height of his career, but there were as yet no plans for concerts outside the Soviet Union. It was almost as difficult to organize appearances with visiting foreign artists. Ernest Krause in his biography *David*

Oistrakh, published in East Germany in 1973, states that he played the Bach double concerto in Moscow with Menuhin in 1945, but this is incorrect. The two men certainly met for the first time that year in Moscow, however, and Menuhin records the occasion in touching detail in his autobiography, *Unfinished Journey*. Excited at the thought of meeting this great violinist, of whom he had heard so much, Menuhin arrived at the airport to find Oistrakh waiting on the tarmac, 'in the wind and wet of the November afternoon' to welcome a fellow artist to his country. An immediate affinity sprang up between the two and resulted in a friendship which endured for almost thirty years. Menuhin recalls the visit as being fraught with rebuffs and bureaucratic obstacles. He had to leave Moscow without even hearing Oistrakh play, let alone taking part in a joint performance.

Oistrakh's earliest appearance outside the Soviet Union after the war was at the First Prague Spring Festival in 1946. A year later at the same festival, Menuhin and Oistrakh were finally brought together professionally to play the Bach double concerto. For Menuhin the experience was significant.

> We were to play the same work together in Paris and Brussels and many other places. Playing this was interesting, not only because of the personal rapport that existed between us but because it gave me an insight of what was still Russian to me. My parents had come from Russia and we shared the same Russian-Jewish background. It was curious how our styles seemed to be almost identical when we played together. We both gained so much from this contact. I for the reasons already stated and he, perhaps something that was useful to him right after the war, when he had been immured in Russia all his life and knew little of what was going on in the Western world.[6]

When restrictions were finally lifted and opportunities to travel abroad became a reality, it was not to satisfy the egocentric ambitions of a star performer that Oistrakh set forth on his journeys. He was convinced that he had a mission to use his influence in representing the traditions of the Russian school of violin playing, and was particularly keen to pass on his ideas to the younger generation.

The Strad critic wrote of a performance in Paris in the early fifties that 'he fully justified his reputation'. The qualities of his playing 'lift it into a class by itself . . . His playing of the Mozart Fifth Concerto in A (K.219) with Jacques Thibaud conducting was

"spacious, gracious and virile", with no signs of affected pretti-
ness in the beautiful phrasing. Though always alive with a
compelling interior warmth and strength, his feelings never
ill-treat either the music or the violin.' One of the qualities that
particularly struck this critic was that 'he never seemed to be in a
hurry, a feature we have now come to accept as almost inevitable
in anyone under sixty! The keynotes of his playing are nobility,
sincerity and the simplicity which goes with profound and
balanced musicianship.'

England did not see Oistrakh officially until 1954, although he
had been sent on a delegation to London some years previously
and had played at a private party at the Soviet Embassy. The
impresario Victor Hochhauser was responsible for bringing Oistrakh to Britain. He had heard him play at the Prague Spring
Festival in 1949 and recognized an extraordinary talent. After a
long campaign of bombarding the Soviet Embassy, in 1953
Hochhauser managed to organize a London concert by Oistrakh's
son, Igor, who was by then a fully-fledged performer in his own
right. A year later Hochhauser brought David Oistrakh to
London.

Accompanied on the piano by V. Yampolsky, Oistrakh gave
his long-awaited recital to a packed Royal Albert Hall on 10
November 1954. He played Beethoven's first sonata in D and
Prokofiev's F minor sonata, which the composer had dedicated to
him. An unusual choice was Schumann's rarely played Fantasia in
C, 'composed for Joachim and touched up by Kreisler', and
unpopular on account of its fiendishly unviolinistic passages. In
this work and Ysaÿe's Ballade No. 3 'the multiple stopping was
carried with such truth of intonation and such smoothness of bow
that one almost overlooked its difficulty'.[7]

Oistrakh's British orchestral début took place at the Royal
Albert Hall on 26 November 1954 with the Philharmonic Orchestra conducted by Norman del Mar. He played concertos by
Brahms and Khachaturian, the latter being conducted by the
composer. In the Brahms, Oistrakh was inevitably compared with
Heifetz who had played it in London the previous week. The
Times critic appears to prefer Oistrakh. Heifetz 'was all objectiv-
ity, Oistrakh's performance . . . had a more classical feeling, more
identification of himself with the composer, than Heifetz'. The
slow movement was 'reminiscent of Kreisler in his gentleness and
sweetness'. Since the end of the war Oistrakh's recordings had

appeared in Europe and America on a variety of labels and had built him a reputation as a violinist possessing a large, luscious tone with tremendous intensity and power. When he finally played to Western audiences in the flesh, they responded not only to his simple unaffected manner, but found that his tone was not overwhelming. It had a refinement and delicacy that was different from and superior to that which had been over-amplified on disc.

Oistrakh made his début in New York at a recital at the Carnegie Hall on 20 November 1955. The audience filled every seat and overflowed onto the stage. Several times they broke into cheers and would not let him go before he had played several encores. Next morning, Howard Taubman wrote in the *New York Times*:

> In Tartini's 'Devil's Trill' sonata he had a masterful command of all the bravura requirements [but] ... the most impressive thing about Mr Oistrakh was the thoughtfulness and sensitivity of his musicianship. He is unmistakably a violinist who does not begin by thinking how to subdue an audience through sheer brilliance.

Taubman illustrates his point by describing Oistrakh's playing of the Sonata No. 1 in D, Op. 12 by Beethoven. In the slow movement 'the framework of the conception was classic, but the feeling had a romantic glow.'

This particular November day is probably unique in the history of this famous hall. At two-thirty that afternoon, Mischa Elman gave a recital. Oistrakh was at five-thirty. Three hours later, Milstein took the stage. In Oistrakh's audience was a galaxy of famous musicians.'But the presence of Kreisler excited me more than anything else. When I saw him deep in thought listening to my playing, and then rising to applaud, I was so overcome I thought I was dreaming.'[8]

By this time, in addition to his foreign tours and international recordings, Oistrakh was giving some ninety concerts a year in the Soviet Union. But however much his performing talents demanded of him he always left time for teaching. He had about fifteen master pupils at the Moscow Conservatory who came from all over the world. He loved his students and they adored him. He would travel any distance to be with them when they were entering international competitions and the high rate of success of his pupils is proof of the excellence of his teaching: Victor Tretiakov, Valery Klimov, Victor Pickeisen and Oleg Kagan are some of the most outstanding.

The Russians claim that the superb technical equipment with which their soloists are blessed is largely due to the fact that all their great players are teachers. They acknowledge their debt to Auer and his school. Although modified by intervening generations, modern Russian traditions are firmly based on his principles which, through his predecessors Vieuxtemps and Wieniawski, are linked to the Italians through Viotti and his pupils.

The most outstanding characteristic of Oistrakh's playing was aptly described by Howard Taubman in the *New York Times* after his orchestral début in that city in 1955: 'a warm, enkindling sensitivity with head and heart inextricably linked'. Time and time again, critics and colleagues alike were to remark upon this quality. In the Tchaikovsky concerto, Oistrakh 'took its lush tones and gave them dignity without robbing them of their essential character. It was lyrical without being maudlin.' And yet, when it came to Mozart, Oistrakh's individual approach seemed to embrace the eighteenth-century style with virility as well as refinement. In his performances of contemporary works by Soviet composers, Oistrakh was regarded as an important propagandist by the Russian government. Shostakovitch dedicated both his concertos to him.

On the platform his playing seemed effortless. One London critic expressed something approaching regret at his making the difficulties imperceptible on the grounds that half the enjoyment of listening to a virtuoso is to witness the phenomenon. Behind this apparent ease was a fine analytical musical mind. Oistrakh would spend hours studying scores and listening to tape-recordings in precise detail. He had always overcome the technical and mechanical aspects before he mounted the platform. After that it was between Oistrakh and the music itself, and he played the way he was, honestly and without vanity. He never took liberties with the music.

Technically he was a master by any standards. Despite his heavy build his bowing was elegant and consistent for the whole length of the bow. After his first appearance in Paris in 1953, the *Strad* critic wrote: 'With only about two inches left at the heel on an up bow, he is able to add another note which is perfectly phrased and clear, only then going to a down bow at the extreme limit and with complete smoothness.' Frederick Riddle, principal viola of the Royal Philharmonic Orchestra for many years, was able to study Oistrakh's playing at close quarters. He says: 'His bowing was a lovely example of the Auer school — the little finger comes off at the point of the bow and the first finger comes out so that the wrist is kept well down as the bow is drawn up. A beautiful motion to watch. And a great influence on violin playing the world over.'[9]

Ricci tells a revealing story about Oistrakh's approach to music. It seems that someone once asked him: 'What is the most difficult piece you play?' Oistrakh replied: 'I don't play the most difficult pieces.' Oistrakh, like Busch and Szigeti, belonged in the very good company of those who place music above pyrotechnics.

One of Oistrakh's greatest pleasures was to perform with his son Igor. When they played the double concertos by Bach and Vivaldi in London in 1961, *The Times* described them as being 'in perfect sympathy, in both thought and expression, their two personalities fused into a single overall conception'.

In private life, Oistrakh was an inveterate collector. His Moscow flat was crowded with instruments, music, books and mementoes of all kinds. Cameras and small mechanical toys always held a fascination for him, and his colleagues would smile at his boyish enthusiasm as he proudly demonstrated his newest acquisition. He was also a fine chess player and followed the international competitions with interest. Best of all he liked to play chess with his son.

Oistrakh's continuing close relationship with his orchestral colleagues long after he had become an internationally famous soloist is reminiscent of Kreisler — a man who never became proud. His friend and impresario Victor Hochhauser considered him to be:

> quite the most outstanding man I have ever known — and I don't exclude all the great names. He was a character who combined the sense of tragedy of the Russian and the Jewish people. He just wanted to be left alone to play the violin, to teach and give pleasure to the masses. He was great fun to be with. His sense of humour was delightful — never cruel or cynical at someone else's expense. Mostly he laughed at himself.[10]

Yehudi Menuhin sums up Oistrakh's achievement:

> The Revolution and World War I having interrupted the regenerating contribution of the great Russian school to our violin world, Oistrakh was the first to rekindle it. For decades Jascha Heifetz and Mischa Elman had carried the torch and I am modestly proud to have been

David Oistrakh, first Soviet violinist to achieve international acclaim

Yehudi Menuhin, supreme musician and humanitarian

instrumental in persuading Oistrakh at a time when relations between Russia and America were strained that he would be welcomed by the great American public. Indeed he evoked unbounded affection, admiration and gratitude and picked up and renewed the current of great Russian violinists that had crossed the Atlantic thirty years previously.[11]

A Man for all Music

Yehudi Menuhin

There can be few violinists who have made a greater impact on the musical world than the young Yehudi Menuhin. His name became known internationally before he had the strength to tune his own fiddle. When he played at a concert in Philadelphia on 26 June 1978 in a series to celebrate his fiftieth year on the concert platform, James Felton of the *Evening Bulletin* wrote:

> The man seems truly ageless, ever modest, still the elegant violinist who avoids virtuoso tricks, ever in search of melody in all its sweetness. He doesn't tune slightly sharp, as some others do, to get a deliberately sharp, commanding tone. He doesn't grind the threads of his bow to tatters in passionate frenzy. Mendelssohn's Violin Concerto was a perfect choice for him ... Menuhin handled it with gentle, loving care, and a slight private smile as if he and his instrument were revealing themselves as partners ... His solo cadenzas didn't capitalize on showiness but rather moved deliberately and thoughtfully, remaining faithful to this overwhelmingly lyrical work. A performance of taste. Menuhin typically insisted on sharing the applause with everyone on stage, as if they had all been playing chamber music together.

Yehudi Menuhin was born on 22 April 1916 in New York, the son of a poor Jewish schoolmaster who shared with his wife a great love of music. They took their child to concerts from the age of fourteen months. He responded so well to musical sound that when he was four they gave him a small violin.

His first teacher was a 'drill-sergeant'[1] who knew little of the classics and less of the subtleties of violin playing, but in 1921, when Yehudi was five, he began lessons with Louis Persinger. Accompanied by Persinger on the piano, the seven-year-old

Yehudi played de Bériot's 'Scène de Ballet' as an item inserted into an orchestral programme at the Oakland Auditorium on 29 February 1924. The following year saw his first appearance with the San Francisco Symphony Orchestra, playing Lalo's 'Symphonie Espagnole' to an excited and appreciative audience. Menuhin's most vivid memory of the occasion was being picked up and embraced by the conductor whose beard 'felt like a moist whisk broom'.[2] A month before his ninth birthday, he gave his first full-length recital, in the Scottish Rite Hall in San Francisco. In the autumn of the same year, 1925, Persinger moved to New York. The Menuhins followed.

Yehudi's New York début was not the Carnegie Hall concert that was to bring him fame overnight a year later, but a recital at the Manhattan Opera House on 17 January 1926 with Persinger accompanying. With the exception of the impresario, Walter Damrosch, the audience lacked any distinguished musicians. But there were three elderly gentlemen sitting in the front row who had good reason to attend. They were Papa Heifetz, Papa Elman and Papa Max Rosen.

In the autumn of 1926 the entire Menuhin family — father, mother, Yehudi and his two sisters, Hephzibah and Yaltah — sailed for Europe, an undertaking sponsored by Sidney Ehrman, a wealthy lawyer and one of the best-known Jewish philanthropists in New York. Yehudi made his European orchestral début by appearing in two highly successful concerts in Paris with the Lamoureaux Orchestra under Paul Paray, playing the Lalo 'Symphonie Espagnole' and the Tchaikovsky concerto.

It was also at this time that he was taken to audition with Ysaÿe in Brussels. As a former student of Ysaÿe, Persinger had created an image that had filled his young pupil with awe. When the boy and the legend came face to face, Yehudi was disappointed: 'In place of the giant of my childish vision, I found a too human man in too human surroundings.'[3] Menuhin played the first movement of the 'Symphonie Espagnole' by Lalo whilst Ysaÿe pizzicatoed chords to provide the illusion of an orchestral accompaniment. When Menuhin had finished, Ysaÿe said, 'You have made me happy, little boy, very happy indeed'. Then he asked Yehudi to play an A major arpeggio in four octaves. The astonished boy 'groped all over the fingerboard like a blind mouse'. Ysaÿe not only offered to teach him but gave him some advice: 'You would do well, Yehudi, to practise scales and arpeggios.'[4] In retrospect,

Menuhin thinks he might have shortened his long search for understanding had he accepted Ysaÿe's offer. But even as a ten-year-old he instinctively resisted learning an imposed method and was unable to accept anything ready-made. 'Music was something very alive to me, an essential means of expression, and I suspect that unending hours of work on dull material might well have blunted rather than polished my interpretation of it.'[5]

One of the most important later influences on Yehudi's playing was Georges Enesco. The association had begun in a legendary encounter at a concert in San Francisco when he was about eight years old. 'Before a note was sounded he had me in thrall. His countenance, his stance, his wonderful mane of black hair — everything about him proclaimed the free . . . man who is strong with the freedom of gipsies, of spontaneity, of creative genius, of fire.'[6]

Much later Yehudi was taken to an Enesco concert in Paris. He went alone to the artists' room after the concert and persuaded Enesco to hear him at six o'clock the following morning, whilst he was packing his bags to leave Paris. As soon as Enesco heard the boy play, he agreed to give him some lessons, each of which was

> an inspiration, not a stage reached in a course of instruction. It was the making of music . . . While he accompanied me at the piano he also sang the different voices of the score . . . What I received from him — by compelling example, not by word — was the note transformed into vital message, the phrase given shape and meaning, the structure of music made vivid.[7]

Looking back on these early studies with Enesco, Menuhin finds that his direct influence is submerged in the very conception of a work, a conception which is unified, its elements no longer traceable to direct sources. 'I must make an effort now to recall any specific things he said, but I know that everything I do carries his imprint yet.'[8]

The autumn of 1927 saw the Menuhins back in New York so that Yehudi could fulfil two concert engagements — one on 26 November at Carnegie Hall with the New York Philharmonic Orchestra. When Fritz Busch learnt that he was to conduct an eleven-year-old boy playing the Beethoven concerto, he said 'One doesn't hire Jackie Coogan to play Hamlet'. But after the audition he revised his opinion: 'My dear child, you can play anything with me, anytime, anywhere.' The orchestra remained unconvinced, especially when the small boy handed his violin to the leader to be tuned. Menuhin recalls: 'By the end of the first movement, however, I knew they were on my side.'⁹ It was not only the triumph over scepticism that had so pleased the young performer — it was being accepted by the hard rank-and-file members of the orchestra, who knew what they were about.

The concert was an unqualified success. There were three thousand in the audience and tears streamed unashamedly from their eyes as Fritz Busch came down from the rostrum and embraced the small boy who had played like a virtuoso with a lifetime of experience behind him.

Next morning, Olin Downes wrote in the *New York Times*:

> Menuhin has a technique that is not only brilliant but finely tempered. It is not a technique of tricks, but one much more solidly established, and governed by innate sensitivity and taste. It seems ridiculous to say he showed a mature conception of Beethoven's Concerto, but that is the fact. Few violinists of years of experience, known to the public, have played Beethoven with as true a feeling for his form and content.

Early in 1929, the Menuhins departed once more for Europe. A few days before Yehudi's thirteenth birthday came the concert that marked the start of his adult career. On 12 April 1929, conducted by Bruno Walter with the Berlin Philharmonic Orchestra, Yehudi played the Bach, Beethoven and Brahms concertos. Berlin was then the musical centre of the western world. Adolf Busch and many like him were able, at this time, to make a good living out of music without ever crossing the German frontier. This was not possible in any other country. In the USA where the musical scene was still largely German, it was essential that any artist seeking international status must first compete with and succeed in the German arena.

The original idea of returning to Europe was following Enesco's advice that Yehudi should study with Adolf Busch in Basle. Enesco had occasionally to check Yehudi's over-passionate rendering and it was probably this fault that led him to suggest a totally different type of teaching. Yehudi spent two summers with Busch. His methods were 'musical rather than violinistic. If he didn't have Enesco's flair or glamour, as a musician he was extremely serious and deep, a passionate fundamentalist who ate, breathed and slept Bach and Beethoven. I think that musicians, more particularly chamber musicians, are to this day, whether knowingly or not, in debt to his combined passion and profundity'.[10]

In November 1929 Yehudi and his family made their first trip to England. His début at the Queen's Hall on 4 November and a recital at the Albert Hall a few days later were both sell-outs. The London critics were, as always, reserved in their judgement on child prodigies. Of his concert at the Queen's Hall with the London Symphony Orchestra conducted by Fritz Busch, *The Times* of 5 November 1929 made the point that however remarkable he was for his age, we must not make allowances on that account, but:

> Judged by the absolute standards, Menuhin's performance was very good. His command of technique is remarkable . . . and the tone was always musical if not very full. But whilst there was something more than a mere cold perfection in his playing there was little real feeling. All the obvious points were duly made but the subtleties escaped him . . . Yet it is the measure of the boy's ability that his performance of a work so exacting both technically and emotionally, can be judged by the same standards as that of his elders.

It is Yehudi's second visit to Britain, in 1932, that has now slipped into musical history and remains clearly in the violinist's memory today. It came about through Frederick Gaisberg, recording manager of HMV, who felt that the Elgar violin concerto had been neglected. The magnificent recording by Albert Sammons made in 1929 would in his opinion never be bettered, but he hankered after making a recording with Elgar himself conducting the work. He thought that 'as a youthful and pliant performer without prejudice'[11] Yehudi would respond best to Sir Edward's wishes and instructions. The septuagenarian composer and the sixteen-year-old Yehudi met for the first time in the spring of 1932 at the recording studios in Abbey Road. Gaisberg writes: 'Yehudi's fresh, agile mind, so quick to grasp the instructions, drew from Sir Edward high praise and encouragement.'[12] Menuhin recalled that Sir Edward arrived looking not in the least like a composer but more like a 'country gentleman' who should have had hounds at his heels. With Ivor Newton as his accompanist, they started to play, but a few bars after the soloist's entry, Elgar stopped them saying he was sure that everything would go beautifully and if they would excuse him he was off to the races. The feeling of trust he inspired was well-founded. 'At the recording studio Elgar was a figure of great dignity but without a shred of self importance. I had never seen anyone conduct less, or show less determination to impose himself. All was ease and equanimity.'[13]

Some months later, following the success of the recording, the concerto was performed again in the Royal Albert Hall. This was a concert to make the young performer both proud and humble. In the first half Sir Thomas Beecham conducted him in concertos by Bach and Mozart and in the second, Elgar, 'propped on a red velvet stool', [14] conducted his own concerto. 'To appear with England's most beloved composer as well as with her most distinguished conductor was like being given the freedom of the city or made a member of the family'.

Gaisberg recalls the occasion:

> The Albert Hall was filled to the last seat. A brilliant and expectant audience such as only London could produce had come to hear the fifteen-[sic]year-old boy and seventy-five year old composer collaborate in what proved to be a thrilling and moving performance. I have never seen such spontaneous enthusiasm as that which recalled to the platform again and again the old man and the young boy hand in hand.[15]

Next morning *The Times* said: 'Menuhin's playing has a singularly musical quality, and if he does not produce a tone of exceptional power it is always beautifully smooth and his execution is of masterly ease. Throughout one was impressed by the sympathy of the phrasing and the general vitality of the playing.'

Elgar, too, was pleased. Afterwards he wrote to Gaisberg thanking him for 'bringing about the wonderful performance. Yehudi was marvellous and I am sure would never have heard of the concerto if you had not set the thing in motion.'[16]

In the years that followed Menuhin became known the world over and earned a vast income from concert appearances and recordings. But in 1936, twelve months before his twenty-first birthday, he took a year off from concert-giving in order to study and to live a little of the private life denied him through the relentless demands of being a travelling virtuoso. The war years and an unsuccessful youthful marriage brought Menuhin into a state of unrest and indecision. It was at this time that he first began to analyse his own performing. He had always played the violin instinctively. He writes:

Considering that I played without thinking, without analysis, without as it were, taking the machine apart for overhaul, just keeping it running at any cost, my performance stood up remarkably well; but there were times when I knew I wouldn't be able to go on until I understood technique and could recapture that ease I had once possessed without thinking and which was now deserting me. I also knew I had fallen into bad habits. This double warning drove me to a search for first principles which was to last for years (indeed it has not ended: every day brings new discoveries).[17]

He studied the manuals of Carl Flesch and D.C. Dounis from cover to cover, he discussed the situation with his friends and took more lessons. But still he made no progress.

It was Antal Dorati, a pupil of Bartók's in Budapest, who brought an end to Menuhin's period of doubt. At a friend's house in New York he was introduced to Bartók. He played the composer's first violin sonata and at the end of the first movement Bartók stood up and said: 'I did not think music could be played like that until long after the composer was dead.'[18]

At that first meeting Menuhin asked if he might commission Bartók to compose a work for him. 'I was not hoping for a third concerto, just a work for violin alone.'[19] Menuhin did not foresee that he would be rewarded with a masterpiece. When Menuhin received the score in March 1944 he was shaken. It seemed to him almost unplayable. Later he realized that this first hasty impression was ill-judged.

The Solo Sonata is eminently playable, beautifully composed for the violin, one of the most dramatic and fulfilling works that I know of, the most important composition for violin alone since Bach. It is a work of wild contrasts. The Tempo di Ciaconna, the first movement, translates the greatest of Bach's own works for solo violin ... That I should have evoked this magnificent music is a source of infinite satisfaction to me; that I should have played it to Bartók before he died remains one of the great milestones of my life'.[20]

The collaboration between composer and performer is interesting. In Bartók's original conception of the work, the recurring passages in semiquavers in the last movement were to be played in quarter tones — the notes between the semitones of the tempered chromatic scale, which long ago virtually died out in western music, but which are still used in oriental and gipsy music. Bartók gave Menuhin the option of playing these passages in semitones, and since he had only a few weeks to prepare the work for performance he chose the latter. He found the playing of accurate quarter-tones too demanding.

Bartók was dying of leukaemia when he wrote to Menuhin from Asheville, North Carolina:

> I am rather worried about the 'playability' of some of the double-stops, etc. On the last page I give you some of the alternatives. In any case, I should like to have your advice. I sent you two copies. Would you be so kind as to introduce in one of them the necessary changes in bowing, and perhaps the absolutely necessary fingering and other suggestions, and return it to me? And also indicate the impracticable difficulties? I would try to change them.[21]

Menuhin suggested very little changes. Their correspondence is mainly concerned with working out technical points.

The work received its first performance on 26 November at the Carnegie Hall, packed to the rafters, with hundreds of men and women from the armed forces seated upon the stage. Olin Downes of the *New York Times* declared the sonata to be in Bartók's 'latest and most boldly dissonant style . . . The work is a test for the ears, the intelligence, the receptiveness of the most learned listener.' The critics would not commit themselves as to the intrinsic value of the sonata at a single hearing, but with hindsight we now acknowledge it to be one of the great solo works of our time.

Menuhin's next step was to re-establish himself with audiences at home and abroad. He encountered little difficulty in this quarter. His private life also began to take on a more optimistic pattern. His first marriage ended in an amicable divorce and in 1947 he married Diana Gould, 'the beautiful and distinguished dancer,' and they have since 'shared total devotion to each other'.[22]

Menuhin's interest in humanitarian causes has always been as important as his own performances. Shortly after the war he toured Europe with Benjamin Britten as his partner on the piano. One of their saddest appearances was playing to the recently-liberated inmates of the concentration camps. Over the years he has given concerts in support of refugees from war, want, famine and flood in every corner of the world: there is scarcely a country in which he has not appeared. He was invited to India in 1952 at the invitation of the Prime Minister and has since promoted visits of Indian artists to the West. He founded the still-flourishing Gstaad Music Festival in 1957 and, at the invitation of Ian Hunter, took over the artistic direction of the Bath Festival from 1959 to 1968. At Bath he founded a new orchestra and was responsible for bringing many internationally famous artists to perform there. He organized programmes which contained many classic favourites but were always balanced with an infusion of new works, and he introduced many unusual ideas such as Margot Fonteyn and Nureyev dancing to his playing of a movement from Bartók's solo sonata.

Perhaps the achievement that is closest to Menuhin's own heart is the school that bears his name in Stoke d'Abernon in Surrey, founded in 1963 to provide talented youngsters with a full-time musical education. The tutors are drawn from some of the finest string players in the world. Menuhin claims that the chamber music playing in his school is in advance of anything in Russia or the USA.

> The important thing is to train young people so that they can take their place according to their talents. Opportunities dictate the need for soloists, orchestral players, quartet players or teachers. One boy has decided he wants to be a composer. It is also possible that some will go on to university and become ethnomusicologists. That kind of musical background cannot be found everywhere. In Russia and elsewhere they are trained as soloists and if they end up in an orchestra they are disappointed.'[23]

Menuhin applauds the fact that in Britain the democratization of life has had its effect on musical values. The discrepancy between the soloist and the orchestral player or the teacher is nowhere near as great as it used to be. The idea of stratification is now becoming a thing of the past.

> There is [still] specialization of a sort but each one of us is as important as the other and that is what my school is achieving. It is also true that with this broader preparation the young musician can achieve a higher degree of expression and response; a sensitivity in hearing other voices and lending an ear to what happens in the orchestra.[24]

The classic style of Menuhin's own playing is in a direct line from the old Italian masters through Enesco, Marsick, Habeneck and Baillot to Viotti on one side, and through Busch, Hess, Joachim, Böhm, Rode back to Viotti on the other. This is playing where virtuosity takes second place to musicianship, and it is nowhere better displayed than in his sonata performances with his sister Hepzibah, especially of Beethoven.

Menuhin has enriched the art of violin playing in many ways. Perhaps the most compelling example of his art is his playing of the slow movement of the Beethoven concerto. His recordings of the complete set of J.S. Bach's partitas and sonatas for solo violin show not only sensitivity towards the composer but humility towards the music itself.

And yet Menuhin has played Indian music with Ravi Shankar, the celebrated sitar player, and has joined Stephane Grappelli in jazz. He is, above all, a man for all music.

32

The Born Virtuoso

Ruggiero Ricci

Two years after launching the young Menuhin, Persinger brought another Wunderkind before the public of San Francisco, Ruggiero Ricci. Not only has he survived the hazardous transition from prodigy to adult virtuoso without artistic mishap, but is still acknowledged today as one of the world's greatest violinists.

Ruggiero Ricci was born in 1918 in San Bruno, California, the third of seven children of a poor Italian immigrant trombonist. The family had anglicized their name to Rich and, in a burst of enthusiasm, had called their son 'Woodrow Wilson' after the current President of their adopted country. It was only when Ruggiero showed marked musical talent that they reverted to the more mellifluous Italian. But 'Woodrow Wilson Rich' is still the name on Ricci's passport.

Ruggiero received his first musical instruction from his father and cannot remember a time when he did not have a violin in his hands. Not only was there the possibility of his becoming a second Menuhin, but a poor family could use the money earned by a child prodigy. To make an even more convincing display, they lopped two years off the child's age.

When Ruggiero was seven he was auditioned by Persinger but passed over to his assistant, Elizabeth Lackey. So convinced was Persinger of his talent that he arranged for Miss Lackey to take him into her home, thus fulfilling the role of foster-mother and teacher. In addition to his daily lessons the young child also received regular instruction from Persinger and was rewarded by winning a gold medal in a local contest at the age of eight. A year later in 1927, he was awarded the Oscar Weil Scholarship, the youngest contestant in a field of twenty-three aspirants of all ages.

Wearing a black velvet suit and playing a thirty-dollar three-quarter-size fiddle, he gave his first public recital on 15 November 1928 at the Scottish Rite Hall in San Francisco. Accompanied by Persinger on the piano he played music by Vieuxtemps, Saint-Saëns and Wieniawski, rounding off his programme by a dazzling performance of the Mendelssohn concerto. By audience and critics he was hailed as 'nothing short of genius'.

A year later, Ruggiero made his orchestral début playing the Mendelssohn concerto with the Manhattan Symphony Orchestra under Henry Hadley at the Mecca Temple in New York. Olin Downes wrote: 'It was immediately apparent that the boy had something to say, that he was playing with a native fire, musical sensitiveness and taste which are much more phenomenal than the mere physical dexterity . . . It was the playing of one born to play his instrument.'

A capacity audience who had paid a then record $6,000 greeted the ten-year-old Ruggiero for his recital début at the Carnegie Hall the following year. They cheered and cheered and would not let him go. Instead of the usual floral tributes, the young performer was handed a model aeroplane whilst his dressing room was heaped with toys and boxes of sweets.

A series of concert tours throughout the USA brought him countless admirers, but the pressures and loneliness of the travelling prodigy gave him scars in his formative years. He was once the central figure in a legal battle that obliged New York's Mayor 'Jimmy' Walker to cancel a sold-out Carnegie Hall concert whilst charges of 'juvenile exploitation' were brought against his guardian. He once said: 'At nine, some uninhibited critic called me the greatest violinist playing. I have had to fight that kind of competition ever since.' But Ricci has a remedy for precocity: 'First shoot the parents of all prodigies and then put the kid up against the wall and finish the job.'[1]

The London public first heard Ruggiero at the age of fourteen with the London Symphony Orchestra under Sir Hamilton Harty. Critics were loath to believe the extravagant claims made by the American press. But 'He played Mendelssohn's concerto with complete assurance as though he had been born playing it, even as though he were already a little tired of playing it', wrote *The Times* critic. He further praised the child's technical equipment in a series of virtuoso short pieces, and concluded: 'Finally, as an encore he gave an unaccompanied prelude by Bach, and in doing so convinced us of his musical sense more thoroughly than by anything else. Here was something more than the faithful copy of a mature performance. It had spontaneous impulse and rhythmic vitality. It showed the artist in the child.'

Ricci repeated this success in every capital city in Europe. In Berlin, Germany's Chancellor, von Papen, cheered from one box, the playwright Gerhard Hauptmann from another, and Professor Albert Einstein from another. When he played in Budapest under Dohnányi, Kreisler called him the greatest musical genius since Mozart. A more analytical approach to the young Ricci comes from the critic and musicologist Henry Roth, who first heard him at the Hollywood Bowl when he was about fourteen.

After breezing through the difficult Vieuxtemps Concerto No. 5 [with the Hollywood Bowl Orchestra] he returned to play several solos with piano accompaniment, among them the Tchaikovsky-Auer 'Waltz No. 2 from Serenade in C', and Sarasate's 'Introduction and Tarantella'. No doubt about this — it was a blazing violin talent. His tone was large and penetrating, with the intense vibrance necessary for a modern soloist career, and his technique was already of virtuoso proportions. Purity of line, clarity of phrasing and neatness of detail characterized his musical approach, and all was infused with an audacious flair. There was not the imaginative expressiveness and inner spirit of the boy Menuhin, but the Ricci muse had a distinctive aura of its own, rich in the promise blossoming into artistry of extraordinary stature. At that time, the boy Ricci already projected, in adolescent form, the best elements of the adult Ricci.[2]

After some fourteen years of concert-giving with an annual income higher than that of the President of the United States, Ricci, at the age of twenty-four, was called up to serve in the US Army Air Force for three years. He performed frequently in entertainments at army camps and hospitals where no suitable piano was available. This exigency prompted Ricci to explore the unaccompanied literature for his instrument. Impressed with the variety of opportunities for projecting a single interpretative point of view unaffected by the inevitable differences between soloist and accompanist, he made a feature of this form of recital. In November 1946, immediately after his discharge from the forces, he gave a recital at the Town Hall, New York, which included the Bach solo sonata in A minor, Ysaÿe's E minor sonata Op. 27 No. 4, Hindemith's sonata Op. 31 No. 2, two Paganini Caprices, and other unaccompanied pieces by Wieniawski and Kreisler. Since that time Ricci has given unaccompanied recitals in New York, London, Paris and Berlin. He is convinced that there is ample variety in the literature for the solo instrument and that it is especially suitable for highlighting the particularly varied sonorities of the violin.

However, it was through an intense period of study of Paganini that Ricci overcame many of the technical difficulties inherent in the solo repertoire. Consequently he is sometimes branded a Paganini 'expert' by those who cannot, despite the ample proof of history, equate a flawless technique with musicianship. Yet Ricci not only possesses a fine musical mind but is also something of a purist. He is aware that this may stem from an early reaction to Persinger, a very stylish player who loved the *portamento*. Ricci has an aversion to slides and *glissandos*. In his opinion too much 'feeling' can lead to over-interpretation.

As a child, Ricci began to see patterns in music. 'None of my teachers taught me this. I had to find out by myself what they meant.'[3] He began by concentrating on Paganini and his music. He carefully analysed all the twenty-four Caprices, breaking them down into a system so that he could see Paganini's manner of fingering, shifting and bowing. 'I learnt more about technique from Paganini than I did from any of my teachers.'[4] Ricci is one of the few violinists who has played all the Caprices at a single recital. He was also the first to record them, and the records have been selling for over twenty years. Recently he has re-recorded the Caprices on the Direct-Disc recording process: this gives an authentic 'live' performance but is much more exacting than the method of recording normally used, where the best of several 'takes' are assembled for the final disc.

Ricci's tone is round and intense and his *vibrato* can vary at will. His bow arm is extremely powerful. Although his fingers are not long, his hand is broad and his stretch from the lower positions can reach notes high up on the strings. This he achieves by shifting very little and using the thumb as a pivot. As a brilliant technician Ricci has few rivals. His left-hand pizzicato has been described as 'hair-raising', his trills 'electric' and his harmonics 'airily transparent'.[5] His staccatos and *spiccatos* evoke similar superlatives. This technical prowess and perfect intonation has been accomplished by the concentrated practice of scales in thirds, sixths and octaves, and the playing of piano music on the violin. 'Keyboard studies are invaluable for developing technique on the fiddle, especially extensions.' Milstein also shares this opinion. These two violinists once took the same train together on a long journey and entertained each other by playing all the Chopin Études, which they both knew from memory.

The effect of Ricci's brilliant technical gifts tends to obscure other facets of his career. It is not always recognized that he has another image in which he stands on common ground with Joachim and Szigeti, that of a programme innovator. His is probably the largest and most original repertoire of any living violinist. A recital he gave in 1969 included the Prokoviev sonata for two violins, a set of songs for soprano and violin by Villa-Lobos, and the Saint-Saëns 'Fantasie' for violin and harp. His unusual programme building struck Ronald Crichton of the London *Financial Times* as 'a taste eclectic and enquiring to a degree rarely found in star violinists or indeed in star performers of any kind'. Ricci was the first to perform in New York the D major sonata for unaccompanied violin by Prokofiev. In 1964 he played fifteen great violin concertos in a series of four concerts in New York, tracing the influences from the baroque to the avant-garde, and in 1977 he partnered Ernest Bitetti in a programme of duos for violin and guitar. With the New York Philharmonic under Bernstein he gave the world premiére of a violin concerto by Ginastera. Gottfried von Einem, Alexander Goehr and Joseph White have all received first performances of their works by Ricci. In 1978, Gerard Schurmann worked closely with Ricci when composing his first violin concerto, written to celebrate the violinist's fifty years on the concert platform.

On the platform the diminutive Ricci — he is only five feet four — is an undemonstrative performer. Everything appears to fall into place with the utmost ease. And yet he does not over-practise any work before a concert, especially Romantic music. 'I can *play* Romantic music but I can't practise it. If my performance has to be emotionally spontaneous then I must walk on to the platform ready to be spontaneous. It is the only time that I really surprise myself.'[6]

Surprise is an element never far from Ricci's daily life. More than once he has tucked his fiddle under his chin at a rehearsal about to play a Mozart concerto, only to find the orchestra striking up one by the same composer but in a different key. Fortunately he has always managed to switch over in time.

But there was another occasion when Ricci was due to play in Boston and had arranged with the management to leave after the final item without playing an encore. He had a plane to catch for Lisbon within an hour of the finishing time. The recital went well until he had played the final movement of the last item. He was greeted with a chilling silence. He stood for a minute thinking his audience might be too moved to applaud, but no-one moved a muscle. He laughed nervously and retreated from the stage. During the drive to the airport the manager asked: 'Why didn't you play the last two movements of the Hindemith sonata?' Ricci gasped. 'Hindemith! I was playing the Prokofiev!'[7]

Ricci is not only a prodigy who has survived: he is one of the few great violinists who concentrates all his energies on performing. So many top-ranking artists of today have commitments outside their platform appearances; but teaching apart, Ricci lays no claims to anything but 'fiddling'.

Exhaustive researches into the art of technique have led Ricci to a knowledge and execution that have few equals. His dazzling but always *musical* performances of some of the most difficult pieces in the repertoire remain among the best of modern recordings. Ricci is concerned about some of the attitudes of today:

> Somehow there has been for some time a stigma on virtuosity as though it were socially unacceptable. But this is nonsense. It should signify that one is master of one's instrument. The fiddle is a virtuoso instrument. When you start going in the opposite direction you eradicate the fiddle. In the years since World War II when soloists stopped playing short pieces, we began to lose our audiences. We started to play sonatas at every recital, and the people who wanted to hear virtuoso pieces stayed away. Fortunately I think they are beginning to change this rigid attitude to programme building. Recently I heard Kremer, the great Russian violinist, play 'The Last Rose of Summer' and it was beautiful.[8]

'I love the violin as Kreisler played it,' says Ricci, 'and I would rather hear "Liebesleid" played well than Beethoven played badly.' Like his eminent predecessor, Ricci can do justice to both composers.

33

'Aim high — aim at beauty'

Ginette Neveu;
Ida Haendel

In Flesch's Paris studio Ida Haendel recalls her first meeting with another of his pupils, a young woman of about sixteen. Only seven years old, Ida was overawed by the girl's great height and strong build. Her deep, husky voice, close-cropped hair and wide neck made her look very masculine. When she attacked the Wieniawski F sharp minor concerto, Ida was dumbfounded. 'I stared at her fascinated, and, child though I was, I realized that I was listening to an extraordinary artist, totally dedicated to music and absorbed in it to the exclusion of all else ... Even then her playing was intense and passionate, her tone large and *vibrato* wide ... Her dramatic approach had the impact of a volcano.'[1] The girl was Ginette Neveu.

Ginette was born in Paris into a musical family of several generations. Her father was an amateur string player and her mother a teacher of the violin. Her brother Jean was a fine pianist who later became her accompanist.

Whilst a baby in her pram, Ginette could sing tunes after a single hearing. As a small child she was taken to a concert and on hearing the music of Chopin, was moved to tears. She was given a quarter-size violin, and received her first instruction from her mother. Her swift progress merited further study with Madame Talluel at the École Supérieur de Musique, already with a view to entering the Paris Conservatoire in the near future. Madame Talluel recalled that at the age of five Ginette displayed sensational gifts, and possessed a capacity for work quite unique in so young a child. She would practise quite easy phrases some fifty times, and if Madame said 'Enough', Ginette would argue. 'But it has got to be beautiful'.[2]

When she was seven Ginette made her concert début at the Salle Gaveau in Paris, playing the Max Bruch concerto. Two years later she won both the first prize at the École Supérieure de Musique and the Prix d'Honneur awarded by the City of Paris for her playing of the Mendelssohn concerto. As a result, she was invited to play the Nardini and Mendelssohn concertos at Winterthur in Switzerland under Ernst Walter. She was described as 'Mozart in petticoats who already possesses a very extensive technique, a full, even tone of great beauty, masterly bowing, clear-cut articulation'.[3]

On her return to Paris she took some lessons from Enesco, who was greatly impressed by her fire. One day, when working on the Bach Chaconne, Enesco stopped her and said 'I don't play that passage like that.' Without batting an eyelid, Ginette replied 'I play this music as I understand it; not in a way which escapes my comprehension.'[4] Enesco would not have taken such a retort from anyone but Ginette. He simply smiled and motioned that she should continue.

In November 1930 Ginette was accepted at the Conservatoire under Jules, and she also studied composition with Nadia Boulanger. In June of the following year she won the Premier Prix. Such a triumph had not occurred since Wieniawski carried off the prize fifty years before. The following year she went in for the Vienna International Competition and came fourth. The disappointment was to have an interesting sequel. One of the adjudicators on the panel was so impressed by her playing that he sent a message scribbled on the back of a visiting card to her hotel. It said: 'If you can come to Berlin, I undertake, without any thought of personal gain, to make myself responsible for the young violinist's musical education.' It was from Carl Flesch.[5]

All the family resources had been used up for the trip to Vienna so two years elapsed before Ginette and her mother were able to make the trip to Berlin. When Flesch heard her play for the second time he said: 'My child, you have received a gift from heaven, and I have no wish to touch it. All I can do for you is to give you some purely technical advice.'[6] Ginette studied for four years with Flesch in Germany and Belgium, and regarded it as the most important period in her life.

At sixteen she entered the Warsaw Competition and won first prize, with the twenty-six-year-old David Oistrakh in second place. She took the Germans by storm when she made her début in Hamburg, playing the Brahms concerto under Jochum. Ginette Neveu was now acclaimed all over Europe as a virtuoso of the first rank. From Germany, she went to Russia, where she met with the same adulation, from Moscow to Baku. In the latter town she played to an audience of ten thousand in an outdoor amphitheatre, with the temperature well up into the nineties. At every stop on the fifteen thousand mile train journey she was presented with a bouquet of flowers, so that by the end of the journey there was no room in her compartment even to sit, let alone practise her violin.

Berlin, Paris, Amsterdam — all clamoured to hear this brilliant girl, and life was a constant round of packing and travelling. In 1936 she crossed the Atlantic and the Americans could not find words to express their delight in her playing.

When war broke out in 1939, Neveu continued concert-giving in France until the German occupation of 1940 put a stop to her travelling. During this time she led a secluded life in her studio, practising and writing; she was a composer of some substance. Occasionally she gave a concert. The Germans offered her enormous fees to undertake a concert tour from Berlin to Stuttgart, but she refused categorically. In the four years of occupation, except for a few concerts, she kept out of the public eye.

For her London orchestral début on 24 March 1945 at the Royal Albert Hall she chose the Beethoven concerto. *The Strad* commented on her 'masterly technique, with a phenomenal range of tone values and a bow-arm which is a joy to watch'. The following year, in the same hall, she played the Brahms concerto with the Ravel 'Tzigane' as an encore. The *Daily Mail* critic wrote: 'Her performance is the best we have heard since Kreisler. I know no woman violinist, and very few men, to equal her.'[7]

For the next three years, Neveu had the world at her feet. Of her New York début at the Carnegie Hall on 13 November 1947, Virgil Thomson, that most exacting of American critics, wrote:

Ginette Neveu ... is the finest, from every point of view, of the younger European artists whom we have had the pleasure of hearing since the war ... She is a great artist because she has tone, technique and temperament. And she is an interesting artist because she has rhythm and a special intensity of communication all her own. It is not often that we hear the Brahms Violin Concerto read with such breadth and nobility and withal so graciously.

The following year, after her one appearance with the Philadelphia

Symphony Orchestra under Ormandy, he wrote: 'Ginette Neveu is unquestionably the greatest woman violinist there is and I will go so far as to claim that she is one of the greatest violinists of our time.'[8] Everywhere she went, Neveu had the same effect upon audiences. After she appeared in Budapest, the city where violin playing is in the blood, one critic wrote: 'Two of the greatest present-day violinists do not add up to one Ginette Neveu.' When the French Ambassador saw her off on the station platform, he said, 'You have done more for our country than I can do myself.'[9]

Despite having been trained by Flesch and Enesco, Ginette Neveu represented no one particular school. She borrowed from the French, Belgian or Russian schools whatever seemed to suit her best by way of solving technical problems. The only difficulty she ever encountered was that of staccato; in this respect she experimented for many years to attain the absolute perfection that became her hallmark.

Her manner of holding the bow baffled all authorities on violin playing. One day she would hold it like Heifetz, another like Francescatti: sometimes she appeared to bow like Thibaud. A Viennese critic who had observed this enigma wrote:

> What one finds so fascinating about her is the perfect harmony which exists between her actual playing and her very remarkable personality. Without showing the slightest bias towards any particular school, her right hand with incomparable concentration and guided by a noble sensitive mind, governs all the technical variations of tone. But the tone which, in all its splendour, forms the melody, and that incredible assurance with which she handles her bow in a diabolical pizzicato are not the only outstanding characteristics of the personality of Ginette Neveu. To create and re-create; there lies her talent.[10]

As a person, Ginette Neveu was a curious mixture. From an early age she had possessed the gift of being able to withdraw into isolation, showing a mask of seeming indifference to the outside world. Her spiritual strength came from within. Before going on to the concert platform she would make a point of being quite alone in the artists' room in order to prepare herself for performance.

In complete contrast was the vigorous, vivacious, fearless young woman with seemingly boundless energy who walked for miles, swam, rode and played ping-pong and was a superb chess player. On holiday she was gregarious and game for anything.

Everything Ginette did was intensive and on a large scale. She would say 'Aim high — aim at beauty'[11]: this was her maxim for life and for music — which were for her inseparable.

She would jot down random thoughts in a notebook. Her scruples cannot be better defined than in the following excerpt:

> To play well, to play better, that must be the sole aim of a virtuoso; a matter of prime importance to the concert artist is an individuality which must ever become more clearly defined. As far as I am concerned, the truly technical problems which are the most disconcerting and the most fruitful are those posed by composers who have a strong personality and pursue the essence of their musical idea to its logical conclusion without wasting too much sympathy on the performer.[12]

At the height of her phenomenally successful career, at the age of thirty, Ginette Neveu met her death in a plane crash in the Azores on the way to America. Clutching her precious Stradivari to her chest, she 'died as she lived, with the wheels of her life in full motion'.[13] Her brother Jean died with her. Ginette had just written in her notebook:

> Nothing great is achieved without the solitude of vocation, and true greatness is, perhaps, radiant solitude . . . Men are sometimes faint-hearted because they fear death. But death is something sublime which one must deserve according to the life and the ideals one has within oneself. This sad sojourn which we make on this earth is but a time of great suffering which men have no wish to accept.[14]

'Her skill is remarkable even in the days when violinists seem to be born with a command of the fingerboard that their forebears achieved only after long and industrious study. There was no sense of strain or lack of polish in her playing of the most florid passages of the concerto and the cadenza. More striking still in one so young was the justness of an interpretation which suggested not only a ripe lesson and young energy, but temperamental force.'

So wrote Ferrucio Bonavia in the *Daily Telegraph* on 1 February 1937, after Ida Haendel's orchestral début at the Queen's Hall playing the Brahms concerto under Sir Henry Wood. She was nine years old.

More than forty years later, she is still playing in a ceaseless round of concerts, recitals and recordings all over the world. She is one of the few child prodigies who has fulfilled her early promise as an adult performer, and is today recognized as one of the world's greatest violinists.

Ida Haendel was born in 1928 into a poor Jewish family in the little Polish town of Chelm. Her father had himself wanted to play the violin but was forbidden to do so by an over-zealous and strict orthodox parent who was convinced that fiddlers only played at weddings. Nathan Haendel ran away from home and eventually became a painter, but his own frustrated ambition prompted him to vow that if ever he had a child with musical talent he would do everything within his power to guide and develop it. At the age of three and a half Ida picked up her sister's violin and taught herself to play perfectly by ear. Her father then knew his pledge had to be kept. Over the years, Nathan Haendel has had many accusations levelled at him for over-protectiveness and for his prodigious shaping of his daughter's career. But ambition and talent are tempting partners, and when a father is faced with an abundance of the latter in his own child, it is difficult to isolate his motives.

In the first few years of her life, Ida's accomplishments were phenomenal. At the age of four she was accepted without fees at the Chopin School of Music in Warsaw under Michalowicz, an ex-pupil of Auer at St Petersburg, who was also Huberman's teacher. A year later, she won the first prize in the Huberman Competition, playing the Beethoven concerto.

The Haendels went to Paris in 1935 with the intention of studying with Szigeti, who had heard Ida in Warsaw. But his plans were suddenly changed. Fortunately, through a chance meeting with Ignace, brother of the pianist, Artur Rubinstein, contact was made with Carl Flesch. The latter was so impressed he agreed to teach Ida for nothing. After only a short period of tuition Ida returned to Warsaw to enter the National Competition, and carried off the first Polish prize for her playing of the Wieniawski concerto in D minor.

Flesch never considered it necessary to give Ida technical exercises: he put her straight away on the Paganini Caprices. The first piece she ever studied with him was Sarasate's 'Carmen Fantasie', and she played it entirely to Flesch's satisfaction before one of his terrifying little audiences. But when Flesch introduced Ida to the classics, she who played the most difficult virtuoso pieces without experiencing technical difficulty came up against a new and unexpected problem. Flesch gave her the Kreutzer sonata, which she learned in a matter of hours. But when

Ginette Neveu, a
brilliant Flesch pupil
who died tragically at
thirty

The Polish-born Ida
Haendel, also a Flesch
pupil

confronted with a pianist as partner instead of accompanist, she was hopelessly out of step. Flesch was furious. Later that evening Ida asked her father if all those dashes and numbers could possibly mean something. He gasped. 'Do you mean to say you didn't know?' 'Of course not!' retorted Ida. 'Nobody told me!'[15] This poor little wonder child could not read music properly; so perfect was her memory that no one ever doubted that she was acquainted with the theory of music. This exigency was soon remedied. 'As soon as I had mastered a work technically, no other problems existed. I played musically by instinct ... It took me years to understand that it was necessary to analyse and study the thoughts, structure and style which make up a great composition by a great composer.'[16]

Ida's Paris début took place in 1935 at a recital at the Salle Gaveau when she was only seven years old; her first professional concert appearance was at the Casino in Monte Carlo. Following these successes, Flesch, then resident in London, considered that Ida was ready for her concert début in that city. The Haendels duly arrived, but were painfully short of money. Nathan Haendel painted portraits and Ida made some pocket money by playing occasionally at fashionable houses. Flesch eventually brought the Haendels into contact with the impresario Harold Holt, who obtained an engagement for Ida to play at a Beecham Sunday Concert. But a serious problem arose. In England, at this time, no child under fourteen was allowed on the concert platform. To wait another four years would have been disastrous, so Harold Holt falsified her age and told the papers that a mistake had been made. It worked, but the fact remains that Ida Haendel was a fully-fledged virtuoso at the age of ten.

Even as a child, Ida Haendel was aware of the isolation of the prodigy: 'The more I was left to myself the more I withdrew; as I grew older, I built a wall round me ever more difficult for others to penetrate. I have now come to the conclusion that the upbringing of an artist, particularly one who begins as a prodigy, leads to a life of loneliness and introspection. The fact that one doesn't go to school, where a child first learns to mix and integrate, must also have a bearing on the problem.'[17]

Her first recital at the Queen's Hall, with Ivor Newton as her accompanist, was not an unqualified success. Flesch had borrowed a full-sized Stradivari violin from one of his pupils for the occasion but it was too large for Ida's tiny hands. For the first time in her life she was nervous and even fluffed a passage in the Mozart concerto. Although the critics were on the cautious side, they admitted that she was a remarkably gifted child and played with great skill. However, Ida had a violin of the right size when she played the Brahms concerto in February 1937, on which performance a comment has already been quoted.

In the summer of that year the Haendels felt the need for a family reunion and decided to take a trip to Poland. Flesch protested that Ida now needed his guidance more than ever, and told them that if they persisted in their plan, he would wash his hands of them. Undaunted, they ignored his threats. In Paris *en route*, Ida had the opportunity to have some lessons with Enesco. She recalls: 'The difference between Flesch and Enesco is difficult to assess. Flesch was a fabulous teacher and knew exactly how to correct your faults. He was like a surgeon in that he could pin-point exactly what you needed to do, and he made sure that you understood. Enesco would not waste time telling you that it should be this way or that; he would show you, get you to try to see what he was driving at, and then he would say "Go home and get it right". And somehow you did.'[18] When Flesch heard about the lessons with Enesco, he took umbrage, and wrote Mr. Haendel a sharp letter of protest. When they met again in London, Flesch told him that it was a slur on his reputation if a pupil of his went to another teacher. He refused to concede he had washed his hands of them. However, lessons were resumed and the incident was forgotten.

During the war years Ida Haendel travelled throughout Britain giving concerts to the troops, to the wounded in hospital, and in factory canteens. When hostilities ceased she began touring the USA and Canada and went to South Africa in 1949. She achieved phenomenal success on her first visit to the Soviet Union in 1959.

Although she has been on the concert platform for more than forty years, Ida Haendel's playing has never become stale or even predictable. Each performance is a new experience and her total commitment to the music itself is liable to send the toughest critic home in a state of euphoria. After her performance of the Beethoven with the Montreal Symphony Orchestra in October 1975, Jacob Siskind of the *Montreal Gazette* admits arriving home 'totally lost for words'. He was completely unprepared for the performance, despite the fact that Haendel had played the same work several times before in the area. It was 'inspired far beyond what I have heard from this fine artist before. The finale, so often an anticlimax . . . was hewn from flawless marble, and the entire reading was capped with a sense of inevitability that swept the listener along until resistance was impossible'.[19]

The Brahms concerto is considered by many to be one of Ida Haendel's prime achievements. Although she has played it since childhood, much of the maturity in her interpretation was brought about by her association with the Rumanian conductor Sergiu Celibidache. Her recording of this concerto in London with Celibidache was 'undoubtedly . . . a landmark in my life as a musician'.[20] At the time it was a bestseller and in her opinion it still is the most outstanding performance of her life.

> Celibidache . . . brought an incomparable grandeur and breadth of line to the music. My real worship of Brahms began then. Brahms now seemed the most integral of composers to me, with his wealth of heart-rending themes and original harmonies. I felt a stirring of the soul with Brahms when he was lyrical, as with no other composer: and his structural designs which were of breath-taking grandeur, quickened my pulse and made me giddy.[21]

Although she exudes confidence without conceit on the concert platform, Ida Haendel is a shy and private person offstage. She speaks eight languages and reads a good deal. Tiny, with beautiful grey-green eyes that dominate her pale face, she has a warmth of personality which is rewarding in personal contact. A simple and direct person, she has none of the affectations that sometimes attend success. For her, indifference is the cardinal sin; an affront to human dignity.

34

The Elder Statesman

Isaac Stern

For 'a life's work dedicated to music and devoted to humanity',[1] Isaac Stern received the first Albert Schweitzer Award in 1975. As 'the elder statesman' of violin playing, there is probably no other figure on the American violin scene today who is more respected by his colleagues. His ability as a performer is taken for granted. But he is also a tireless organizer in musical affairs, from saving the Carnegie Hall to finding a dentist for an immigrant prodigy.

Isaac Stern was born in 1920 in Kriminiesz, a small town on the Polish-Russian border and brought to San Francisco when he was a few months old. His musical studies began with the piano when he was six, but two years later, when he heard a neighbour practising the violin he decided that he preferred that instrument. He entered the San Francisco Conservatoire of Music and studied with Naoum Blinder, leader of the San Francisco Symphony Orchestra. Blinder was a pupil of Brodsky who had studied with Hellmesberger in Vienna, thus forming a direct link with Viotti through his teacher Robberechts. When he was fifteen, Isaac made his début playing the Bach double concerto with his teacher and the San Francisco Symphony Orchestra.

The young Stern subsequently gave a number of recitals in Pacific coast cities and appeared with the Los Angeles Symphony Orchestra. His New York recital début came in October 1937, when he was seventeen. At the New York Town Hall with Arpad Sandor accompanying him at the piano, he played an ambitious programme which included Tartini's 'Devil's Trill' Sonata and the Glazunov concerto, and attracted a large audience. The *New York*

Isaac Stern, philanthropic virtuoso

Ruggiero Ricci, whose repertoire is perhaps largest of any living virtuoso's

Times praised the 'extent of his technique and his spirited straight forward playing', but was critical of the fact that 'his bow presses too hard and vibrates the string too little', arguing that it gave 'a fine sonority on the lower strings but frequent stridency in upper registers'.[2] Stern's New York recital the following year was declared an unqualified success by public and critics alike. His career as a concert artist of the first rank had begun.

If asked today exactly where or when these early concerts took place, Stern is himself unable to say with accuracy. He has never collected press cuttings, nor requested an agent to do so, because he has never felt they would be of any interest to anyone but himself.

After the age of seventeen, Stern had no more formal lessons. He says: 'I was responsible for my own mistakes. It is a process of intellectual and personal involvement with music as an idea and a way of life, not as a profession or career, but a rapport with people who think and feel and care about something — you have to find your own way of thinking, feeling and caring.'[3] That this philosophy had borne fruit was evident at his Carnegie Hall recital début in 1943. The *New York Times* was in no doubt this time. 'He produced a voluminous, round, singing tone from the strings capable of a wide range of dynamic effects and most sensitive gradations. The bow was under admirable control, the left hand unswervingly accurate. It seems the youthful artist made known every asset needed for the negotiation of the exacting compositions he had chosen to expound.'[4] The programme included the Bach G minor sonata for unaccompanied violin, the Mozart sonata in E minor and the Brahms D minor.

In the intervening years Isaac Stern has played with almost every major orchestra in the world and under most of the great conductors. This versatile artist has recorded virtually all the significant classical and contemporary violin literature and has appeared on TV and in films — once as Ysaÿe in 'Tonight We Sing'.

Stern is not only a great violinist, but an accomplished musician. For him, the two are as inextricably linked as a man with his own shadow. Stern is familiar with the orchestral score of any music he undertakes. He can relate his own phrasing and style to the orchestral requirements, and has the patience to work with the players until everyone is satisfied. He is aware of the structure of the music and instinctively feels the harmonies underlying every phrase. For him 'the inevitability of the harmonic structure is automatically part and parcel of the ear'.[5] It must then follow that the same principle applies to the hand. It is for this reason that Stern's phrasing has such meaning. There is a deep logic underlying each phrase. If asked he could probably give a reason for every note he plays.

As a musician he is totally committed to the composer's intentions as he understands them. If we first observe Stern playing Mozart and he then turns to Tchaikovsky we see that not only does his style change but his face and body also are transformed. It is the total commitment to the music that is the hallmark of his interpretations.

How and why did this development take place? Stern believes that his earliest and most important musical influences were playing chamber music with members of the San Francisco Symphony Orchestra. 'I was the young kid around town who played the fiddle not too badly, who was interested, and the older men took me through the entire chamber music repertoire.'[6] Stern has retained a lifelong interest in chamber music. Even today, with spare time reduced to a minimum, he will find three friends to play quartets. At the end of the longest day, these sessions have been known to extend well into the night. The public side of this chamber music passion is the famous Trio with pianist Eugène Istomin and cellist Leonard Rose, one of the most sought-after ensembles in the USA. They have recorded the complete trios of Beethoven, Brahms and Schubert and made television films of the complete Beethoven and Brahms.

For most of his performing life, Stern has been in constant contact with two of the most important influences in the world of string playing: Casals and Galamian. His close personal and professional relationship with Galamian must have coloured his ideas on violin playing, especially from the analytical aspect. Stern was playing chamber music with Casals at Prades when the latter was in his prime. Someone once remarked that you could not sit in the same room with Casals and emerge unchanged. Many of Stern's approaches to music resemble those of Casals. A story told about him could as easily apply to Stern. A conductor once asked: 'Maître, what tempo would you like?' Casals chewed his pipe and replied quietly, 'The *right* one.'[7] This is the essence of Stern. Whatever he plays is right for him. And at the time, for the listener, there is no other way.

This single mindedness is another of the ingrained qualities in Stern. It is epitomized in his efforts to save the Carnegie Hall. In 1959 civilized America was shocked by the announcement that the owners of the Carnegie Hall had contracted to have it demolished in order to erect a new building on the site. A deadline was set for May 1960 to complete negotiations. Isaac Stern immediately approached the Mayor of New York. On discovering that Federal aid was not possible, he swiftly gathered together a group of people interested in a campaign to save the hall. On the eve of his departure for an extended European tour, Stern held a meeting at his home and the Citizens Committee for Carnegie Hall became a reality.

As a result of the Committee's prompt action two bills were passed by the State Legislature and, as a measure of support for the approval of the City's Board of Estimate, the Committee sent a telegram to Mayor Wagner of New York: 'To destroy Carnegie Hall now for "practical reasons" is an act of irresponsibility damaging to the United States and our prestige in the entire civilized world.'[8] Signatures included Casals, Bernstein, Piatigorsky, Heifetz, Horowitz, Ormandy, Szell, Kreisler, Elman, Munch and Stern.

Authorization for the hall's acquisition was obtained in April 1960. In May, the Board of the Carnegie Hall Corporation was formed with Isaac Stern as President. At the historic reopening concert on 25 September, with the New York Philharmonic Orchestra conducted by Bernstein, Stern flew to New York in between performances in Geneva and London in order to take part. This was the culmination of countless projects to raise millions of dollars, that had been organized in every detail by Stern. He arranged a gala concert in which many international star performers in the musical world participated: for example, Fischer-Dieskau was accompanied on the piano by Horowitz. But on the other hand, no organization was too small to be approached personally by Stern, if he thought they could help in the campaign.

Stern has another important role— that of fairy godfather to promising youngsters:

> It gives me particular pleasure to hear the magnificent work, the power, the brilliance, the authority, the joy of young colleagues like Pinchas Zukerman, Itzhak Perlman, Miriam Fried, Sergiu Luca and others ... all these young people we heard when they were little

children . . . To be on the stage next to them from time to time, to see these healthy, vital, gifted young people carrying on traditional violin playing as brilliantly as they do, and to know you have been a part of it . . . to me is the greatest of all satisfactions.[9]

Stern is aware that standards of performance are continually rising, and that competition for places at the top is fiercer than it has ever been. But he thinks that we sometimes underestimate the giants of the past — Huberman, Kreisler, Joachim, Sarasate. He says:

These men not only had the agility and grace but they had a mastery and a kind of majestic authority over their playing that stamped them as very special people. It's this individuality I think that we see less of today except in a very few cases. I think that one of the things that pleases me most about the young people that I've mentioned is that each of them plays well but entirely different. Each has an individual view, an individual approach. But one thing they have in common — they don't *ask* you to listen . . . they demand your ears.[10]

Stern's playing reflects this approach; feet firmly planted on the earth, but with a spirit that soars in a common emotion that all can share. Stern has never seen the need to invent the wheel, musically. His roots are positively and healthily in the past; the Classical and nineteenth-century masters have all been his teachers. He has also heard and learned from as many contemporary influences as possible and then found a personal self. Then, and only then, can the total commitment begin: the total commitment that is the beginning of artistry. For as Stern says with characteristic logic: 'If you do not speak with the violin, and just play it, you might as well get a machine to do it better.'[11]

35

The Musician's Musician

Arthur Grumiaux

For Arthur Grumiaux, virtuosity is a means to an end. The musicality of his performance is always the main consideration. As the natural successor to Vieuxtemps, Ysaÿe and César Thomson in the great Belgian school, Grumiaux is one of the most important violinists of our time. His faithful interpretations of the classics and his musicianly readings of modern works have exerted considerable influence not only upon his contemporaries but on the younger generation as well. In an age when everyone aspires to play like Heifetz, it is refreshing to find a violinist who strikes a harmonious balance between virtuosity and the musical demands of the composer.

Arthur Grumiaux was born in 1921 in the little village of Villers-Perwin in the Walloon province of Brabant in Belgium. Brought up in the home of his maternal grandparents, it was his grandfather, an all-round, self-taught musician, who first aroused his interest in music. At the age of three he was discovered trying to imitate violin playing by using two pieces of wood. Even with these primitive substitutes, his grandfather noticed the child's keen sense of rhythm in manipulating the 'bow' with exactitude. He bought him a quarter-size fiddle and bow, and gave him some lessons on the instrument together with some elementary instruction in the rudiments of music. Arthur quickly mastered the notes of the scale and within a few days astonished his grandfather by revealing that he possessed the gift of perfect pitch — by naming the notes of the church bells.

Arthur's first concert took place when he was five, in a cinema that held eight hundred people. The audience responded warmly and he was asked to play the National Anthem, the Brabançonne, to end the programme. After a few bars he stopped, complaining that everyone was sitting down. He refused to continue until they were all standing. They not only obeyed his command but remained on their feet to cheer. His reward was a large rocking-horse which he 'rode home triumphantly'[1], entrusting his precious violin to his grandfather. It was the first time it had been out of his hands.

A year later Arthur began lessons on the piano and made such good progress with his combined musical studies that he was admitted to the Conservatoire of Music at Charleroi at the age of six, the normal age of entry being eleven. Five years later he graduated with the highest honours for *both* instruments equally, and was then given a place at the Conservatoire in Brussels. At this point, a heartbreaking choice had to be made between piano and violin since it was impossible to pursue the study of both instruments in addition to the general curriculum. Arthur refused to decide. Finally his grandfather took the matter in hand and chose the violin.

Under the 'admirable teaching and kindness'[2] of Alfred Dubois, a former pupil of Ysaÿe, the boy progressed so well that at fourteen he made his début at the Palais des Beaux Arts in Brussels, playing concertos by Vieuxtemps and Paganini. In 1939, after winning the Prix Vieuxtemps, the eighteen-year-old Grumiaux took Dubois' advice and went to Paris to attend the Enesco summer master-classes in June and July. Grumiaux says: 'The contact with this great master and the privilege of playing before him, and the atmosphere he created in the class, revealed to me that indispensable serenity which is an integral part of the works of the great composers.'[3]

Now ready to embark upon an international career, he returned to Brussels to receive the Special Prize for Virtuosity created by the Belgian Government. He remains today the sole recipient of the honour. The outbreak of war disrupted all plans. The occupation forces decreed that all students and performing artists must apply every three months for exemption from enforced factory work. Grumiaux was appointed assistant to Dubois and managed to obtain some respite. The Germans were not slow to recognize his worth and put pressure on him to become leader of the Dresden State Orchestra. Patriotic reasons prevented him accepting and he was forced to go underground into hiding. From this time he lived the life of a fugitive, flitting from house to house to escape capture until the arrival of the British Army of Liberation.

Following closely behind the British Army came ENSA, the unit responsible for organizing entertainment for the troops. Their musical director, Walter Legge, promptly arranged auditions for Belgian artists. As soon as Legge heard Grumiaux he offered him engagements in Europe and in Britain. The artists who travelled under the auspices of ENSA were a devoted group of international performers who gave concerts wherever it was possible to set up a stage or platform, however primitive. The 'theatre' could be anything from a tent or a factory canteen to a hospital ward. Conditions were sometimes appalling, with freezing halls and cramped, makeshift dressing rooms. At other times the surroundings were almost luxurious, such as Grumiaux's own first concert for ENSA at the Ghent Opera House, when he played the Mendelssohn concerto under Barbirolli. But rehearsals were almost unknown. Grumiaux recalls: 'There was no time for niceties in these troubled times. Sometimes we played under gun-fire and with bombs dropping at the same time. In Holland it was particularly bad.[4]

So impressed was Legge with Grumiaux's playing that he signed him up for his first recording contract with His Master's Voice, and made him a present of the score of William Walton's violin concerto, a romantic work with a solo part of phenomenal difficulty. Grumiaux mastered the work within three weeks for its first European performance on 14 February 1945. The programme survives in a faded sheet of pale green duplicating paper with the information that the concert is organized by NAAFI (Navy, Army, Air Force Institutes), and that they present the Belgian National Orchestra conducted by Constant Lambert.

The concerto had been written for Heifetz, who gave the first performance in Cleveland, Ohio, in December 1937. But he had also reserved the performing rights for two years, so it was not heard in Britain until 1941, when Henry Holst played it in London with the composer conducting. Grumiaux has since made the Walton his own, and has played it under most of the great conductors, and also with the composer.

When the war ended, Grumiaux's reputation quickly spread throughout Europe. Of a performance of the Brahms concerto conducted by Sir Adrian Boult at the Albert Hall on 6 March 1946, *The Times* critic wrote:

His classical purity, alike in style, tone and intonation, was balanced by a romantic warmth, while on the rhythmic side of the account his phrasing was supple, and withal beautifully moulded, without liberties being taken with the time. Could any combination of qualities better suit Brahms?

Grumiaux first crossed the Atlantic in 1951 and made his début in Boston playing the Mozart concerto in G (K. 216) and Ravel's 'Tzigane' with the Boston Symphony conducted by Ernest Ansermet. It was a triumph. At his next appearance, with the Chicago Symphony Orchestra conducted by Rafael Kubelik, the 'no encores' rule for soloists had to be relaxed because the audience refused to stop applauding until Grumiaux put his violin back under his chin.

The following season Grumiaux was invited back as guest soloist with six of America's leading orchestras, whose conductors had heard him in Europe. He had now become identified with the Mozart concerto K. 216 and was always asked to play it. The *Minneapolis Morning Tribune* commented: 'He has that subtle knack of within-the-phrase varying of tone colour and weight that creates a cogent and significant musical sentence ... The whispered cadenza of the second movement had all the customers breathless.' Another critic wrote: 'Everything was played with a silken tone which seemed to come from the instrument without any effort on the part of the performer.'[5]

In the mid-fifties Grumiaux gave the first modern performance of the rediscovered Paganini Concerto No. 4 in D minor. Originally performed by Paganini in Paris, it was then lost. Obsessed by his constant fear of theft, Paganini had separated the solo and orchestral parts and deposited them in different places. An Italian collector named Gallini subsequently came into possession of the solo part. Many years later the orchestral score was found amongst a bunch of papers offered for sale by a beggar, and eventually acquired by Gallini. Grumiaux performed the concerto at the Salle Pleyel in Paris on 7 November 1954, with the Lamoureux Orchestra directed by Gallini, son of the collector. A recording was made the following day. So great was the advance demand for this disc that it was issued within three days of the performance.

Grumiaux today is in constant demand all over the world, though unfortunately he is seldom heard in Britain. His recordings include a number of classic performances, for example the

Bach sonatas and partitas for solo violin. But it is his sensitive playing of Mozart that has won him the respect and admiration of his colleagues. His line, his attention to detail and immaculate phrasing, allied to the emotional expression that is an integral part of Mozart's music, seem to be inborn. His recording of the Mozart concertos made in Vienna for the Mozart Jubilee in 1956 is a masterpiece. The slow movement of the divertimento for string trio (K. 563) must surely be one of the great moments of recorded sound. François Poulenc, after hearing Grumiaux play Mozart, wrote: 'I have for a few seconds tasted the great and exceptional delight of shedding tears of joy.'[6]

Shortly before he died Dinu Lipatti wrote to Grumiaux asking him to form a duo to record the sonatas of Bach, Beethoven and Brahms. But the untimely death of Lipatti occurred before they were able to meet to work together. Shortly afterwards Grumiaux met Clara Haskil at the Pablo Casals Festival in Prades. Here they played together in the first of innumerable concerts. The recordings they made of the sonatas by Mozart and Beethoven are examples not only of superb musicianship, but of the rapport that must exist between artists in such an undertaking. Grumiaux sets great store by his friendship with Clara Haskil. For him it was one of those professional associations that happen only once in a lifetime. He says: 'At our first session we rehearsed for less than an hour and were then ready to record. In our approach to the works we had a complete unity of views and feeling.'[7]

In this respect, Grumiaux has a distinct advantage over most of his colleagues. He has always played the piano and is equally familiar with both parts of a duo. Ample proof of his double ability exists in what must be a unique recording made in 1957, of Grumiaux playing both violin and piano in the Brahms Sonata No. 2 in A major, coupled with Mozart's Sonata in E flat major (K.481).

Grumiaux also plays Bartók, Stravinsky and Berg. His recording of the Berg concerto has been described as 'one of his finest accomplishments'. A reviewer says that although he has the technique to 'sail through its difficulties with no sense of strain', unlike so many exponents who do have the technique 'he does not play it so as to show you what a big violinist he is'.[8]

Avant-garde music has no appeal for Grumiaux. He is yet another who says: 'The violin is a "singing" instrument and not built for peculiar effects or sounds.'[9] He is proud of the Belgian school's rich heritage of violin playing, established as a primary world influence by Viotti, de Bériot and Vieuxtemps, continued by Massart and Marsick in Paris, Musin in New York, and more recently Thomson and Ysaÿe, and numbering amongst its international heirs Kreisler, Thibaud, Wieniawski and Sarasate. It is the wealth of this tradition that Grumiaux brings to his own students at the Conservatoire in Brussels.

With a platform manner that is reserved and totally lacking in showmanship, Grumiaux speaks to his audience through the sonority of his violin. His approach is the opposite of the head tossing and agonized gestures of the exhibitionist player. His inborn sense of style permeates every movement right down to his bow grip with the second phalanx of his index finger on the stick — the classic Franco–Belgian hold. He has no exalted opinion of himself as a great virtuoso. His greatest pleasure is when he gathers fellow artists around him to perform chamber music for a festival in a small mountain town in Belgium every summer. His colleagues rightly call him 'the musician's musician'.[10]

Arthur Grumiaux, the immaculate recording artist

Henryk Szeryng, who premièred the 'lost'
Third Concerto of Paganini in 1971

Josef Hassid, considered by Flesch to have
been his most gifted pupil. His career ended
tragically in his twenties

36

The Diplomat and 'The Polish Boy'

Henryk Szeryng;
Josef Hassid

Today the name of Henryk Szeryng is universally familiar, but few could identify that of Josef Hassid. Both artists were born in Poland, five years apart. At sixty-one Szeryng travels the world in luxury on a diplomatic passport. Hassid died at the age of twenty-seven after an unsuccessful brain operation in a mental hospital. He was a schizophrenic.

Szeryng was born in 1918 in Warsaw into a rich industrialist Jewish family who loved music. He had his first piano lessons from his mother at the age of five and two years later some tuition on the violin from his brother, a good amateur fiddler and a lawyer by profession. Henryk was intrigued by the violin because it was such a small instrument in comparison with the piano. He wondered how it was possible to fill a large theatre with sound from so small an instrument. His progress soon merited his being sent to study with Maurice Frenkel, former pupil and assistant of Auer in St Petersburg. Only today is it dawning on Szeryng how much he owes to Frenkel, and how the different violin schools are in reality 'interdependent, intertwined and closely related'.[1]

When Huberman heard the ten-year-old Henryk play the Mendelssohn concerto, he was so impressed that he suggested he should go to study with Flesch in Berlin. Henryk took his advice and stayed with Flesch for three years. In 1932 the Szeryng family moved to Paris. Here Henryk met many of the notable poets, painters and composers, and studied composition with Nadia Boulanger. When he first heard Thibaud and Kreisler he was captivated by the French style of playing. Kreisler's elegance, finesse and general approach to the art of violin playing were unlike anything that Szeryng had so far learned from any of his teachers. Of Thibaud he says: 'He never had the technique of Heifetz or the power of Elman, yet his playing, especially when he was in a good mood . . . was second to none.'[2] This dual influence inspired Szeryng to enter the Paris Conservatoire for a further period of study. He graduated in 1937, having been awarded the coveted first prize for violin, and began a performing career.

Szeryng was twenty-one when Hitler invaded Poland, and he immediately joined up in the Polish Army. Since he already spoke six languages with fluency he was appointed to the staff of General Sikorski as liaison officer and interpreter. He was allowed to take his violin with him on his travels and he took part in over three hundred concerts for the sick and wounded and their families. He also played in prisoner-of-war camps. This experience impressed upon him the power of music as a unifying force — linking generals and privates, Anzacs, Czechs, Poles and Mexicans. Szeryng also responds to music of all kinds — folk, pop, rock and jazz, considering them part of the same force that works through classical music. He is a fine pianist and plays jazz for relaxation.

In 1942, Szeryng accompanied the exiled Polish premier to Latin America in search of a home for four thousand Polish refugees who had been displaced by the war. Moved by the warmth with which Mexico accepted the homeless, after the war he returned to Mexico to teach, and in 1946 he became a Mexican citizen. He is today Official Cultural Ambassador to the Mexican government and is chiefly concerned with fostering cultural exchange between countries which have no diplomatic relations; 'because I think that music should be absolutely above politics'.[3]

In the autumn of 1954, Artur Rubinstein went to Mexico to give a series of piano recitals. Szeryng was in the audience and, overcome with the beauty of Rubinstein's playing, went back-stage to congratulate him, speaking in his native Polish. The maestro, intrigued to find a Polish-speaking 'Mexican', suggested a meeting the following day.

When Szeryng played for Rubinstein, he was in turn so struck by the violinist's artistry that he encouraged him to return to the concert platform after an absence of twelve years. An introduction to the impresario Sol Hurok brought about an immediate concert tour of the USA. Szeryng's first European tour took place in 1956.

Szeryng was thirty-six when he made his reappearance on the concert stage. Some three decades later he is playing all over the world, making recordings and leading an extremely active teaching life (he is head of the String Department — which he founded in 1946 — in the Faculty of Music at Mexico University). Szeryng's repertoire comprises all the classical concertos and many modern works which include contemporary compositions by Mexican composers. At the Edinburgh Festival in 1966 he gave the European première of a concerto by his friend Carlos Chavez, of which he had given its first performance a month before.

He caused considerable excitement when he gave the first modern performance of Paganini's 'lost' third violin concerto at the Royal Festival Hall on 10 October 1971 with the London Symphony Orchestra under Alexander Gibson.

The manuscript was believed to have been destroyed in the Napoleonic Wars. It came to light as a result of some lively detective work on Szeryng's part. He had been searching for the concerto for many years and was consequently delighted to make the acquaintance of two octogenarian great-grand-daughters of Paganini. The ladies suggested to Szeryng that he should play more of the maestro's compositions and finally showed him a stack of music that had lain untouched for well over a century. Szeryng worked on reassembling the separate sheets — 'It took us five days to put the first movement together! — Eventually we discovered a complete concerto.'⁴ It was later identified and authenticated by two of Italy's leading musicologists as the missing number three. Szeryng recorded it and the disc was released the day after the London première. Stanley Sadie wrote in *The Times*:

> There were *spiccatos* at a breathtaking pace, the notes as even as a row of pearls; there were handfuls of double-stops in octaves, thirds, sixths and tenths, sometimes in trills thrown in; there were lightning left-hand pizzicatos; there were long passages in harmonics, some-times double-stopped — how many fingers, I begin to wonder, does Mr Szeryng have? ... The harmonics sounded uncommonly sweet and pure, the bowing clean and rhythmic, the tone bright and silvery ... I would have welcomed more passion in the phrasing, and a rhythmically freer, more gipsy-like style. Paganini was, after all, rumoured to be in league with the devil: and devilishly brilliant though Mr Szeryng's was, it had too angelic a purity and simplicity.

This view was borne out by Peter Stadlen, writing in the *Daily Telegraph*: 'Mr Szeryng performed the unperformable with un-ruffled good humour and with at least ninety-nine per cent success, just to dispel any notion of him being in league with the devil.' This pure quality — the hallmark of Szeryng's style — may not be altogether appropriate for Paganini, but in Bach it is an essential ingredient. Szeryng's interpretation of the Bach solo sonatas and partitas is considered by many to be one of the finest on record. Of a performance of the third partita at the Queen Elizabeth Hall in 1973, the *Daily Telegraph* critic wrote: 'The "preludio" unfolded an almost hypnotic impetus as phrase succeeded phrase with tidal inevitability, and Bach's unquenchable melodic invention flowed with ease and strength throughout the remaining movements.'

Szeryng considers that it is important to have a complete knowledge of a composer's life, character and environment, in which historic events also play a part. He has always found it easier to interpret a work after he has been able to identify himself with the general atmosphere with which the composer was surrounded.

In his concert and ambassadorial rovings Szeryng has the opportunity to investigate the musical conditions in many countries. He was dismayed to discover that the State of Israel, despite its outstanding contribution to the art of violin playing, possessed no Stradivari violin. In December 1972, at a concert to celebrate the 25th anniversary of the State of Israel, Szeryng repaired the exigency by presenting that country with a superb example of the master's work, the 'Hercules', dated 1734. This violin once belonged to Ysaÿe, was stolen in St Petersburg after a concert, and reappeared at a shop in Paris in 1925, when it was bought by Mrs Charles Munch for her husband.

Szeryng has renamed it 'Kinor David', the Lyre of David.

When Kreisler heard Josef Hassid as a young boy at Flesch's house, he said: 'A fiddler such as x [mentioning a very famous name] is born every hundred years — one like Hassid, every two hundred.'[5] Josef Hassid was born in 1923, of poor Jewish parentage, in Suwalki, a remote Polish town not far from the Russian border. His mother had died when he was a baby, so the responsibility for his upbringing rested entirely on his father, an accountant by profession who loved music. As a small child Josef taught himself to play the violin and when he was six he was given his first lessons by the local violin teacher. He quickly exhausted his teacher's knowledge, and was taken to Warsaw where he studied for some time with a violinist named Krystal.

At ten he was accepted into Michalowicz's class at the Chopin School of Music in Warsaw. Here he met his first serious rival in a tiny child five years his junior — Ida Haendel. In her autobiography *Woman With Violin* she writes: 'When I heard him I was too young to appreciate his talent and I was not at all impressed by his slow vibrato.' Ida already had a fast vibrato which she had picked up naturally soon after she began to play. 'At that time vibrato seemed to me of prime importance, and since Josef Hassid was also technically less advanced than I, I soon dismissed him entirely. But father did recognize in this boy with his round face, black curly hair and ready smile, a talent of enormous range. And soon we became rivals — at any rate in the eyes of our parents and the public.' Josef subsequently appeared with success at a number of concerts in Warsaw, and at the age of twelve entered the Wieniawski Competition. But he came nowhere, owing to a lapse of memory. This was the historic year that Ginette Neveu won first prize and Oistrakh took second place.

It was also at this time that Huberman first heard Josef play and recommended him to have some lessons with Flesch. Ida Haendel was then studying with him and her father also made approaches to Flesch on Josef's behalf. He was the first to send the news to Hassid's father that his son had been accepted without fees. Hassid wrote by return to Mr Haendel: 'My Josef, upon hearing the news, danced one solid hour for joy.'[6]

In 1937 Josef went to study with Flesch on his summer course at Spa in Belgium. Not only was Flesch greatly impressed with his talent, but also thought that Josef possessed extraordinary musical perception and understanding for his age. Flesch once said that he considered him the most gifted pupil he ever had. He had nothing to teach him technically; he had only to ripen his style.

But something else happened at that summer course. Josef fell deeply in love with one of his fellow students. The feelings were reciprocal but the girl was a gentile. The two families were totally opposed to the match on religious grounds and thwarted every meeting. Eventually they succeeded in destroying the romance and the couple were finally parted. Even today the name of the girl remains a secret. Josef, who had been deprived of female affection from infancy, was shattered by this treatment.

But meanwhile, his career began to take shape. In 1938 he made his first London appearance at a recital in aid of Ben Shemen, the

Palestine training home for refugee children from Central and Eastern Europe, at the house of Sir Philip Sassoon in Park Lane. Critics were enthusiastic and spoke of him as a natural violinist.

When war broke out in 1939, the Hassids decided to stay in London. Harold Holt took Josef under his wing and arranged a recital and several concerts. But what must be an almost unprecedented occurrence — and extraordinary insight on the part of the recording manager, Walter Legge — was that HMV engaged him for a recording of some 'genre' pieces several weeks *before* his first recital. Gerald Moore, who was Hassid's accompanist in these recordings, gives a vivid account of the experience:

> I . . . was at once struck by his genius. He was a very reserved — not to say shy — boy and had no self-confidence *except* when he had his violin under his chin . . . When rehearsing, his concentration was as fierce and well-focussed as that of a virtuoso of maturity. I say this advisedly for we rehearsed several times for one London recital when I was moving house and my goods and chattels were 'housed' temporarily in the large house of a friend — tables, tall-boys, chests, desks, pianoforte, crates of china — all in a medley. Nothing disturbed him.[7]

Gerald Moore also accompanied Hassid at his first recital at the Wigmore Hall, on 3 April 1940. He was billed as 'The Polish Boy Violinist', but his programme would have taxed the skills of a veteran. It included Corelli's 'La Folia', works by Debussy and Schubert, and Paganini's 'I Palpiti'. *The Times* found him a 'mature artist', and admired the 'smooth and full tone' in the Corelli and the 'depth of his musicianship' in an unaccompanied sonata of Bach.

Three weeks later Hassid made his orchestral début playing the Tchaikovsky concerto at the Queen's Hall. It was at a concert for the Polish Relief Fund with the London Philharmonic Orchestra conducted by Gregory Fitelberg, himself a refugee and formerly conductor of the Warsaw Radio Orchestra. *The Times* considered that the strong impression made in his recital 'was more than confirmed . . . when after a rather tentative beginning he grasped Tchaikovsky's bravura style boldly. The beauty of his tone in the lyrical slow movement was striking, and the brilliance of the finale earned him the generous applause which the large audience accorded him'. Ida Haendel, who was at the performance, recalls: 'When we saw him step on to the stage, a charming figure with his unruly black hair and modest manner, we knew he would win all hearts.'[8]

Hassid played in three more concerts and HMV offered him a contract to make more recordings which would have included the first recording of the Walton violin concerto. But the plans never came to fruition. Hassid became moody, depressed and suffered memory lapses. He would not touch his violin for weeks on end. He once attacked his father with a knife. He underwent sporadic sessions of treatment but with only partial success. He was admitted into a mental hospital in Epsom, an incurable schizophrenic.

In the tragic years that followed, Hassid became withdrawn and totally alienated from anything concerned with music. He rejected any idea that he had ever even played the violin. A letter from Carl Flesch dating from this period is a poignant reminder of the hopes he cherished for his pupil's future. 'I hope you will do everything within your will-power to get well again as soon as possible,' he wrote. 'A great artist like you owes it to the world to become active again.'[9] But in November 1950 Hassid underwent a brain operation from which he never recovered. Eight short pieces recorded on four 78 r.p.m. discs are all that remain to remind us of his genius. But they are enough to prove that he was one of the great violinists, and justify Kreisler's recognition of that greatness.

37

Great Teachers of America

Louis Persinger;
Josef Gingold;
Ivan Galamian

With the passing of Auer, Flesch and Enesco, the twentieth century gratefully inherited their pupils. Sascha Lasserson carried on the Auer tradition until his death at eighty-eight in July 1978. Max Rostal has become the best-known disciple of Flesch and teaches in Switzerland, whilst Menuhin and Helen Dowling pass on to their students something of the subtle but powerful influence exerted upon them by Enesco.

In the USA, Louis Persinger and Josef Gingold, two ex-pupils of Ysaÿe, have made a significant contribution to the development of violin playing in that country. And then there is the greatest teacher of our time, Ivan Galamian, who studied with Lucien Capet in Paris and is not affiliated to any of the mainstream 'schools'.

Born in Rochester, Illinois, Persinger (1887–1966) was trained at the Leipzig Conservatoire before finishing with Ysaÿe in Brussels. He held leaderships both in the Berlin Philharmonic Orchestra and the Royal Opera Orchestra in Brussels and in 1915 he was appointed leader and assistant conductor to the San Francisco Symphony Orchestra. After the death of Auer in 1930 he succeeded him at the Juilliard School in New York.

Persinger became best known for his ability to teach gifted children and it was he, as we have seen, who trained and launched Menuhin and Ricci on their careers. Helen Dowling, who also studied with Persinger as a child, praised his faculty for making the music come alive. She says:

He paid great attention to learning the music as a whole. When a new

composition was to be tackled he would begin the lesson by playing
the accompaniment or orchestral part on the piano. You followed the
violin part with your eyes so that you already knew the composition
before you started to play your part. Anything you would eventually
play with orchestra was explained in detail, including where most
orchestras might go wrong, and how you could hold your own part
together regardless. We were only *children*, but it made all the
difference in the world to our performance. You didn't just learn a
violin part.[1]

Helen Dowling also recalled his ability to teach how to phrase
from a technical point of view. As an experienced teacher she says
with conviction:

You may have all the music in the world inside you, but unless you
know *technically* how to bring it out, you are lost. This is what
Persinger did so well. You may not agree with his interpretation, but
phrasing is a technique and once you have learned how to phrase you
can use your own interpretation. It is like learning a language — you
must articulate slowly at first.[2]

Persinger had infinite patience. Menuhin says of him: 'The milk
of human kindness may not lubricate a soloist's career; it made
Persinger an ideal teacher, at least for someone thirsty for instruction.'[3] Menuhin also tells a story showing another side to his
character. Persinger had agreed to allow the eight-year-old Yehudi to tackle the Beethoven violin concerto, provided he had
mastered the one in A major by Mozart. In eight hours of
concentrated practice the child had memorized the Mozart and
played it for Persinger. Menuhin writes:

A crueller man than he would have thrown me a coin, complimented
the monkey and suggested tunes more appropriate to the hurdy-
gurdy, but Persinger mercifully lost his temper for once — in the
middle of the Andante. 'Go home!' he said angrily. 'Use your good
mathematical head and figure out for yourself the exact rhythms. I
don't want to see you again until you have given thought to every
note in each movement.[4]

Josef Gingold was born in Russia in 1909 and emigrated to the
USA in 1920. At first a pupil of Vladimir Graffman in New York,
he later spent two years with Ysaÿe in Brussels.
Gingold was a member of the NBC Symphony Orchestra
under Toscanini and has been leader of both the Detroit and
Cleveland Symphony Orchestras, in the latter under Georg Szell.

The great American teachers:

Above left: Ivan Galamian, teacher of Perlman, Zukerman and Kyung-Wha Chung: portrait by Wayman Adams, 1958

Above: Louis Persinger with his pupil Yehudi Menuhin

Josef Gingold, pupil of Ysaÿe and professor at Indiana University School of Music

He remained in Cleveland for thirteen years, during which time he was the soloist in fifteen concertos. In 1960 he joined the faculty of the Indiana University School of Music at Bloomington, where he is now 'Distinguished Professor of Music'. He has been head of the Chamber Music Department of the Meadowmount School of Music in New York State for the past twenty-five years. In addition to his teaching, recording and concert appearances in the USA, Gingold has given master classes at the National Conservatoire de Musique in Paris and at the Toho School of Music in Tokyo. He has also represented his adopted country on the juries of a number of international violin competitions including the Queen Elisabeth, Paganini, Wieniawski, Leventritt, Sibelius and Tchaikovsky. He has edited over thirty works in the Classical and modern violin repertoire. His recording of Kreisler pieces is a masterpiece of style, always respecting the music and never indulgent.

Gingold's teaching gifts are remarkable and his warm, friendly personality endears him to all who come within his ken. Miriam Fried, who studied with him before going to the Juilliard School under Galamian, says: 'Gingold directed in a way I had never thought about before. He made me aware of sounds. He showed me how the violin differs from the piano and where its possibilities lie. I had neglected this aspect before and have been grateful ever since for his opening up this new dimension for me.'[5]

Born in 1903 in Tabriz, Iran, of Armenian parents, Ivan Galamian was brought to Russia when he was two months old. His father was a businessman who loved music. When at the age of eight Ivan showed interest in the violin, he was sent to the School of the Philharmonic Society in Moscow, where he took lessons with Mostras, a pupil of Sibor. Ivan's graduation coincided with the Revolution of 1917 and he fled to Germany. Finally he reached Paris and it was here that Ivan became a pupil of Lucien Capet, who became 'a strong influence, both musically and pedagogically'.[6]

In his youth Galamian achieved a reputation as a virtuoso performer and in the twenties made many successful European tours. But he had always been interested in teaching from the age of thirteen. He would keep a special diary in which he recorded the progress of his pupils, and sometimes the notes ran into several pages. In 1923, when Capet began to pass on a few of his surplus students, Galamian began to take his teaching seriously.

In 1930 Galamian was appointed Vice President of the Russian

Conservatoire in Paris and from 1936 to 1939 was a member of the faculty at the École Normale de Musique in Paris. In 1939 he emigrated to the USA, taking US citizenship in 1944.

That same year Galamian was invited by Zimbalist, who was then director of the Curtis Institute, to become a member of the faculty. Two years later he was appointed to the staff of the Juilliard School, where he remained to build himself a reputation that can only be compared with that of Auer at St Petersburg.

Today, all Galamian's teaching takes place at his private apartment in New York, except during the summer months when the classes are removed to his famous Meadowmount School in the Adirondack Mountains at Westport, New York, which he founded in 1944. Until recently his day began at eight a.m. and finished at six p.m., but upon reaching his seventy-fifth birthday Galamian has made a concession. He has delayed his start to nine o'clock. However, he is not above telephoning a lazy student before that hour, and will ask 'Why aren't you practising?'

Galamian has firm views on practice. 'If we analyse the development of the well-known artists, we see that in almost every case the success of their entire career was dependent upon the quality of their practising ... The lesson is not all. Children do not know how to work alone. The teacher must constantly teach the child *how* to practise.'[7]

This attention to practice is one of the most important aspects of Galamian's teaching, his main principle being that the player must develop a sense of responsibility for his own technique, particularly in working out a practising routine. At Meadowmount, Galamian and his coaching staff spend considerable time touring the practice-cabins and listening-in. They will then advise on what to practise and for how long. Sidney Mann, who helped the late Frances Kitching to run a Galamian-inspired course in Britain in 1969, said: 'When you hear someone in the next cabin practising two Kreutzer studies, a movement from a concerto and some unaccompanied Bach — most of it from memory — it really makes you improve.'[8]

The underlying strength of the Galamian method is the constructive and economic use of available time. So that 'From an early stage in the pupil's development the teacher should try to encourage a personal initiative while at the same time constantly striving to better the student's understanding and to improve his taste and sense of style'.[9]

Another important aspect of Galamian's teaching is the necessity to keep a balance: evenness and consistency are his maxims. One of his teachers in Russia was moody, so that everything depended upon the way he felt. 'I promised myself I would never react to pupils that way . . . I have patience and I teach my students to have patience. Especially I try to be patient in letting them find their own way.'[10] He stresses: 'The teacher must always bear in mind that the highest goal should be for him to make the student self-sufficient.'[11]

Some of his students find him too strict, but the successful ones have no complaints. Miriam Fried says: 'I found Galamian one of the most organized people I have ever met. His head probably has little drawers in it, and his brain pulls out little bits of information one at a time.' She found him particularly expert at diagnosing problems. 'Students will practise at home and become depressed because they are not achieving the right results. A talk with Galamian will evoke an immediate response. He will demonstrate and say: "Why don't you do it this way". Miraculously the student finds that it works.' 'But,' says Miriam Fried, 'You can't get away with anything less than what *he* wants. He'll make you play the same piece for a week if he doesn't think you have reached your individual maximum.' A classic remark of Galamian's is: 'You do things very well up to ninety-five per cent — now let's do the last five.'[12]

The Korean Kyung-Wha Chung discussed the way in which Galamian prepares his students for the concert platform: 'It is like an actor wearing strong make-up. If you are near it is too strong, but on stage it looks perfect. Galamian bases his teaching on this kind of projection. In a room it can be too strong but on stage it's fantastic.'[13]

Galamian acknowledges that the standards of our present time are higher than they were thirty or even twenty years ago. 'Violinists these days are technically more developed, and from the musical aspect more faithful to the text of the composer's writing.'[14] Repertoire is also much more extensive than before. He says: 'When I studied in Paris with Capet, I had to learn about a dozen concertos: now it is more like fifty.'[15]

There is no doubt that Galamian has made a unique contribution to the development of violin playing. He has devoted a lifetime to the study and practice of every aspect of playing. His book *Principles of Violin Playing and Teaching* contains precise directions and explanations for every mental or physical action. But he also treats each pupil as an individual according to his needs. 'He believes that the differences between *great* players is much bigger than between *good* players.'[16] The list of great violinists who have been trained by Galamian would occupy several pages of a fiddlers' Who's Who.

Galamian sums up his main principles:

> Interpretation is the final goal of all instrumental study, its only raison d'être. Technique is merely the means to this end, the tool to be used in the service of artistic interpretation. For successful performance, therefore, the possession of the technical tools alone is not sufficient. In addition, the player must understand the meaning of the music thoroughly, must have creative imagination and a personal approach to the work if his rendition is to be lifted above the dry and the pedantic. His personality must be neither self-effacing nor aggressively obtruding.[17]

When a reporter once asked Galamian who was the most outstandingly gifted violinist he had ever taught, he replied without hesitation: 'Michael Rabin. There was an extraordinary talent — no weaknesses, never!'[18] Born in 1937, Michael Rabin made an extraordinary impact on the violinistic world when he first appeared as a prodigy. He died in 1972 at the age of thirty-five, at the height of a brilliant but troubled career, undermined by drug problems and mental instability. It would have been interesting to have followed the development of such a talent — reminiscent of Flesch's most promising pupil, young Josef Hassid.

However, still very much alive are three of Galamian's pupils whose names immediately spring to mind as outstanding, even in an age when virtuosity abounds. They are the two Israelis, Itzhak Perlman and Pinchas Zukerman, and the Korean Kyung-Wha Chung.

38

The 'Galamian Trio'

Itzhak Perlman;
Pinchas Zukerman;
Kyung-Wha Chung

The pupils of Galamian dominate late twentieth-century violin playing as did Auer's at its beginning. Amongst the younger generation who have achieved international fame, Perlman, Zukerman and Kyung-Wha Chung, each of whom has an individual way of playing the violin, which is proof of Galamian's insistence that his students must eventually find their own way.

Chung is by far the most overtly emotional player, with a distinct taste for the Romantic repertoire. Perlman and Zukerman are quite different despite their close personal and professional affinity with each other. Perlman is a thoughtful, refined but exciting player, always technically and musically in command. Zukerman is more impetuous. He is the born virtuoso. Gillian Widdecombe says: 'The special delicacy and lightness in his playing seem to be the result of a miraculous bowing arm, which floats *spiccato* so freely it sounds like the most natural thing in the world rather than the zenith of musical and technical control.'[1]

Itzhak Perlman was born in 1945 in Tel Aviv, Israel, the son of an immigrant Polish barber. Music was always present in the home and he cannot recall a time when he did not have the ambition to play the violin.

At the age of four, Itzhak contracted polio which resulted in paralysis of his lower limbs. The illness, and a year's convalescence, left his ambition unchanged. He received his first violin lessons at the Music Academy in Tel Aviv, and by the age of ten he was a veteran performer.

Perlman insists he was not a child prodigy and that no pressure was ever exerted upon him either by parents or teacher. He loved the violin and he liked performing. Since his parents handled his disablement with sound common sense, it never occurred to him that there was anything unusual in a physically-handicapped child seeking a career as a violinist.

When he was thirteen, Itzhak went to America to appear on the Ed Sullivan Show, the success of which resulted in a three-month tour, 'The Ed Sullivan Caravan of Stars'. Shunted around the ballrooms of luxury hotels, a bunch of gifted children played their party pieces to a weary audience who had wined and dined too well. Their dressing room was the kitchen and here they sat until well after midnight for their call. Looking back, Perlman admits that after working under such conditions at the onset of his career, nothing now bothers him.

Despite the hazards of his initial experiences, Itzhak decided to stay on in New York and he was awarded scholarships by the Juilliard School and the American-Israeli Foundation to study with Galamian and his assistant Dorothy Delay.

On 5 March 1963, Perlman made his début at Carnegie Hall, playing the Wieniawski Concerto in F sharp minor with the National Orchestral Association conducted by John Barnett. The concert took place during a newspaper printers' strike and no reviews appeared.

A year later Perlman, after winning the Leventritt Competition at the Carnegie Hall, was engaged for a series of concerts with leading American orchestras, and his old sponsor, Ed Sullivan, invited him back on to his show. Sol Hurok, his newly-acquired agent, sent him on a coast-to-coast tour which took him to fifty major American cities. He was acclaimed, not only as an exciting new talent, but for his ebullient personality.

In January 1965, Perlman returned to his native Israel after five years for a series of eight concerts. He had left as a talented youngster and returned a fully-fledged virtuoso. For him the most emotional experience was when he went on stage at the Mann Auditorium in Tel-Aviv, to play with the Israel Philharmonic Orchestra. The audience gave him a deafening welcome. 'Every kid in Israel dreams that one day he's going to play with the IPO . . . and then the dream comes true . . . '[2]

In May of that same year, Perlman appeared with the New York Philharmonic Orchestra at the Philharmonic Hall conducted by William Steinberg. He was called back to the stage five times. At twenty he had proved himself an artist of the front rank. When he appeared as soloist with the Detroit Symphony Orchestra under Sixten Ehrling at the opening concert of the Carnegie Festival, playing the Sibelius concerto, Howard Klein wrote in the *New York Times*:

> Truly a sensation violinist ... The tone was voluminous — warm, throbbing and dead in tune. The octave playing was only surpassed by the way Mr Perlman whistled through the short section of the harmonics in the last movement ... Listening to him play produced joy on every level — technical, musical and above all the human. For the burly young man has that extra quality that raises music above technicalities and that is heart.[3]

Perlman first came to Britain in March 1968 and made his London début at the Royal Festival Hall playing the Tchaikovsky concerto with the London Symphony Orchestra. In 1968 he toured Britain with the Israel Philharmonic Orchestra, and in August joined the cellist Jacqueline du Pré and Daniel Barenboim in a highly successful series of South Bank Summer Concerts. It was also at this time that he gave his first recital with Vladimir Ashkenazy — a partnership that has endured both personally and professionally for ten years. In the recently issued recording of the complete cycle of Beethoven sonatas for violin and piano, these two artists have proved that the technical level of their playing equals their artistic conceptions.

Perlman and Ashkenazy are natural partners. Perlman maintains that when they make music together his own playing gains an extra dimension. The final result — gained through much hard work — is certainly proof of this statement. Perlman tells us that in the case of the first Beethoven sonata, it took them two and a half years to reach the desired standard of performance and interpretation.

In the light of his seemingly meteoric rise to fame, it is surprising that Perlman himself feels that his development has been steady, with no erratic leaps. Upon reflection, he believes that this could have been different if he had gone in for more competitions after the Leventritt. 'I won it — [I] quit,'[4] he says. He considers that there are inherent problems in winning competitions. In his own case there were nineteen others who were all brilliant performers, and it is daunting to find you are the best of such a bunch. The sudden change in circumstances is too precipitous. An unknown student enters the race and having won, emerges faced with sixty or seventy concerts a year. Perlman is convinced that the highest level of performance cannot be maintained for long periods; there must be a dip when the adrenalin is not flowing in the same way as it is under the stress of competition.

Perlman finds an audience stimulating and does not generally feel nervous. Curiously enough, the microphone makes him nervous — in spite of his regular recording schedule. He finds that playing without an audience is always a problem, and in recording sessions it is difficult for him not to fall into a trance. He recalls the tour of 1975 when he and Pinchas Zukerman travelled all over Europe recording and filming their performances of violin duos. These two are not only colleagues but close friends and it was a pleasurable experience. Perlman said: 'The formality just goes out of the window ... no keeping up appearances. Especially with Pinky, we know exactly what each one wants to do. We do it on the spur of the moment.' Here he is putting into practice one of his teacher's firm principles. 'The best performance always partakes of the nature of an improvisation in which the artist is moved by the music he plays, forgets about technique, and abandons himself with improvisatory freedom to the inspiration of the moment.'[5]

Perlman's impeccable left-hand technique and his bow hold with fingers curved in a natural, relaxed way, ready to spring into action for every kind of bowing, are a source of amazement even to orchestral players who witness the operation from close quarters. This technique clearly has its effect. 'There is a joy and bounce to his playing that had old-timers at Carnegie Hall reaching back in their memories to the days of the youthful Heifetz to find a parallel',[6] wrote William Bender in 1964. And this 'joy and bounce' are also the key elements to Perlman as a man. He has ignored a disability that one might have thought crippling to scale the heights.

'He could be described as a violinist born; one of those rare musicians who play as if by light or nature, without effort. His violin seemed part of him',[7] wrote Joan Chissell in The Times after the twenty-one-year old Zukerman's London recital début at the Queen Elizabeth Hall in August 1969. He was accompanied by Daniel Barenboim in Mozart, Beethoven, Brahms and Schoenberg.

Pinchas Zukerman was born in 1948 in a village outside Tel

Aviv, the son of a Jewish fiddler-cum-clarinettist. Before he was six, Pinchas had mastered the recorder and clarinet well enough to accompany his father and the *ad hoc* ensembles who toured the hotels at weddings and other social events. At six Pinchas took up the violin and received his first lessons from his father. At eight he was admitted to both the Academy of Music at Tel Aviv and the Israel Conservatoire. Here he was in the care of Ilona Seher, who had herself been a pupil of Hubay in Budapest. He became Seher's prize pupil and in addition to his lessons at the Academy spent many hours each day at her house playing duets and chamber music.

By the time he was thirteen, Pinchas had studied some eighty-five per cent of the general violin repertoire. 'In physical terms,' Gillian Widdecombe tells us, 'he was able to cope with anything from the Paganini Caprices to the standard concertos, though of course he played them in a childishly imitative way.'[8]

In 1961, Casals and Stern were visiting Israel and heard him play. They were greatly impressed and Stern recommended that the boy should go to New York for further training, and that he would be his legal guardian. Although Stern was never his teacher, he kept a vigilant eye on his prodigy. Stern arranged for Zukerman to live with the parents of Eugene Istomin, pianist of the Stern Trio. It was the Istomins who abbreviated 'Pinchas' into the 'Pinky' by which he is now universally known.

A scholarship awarded by the America-Israeli Cultural Foundation financed his studies with Galamian at the Juilliard School, where his talent quickly developed. He studied for five years with Galamian in a vintage period when Perlman and Kyung-Wha Chung sat beside him on the front desks of the student orchestra. Zukerman is convinced that Galamian's genius as a teacher lies in his flexibility, an opinion echoed by almost every pupil.

In 1967 Zukerman shared the Leventritt award with Kyung-Wha Chung. This led to a number of concerts and recitals in many of the leading cities of North America. Audiences responded warmly to this gifted young player who seemed able to tackle anything on the violin without difficulty, and whose superb tone was being compared to all the great names in history.

A year later, CBS signed Zukerman up on an exclusive recording contract. His first recording — of the Tchaikovsky concerto — was made in Britain with the London Symphony Orchestra under Antal Dorati. His mastery of technique and musicianship so astonished the tough rank-and-file of the orchestra that they shook their heads in disbelief.

Zukerman's New York début was in February 1969 at the Philharmonic Hall. He played the Mendelssohn concerto with the New York Philharmonic Orchestra under Bernstein. The *New York Times* tells us that the twenty-year-old 'tossed off the event as it it were a nursery rhyme' and that he 'has the physical equipment to be a top virtuoso. His bowing and fingering are perfectly in hand and he negotiates the most difficult passages with ease. His tone is not huge but it is flexible and has a pleasing, poetic quality.'9

In the spring of the same year Zukerman crossed the Atlantic to make his first appearance before the British public, at the Brighton Festival. He and Daniel Barenboim gave a violin and piano recital at the Royal Pavilion, and later they were joined by Jacqueline du Pré to give a compelling performance of the Brahms double concerto with Barenboim conducting the New Philharmonic Orchestra.

Barenboim and Zukerman had first met in New York only a few months before. Barenboim had conducted when Zukerman was the soloist with the English Chamber Orchestra at a Carnegie Hall concert. They were so impressed with his playing of Mozart's Violin Concerto No. 4 in D major (K.218) that they rearranged their Queen Elizabeth Hall concert to enable him to repeat his performance before a London audience. This association has since ripened into a close friendship which also includes Perlman. Together with Jacqueline du Pré they have made some memorable music — including the 1969 film of the Schubert 'Trout' Quintet with Zukerman playing the viola (on which he is also first class), Zubin Mehta in the less familiar role of double bass, and Daniel Barenboim, piano.

Zukerman has the physique of an athlete and an inexaustible supply of energy to match. His friend and colleague Christopher Nupen describes him as: 'Quite the most spiritually and materially generous person I know — he is always ready to give.'10 His tremendous sense of fun sometimes gives the impression that he is happy-go-lucky: he may not take himself very seriously, but those close to him know that his music is quite another matter. His abundant natural talent makes everything look easy to the casual observer, but behind this apparent effortlessness lies a musical conceptual certainty that continually surprises his fellow artists.

A development of this aspect can be seen in Zukerman's increasing interest in conducting and directing specialist chamber orchestras. He needs to expand his musical activities far beyond the solo violin repertoire. In Britain he has always enjoyed playing with the English Chamber Orchestra, and in September 1980 he took up an official appointment as musical director of the St Paul Chamber Orchestra in Minnesota, considered by many to be the finest chamber orchestra in the USA.

Kyung-Wha Chung was born in 1948 in Seoul, South Korea, the daughter of a lawyer. She is one of seven children, six of whom are trained musicians now pursuing careers in the western world. Kyung took piano lessons when she was four but found no affinity with the instrument. She played all her exercises by ear and gave such good performances that nobody suspected that she had not learned to read the notes. She was then given a small violin on which she proceeded to teach herself. From the first sound of the bow on the string, she says: 'I knew it would be my life.'[11]

At nine Kyung played the Mendelssohn concerto with the Seoul Philharmonic Orchestra. She then passed through the hands of at least six teachers, and at twelve went on a successful concert tour of Japan sponsored by the Korean government. In 1961 her parents took her to the USA where she had private lessons with Galamian: subsequently she won a full-time scholarship to the Juilliard School. Chung displays the same respect and admiration for Galamian that is apparent in all his pupils.

Unashamedly a performer, Chung has no interest in teaching. She says: 'I have always loved audiences, and the more people there are, the more exciting it is. Galamian can see this immediately. He can tell if you are a performer or teacher — or both. He has something for everyone so that you bloom in your own way.'[12] In 1967, when she was nineteen, Kyung shared the first prize in the Leventritt Competition with Zukerman. Shortly afterwards she made her début with the New York Philharmonic Orchestra. Offers of engagements came thick and fast, but Chung did not feel that she was ready to embark upon an international career. Instead she decided to study for a further year.

In 1970 Chung came to Europe with one engagement in her diary. It was at the Royal Festival Hall on 13 May to play the Tchaikovsky concerto in a Charity Gala Concert with the London Symphony Orchestra under André Previn. She walked on to the

Itzhak Perlman, who first appeared in the USA on the Ed Sullivan Show

Eugene Fodor, pupil of Heifetz and the first American to win a top prize in the Tchaikovsky Competition in Moscow

Pinchas Zukerman, a born virtuoso

Ralph Holmes: every seat was sold before the doors opened for his first recital

The Korean Kyung-Wha Chung

stage completely unknown. She left it to a standing ovation. Critics tend not to review such concerts for fear of causing embarrassment to artists who are providing their services free. Gillian Widdecombe, in the *Financial Times*, broke the unwritten law because it was 'an event of such musical excitement that it sincerely deserved more than the compliment of a full house and fulsome applause; more even than the compliment of the London Symphony Orchestra glued to their chairs in praise at the end'. 'I doubt whether Heifetz ever played the notes more accurately,' wrote this critic,

> and it's certainly a long time since Oistrakh or Stern played nearly as many. But what was so magnificent and moving about this perform-ance was not its proud virtuosity, nor the vitality and intensity in the first movement, nor even the ruthless dominance Miss Chung exerted over every awkward corner of this unwieldy work. No, these points were marvellous features, but even more rare and rewarding was the expressive force of her performance: sweet, silken phrasing, soft and tender in the slow movement; beautiful playing, immeasurably mature.[13]

Within three days of her spectacular success at the Festival Hall, Chung was booked for thirty more concerts throughout Britain. There were five BBC TV appearances and a concert tour of the Far East with Previn and the London Symphony Orchestra.

Edward Greenfield, music critic of *The Guardian*, accompanied this tour. He tells a story that reveals the rapport that exists between the tiny virtuoso and an all-male orchestra. They were about to rehearse the Tchaikovsky and Chung was ready, tense and poised. The first violins began to play the introduction — not to the Tchaikovsky, but the Mendelssohn. Chung's lightning reflexes had her whip her violin under her chin ready for the much earlier attack. Then she realized they were playing a trick on her. 'She stamped her foot in giggling anger, irritated to have been taken in but obviously delighted that she could inspire such joke-playing from the LSO.'[14]

Chung's repertoire includes most of the standard works, many of which she learnt long before her American début. But there are some eminent additions which show that she not only has the courage of her own choice, but can also meet a challenge with impunity. It was André Previn who persuaded her to learn the Walton concerto. At first she was not happy with the idea. It is a difficult work and Chung, with characteristic humility, was not sure that she could do it justice. Now she finds it a 'rich and rewarding work'.[15] Chung's recording of this concerto coupled with the Stravinsky confirms this opinion.

Another work with which Chung has become closely identified is the Elgar concerto. Her recording of it was released in 1977 and was exceptionally well received. How did Chung come to find an affinity with this very English work, redolent with Edwardian graciousness? She explains: 'I can't say it is English or anything else. In Europe you have a tradition and you can compare performances with the familiar ones. But for me it is a new work and I must study it first as *music*. I must learn its structure, its form and its key. But I can only imagine what it sounds like to English people. We in the East have no models on which to build.'[16] The lack of tradition inevitably means the absence of preconceived ideas. Perhaps it is this very freshness that makes her performances so compelling.

Chung has a healthy respect for the Romantic repertoire. Although she plays Bach, Mozart, Bartók, Prokofiev, Sibelius, Stravinsky and Berg, she also includes Chausson's 'Poème', concertos by Dvořák, Kreisler, Saint-Saëns and Wieniawski. She is one of the few violinists who plays the Vieuxtemps concerto. She says with conviction: 'These composers from the nineteenth century are so neglected. It is music written for the instrument which in itself is very important.' Chung admits that she came up against considerable scepticism when she wanted to learn Bruch's 'Scottish Fantasia', which other than Heifetz few violinists have played. Galamian was puzzled at her choice and tried to dissuade her. 'But,' says Chung, 'I was determined and I know that I was right.'[17]

Galamian can be forceful in exerting pressure on his pupils in the earlier stages. It was he who advised Chung against entering the Brussels competition, because he did not consider she was ready to come to Europe. He made a concession with the Leventritt because it was on her own doorstep. His judgement was evidently well-placed, for Chung's career has gained momentum from the onset and in performance she seems always to be at the top of her form.

At first sight Kyung-Wha Chung appears deceptively fragile. But after minutes in her company one is aware of her great reserves of mental and physical strength. Highly disciplined, she aims at perfection in every aspect of her playing. She is a born performer and as soon as she appears she has her audience in the palm of her hand. She has a warmth of personality that is the hallmark of the communicator — Kreisler had it, and so does Menuhin. But Chung does not rely upon this quality alone to capture her audiences. She has another side to her character that searches beyond the music in order to understand it. Looking back again to the nineteenth century, she reflects how violinists of that time were nearly all violinist-composers. 'Concerts for them consisted of their own music, and that of their friends. Music was only a part of their lives. They were interested in philosophy, art and literature. They were complete human beings. Today we are all part of a gigantic mechanism. There is a great danger that we shall all be swept up into this mechanism and forget that there are other sides to being a musician.'[18]

Chung thinks that our perfectionism — largely brought about by the gramophone industry — makes us too conscious of the metronome. She says: 'Players like Kreisler made such fantastic *glissandos* and they were absolutely beautiful. If we would do things like that today, everyone would think we were mad. Our style is the reflection of our present society and sometimes I feel we are too inflexible.'[19]

In her early thirties like her coeval and co-prizewinner Zukerman, Chung has achieved a reputation upon which she could rest for many years to come. But she is always seeking a new dimension to her playing, and consequently it grows accordingly. She has played the Elgar concerto many times, yet at a London performance early in 1979, her reading 'seemed to have grown in emotional relevance'[20]; additional beauties of sustained tone and a carefully controlled *rubato* lifted it to the heights.

All three 'Galamians' have contributed immeasurably to the art of violin playing in less than a decade. It will be interesting to reassess this contribution when time has shaped their maturity.

39

The English Phenomenon

Ralph Holmes

The Anglo-Saxon virtuoso violinist is a rare bird and only a handful of names have survived the centuries. We have already touched upon John Bannister and Henry Holmes. John Dunn (1866–1940), who studied under Shradieck at the Leipzig Conservatoire, achieved considerable fame as a soloist and was a brilliant exponent of Paganini's works. Until recently Albert Sammons, born twenty years later, was the only English violinist whose talents were considered to reach international standards.

One of Sammons' pupils is the New Zealander Alan Loveday. Today a professor at the Royal College of Music in London, he remains a distinguished soloist.

The son of a professional violinist, Loveday began to play when he was three on an eighth-size fiddle made especially for him. He received his first instruction from his father. At nine he was heard by the Budapest String Quartet when they were touring New Zealand. So impressed were they by the child's talent that they gave a benefit concert at his home town of Palmerston to start a fund to finance his studies in Britain. Sammons heard the eleven-year-old boy soon after his arrival in 1939, and, recognizing his talent, predicted a bright future. Loveday became a private pupil of Sammons and later continued under his care at the RCM.

When in August 1946 Loveday gave a Prom performance of the Tchaikovsky concerto, *The Strad* critic commented on his 'beautiful velvety tone produced without apparent effort' and also remarked upon his pure intonation. Loveday's playing has always been distinguished by his ability to maintain this purity even at speed in the highest positions.

Then there is Ralph Holmes. In 1966, after his solo début at Carnegie Hall in New York — playing Vaughan Williams's 'The Lark Ascending' and Ravel's 'Tzigane' with the Houston Symphony Orchestra and Sir John Barbirolli — Louis Biancolli, critic of the *World Telegram*, described him as 'that rare English phenomenon, a concert violinist to be reckoned with the upper echelon of the international string set'.[1] Today Ralph Holmes enjoys an established place in those upper echelons. In July 1978 he was a member of the jury of the Carl Flesch International Violin Competition alongside Yehudi Menuhin, Yfrah Neaman, Wolfgang Schneiderhan, Spivakov and other great violinists of international reputation.

Ralph Holmes was born in Kent in 1937 into a family where music was part of the furniture. His father, a schoolmaster, played both violin and piano, and his mother was a trained singer who relinquished her professional ambitions when she married.

In 1941, when his father was serving in the army, the four-year-old Ralph, hiding under the grand piano, tried out his skill on his father's violin. He says: 'I can remember the frustration of only being able to make scratchy noises and longed to make a beautiful sound.' Ralph's mother then bought him a small fiddle and put him with a local teacher, 'more in the interest of my father's violin than the idea that she might have a virtuoso on her hands. We hoped that by the time my father came home in a few months time I might be able to play a scale.'[2]

When the war ended four years later, Ralph's progress was considerably in advance of the anticipated single scale. He had passed the Final Grade in the Associated Board examinations with the highest marks in the British Isles for violin playing, and had appeared in a number of local concerts.

Ralph was just eight when he began taking holiday lessons with the distinguished Canadian-born chamber musician David Martin. He was beginning to make progress when he was awarded a choral scholarship to the choir school of New College Oxford. It was not a welcome move. Although the standards of music were high and Ralph's musical education improved, he was unhappy. 'I was neither fish nor fowl and my violin practice suffered.'[3] In retrospect, Holmes feels that this incompatibility stemmed from the fact that during the war he had been living an insulated existence with his mother, having regular lessons, with most of his practice supervised. The sudden change to communal living was too abrupt. But matters improved when, at ten, Ralph won a junior scholarship to the Royal Academy of Music. Here he was fortunate in being placed with David Martin.

Three years later Martin suggested that Ralph should attend the Junior Orchestral Summer Course at Sherborne, directed by Ernest Read. Read was so impressed with his playing that he invited him to perform the Mendelssohn concerto with the Royal Philharmonic Orchestra at the Central Hall, Westminster. At these children's concerts it was customary for only one movement to be played, but Ralph was asked to play the entire concerto.

Ten days later Ralph gave a recital at the Royal Academy of Music which included works by Wieniawski, Paganini and the Bach Chaconne, with Peter Stone at the piano. Richard Capell from the *Daily Telegraph* was impressed: 'Here was unmistakably a talent. It was the playing not of a child but of a robust young man. His technical achievement is surprising, and from end to end the performance was without a shadow of diffidence.'[4] Ralph was just thirteen.

During the next two summers Ralph had the opportunity to study with Enesco in Paris. At the time, his father was running an Anglo-French school and Ralph went with his class-mates to Paris, ostensibly to improve his French but in reality to study with Enesco. The experience has remained a landmark in his musical life. He says:

> He was a very real inspiration to me as he was to many and had a profound influence upon my musical development. He helped me to understand the role of the violinist as interpreter and gave me vital help in grasping the essence of differing musical styles. Master of many languages, he would speak fluently in whatever the native tongue of his pupil and could accompany numerous concertos beautifully on the piano — naturally, from memory. And yet, with all his accomplishments, as violinist, composer, conductor, teacher, he also radiated a deep humility. A truly great man.

Enesco was meticulous over fingering. Holmes can recall working into the small hours fingering as the master had shown him. He says 'It was particularly important in Bach, where each partita became a hobby. Enesco was insistent that in fingering the fugues one should maintain the integrity of each voice and not go careering over to other strings for odd notes. Conversely, however, he frowned upon shooting up to the top of the G string just for effect. His creed was honesty.'[5]

Holmes recalls a lesson on Ravel's 'Tzigane' from nearly thirty years ago. 'Enesco made so clear to me the comparison between the French Ravel writing in the *manner* of the gipsy idiom, and Sarasate's "Zigeunerweisen" where the composer was writing from the roots.' The experience remains vivid: 'Even today when I am playing any of the works that I did with Enesco, such as the Beethoven C minor sonata or the Bach unaccompanied partita, much of what he said comes winging over the years as if it had been said yesterday.'[6]

There seems to have been no point at which Holmes decided he wanted to become a professional violinist. 'The idea of performing in public and taking it up as a career was taken for granted at an early age. After my studies with Enesco, everything appeared to fall into place.'[7]

In April 1953, when he was sixteen, Ralph played the Mendelssohn concerto under Walter Susskind with the National Youth Orchestra at their first Royal Festival Hall concert. Then followed a year of intensive study in preparation for the all-important recital début.

Every seat was sold out before the doors opened for Ralph's first Wigmore Hall recital on 29 October 1954. Gerald Moore was his 'most helpful'[8] partner at the piano. All the critics were enthusiastic. *The Times* judged: 'There is everything to suggest that he will end his career as one of the finest violinists this country has produced . . . '[9]

Inevitably there were many forecasts as to the heights to which the young Holmes might aspire. On one occasion Yehudi Menuhin could not reach the studios in time for a rehearsal for the BBC TV programme 'Music For You'. The producer rang the Royal Academy of Music for a student to 'stand-in'. 'He needn't play much,' she said: 'Just enough for the cameramen.' They sent along the eighteen-year-old Ralph Holmes, who proceeded to play Menuhin's programme right through without batting an eyelid. During the rehearsal Menuhin arrived but listened behind a curtain, delighted as always to discover young talent from an unexpected source. The conductor Eric Robinson's comment must have been the understatement of the year: 'Given ordinary luck, this young British violinist will become a successful concert artist.'[10]

On leaving the Academy, Holmes completed two years of national service in the Grenadier Guards. Here he found himself in the string orchestra, a body that played at official functions. A special pass was granted to enable him to fulfil concert engagements. It was on such a pass that he played Max Bruch's Violin Concerto No. 1 in G minor in his first Prom with the National Youth Orchestra under Boult.

With national service behind him and as many concert engagements as he could manage, all seemed to be set fair for the future. But in 1964 Holmes experienced a crisis. Although the critics were always kind, he himself began to have private doubts about his playing. He was particularly concerned about his bowing, but ignored possible causes. Then suddenly in the middle of a performance of the Tchaikovsky at the Albert Hall, he felt his bow arm tighten. When his *vibrato* also began giving him trouble, Holmes knew something was wrong. He consulted Sir Thomas Armstrong, the then Principal of the Royal Academy of Music, who thought he might benefit from a further period of study. 'At the time,' says Holmes, 'I didn't put it down to technical problems. I felt it was due to a stultification of ideas. But when Sir Thomas made his suggestion I realized that it was not so much the lack of ideas but the means to express them.' It was ten years since Holmes had had his last lesson with David Martin. He therefore decided upon a refresher course, and chose to go to Galamian in New York.

The next four months were spent in an intensive period of study with Galamian who worked hard on Holmes's bowing. 'He greeted me with the news that he was going to make me my own doctor. And in the end he did.[1] But in New York Holmes was not readily able to change his bow-hold — understandably when one considers that by that time he had already been playing for twenty-three years. 'I realized that he was a wonderful teacher and naturally much of his general advice was invaluable, but the overall approach did not appear to be solving my particular problem.' On his return to Britain, Holmes was further discouraged to find that he was gradually returning to his old style. Then one day he tried out a beautiful Peccatte bow that belonged to a friend and could not make it work properly:

> I knew then it was not the bow but *me*; I then went over everything that Galamian had taught me, analyzing every detail. Suddenly I saw what he meant and in a few days I was able to put it into practice. Basically, as I saw it, was the necessity for me to make 'second nature' in the bow-hold the see-saw action of the fingers over the

thumb as the bow travelled up and down the string, together with a much freer upper arm. And the vital concept of the arm as the lungs to a singer.[12]

Today it is difficult to imagine that Holmes has ever experienced difficulty with bowing. The tone seems to flow from an arm that distils by instinct. His effortless technique is always subservient to the music. He can make a melodic line sing like a bird, but his slashing bow-strokes as in the Ravel 'Tzigane' or the Bartók solo sonata can bite with a vengeance.

Holmes has a varied and extensive repertoire that embraces some fifty-three concertos from Bach to Havergal Brian. He plays the difficult Schoenberg — said to need a violinist with six fingers — and is equally at home with all the Mozart concertos. In May 1978 he deputized — at short notice — for the indisposed Josef Suk in two all-Mozart programmes at the Royal Festival Hall. When he played the Berg concerto with the National British Students Orchestra under Norman del Mar in Vienna, the *Kurier* wrote: 'An Englishman . . . had to come and show us what a subtle romantic Alban Berg was.'[13] In 1979 Holmes played the Hamilton Harty violin concerto, a work rarely heard since Szigeti played it in 1909, in Ireland with the Ulster Orchestra and in Manchester with the Hallé; he also recorded it with the Ulster Orchestra, together with Harty's very beautiful *Variations on a Dublin Air*.

On the concert platform Holmes has that 'giving' quality that brings a warm response from his audience before he has played a note. He always looks as if he is enjoying himself. And yet each performance is born of a serious respect for the music itself. As one critic put it: 'At the heart of his playing was a great sense of integrity . . . no effects for the sake of effects, no extra trimmings. Always the style seemed to evolve from within the fabric.'[14]

40

Great Quartet Leaders

The string quartet — that most pure form of music — has some unlikely ancestors in the mid-eighteenth-century divertimento and serenade, originally designed to be played in the open air after nightfall. It was Haydn who developed the form and brought it into the salon. He composed his Opp. 1 and 2 out of necessity, when he was visiting music master at the country house of the family of Baron von Furnberg. He found that the musical resources of the house consisted of the parish priest and the steward — who both played the violin — and Albrechtsberger the cellist. Haydn himself played the viola.

The string quartet rapidly became the music of the connoisseur, performed in the salon of the music-loving nobleman. From the difficulty of much of the music it is apparent that standards of playing were high. Often quartet music was written for specific players. The virtuoso first violin parts of Haydn's Opp. 9 and 17 quartets were tailor-made for Luigi Tomasini (1741–1808), an Italian from Pesaro who came to Prince Esterházy as his valet. In 1761, when Haydn became Kapellmeister to the Prince, he appointed Tomasini leader of the chapel orchestra. He and Haydn became close friends and the latter would say: 'Nobody plays my quartets so much to my satisfaction as you.'[1]

The first musician to play quartets at public performances was Ignaz Schuppanzigh (1776–1830), conductor and viola player who later turned to the violin. From 1794 to 1795 he was a member of the party of musicians who met every Friday evening at Prince Carl Lichnowsky's. Schuppanzigh led the quartet with the Prince as second violin.

In the winter of 1804–5 Schuppanzigh gave the first of his quartet 'Academies' with his pupil Mayseder second violin, Prince Lobkowitz, viola, and Anton Kraft, cello. When Schuppanzigh entered the service of Count (afterwards Prince) Rasumovsky in 1808, he founded the Rasumovsky Quartet with himself as leader; Sina, second violin; Weiss, viola; and Kraft, cello. The staple diet of their performances were the Beethoven quartets, usually under guidance from the composer.

It was only after the Rasumovsky Palace was burnt down in 1815 that Schuppanzigh took his quartet on tour through Germany, Poland and Russia. They were so well received that they did not return until 1824.

One of the most popular quartet leaders of the early nineteenth century was Spohr: but according to his contemporaries, he was guilty of over-emphasizing the first violin part. His own quartets are little more than solos with three accompanying parts. His pupil Ferdinand David led the Leipzig Quartet for over forty years, but went even further than his master in manipulating the first violin part to display his own virtuosity.

Joseph Hellmesberger (1828–93) founded the quartet that bore his name and the quartet parties he led from 1849 to 1887 were the first to awaken interest in Beethoven's late quartets. C. Ferdinand Pohl wrote: 'The fine tone, grace and poetic feeling which marked Hellmesberger's execution as a solo and quartet player were equally conspicuous in the orchestra, of which he was a brilliant leader.'[2]

Joseph Joachim was without doubt the greatest quartet leader of the nineteenth century. He founded the Joachim Quartet in 1869 with Ernst Schiever (second violin), Heinrich de Ahna (viola) and Wilhelm Muller (cello). Joachim was a rare exception to the general rule that soloists are bad leaders. Normally they have difficulty in keeping within the strict discipline of the medium, but Joachim never allowed his virtuosity to predominate. He also took care to select artists who were not only technical masters of their instruments, but who were in sympathy with his own artistic ideals. He insisted upon a pure and classic approach to the music and would tolerate no excesses of *rubato* or *portamento*: *vibrato* was also kept to the minimum. The quartet gave concerts all over Germany and became so popular that no festival was considered complete unless they were included in the programme. In the spring of 1905 they visited Rome and performed all the Beethoven

quartets at the Farnese Palace. Their English début was comparatively late. They first appeared in London at the St James's Hall on
25 April 1900, and later played the whole of Brahms's chamber
music works in the Bechstein and Queen's Halls. Joachim also
formed a second quartet in London that he ran from January to
March each year, with Franz Ries as second violin and Webb and
Piatti on viola and cello. When Joachim was absent, either Lady
Hallé or Ysaÿe would take his place as leader. A unique feature of
the Joachim Quartet was that the four members each possessed a
Stradivari instrument of the best period. Therefore, the tone they
produced was not only pure but blended perfectly throughout
their range.

Sir Adrian Boult recalls hearing the Joachim Quartet at one of
their last appearances before Joachim's death in 1907. He writes:

> Joachim, apparently, was a player whose tone became weaker in his
> last days, and it was an example of perfect loyalty to hear how the
> whole quartet brought their tone down to balance that of their leader.
> I still remember the slow movement in Beethoven's Op. 18 No. 3
> when Halir's second violin rose to the surface above the first violin for
> four bars and let us hear a beautiful *cantabile* which came from him at
> no other time.[3]

Adolf Brodsky (1851–1929), from Taganrog in Russia, formed
the Brodsky Quartet in 1870 with Becker, Sitt and Klengel. He
had shown talent as a small child and had been sent to study with
Hellmesberger in Vienna at the Conservatoire. He became a
member of the Hellmesberger Quartet and in 1890 went to the
USA to lead Damrosch's Symphony Society. He returned to
Europe in 1894 as leader of Sir Charles Hallé's Orchestra in
Manchester. Later, as principal of the Royal Manchester (now
Northern) College of Music, he organized quartet concerts with
Briggs, Spielman and Fuchs and greatly influenced the musical life
of that city.

A man who did more than anyone else at the time to awaken
interest in chamber music in the USA — amongst people with
very little culture — was Franz Kneisel (1865–1926). Born in
Bucharest, he studied in Vienna with J. Grün and Josef Hellmesberger. In 1885 he went to the USA as leader of the Boston
Symphony Orchestra. Under his influence the string playing
section of the orchestra greatly improved. That same year he
formed the Kneisel Quartet and took them all over the USA. In

addition to giving concerts in halls in the large cities, they visited small towns, engineering camps in the Wild West, and coal mines. Many who later sent their children to study in the American academies had first heard chamber music played by the Kneisel Quartet.

The Flonzaley Quartet, with Adolfo Betti as leader, was founded in New York in 1902 by Edward J. De Coppet, a banker of Swiss descent. 'Flonzaley' was the name of his summer estate near Lake Geneva, where some of the first rehearsals took place. First formed for private performances in De Coppet's home, the Flonzaley later gained an international reputation for their impeccable playing and beautiful tone. From the outset, De Coppet insisted that the players should devote themselves entirely to quartet playing, and they were the first ever to specialize in the medium.

The Brosa Quartet, formed in 1925 by Antonio Brosa (1894–1979), was one of the great string quartets dating from the period between the two wars. A native of Tarragona, educated at the Ainaud Academy in Barcelona and later with Crickboom in Brussels, Brosa's playing was both brilliant and fluent, with a bow arm capable of every nuance. The quartet are memorable for their interpretations of modern works at a time when string quartets tended not to venture outside the Classical repertoire. Elgar, Vaughan Williams, Bax, Frank Bridge, Britten, Berkeley and Tippett all found a willing interpreter for their music in the Brosa Quartet.

Originally, Brosa had had ambitions of concentrating upon solo work. When he formed the Brosa Quartet he nursed a secret hope that their success would not be too great. 'I decided that we should have our début in Paris, where the audience was very critical. Then, if we had bad reviews I could say "you see we are no good" — and we would give up the idea. But to our amazement we were a great success. Then we went on to Berlin, where I was sure they would not like us at all, especially as I had included the Haydn Quartet Op. 76 No. 3 that included the Emperor's National Hymn. But they went mad for us too, and said they had never heard the Haydn played better. That was how we started. So we had to continue.'[4]

However, owing to increasing demands for solo work, Brosa did disband his quartet in 1939. A year later he went to the USA to give the first performance of the Britten violin concerto with the

New York Philharmonic Orchestra under Barbirolli. He stayed for eight years. When Onnue, leader of the Pro Arte Quartet, died, Brosa took his place and toured the USA for four years. The Pro Arte were the first quartet to become attached to an American University as 'Artists in Residence', combining a performing and teaching appointment.

Adolf Busch (1891–1952), leader of one of the finest string quartets of all, was also a successful soloist, sonata player, composer and arranger. Born in Siegen in Germany, Busch was the son of a cabinet-maker and amateur musician who also made and played violins. Busch studied at the Cologne Hochschule, at first under Willy Hess and then under Bram Eldering. There is an interesting link here in that the Dutch Eldering had studied with Hubay in Brussels and had followed him to Budapest, where he played in the Hubay-Popper Quartet. It was not until 1888 that Eldering renewed his studies with Joachim at the Hochschule in Berlin, so that when Busch became his pupil about 1904, the latter would have benefited from the fusion of teaching elements present in his master.

Busch played the Brahms concerto at his London début in 1912. *The Strad* critic wrote: 'No-one short of Kreisler could approach him for purity of style and intense beauty of phrasing.'

At twenty-one, Busch took over the leadership of the Konzert-verein Orchestra in Vienna and it was here that he formed the first Busch Quartet. In 1917, when only twenty-six, he succeeded Henri Marteau as chief professor of violin at the Hochschule in Berlin, where ten years previously Joachim had held the same post. It was then that he founded the string quartet which was to become famous throughout the world.

But his solo career also continued to flourish and in 1931 he made his American début. In so doing he caught the attention of Toscanini, who was so impressed that he invited Busch to tour the USA with him. This close contact bred a friendship between these two great opposites which lasted until the younger man's death in 1952.

Flesch called Busch 'a character ... a personality ... a thoroughly sympathetic figure in every respect ... By and large, he is the greatest purely German violinist of his age.'[5] This view is borne out by Yehudi Menuhin, who acknowledges a great debt to Busch, with whom he studied: 'He presented me with German culture; in after-years the people and the literature would improve my acquaintance with it; but to him I owe the entry through music, and music expressed in a sensibility which combined scholarship and passion and was never dry.'[6]

To many, Busch had one of the finest bow arms in existence, and his 'elastic' *cantilena* and faultless phrasing can be heard in his numerous recordings, many of which are of the quartet. When he and Rudolf Serkin played all the violin sonatas of Beethoven at the Carnegie Hall in the 1937–8 season, it was declared that the highest ideals of ensemble playing had been realized. One of the features of their playing was that they 'never use their magnificent technical equipment save as a means to express the full power and beauty of the music'.[7]

The Lener Quartet had its origins in the Opera Orchestra in Budapest. When the Revolution broke out in Hungary in 1918, Teno Lener and three of his friends from the orchestra retired to a remote Hungarian village to play chamber music together. They made their first apperance in Vienna in 1920, and Ravel, who was in the audience, invited them to Paris. They became the most celebrated European quartet up until the late forties. In the USA, the Budapest Quartet enjoyed similar acclaim at about the same time.

Another great quartet from central Europe, the Hungarian, was formed in 1935 and led by Zoltan Székely (b.1903) with Sandor Végh (b.1905) as second violin; both were pupils of Hubay at the Budapest Conservatoire. The Hungarian Quartet have made what is widely regarded as one of the best recordings of the Beethoven cycle. In 1940 Végh founded the Végh Quartet which, not surprisingly, is universally known for its 'Hungarian' tone colour, especially evident in the quartets of Bartók. Today Végh is regarded as one of the outstanding teachers of our time and has greatly influenced the performance of chamber music, which he describes as 'an ideal form of democracy; all the players are equal.'

The Russians have also produced some excellent string quartet players. The Borodin Quartet was formed in 1945 whilst the players were still at the Moscow Conservatoire. They specialize in works by Russian composers, and their playing of the Shostako-vich quartets is particularly exciting. In Czechoslovakia, the Prague Quartet, particularly under the leadership of Bretislav Novotny (b.1924) from the early fifties, established a reputation with their interpretations of the music of Smetana and Dvořák.

Emanuel Hurwitz (b.1919), leader of the Aeolian Quartet,

recalls hearing the Busch Quartet when he was a boy and in the late forties and early fifties.

> I always admired them for the sheer ruggedness of their late Beethoven quartets. They had a marvellous sense of urgency and nobility. Busch was a wonderful man for spinning out bow, making a Mozart or a Beethoven tune have a tremendous sense of line. He had an honesty and directness of approach. Today's violinists aim for tone that tries to be beautiful and ingratiating. Busch and the older style of playing had a more stark left hand and relied much more upon accent and punctuation. There were, of course, more slides in the position changes. I find that I have to make my own students listen several times to a Busch recording before they can hear past the older style into the greatness of the playing.[8]

Recent reissues of the Busch Quartet recordings on LP have aroused considerable interest.

It was hearing the Budapest Quartet as a boy that made Hurwitz want to dedicate his life to the medium. He draws an interesting comparison between the style of the Busch and the Budapest Quartets:

> The one Beethoven late quartet that the Busch happened not to have recorded in those days was the Op. 130, but the Budapest Quartet had, with Roisman as their leader — an incredibly elegant player. Although I found it very beautiful, I felt that for the Beethoven it was too easy, too comfortable. But when the Busch eventually recorded it I found theirs a little *too* heavy. It just shows how easy it is to get too used to a certain way of listening and then being jolted into quite another direction.[9]

Hurwitz's training with Leon Bergman, an Auer student, and Robjohns, a pupil of Joachim, places him in a direct line to the Italians. He joined the Aeolian Quartet in 1969: in the next decade they performed all over the world and recorded all the Haydn quartets. In 1979 they recorded the late Beethoven quartets.

The technical demands of string quartet playing are different from those placed upon the soloist. In Hurwitz's opinion, the range of dynamics is one of the most important:

> For a quartet you can play from a whisper up to a *fortissimo* as loud as your collective instruments can produce without going outside the medium. A soloist mostly plays *mezzo forte* to *fortissimo*, and rarely plays softly at all. With an orchestra of up to a hundred players behind him he hasn't the chance. And the soloist who may have exceptional

gymnastic powers may never need to use more than three different bowings for short notes. A really good quartet player might have twenty-five varieties and any number of actual bow starts and finishes. There are subtleties that enter into string quartet playing that the soloist would find unnecessary.[10]

Hurwitz, who has been playing in string quartets since he was fourteen, stresses that it is vital for each player to know all the other parts. He says: 'You may not be able to play the cello part, but you should be able to sing it.' Ultimately it is the 'give and take' of quartet playing that appeals to Hurwitz. 'The parts just flowing across from one to the other makes it such a great joy. It imposes a greater discipline than in any other medium, but it is this very discipline that makes the teamwork of rehearsing a constant pleasure and exploration.'[11]

The teacher of Norbert Brainin (b.1923), Rosa Hochmann-Rosenfeld, arranged for her twelve-year-old student to play the Mozart Quartet in D minor with herself and two of her colleagues. Although he could at the time play the Beethoven concerto, Brainin admits that he was completely at sea when confronted with this second violin part. He had no grasp of what was going on. The experience had a legacy: 'During that session I heard a sound in my inner ear. I knew exactly how it should be if it were done properly.'[12] He vowed if he ever became good enough and chanced to find the right people, he would try to make that sound. Today that sound is a fact. It is known as the Amadeus Quartet, unique in the history of the medium in that — with Brainin as leader — the original four musicians have been playing together for thirty-four years.

Norbert Brainin was born in Vienna into a family who were not particularly musical. At seven he was given a quarter-sized violin, and as soon as he felt it in his hands he knew that somehow he would one day be a violinist.

By his tenth birthday Norbert had made sufficient progress to enter the Vienna Conservatoire under Ricardo Odnoposof, and at twelve he went to Rosa Hochmann-Rosenfeld who trained him in the Viennese school of playing which she had learned from her teacher, Jakob Grün, a pupil of Böhm and contemporary of Joachim. In 1938 when he was fifteen he came to Britain and studied with Carl Flesch for the first six months of the following year. Brainin attaches the greatest importance to this period of his training. In October 1939, shortly after the outbreak of war, at the recommendation of Flesch — who had left for Holland that summer — Brainin went to study with Flesch's pupil, Max Rostal.

During the Blitz of 1940 Brainin was interned as a so-called 'Enemy Alien' at a camp in Shropshire. It was here that he made the acquaintance of a fellow violinist, Peter Schidlof, with whom he became friendly until they were separated and sent to two different camps on the Isle of Man, where Schidlof met another violinist, Siegmund Nissel. Brainin was released after a mere two months of internment but Schidlof and Nissel were detained for over a year. However, by the end of 1941 all three were studying with Max Rostal and it was through another of his pupils, Suzanne Rozsa, that they met her husband, the cellist Martin Lovett.

In 1946 Brainin entered for the Carl Flesch Competition and won the Gold Medal, but despite the opportunity provided by a solo engagement with the London Philharmonic Orchestra at the Royal Albert Hall, his path seemed to be leading in quite a different direction. In the beginning of the following year the four friends teamed up together as a quartet with Schidlof on the viola. They rehearsed almost daily and built up a repertoire so that by the winter they felt they would benefit from giving a recital at the Wigmore Hall. They chose the name 'Amadeus' — suggested by Nissel — because it sounded harmonious and expressed a feeling of agreement. Imogen Holst, who had fostered the ensemble from its inception, made the recital a reality by giving them £100 towards the financial costs.

The concert took place in January 1948 and every seat was sold out before the performance. The ensemble was immediately booked for a BBC broadcast and tours of Spain and Germany followed. Today the Amadeus Quartet gives approximately a hundred performances a year. Its recordings of the Mozart, Schubert, Haydn, Brahms and Beethoven quartets have become classics and sell all over the world.

Brainin always insists upon using the *Urtext*, because there is no other way of knowing what a composer wishes. He avoids those nineteenth-century editions that were fingered and arranged for the amateur rather than the professional musician. Often the bowing, fingering and phrasing were nothing to do with the original. Over a period, Brainin maintains, if enough people add their own ideas on how a piece should be played, you cannot even

The Amadeus Quartet, who have played together for over thirty years: Norbert Brainin, Siegmund Nissel, Peter Schidlof, Martin Lovett

One of America's foremost quartets, the Guarneri: Arnold Steinhardt, John Dalley, Michael Tree, David Soyer

recognize it. 'If you start with an interpretation, all you get is the interpretation of an interpretation.'[13]

The homogeneity of the 'Amadeus' sound is immediately recognizable. In December 1977, after a Beethoven programme in Vienna, Karl Loebel, music editor of the *Kurier*, wrote:

> When the Amadeus play Op. 18 No. 4 and follow this with Op. 131 you do not get interpretations but the whole of Beethoven: his wilfulness, his boisterous abandon, his rage, his infinite imagination. It comes to reshaping themes time and time again, his violence, but also his tenderness, revealing in the slow movements dance-like gestures soon to be hidden. There are no rough edges smoothed over. There is no sentimentality, there is feeling, humour without coyness; nothing prettified. Never is technique displayed for its own sake. Here are four musicians welded into a quartet in four parts. There is no pretension in their playing. It has become a natural utterance.

The string quartet is perhaps the most exacting form of chamber music playing, and the leader's task is formidable. Besides being a faultless technician, he should know exactly the character of sound required for each work and where the emphasis should lie — be it Haydn or Shostakovich — and he is responsible for seeing that each instrumentalist moulds his playing to the other parts. A wise leader will ensure that decisions regarding phrasing, tone quality, tempi and dynamics are taken in collective agreement. As top voice, the leader naturally has the most influence, but a one-to-three, or even two-to-two, decision does not make for artistic concord.

All this is difficult enough to achieve within the classical repertoire, especially the late Beethoven quartets. Contemporary music, in moving away from Classical harmony, form and textures, creates new problems, both technical and musical, yet must still rest within the discipline imposed by the medium. The quartets by Debussy, Ravel, Bartók, Hindemith, Tippett and Shostakovich, for example, explore a variety of colours, textures and rhythms which are altogether more challenging than those by composers of the eighteenth and nineteenth centuries. The six quartets by Bartók in particular are the most complete and widely ranging since the late Beethoven quartets.

One example of the demanding nature of modern string quartet playing is Benjamin Britten's No. 3 Op. 94 written for the Amadeus Quartet and prepared for performance in collaboration with them, shortly before Britten's death in 1976. Here is an instance of the master craftsman writing for a group of superlative musicians whose capabilities were known to him. The result is an alliance of imaginative power and skill in a work as compelling in its valedictory character as it is in its musical content.

In the USA today, several world class quartets are to be heard. The Juilliard Quartet, formed in 1946, are particularly celebrated for their recordings of the Bartók quartets which superlatively portray the mood and colour of this complex writing. The La Salle Quartet was also founded in 1946 whilst its members were at the Juilliard School. They specialize in the playing of twentieth-century music, and have inspired many contemporary composers to write for them. The Guarneri Quartet, formed in 1964, have steadily built up their reputation, playing on superb instruments. Reviewing a performance in Britain in 1979, the *Daily Telegraph* critic found in their playing 'a corporate tone of utmost beauty and a rhythmic sureness rarely to be heard'. The Cleveland Quartet, founded at the Marlboro Festival in 1969, has a wide repertoire extending from Haydn to Eliot Gardiner; their recording of the Brahms quartets is a fine example of their artistry.

Quartet playing is also in a healthy state in Britain today, where a number of young players are turning to the medium. 1971 would seem to be a vintage period, three of the most promising of the youthful quartets being founded in that year: the Chilingirian, led by Levon Chilingirian (b.1948), formed when all the members were students at the Royal College of Music; the Medici, with Paul Robertson as leader, from the Royal Academy of Music; and the Amphion, led by Adrian Levine, formerly resident string quartet at Hatfield Polytechnic and now fulfilling the same function at Liverpool University.

Techniques and styles in quartet playing have been revolutionized over the years. If it were possible to hear the quartets led by Tomasini or Schuppanzigh today, it is unlikely that there would be much resemblance to the playing to which we are accustomed. But the leader's role has remained unchanged throughout the centuries. Without him we have three first-class ensemble musicians: with him they become an entity that is one of the most satisfying of all musical forms.

41

The Way Ahead

In four centuries of the development of violin playing, standards have probably never been higher than they are today. It is not surprising that in striving to reach perfection, the young virtuosos have influenced general standards of performance; although sometimes their facility outstrips their artistic mastery. It is possible for an artist to circle the earth by jet plane and appear in New York on one night and Berlin the next: a formidable contrast to the leisurely travels of Spohr in his carriage or even boat and train journeys of the early part of the present century. The dilemma we face at the present time is that whereas the playing of yesterday's performers matured more slowly naturally, the young virtuoso today is often forced in a hot-house to bloom and be placed on show whilst the shoot is still tender. It is much to their credit that so many players appear to survive these pressures of TV, record-making and ceaseless globe-trotting.

In an age when technical mastery is taken for granted and musicianship is often sacrificed to the inordinate demands of recording, how can a young player make a personal statement that distinguishes him from the uniformity of professional excellence? Only by ignoring fashionable trends and standing rock-firm on the impression the music makes upon the individual performer, can this be achieved, and the full meaning of the music reach the audience. That legendary Hungarian Sandor Végh believes that spontaneity and inspiration must match a player's technical ability. At the biannual International Musicians' Seminar at Prussia Cove in Cornwall, of which he is musical director, he preaches individualism firmly rooted in European traditions. He says: 'I am a chauvinist European. We must preserve what we have from the past or we lose ourselves.'

The individuality of violinists like Ysaÿe, Kreisler, Thibaud and Heifetz can immediately be identified from recordings, however old and scratched. Of the modern violinists, Stern is one of the few whose playing has a personal dimension; Grumiaux is another; and so is the Dutch violinist Herman Krebbers, to whom even the Italians refer as 'Il Paganini'. Among the younger generation, Perlman sometimes falls into this category, and Kyung-Wha Chung has a decidedly 'personal' approach, while the young Japanese Tomotada Soh has that touch of magic that lifts the artist into a class of his own.

Russia and the Eastern European countries continue to produce a steady stream of first-class players. Here there exists an unbroken line of excellence from Viotti to de Bériot through Vieuxtemps and Auer at St Petersburg with Stolyarsky in Odessa. The late David Oistrakh, revered as much as a teacher as an artist, trained many of the brilliant young players who have attained international status or are well on the way to achieving it: Oleg Kagan, Valery Klimov, Gidon Kremer and Victor Pickeisen were all pupils of Oistrakh. Lydia Mordkovich, now resident in Israel, has recently made a superb recording of the César Franck and Ravel sonatas for RCA. The Bulgarian Stoika Milanova has impressed many critics with the poetic and expressive intensity of her playing. Both were Oistrakh pupils.

Another prominent Soviet teacher was the late Yuri Yankelevich, professor of violin at the Gnessin Institute in Moscow. One of his students, Albert Markov (b. 1933), is a late arrival on the American musical scene. He was virtually unknown in the west until his first appearance in New York in 1976 at the age of forty-three. Markov decided to leave the Soviet Union in 1975 because of 'the absence of the possibility to organize an artistic life of my own'.[1]

Markov made his recital début at Alice Tully Hall in New York on 1 November 1976, in a programme that included the Prokofiev Sonata No. 2 in D major and the Schumann Fantasy in C major. He was accompanied by Milton Kaye, for many years Heifetz's personal pianist. The critic from the *New York Post* praised him for not over-romanticizing the Prokofiev: 'His rhythm is vital, dynamic, firmly in his body and blood as well as in his fingers. He performed, altogether, with an actor's sense of drama that arrested the attention and kept it.'[2]

Some virtuosos who have recently emerged:

Pupils of the eminent Soviet teacher Yuri
Yankelevich – Albert Markov *(above)* and
Vladimir Spivakov *(below left)*

Mayumi Fujikawa, one of Japan's most
celebrated cultural exports

Another Yankelevich pupil achieving increasing success in the west is Vladimir Spivakov. His early training was at the Leningrad Conservatoire under Lubov Sigal, who himself studied with Auer. He first appeared in the USA in 1976 at concerts and recitals in New York, Chicago and San Francisco. The critics were unanimous, not only about the beauty of tone and his outstanding technical facility but of his understanding of the music itself. After his début recital at the Carnegie Hall on 28 October, *Musical America* commented that Spivakov descends 'so deeply within himself that the full breadth of the musical meaning lying beneath the subjectives of both performer and composer is expressed with a profundity I have never heard from any performer'.

Most of the musicians mentioned in this chapter have been winners in one or more of the international competitions. The twentieth century could well be called 'The Century of the Competition'. Most aspiring virtuosos enter at least one of these contests — regarded by many to be of dubious worth. On the one hand, a prize can bring a violinist out of obscurity into the limelight, and, provided he or she can face the heat, it may well be the start of an international career. But it is also a further example of how a budding artist can be exposed to the elements too soon. Many prizewinners become competition casualties and never fully recover.

Of the lucky ones, Perlman, Zukerman and Chung all used the Leventritt Prize as a spring-board, as did Eugene Fodor with the Tchaikovsky Competition in Moscow, and survived. The twenty-nine-year-old David Oistrakh was completely unknown in the west when he became the first ever prizewinner in the Ysaÿe Contest in Brussels (now the Queen Elisabeth of the Belgians Concours).

The first International Tchaikovsky Competition was held in Moscow in 1972. Although its technical demands are formidable, the challenge appears to attract an ever-increasing number of applicants. There are three rounds in which the contestant must play — from memory — music that ranges from a Bach sonata to the Tchaikovsky concerto with orchestra. It is only in the first round that the competitor is called upon to play Bach and Mozart. In rounds two and three the pieces are all drawn from the Romantic or contemporary repertoire, a practice that has brought forth the argument that technical facility rather than musical ability is the criterion by which the judges make their decisions.

The young American-Portuguese Elmar Oliveira (b. 1950) caused a stir in July 1978 when he became the first non-Russian to win the gold medal in the Tchaikovsky Competition. A pupil of Raphael Bronstein, he has since given some eighty concerts in North and South America. He is scheduled to visit Europe in 1980. For him, the winning of the competition brought immediate recognition and offers of engagements from those who previously were scarcely aware of his existence.

Until recently, the Leventritt was one of the most prestigious of the US competitions. Held in New York, it awarded the winners a cash prize and a series of engagements with leading American orchestras. It now operates as a scholarship offering a bursary for winners to continue their studies, after which the concert series is undertaken.

The Paganini Competition has been held in Genoa for the last twenty-four years. The first prize-winner receives 5,000,000 lire and is allowed to play Paganini's violin both at a concert to celebrate the close of the event and at another during the season following the competition. Many Japanese have taken prizes in this competition, and a number of French and Italians: Salvatore Accardo (b.1943), one of the most celebrated of the Italian nationals, won the first prize at the age of fifteen.

The Carl Flesch International Competition is Britain's most important contribution. Held every two years, it was instituted at the Guildhall School of Music and Drama in 1945 'for excellence in violin playing' to commemorate the life and work of Carl Flesch. The joint idea of Max Rostal — a Flesch pupil — and Edric Cundell — then Principal of the GSMD, it has gradually expanded from modest beginnings into becoming one of the world's major international competitions and now ranks with the Tchaikovsky in Moscow and the Queen Elisabeth in Brussels.

For several years the Competition was held inside the school with little publicity, and the Carl Flesch medal and one engagement promised to the winner by the London Philharmonic Orchestra were the only tangible rewards; the general public was hardly aware of its existence.

Now incorporated into the Festival of London, the Competition has expanded to offer eight money prizes totalling over £7,000 and is held in three stages in which the entrants are required to play a sonata by Bach, a piece by Sarasate and a modern work specially composed for the occasion. Finalists have to play a Beethoven sonata and one of the major concertos with orchestra. A distinguished international panel of judges under the chairmanship of Yehudi Menuhin attends every stage of the competition.

The Competition director, Yfrah Neaman, himself a pupil of Flesch, Thibaud and Rostal, is widely acclaimed as a teacher and has made a speciality of the performance of modern works, many of which have been written for him.

The first winner of the Carl Flesch medal in 1945 was Raymond Cohen (b. 1919), an important soloist and chamber music player, also much sought after as a teacher. Erich Gruenberg (b. 1924), took the prize in 1947. He came to London in 1946 to study with Max Rostal and stayed to make Britain his home. He has enjoyed a distinguished career in chamber music and as leader of both the London Symphony and Royal Philharmonic Orchestras. He turned to full-time solo work in 1976. An artist whose musical integrity matches his technical facility, Gruenberg has achieved international success. He is 'a player's player': when he gives a London recital, the audience will certainly include a number of his fellow violinists.

In 1970, the Bulgarian Stoika Milanova took first prize in the Carl Flesch and the Japanese Takayoshi Wanami fourth prize. The latter, a sensitive and lyrical player, is the first blind-from-birth virtuoso violinist to gain recognition on an international level. In 1972 the first prize was awarded to a Hungarian violist Csaba Erdelyi, with Michael Bochmann from Britain in fourth place. 1974 saw another Bulgarian, Mincho Minchev, as first prizewinner with the Korean Dong-suk Kang second; Kang has been greatly encouraged by Menuhin, and is now a much sought-after artist. Dora Schwarzberg from Israel was awarded first prize in 1976 with British-born Andrew Watkinson in second place. A product of the Menuhin School, who has also studied with Neaman, the latter is emerging as a soloist whom Neaman compares with Sammons or Szigeti: already he shows signs of turning to quartet playing on a high level of performance. In complete contrast is the 1978 winner of the competition, Eugene Sarbu from Rumania. He studied with Galamian at the Juilliard and in London with Neaman. He possesses a consummate technical facility and excels in the short pieces, which he plays with ease and considerable charm: the true recitalist.

Looking back over the centuries we observe that certain nationalities appear to produce an abundance of great players, whereas others yield only an occasional virtuoso of outstanding significance. From early in the nineteenth century up to the present time the Jewish race would seem to have a monopoly of great soloists, with their origins mainly in Hungary, Poland and Russia. The large number of Jewish violinists born in and around Odessa, makes nonsense of coincidence. The exodus of so many who have achieved international status in the USA, caused Stern to remark: 'They send us their Jews from Odessa, and we send them our Jews from Odessa.'[3]

A significant feature of the seventies is the upsurge of talent from the Far East in less than a decade: Dong-Suk Kang (b. 1954) from Korea, a Carl Flesch Competition prizewinner in 1974, and the Japanese Mayumi Fujikawa (b. 1946) are two outstanding examples of players who have achieved international status. The technique, dedication and musicality manifest in the oriental virtuosos — despite not having been reared in a western culture — is not only surprising, but seemingly inexplicable.

Nevertheless, there is a link here of some significance. The origins of the violin itself — in its most primitive state — rest in the ancient Eastern instruments played with a bow: the ravanastron from Ceylon and the Chinese fiddle. Centuries later the rebec was brought to the west by the Arabs. Played and perfected by the Latins, the violin reached its zenith of performance in the hands of Hebrews. It would seem that the orientals have now come full circle, and will, in the future, play a prominent part in the history of violin playing.

The high standards of performance engendered by this multiracial excellence presages well for the future. The superlative quality of contemporary recorded sound will provide definitive examples by which unprecedented comparisons may be made by succeeding generations.

However, whether we learn about technique and style from eighteenth-century journals or the latest digital recording, one quality is shared by them all. The great violinists are the supreme romantics, and it is through their gift of direct communication that we have experienced and will continue to experience the impact of music as a living force.

Notes

For full details of publications cited, see Bibliography.

PROLOGUE: TOOLS OF THE TRADE

1 Boyden, p. 32.
2 Farga, p. 54.

I. BEGINNINGS

1 Van der Straeten, *Romance*, p. 68.
2 Burney, iii, p. 462.
3 Quoted in van der Straeten, *History*, i, p.151.

2. THE ARCHANGEL AND THE RED PRIEST: *Corelli; Vivaldi*

1 Quoted in van der Straeten, *History*, i, p. 143.
2 Ferris, p. 12.
3 Quoted in van der Straeten, *History*, i, p. 139.
4 Quoted in Kolneder, p. 31.
5 Pincherle, p. 43.
6 Ibid., p. 91.
7 Busby, ii, p. 205.
8 Quoted in van der Straeten, *History*, i, p. 153.

3. MASTER OF THE NATIONS: *Tartini*

1 Menuhin, p. 224.

2 Boyden, p. 344.
3 Quoted in E. Heron-Allen, Grove 5, viii, p. 313.
4 Ibid.
5 Tartini, pp. 11–13.
6 Quoted in van der Straeten, ii, p. 9.

4. VIOTTI AND THE FRENCH TRIO: *Viotti; Baillot de Sales; Rode; Kreutzer*

1 Chappell White, Grove 6, p. 3076.
2 Ibid.
3 Quoted in Ferris, p. 29.
4 Adrienne Simpson, 'An Introduction to Czech Baroque Music', *The Consort*, 1978 (No. 34), p. 288.
5 Perceval Graves, Grove 5, v, p. 554.
6 Spohr, i. p. 13.
7 Quoted in Farga, p. 150.
8 Quoted in E. Heron-Allen, Grove 5, viii, p. 827.
9 Quoted in F.O. Souper, *The Strad*, May 1930, p. 25.
10 P. Donostia, Grove 5, i. p. 356.
11 Quoted in Blunt, p. 144.

5. 'NIGHTINGALE OF VIOLINISTS': *Spohr*

1 Quoted in Pleasants, p. 53.
2 Spohr, i, p. 4.
3 Ibid., p. 13.
4 Quoted in P. Donostia, Grove 5, ii, p. 879.
5 Quoted in Pleasants, p. 16.
6 Quoted ibid., p. 85.
7 *Wienertheaterzeitung*, December 1806.
8 Quoted in Sonneck, p. 95.
9 Spohr, i, p. 302.
10 Ibid., p. 280.
11 Ibid., p. 281.
12 Ibid., ii, p. 168.
13 Ibid., ii, p. 189.
14 Quoted in Herman Klein, Grove 5, ii, p. 219.

6. THE CATALYST: *Paganini*

1 Pulver, p. 44.
2 Quoted in De Courcey, i, p. 44.

3 Ibid., i, p. 27.
4 Ibid., i, pp. 34–5.
5 Quoted ibid., i, p. 56.
6 Quoted ibid., i, p. 67.
7 Quoted ibid., i, p. 99.
8 Ibid., i, p. 265.
9 Open University, Course A202, 'The Age of Revolutions'.
10 Quoted ibid.
11 Ibid.
12 De Courcey, ii, p. 55.
13 Quoted ibid.
14 Quoted ibid.
15 Quoted in Haweis, p. 383.
16 Quoted in De Courcey, i. p. 47.

7. DISCIPLES OF PAGANINI: *Sivori; Ernst; Bazzini; Bull*

1 *The Times*, 30 June 1846.
2 Van der Straeten, *History*, ii, p. 353.
3 Laurie, p. 61.
4 Berlioz, pp. 538–9.
5 Ibid., p. 538.
6 Auer, p. 91.
7 Ibid., p. 5.
8 Spohr, ii, p. 17.
9 Lahee, p. 200.
10 Quoted ibid., p. 183.
11 Quoted ibid., p. 188.
12 Ibid., p. 193.
13 Ibid., p. 203.

8. AGE OF TRANSITION: *Böhm; David; de Bériot*

1 Quoted in Blunt, pp. 241–2.
2 Quoted in van der Straeten, p. 134.

9. THE HOT-BED OF LIÈGE: *Massart; Marsick; Thomson*

1 Flesch, *Memoirs*, pp. 65–6. See quotation on p. 143.
2 Lahee, p. 269.
3 Flesch, op. cit., p. 44.

4   Lahee, p. 268/9.
5   Quoted in van der Straeten, ii, p. 180.

10. 'HE HOLDS YOU IN A MAGIC CIRCLE': *Vieuxtemps*

1   Robert Schumann, *Gesammelte Schriften*, 1834.
2   Berlioz, p. 538.
3   Laurie, p. 112.

11. THE SLAVONIC WIZARD: *Wieniawski*

1   Harold Schonberg, *The Great Pianists* (London, 1974), p. 260.
2   Lahee, p. 224.
3   Quoted in C. R. Halski, Grove 5, ix, p. 288.
4   Ibid.

12. SERVANT OF ART: *Joachim*

1   Moser, p. 57.
2   *Honmuvesz*, 21 March 1839.
3   Quoted in Moser, p. 7.
4   Quoted ibid., p. 39.
5   Quoted ibid., pp. 51–2.
6   Quoted ibid., p. 173.
7   Auer, p. 6.
8   Flesch, *Memoirs*, p. 34.
9   Joachim to Brahms, 24 August 1878.
10 Ibid., 20 May 1879.
11 Brahms to Joachim, May 1879.
12 Joachim to Brahms, end of March 1879.
13 Quoted in Moser, p. 263.
14 Quoted in Hill, p. 152.
15 Hanslick, pp. 78–91.
16 Flesch, *Memoirs*, p. 32.
17 Ibid., p. 36.
18 Ibid., p. 37.
19 Quoted in Lochner, p. 50.
20 Quoted in Moser, pp. 286–7.

13. LADY OF THE BOW: *Wilma Norman-Neruda*

1 Quoted in Haweis, p. 296.
2 Lahee, p. 302.
3 Quoted in *The Strad*, August 1897, p. 107.
4 Quoted in Scholes, ii, pp. 834–5.
5 Quoted in Lahee, p. 315.
6 Gibson, p. 50.

14. INCOMPARABLE CHARMER: *Sarasate*

1 Van der Straeten, ii. p. 419.
2 Quoted in Lahee, p. 229.
3 Quoted in Scholes, i. p. 347.
4 Quoted ibid.
5 Quoted ibid.
6 Lahee, p. 231.
7 Flesch, *Memoirs*, p. 38.
8 Arthur Symons, *Illustrated London News*, 21 November 1891, p. 658.
9 Arthur Symons, *Double Dealer* (New Orleans), November 1921.
10 Flesch, *Memoirs*, p. 42.
11 D. C. Parker, *The Strad*, January 1966. p. 323.
12 Flesch, *Memoirs*, p. 43.
13 Ibid., p. 42.
14 Ibid., p. 43.
15 Ibid., pp. 38–9.

15. THE GREAT TEACHERS: *Wilhelmj; Auer; Ševčik; Hubay; Flesch*

1 Quoted by Dettmar Dressel, *The Strad*, February 1952, p. 296.
2 Flesch, *Memoirs*, p. 33.
3 Van der Straeten, *History*, ii. p. 264.
4 Interview, MC.
5 Quoted in Flesch, *Memoirs*, p. 253.
6 Ibid., p. 254.
7 Quoted by Reid Stewart, *The Strad*, June 1933, p. 59.
8 Quoted ibid., p. 58.
9 Quoted by Granville Casey, *The Strad*, October 1966, p. 207.
10 Quoted by Reid Stewart, *The Strad*, June 1933, p. 58.
11 Quoted by Andrée Alvin, *Monde Musical*, 28 February 1934.
12 Ibid.
13 Flesch, *Memoirs*, p. 153.

14   Ibid., p. 154.
15   Szigeti, *With Strings Attached*, pp. 87–8.
16   Flesch, *Memoirs*, p. 66.
17   Ibid., p. 161.
18   Ibid., p. 174.
19   Haendel, p. 43.
20   Ibid.
21   Quoted in Flesch, *Memoirs*, p. 371.
22   Interview, MC.

16. 'AS THE BIRDS SING': *Ysaÿe*

1   Ysaÿe, p. 21.
2   Ibid., p. 29.
3   Quoted ibid., p. 47.
4   George Bernard Shaw, *The World*, 1 April 1891.
5   Ibid., 20 May 1891.
6   Flesch, *Memoirs*, p. 78.
7   Ibid., p. 79.
8   Interview, MC.
9   Lahee, pp. 272–3.
10   Ysaÿe, p. 155.
11   Interview, MC.
12   Ibid.
13   Ysaÿe, p. 154.
14   Van der Straeten, *History*, p. 145.
15   Ysaÿe, p. 90.

17. SYMBOL OF AN EPOCH: *Kreisler*

1   Szigeti, *With Strings Attached*, pp. 88–9.
2   Hanslick, *Neue Freie Presse*, 25 January 1898.
3   *Neues Wiener Journal*, 26 January 1898.
4   Lochner, p. 196.
5   Quoted ibid., p. 365.
6   Quoted ibid., p. 38.
7   Ibid., p. 353.
8   Flesch, *Memoirs*, p. 125.
9   Josef Gingold, speech given at the Kreisler Centennial Concert held at
     Indiana University, 2 February 1975.

18. THE FRENCH PHENOMENON: *Thibaud*

1 Flesch, *Memoirs*, p. 196.
2 Ibid., p. 197.
3 Ibid.
4 Brook, p. 178.
5 Interview, MC.

19. TO DANCE IN CHAINS: *Enesco; Kubelik*

1 Quoted in Menuhin, p. 68.
2 Interview, MC.
3 Quoted in Menuhin, p. 69.
4 Interview, MC.
5 Ibid.
6 Flesch, *Memoirs*, p. 178.
7 Boult, p. 141.
8 Interview, MC.
9 Haendel, p. 90.
10 Ibid.
11 Ibid., p. 172.
12 Menuhin, p. 71.
13 Aldrich, p. 118.
14 Lochner, p. 70.
15 *The Strad*, December 1938, p. 352.

20. THE UNBRIDLED INDIVIDUALIST: *Huberman*

1 Haendel, pp. 30–1.
2 Arthur Herman, *The Strad*, February 1932, p. 531.
3 A. S. Ruppa, *The Strad*, March 1934, p. 464.
4 Quoted by A. S. Ruppa, *The Strad*, February 1936, p. 439.
5 Menuhin, p. 97.
6 Arthur Herman, *The Strad*, February 1932, p. 530.
7 Quoted ibid.
8 Flesch, *Memoirs*, p. 178.
9 Hans Keller, Appendix I in Flesch, *Memoirs*, p. 368.

21. 'OUR OWN ALBERT': *Sammons*

1 Brook, p. 145.

2 Beecham, p. 81.
3 Quoted in Brook, p. 148.
4 Quoted ibid., p. 156.
5 Interview, MC.
6 Ibid.
7 Ibid.
8 Quoted in Brook, p. 155.

22. THE RUSSIAN VANGUARD: *Zimbalist; Elman*

1 Aldrich, p. 338.
2 Ibid. p. 339.
3 Brook, p. 191.
4 Quoted in Applebaum, p. 2.
5 Brook, p. 37.
6 Auer, pp. 42–3.
7 Brook, p. 37.
8 Gaisberg, p. 207.
9 Flesch, *The Art of Violin Playing*, p. 51.
10 Flesch, *Memoirs*, p. 254.
11 Brook, p. 38.

23. THE SCHOLARLY VIRTUOSO: *Szigeti*

1 *The Strad*, April 1951, p. 432 (book review).
2 Szigeti, *With Strings Attached*, p. 29.
3 Ibid., p. 46.
4 Ibid., p. 48.
5 Ibid., p. 245.
6 Ibid., p. 250.
7 Brook, p. 172.
8 Ibid., p. 171.
9 Flesch, *Memoirs*, p. 292.
10 Interview, MC.
11 Henry Roth, *The Strad*, December 1972, p. 413.
12 Quoted in Szigeti, op. cit., p. 83.

24. 'KING OF VIOLINISTS': *Heifetz*

1 Letter from George Bernard Shaw, 5 May 1920.
2 Axelrod (ed.), p. 33.
3 Ibid., p. 126.

4 Ibid., p. 128.
5 Ibid., p. 46.
6 Ibid.
7 Flesch, *Memoirs*, p. 337.
8 Richard Aldrich, *New York Times*, 28 October 1917.
9 *Musical Times*, June 1920.
10 A. Bryan, *The Strad*, July 1930, p. 148.
11 Axelrod (ed.), p. 280.
12 Ibid., p. 263.
13 Ibid.
14 Flesch, *Memoirs*, p. 335–6.
15 Ibid., p. 337.
16 Applebaum, p. 38.
17 Axelrod (ed.), p. 277.
18 Interview, MC.
19 Axelrod (ed.), p. 473.
20 Interview, MC.
21 Ibid.

25. CHILD OF THE REVOLUTION: *Milstein*

1 Szigeti, *With Strings Attached*, p. 221.
2 Interview, MC.
3 Ibid.
4 Ibid.
5 Ibid.
6 Ibid.
7 Simon Collins, *The Strad*, August 1976, p. 267.
8 Interview, MC.

26. THE *Bel Canto* VIRTUOSO: *Campoli*

1 Interview, MC.
2 *Morning Post*, 19 May 1923.
3 *Westminster Gazette*, 19 May 1923.
4 *Daily Express*, 23 May 1923.
5 Interview, MC.
6 Ibid.
7 Ibid.
8 Ibid.
9 Ibid.
10 Ibid.
11 Ibid.

12   *Daily Mail*, 4 September 1945.
13   Interview, MC.

27. THE ENTERTAINERS: *Sandler; Jenkins; Jaffa; Leopold; Georgiadis*

1   Robert Lewin, *The Strad*, March 1978, p. 1049.
2   Ibid., April 1929, p. 706.
3   Interview, MC.
4   *The Strad*, March 1934, p. 448 (anon.).
5   *Hastings and St Leonards Observer* (concert at Brahms Festival, 25 April 1933).
6   Jonah Barrington, *Daily Graphic*, 8 July 1949.
7   *Hastings and St Leonards Observer*, 24 June 1950.
8   Quoted in 'Max Jaffa', (BBC radio broadcast by Gale Pedrick.)
9   Quoted ibid.
10   Interview, MC.
11   Ibid.
12   Ibid.
13   Interview, MC.
14   Ibid.
15   Ibid.
16   Ibid.
17   Ibid.

28. THE VIOLIN 'HOT': *South; Smith; Venuti; Grappelli*

1   Gunther Schuller, *Early Jazz: Its Roots and Musical Development* (New York, 1968), Appendix.
2   Ibid., p. 368.
3   Ibid., p. 372.
4   Charles Fox, Peter Gammond, Alun Morgan, *Jazz on Record: A Critical Guide* (London, 1960), p. 287.
5   Ibid., p. 285.
6   *Jazz Journal International*, November 1978.
7   Interview, MC.
8   Ibid.
9   Ibid.
10   Ibid.
11   Ibid.
12   Ibid.
13   Whitney Balliett, *New Yorker*, 19 January 1976.
14   Interview, MC.

15 Ibid.
16 Interview, MC.
17 Programme Notes.

29. MORE LADIES OF THE BOW: *Hall; Powell; Morini; de Vito*

1   Morini, letter to MC.
2   Ibid.
3   Quoted ibid.
4   *New York Post*, 9 February 1976.
5   Morini, letter to MC.
6   Ibid.
7   Applebaum, p. 88.
8   Interview, MC.
9   Simon Collins, *The Strad*, October 1977, p. 481.
10 Eric Blom, Grove 5, ix, p. 23.

30. THE ENKINDLING SPIRIT: *Oistrakh*

1   Interview, MC.
2   Quoted in Krause, p. 13.
3   Ibid.
4   Haendel, p. 51.
5   Ysaÿe, extract in *Journal des Beaux-Arts*, 1955, p. 175.
6   Interview, MC.
7   *The Times*, 11 November 1954.
8   Quoted in Krause, p. 19.
9   Interview, MC.
10 Interview, MC.
11 Menuhin, letter to MC, 30 October 1978.

31. A MAN FOR ALL MUSIC: *Menuhin*

1   Menuhin, p. 27.
2   Ibid., p. 50.
3   Ibid., p. 66.
4   Ibid.
5   Ibid., p. 67.
6   Ibid., p. 57.
7   Ibid., p. 71.
8   Ibid., p. 72.

9 Ibid., pp. 85–6.
10 Ibid., p. 102.
11 Gaisberg, p. 237.
12 Ibid.
13 Menuhin, pp. 122–3.
14 Ibid.
15 Gaisberg, p. 238.
16 Gaisberg, op. cit. (letter dated 22 November 1932).
17 Menuhin, p. 162.
18 Quoted ibid, p. 164.
19 Ibid., p. 166.
20 Ibid.
21 Quoted ibid., p. 167.
22 Interview, MC.
23 Ibid.
24 Ibid.

32. THE BORN VIRTUOSO: *Ricci*

1 Alix B. Williamson, publicity brochure.
2 Henry Roth, *The Strad*, August 1976, p. 303.
3 Interview, MC.
4 Ibid.
5 Henry Roth, *The Strad*, August 1976, p. 303.
6 Interview, MC.
7 Ibid.
8 Ibid.

33. 'AIM HIGH — AIM AT BEAUTY': *Neveu; Haendel*

1 Haendel, p. 45.
2 Quoted in Ronze-Neveu, p. 31.
3 Ibid., p. 36.
4 Quoted ibid., pp. 36–7.
5 Ibid., p. 41.
6 Quoted in ibid., pp. 41–2.
7 Quoted ibid., p. 67.
8 Quoted ibid., p. 90.
9 Quoted ibid., p. 92.
10 Quoted ibid., pp. 49–50.
11 Quoted ibid., p. 79.
12 Quoted ibid., p. 52.
13 Quoted Haendel, p. 201.
14 Ronze-Neveu, p. 81.

15 Haendel, p. 54.
16 Ibid., p. 53.
17 Ibid., p. 56.
18 Interview, MC.
19 *The Gazette*, Montreal, 7 October 1975.
20 Haendel, p. 224.
21 Ibid.

34. THE ELDER STATESMAN: *Stern*

1   Simon Collins, *The Strad*, August 1977.
2   Olin Downes, *New York Times*, 12 October 1937.
3   Quoted by Simon Collins, *The Strad*, August 1977, p. 293.
4   *New York Times*, 9 January 1943.
5   Interview, MC.
6   Quoted by Simon Collins, *The Strad*, August 1977, p. 291.
7   Interview, MC.
8   Carnegie Hall: 'Looking Ahead'.
9   *Philadelphia Guide*, 'Master Fiddler', June 1978.
10 Ibid.
11 Quoted by Simon Collins, *The Strad*, August 1977, p. 295.

35. THE MUSICIAN'S MUSICIAN: *Grumiaux*

1   Grumiaux, letter to MC.
2   Ibid.
3   Ibid.
4   Ibid.
5   *Brooklyn Eagle*, 16 January 1953.
6   Philips publicity brochure.
7   Interview, Bernadette Morand (Grumiaux).
8   *Stereo Review*, November 1968, p. 87.
9   Interview, Bernadette Morand (Grumiaux).
10 Philips publicity brochure.

36. THE DIPLOMAT AND 'THE POLISH BOY': *Szeryng; Hassid*

1   Simon Collins, *The Strad*, May 1978, p. 11.
2   Quoted ibid., May 1978, p. 13.
3   Quoted ibid., May 1978, p. 57.
4   *International Herald Tribune*, 29 January 1973.

5 Flesch, *Memoirs*, p. 360.
6 Quoted in Haendel, p. 65.
7 Gerald Moore, letter to MC, 2 December 1978.
8 Haendel, p. 115.
9 Carl Flesch to Josef Hassid, 6 June 1943.

37. GREAT TEACHERS OF AMERICA: *Persinger; Gingold; Galamian*

1 Interview, MC.
2 Ibid.
3 Menuhin, p. 34.
4 Ibid., p. 36.
5 Interview, MC.
6 Applebaum, p. 282.
7 Quoted ibid.
8 Interview, MC.
9 Galamian, p. 8.
10 *New York Times*, 23 November 1977.
11 Galamian, p. 8.
12 Interview, MC.
13 Ibid.
14 Galamian, letter to MC, 12 May 1977.
15 *New York Times*, 23 November 1977.
16 Ibid.
17 Galamian, p. 6.
18 *New York Times*, 23 November 1977.

38. THE 'GALAMIAN TRIO' *Perlman; Zukerman; Kyung-Wha Chung*

1 Gillian Widdecombe, *Records and Recording*, May 1973.
2 *Violin Society of USA Journal*, Vol. III, No. 2 (Spring 1977), p. 21.
3 *New York Times*, 30 October 1965.
4 *Violin Society of USA Journal*, Vol. III, No. 2 (Spring 1977), p. 12.
5 Galamian, p. 7.
6 William Bender, *New York Herald Tribune*, 30 October 1964.
7 Joan Chissell, *The Times*, 25 August 1969.
8 Gillian Widdecombe, *Records and Recording*, May 1973.
9 *New York Times*, 6 February 1969.
10 Interview, MC.
11 Interview , MC.
12 Ibid.
13 Gillian Widdecombe, *Financial Times*, 14 May 1970.

14 Edward Greenfield, *The Guardian*, 11 June 1971.
15 Interview, MC.
16 Ibid.
17 Ibid.
18 Ibid.
19 Ibid
20 *Daily Telegraph*, 31 January 1979.

39. THE ENGLISH PHENOMENON: *Holmes*

1 Louis Biancolli, *World Telegram* (New York), 1 April 1966.
2 Interview, MC.
3 Ibid.
4 *Daily Telegraph*, 9 February 1951.
5 Interview, MC.
6 Ibid.
7 Ibid.
8 Ibid.
9 *The Times*, 1 November 1954.
10 Quoted in *The Strad*, February 1956, p. 365.
11 Interview, MC.
12 Ibid.
13 *Kurier*, Vienna, 23 December 1959.
14 Louis Biancolli, *World Telegram* (New York), 1 April 1966.

40. GREAT QUARTET LEADERS

1 Van der Straeten, ii, p. 37.
2 C. Ferdinand Pohl, Grove 5, iv. p. 230.
3 Boult, p. 18.
4 Interview, MC.
5 Flesch, *Memoirs*, p. 265.
6 Menuhin, p. 97.
7 *New York Times*.
8 Interview, MC.
9 Ibid.
10 Ibid.
11 Ibid.
12 Interview, MC.
13 Ibid.

41. THE WAY AHEAD

1   Quoted by Leighton Kerner, *The Voice*, 1 November 1976.
2   Harriett Johnson, *New York Post*, 12 November 1976.
3   *Stagebill*, Vol. II, No. 1 (Philadelphia), 1978.

Bibliography

First-mentioned editions are those I have consulted and to which reference is made in the Notes.

Abraham, Gerald. *A Hundred Years of Music*, Duckworth (London, 1966)

Aldrich, Richard. *Concert Life in New York*, Putnam (New York, 1941)

Applebaum, Samuel and Sada. *With the Artists*, Markert (New York, 1955)

Auer, Leopold. *Violin Playing as I Teach it*, Duckworth (London, 1960)

Axelrod, Dr Herbert R. (ed.). *Heifetz*, Paganiniana Publications (New Jersey, 1976)

Bacharach, A. L. (ed.). *The Musical Companion*, Victor Gollancz (London, 1934)

Bachmann, Alberto. *An Encyclopedia of the Violin*, Da Capo (New York, 1975; London, 1976)

Beecham, Sir Thomas. *A Mingled Chime*, White Lion; Da Capo (London; New York, 1973)

Berlioz, Hector. *The Memoirs of Berlioz*, ed. D. Cairns, Panther (London, 1970); W. W. Norton (New York, 1975)

Blunt, Wilfrid. *On Wings of Song*, Hamish Hamilton; Scribner's (London; New York, 1974)

Boult, Sir Adrian. *My Own Trumpet*, Hamish Hamilton (London, 1973)

Boyden, David D. *The History of Violin Playing*, Oxford University Press (London; New York, 1965)

Brook, Donald. *Violinists of Today*, Rockliff (London, 1948)

Burney, Charles. *A General History of Music*, ed. Mercer, Dover; Constable (New York; London, 1957)

Busby, Thomas. *Concert Room and Orchestra Anecdotes*, (London, 1825)

Courcey, G. I. G. De. *Paganini the Genoese*, 2 vols, Oklahoma Press (Oklahoma, 1957)

Elkin, Robert. *Queen's Hall (1893–1941)*, Rider (London, 1944)

—— *Royal Philharmonic (1893–1941)*, Rider (London, 1946)

—— *The Old Concert Rooms of London*, Arnold (London, 1955)

Emery, Frederic B. *The Violin Concerto*, 2 vols, Da Capo (New York, 1969)

Evans, Edwin. *Brahms Chamber and Orchestral Music*, Reeves (London, undated)

Farga, Franz. *Violins and Violinists*, Rockliff (London, 1950)

Ferris, George T. *Great Pianists and Great Violinists*, 3rd ed., Reeves (London, undated)

Flesch, Carl. *The Art of Violin Playing*, Carl Fischer (New York, 1939)

—— *The Memoirs of Carl Flesch*, trans. Hans Keller, Bois de Boulogne: W. Reeves/Rockliff (London, 1973)

Fuller-Maitland, J. A. *Brahms*, Methuen (London, undated)

Gaisberg, Fred W. *Music on Record*, Robert Hale (London, 1946)

Galamian, Ivan. *Principles of Violin Playing and Teaching*, Prentice-Hall; Faber & Faber (New York; London, 1962)

Gibson, J. C. *A Musician's Life*, Frederick Books (London, undated)

Greer, David. *Hamilton Harty, His Life and Music*, Blackstaff Press, (Belfast 1979)

Grove's *Dictionary of Music and Musicians*, 5th and 6th eds, Macmillan; St. Martin's Press (London; New York, 1954, 1980)

Haendel, Ida. *Woman with Violin*, Victor Gollancz (London 1970)

Hanslick, Eduard. *Music Criticisms 1846–99*, trans. and ed. Henry Pleasants, Penguin (London, 1950; Baltimore, 1964)

Harley, John. *Music in Purcell's London*, Dobson (London, 1968)

Haweis, R. H. *My Musical Life*, W. H. Allen (London, 1884)

Hill, Ralph. *Brahms: A Study in Musical Biography*, Dennis Archer (London, 1933)

Hill, W. Henry, Arthur F. and Alfred E. *Antonio Stradivari*, Dover; W. E. Hill (New York; London, 1963)

Horton, John. *Brahms Orchestral Music*, BBC Music Guides (London, 1968)

International Cyclopedia of Music and Musicians, ed. A. Thompson, 10th ed., Dodd, Mead; Dent (New York; London, 1975)

Kolneder, Walter. *Antonio Vivaldi, His Life and Work*, Faber & Faber; California University Press (London; Berkeley, Calif., 1970)

Krause, Ernst. *David Oistrakh* (Berlin, 1973)

Lahee, Henry C. *Famous Violinists of Today and Yesterday*, Page (Boston, 1899)

Laurie, David. *Reminiscences of a Fiddle Dealer*, Virtuoso Publications (Cape Coral, 1977)

Lochner, Louis P. *Fritz Kreisler*, Rockliff (London, 1951)

Macleod, Joseph. *The Sisters d'Aranyi*, George Allen & Unwin (London, 1969)

Menuhin, Yehudi. *Unfinished Journey*, Macdonald & Jane's; Alfred A. Knopf (London; New York, 1977)

—— *Violin and Viola*, Macdonald & Jane's; Macmillan (London; New York, 1976)

Moser, Andreas. *Joseph Joachim*, trans. Lilla Durham, Philip Welby (London, 1901)

—— *Briefe an Brahms und Joachim*, ed. Moser, Verlag der Deutschen Brahms Gesellschaft, Berlin (vol. i 1908, vol. ii 1912)

Mozart, Leopold. *A Treatise on the Fundamental Principles of Violin Playing*, trans. Editha Knocker, Oxford University Press (London, 1948; New York, 1951)

Neumann, Werner. *Bach and His World*, Thames & Hudson (London, 1961)

Roger North on Music, ed. John Wilson, Novello (London, 1959)

Penguin Stereo Record Guide, 2nd edition, ed. Edward Greenfield, Robert Layton, Ivan March, Penguin (London; Baltimore, 1977)

Pincherle, Marc. *Vivaldi, Genius of the Baroque*, Norton; Gollancz (New York, 1957; London, 1958)

Pleasants, Henry. *The Musical Journeys of Louis Spohr*, Oklahoma Press (Oklahoma, 1961)

Pulver, Jeffrey. *Paganini the Romantic Virtuoso*, Herbert Joseph (London, 1936); repr. Da Capo (New York, 1970)

Ronze-Neveu, M. J. *Ginette Neveu*, Rockliff (London, 1957)

Salter, Lionel. *The Gramophone Guide to Classical Composers and Recordings*, Book Club Associates (London, 1978)

Scholes, Percy A. *The Mirror of Music 1844–1944*, 2 vols, Novello and Oxford University Press; Arno (London; Oxford; New York, 1947)

Sonneck, O. G. *Beethoven: Impressions by his Contemporaries*, Dover; Constable (New York; London, 1968)

Spohr, Louis. *Louis Spohr's Autobiography*, Da Capo (New York, 1969)

The Strad, Novello (London, 1898–1979)

Straeten E. van der. *The History of the Violin*, 2 vols, Da Capo (New York, 1968)

—— *The Romance of the Fiddle*, Rebman (London, 1911)

Szigeti, Joseph. *With Strings Attached*, Alfred A. Knopf (New York, 1967)

—— *On the Violin*, Cassell; Praeger (London, 1969; New York, 1970)

Tartini, G. *Letter to Maddalena Lombardini*, trans. Charles Burney (London 1779); Johnson Repr. (New York)

Ysaÿe, Antoine. *Eugène Ysaÿe*, Editions Ysaÿe (Brussels, 1974)

Discography

*signifies 'unavailable'.

Abbreviations: BSO   Boston Symphony Orchestra
                CO   Concertgebouw Orchestra
     ... CO ... Chamber Orchestra
                ECO   English Chamber Orchestra
                LPO   London Philharmonic Orchestra
                LSO   London Symphony Orchestra
                NPO   New Philharmonia Orchestra
                NSO   New Symphony Orchestra
                NYPO New York Philharmonic Orchestra
                PO   Philharmonia Orchestra
                RPO   Royal Philharmonic Orchestra
     ... SO ... Symphony Orchestra
                VPO   Vienna Philharmonic Orchestra

In names of further orchestras, the word 'Orchestra' is understood throughout.

		UK no.	US no.
Accardo, Salvatore	PAGANINI Concertos Nos 1–6; LPO, Dutoit	DGG 2740 121 (5 discs)	id.
Aeolian Quartet	HAYDN Quartets complete, Nos 1–80:		Lon.
	0–12	HD NM 52–56	STS 15328–32
	13–18+50–56	HD NV 82–84	
	19–24+25–30	HD NQ 61–66	STS 15337–8

			UK no.	US no.
		31–36+63–68	HD NT 70–75	STS 15447–52
		37–49	HD NU 76–81	STS 15453–8
		57–59+60–62	HD NS 67–69	STS 15346–8
		69–74	HD NL 49–51	STS 15325–7
		75–80	HD NP 57–60	STS 15333–6
Allegri Quartet	BRITTEN Quartets Nos 1 in D major Op.25; 2 in C major Op.36		Decca SXL 6564	Lon. STS 15303
Amadeus Quartet	BEETHOVEN Quartets Nos 1–16; Grosse Fugue		DGG 2721 071	
——	BRITTEN Quartets Nos 3 Op.94; 2 in C major Op.36		Decca SXL 6893	
Bean, Hugh	VAUGHAN WILLIAMS The Lark Ascending; (Symphony No. 6); NPO, Boult		EMI ASD 2329	Angel 36469
Borodin Quartet	SHOSTAKOVICH Quartets Nos 1–13		HMV SLS 879 (6 discs)	Angel SIC 6034/5
Bress, Hyman	SPOHR 'Gesangsscene', Concerto No. 8 in A minor Op. 47; 9 in D minor Op. 55; SO of Beck		Oiseau-Lyre SOL 278	SOL 278
Budapest Quartet	BEETHOVEN Quartet No. 14 in C sharp minor Op. 131			★AmC 70685/9D
——	BEETHOVEN Quartet No. 15 in A minor Op. 132			★AmC 71499/503D
Busch Quartet	BEETHOVEN Quartets Op.95, Op.127, Op.130, Op.131, Op.132, Op.135		EMI World Records SHB 38 (set) LP Reissue	
Busch, Adolf	BEETHOVEN Sonatas for violin and piano; Serkin (pre-1936 rec.)		★HMV DB 1973/5 (set)	★Vic 8351/3 (set)
Campoli. Alfredo	BAZZINI 'Ronde des Lutins', etc.		★Decca Eclipse ECS 639	

		UK no.	US no.
——	BEETHOVEN Concerto; LSO, Krips	Decca ECS 521	Lon. LL 560
——	ELGAR Concerto; LPO, Boult	Decca ECS 675	Lon. LL 1168
——	BRUCH Concerto No. 1 in G minor; NSO, Kisch; MENDELSSOHN Concerto in E minor; LPO, Van Beinum	Decca Eclipse ECS 505	Richmond R 19021
——	SARASATE *Zigeunerweisen* Op.20/21; SAINT-SAËNS Concerto No.3 in B minor Op.61; WIENIAWSKI *Légende*; LPO, Gamba	Decca Eclipse ECS 663	Lon. STS 15142
——	SARASATE 'Eight Spanish Dances'; Daphne Ibbott, piano; 'Navarra' for two violins; Belinda Bunt, violin	Oiseau-Lyre DSLO 22	
——	TCHAIKOVSKY Concerto; PAGANINI Concerto No.1 in D major Op.6; LSO, Argenta	Decca SPA 183	Lon. STS 15263
Chilingirian Quartet	KORNGOLD Quartet No.1 in A; 3 in D	RCA RL 25097	
Chung, Kyung-Wha	BRUCH Concerto No.1 in G minor Op.26; Scottish Fantasia; RPO, Kempe	Decca SXL 6573	Lon. CS 6795
——	PROKOFIEV Concertos Nos 1 in D major Op.19, 2 in G minor Op.63; LSO, Previn	Decca SXL 6773	Lon. CS 6997
——	TCHAIKOVSKY and SIBELIUS Concertos; LSO, Previn	Decca SXL 6493	Lon. CS 6710
——	VIEUXTEMPS Concerto No.5 in A minor Op.37; SAINT-SAËNS Concerto No.3 in B minor Op.61; LSO, Foster	Decca SXL 6759	Lon. CS 6992

		UK no.	US no.
——	WALTON and STRAVINSKY Concertos; LSO, Previn	Decca SXL 6601	LON. CS 6819
Elman, Mischa	BEETHOVEN Concerto; LPO, Solti	Decca ECS 813	Lon. LL 1257
——	TCHAIKOVSKY Concerto: WIENIAWSKI Concerto No.2 in D minor Op.22; LPO, Boult	Decca ECS 569 ACL 25	Lon. LL 1037
—— (and others)	'Great Virtuosi of the Golden Age', Vol.1: SCHUBERT 'Ave Maria'	Pearl GEMM 101	
Enesco, Georges	ENESCO Sonatas Nos 2–3 for violin and piano; Dinu Lipatti	*DXL 40/41	Everest
——	BACH Sonatas and three Partitas for solo violin	Continental CLP 104/6	
Flesch, Carl and Szigeti, Josef	BACH Concerto for two violins in D minor; orchestra (unnamed), Walter Goehr	HMV HQM 1127	*Col. set X–90
Fodor, Eugene	PAGANINI Concerto No.1 in D; MENDELSSOHN Concerto in E minor; NPO, Maag		RCA ARLI–11565
Fujikawa, Mayumi	BRUCH Concerto No.1 in G minor Op.26; TCHAIKOVSKY Concerto; Rotterdam Philharmonic, Waart	Phonogram 6500 708	
Gabrieli Quartet	BRITTEN Quartet No.1 in D major Op.25; Phantasy Quartet Op.2 (with J. Craxton, oboe); BRIDGE Idylls, Novelletten	Decca Ace of Diamonds SDD 497	Lon. STS 15399
——	DVOŘÁK Quartets Nos 10 (3) in E flat major Op.51; 14 (7) in A flat major Op.105	Decca Ace of Diamonds SDD 479	

		UK no.	US no.
Georgiadis, John	ELGAR Collection of music for violin and piano: *La Capricieuse* Op.17, *Chanson de matin, Chanson de nuit,* Op.15/1 and 2 etc.; John Parry	Pearl SHE 523	
Gingold, Joseph	KODÁLY Duo for violin and cello; Janos Starker, cello; (HEIDEN Sonata for cello and piano; Menahem Pressler, piano)		Fidelio F–003
——	KREISLER Collection: Plays Kreisler		Fidelio F–001
Grappelli, Stephane	'At the Talk of the Town'; Alan Clare, piano and celeste	Logo Black Lion BLP 30165	
——	'Swing '35–'39': 'Lime-house Blues', etc.; Django Reinhardt, Quintet of the Hot Club of France	Decca Eclipse ECM 2051	
——	'Best of Stephane Grappelli'; Barney Kessel, guitar; Diz Disley, guitar, and others	Logo Black Lion BLM 51001	
——	'Violinspiration'; Diz Disley Trio	EMI 68058	
Grappelli, Stephane and Menuhin, Yehudi	'Tea for Two'; Famous standards – 'Crazy Rhythm', etc.; John Etheridge, lead guitar, and others	EMI EMD 5530	Angel S 37533
——	'Fascinatin' Rhythm': Songs by Gershwin, Kern and Cole Porter; Max Harris, Alan Clare, pianos, and others	EMI EMD 5523	Angel S 37156
——	'Jealousy': Hits of the Thirties; Alan Clare Trio	EMI EMD 5504	Angel S 36968

		UK no.	US no.
Gruenberg, Erich	MORGAN Concerto; RPO, Handley	Lyrita SRCS 97	
——	REIZENSTEIN Solo sonatas in G sharp major Op.20, Op.46; Prelude No.11 Op.32; Prelude and Fugue No.8 in D major Op.32; David Wilde, piano	Oiseau-Lyre SOL 348	
Grumiaux, Arthur	BACH Unaccompanied violin sonatas Nos 1 in G minor, 2 in A minor, 3 in C major; Partitas Nos 1 in B minor, 2 in D minor, 3 in E major	Philips SAL 3472/4	835198/200 AY
——	BACH Concertos Nos 1 in A minor; 2 in E major; HAYDN Concerto in C; ECO, Leppard	Philips 6530 004	PHM 5000075 PHS 900075
——	BERG Concerto; CO, Markevitch; STRAVINSKY Concerto; CO, Bour	Philips SAL 3650	Philips 802785 AY
——	BRAHMS Concerto; NPO, C. Davis	Philips 6500 299	id.
——	BRAHMS Sonata No.2 in A major; MOZART Sonata in E flat major K.481; Grumiaux, piano		*Philips 802839 AY
——	MOZART Divertimento in E flat major K.563; Georges Janzer, viola; Eva Czako, cello	Philips SAL 3664	PHS 900173
——	TCHAIKOVSKY Concerto and 'Sérénade mélancholique' Op.26; NPO, Krenz	Philips 9500 086	id.
Guarneri Quartet	BARTÓK Quartets Nos 1–6	RCA RLO 2412	RCA CRL 3 2412

		UK no.	US no.
——	SCHUBERT *Italian Serenade*	RCA RL 11994	ARLI 1994
Haendel, Ida	BRITTEN Concerto; WALTON Concerto; Bournemouth Symphony, Berglund	EMI ASD 3483	
——	ELGAR Concerto; LPO, Boult	EMI ASD 3598	
——	LALO *Symphonie Espagnole* Op.21; RAVEL 'Tzigane'; Czech Philharmonic, Ančerl	Supraphon SUAST 50615	Parliament PLP 620 PLPS 620
——	SIBELIUS Concerto; 'Finlandia'; Bournemouth Symphony, Berglund	HMV ASD 3199	
——	TARTINI 'Devil's Trill' Sonata (transc. Kreisler); CORELLI 'La Folia' (transc. Kreisler); NARDINI (transc. Flesch); VITALI Chaconne (transc. David); Geoffrey Parsons, piano	EMI ASD 3352	
Hall, Marie (and others)	MENDELSSOHN Concerto (Finale exc.); HANDEL Bourrée; RAFF Cavatina	Pearl GEMM 102	
Hassid, Josef	ELGAR *La Capricieuse* Op.17; Gerald Moore, piano; TCHAIKOVSKY 'Mélodie'	HMV B 9074	
——	SARASATE *Spanish Dances* Op.23: 'Playera', 'Zapateado'; Gerald Moore, piano	HMV C 3185	
Heifetz, Jascha	BRUCH *Scottish Fantasia*; Los Angeles PO, Wallenstein; KORNGOLD Concerto; NSO, Sargent	RCA LSB 4105	LSC 2603 LM 1782

		UK no.	*US no.*
——	GLAZUNOV Concerto in A minor Op.82; RCA Symphony Orchestra, Hendl; BRUCH Concerto No.1 in G minor; NSO, Sargent	RCA LSB 4061	LSC 4011
——	MENDELSSOHN Concerto; BRAHMS Concerto; TCHAIKOVSKY Concerto; BSO, Munch	RCA DPS 2002 (set)	VCS 7058
——	PROKOFIEV Concerto No.2 in G minor Op.63; BSO, Munch; SIBELIUS Concerto; Chicago SO, Hendl		LSC 4010
——	R. STRAUSS Sonata in E flat major Op.18; FRANCK Sonata; Brooks Smith, piano		Col. M2 33444
——	VIEUXTEMPS Concerto No.4 in D minor Op.31; LPO, Barbirolli	*HMV DB 2444/6	RCA ARM4 0944
——	WALTON Concerto; PO, Walton; CASTELNUOVO-TEDESCO Concerto; Los Angeles PO, Wallenstein	*RCA LSB 4102	*Victor LM 2740
——	'The Heifetz Collection', 1917–55		RCA ARM4-0942-7
Holmes, Ralph	DELIUS Sonatas Nos 1–3; Fenby, piano	Unicorn UNS 248	Unicorn 72030
——	HARTY 'Orchestral Music of Hamilton Harty' including concerto in D minor for solo violin	DBR 2001	
——	PROKOFIEV Sonata Op.115; REGER Chaconne Op.117 No.4; BARTÓK Sonata for solo violin	ARGO ZK 36	

		UK no.	US no.
Huberman, Bronislav	BEETHOVEN Concerto; VPO, Szell	*Columbia LX 509/13	*CBS ML 4769
Hungarian Quartet	BEETHOVEN Quartets Nos 1–16; Grosse Fugue	HMV SLS 857 (10 discs)	Sera S 6005/6/7
Italian Quartet	BEETHOVEN Quartets Nos 1–16; Grosse Fugue	Philips 6747 272 (10 discs)	
——	DEBUSSY and RAVEL Quartets	Philips SAL 3643	835361 AY
——	MOZART Quartets Nos 1–23; Adagio and Fugue in C minor K.546; Divertimenti for strings Nos 1–3 K.136–8	Philips 6747 097 (9 discs)	
Joachim, Joseph (and others)	'Great Virtuosi of the Golden Age', Vol.1: BRAHMS Hungarian Dance No.1; BACH Prelude in G minor	Pearl GEMM 101	
Juilliard Quartet	BARTÓK Quartets Nos 1–6	CBS Classics 61118/20	Col. D 35717
——	BEETHOVEN Quartets 1–16; Grosse Fugue	CBS GM 101	
Kagaan, Oleg	BEETHOVEN Sonatas Nos 4 in A minor Op.23, 5 in F major (Spring) Op.24; Richter, piano	HMV ASD 3295	
Kogan, Leonid	LALO Symphonie Espagnole Op.21; PO, Kondrashin	Classics for Pleasure CFP 40040	Angel S 35721
Krebbers, Herman	BEETHOVEN Concerto; CO, Haitink	Philips Universo 6580 115	
——	BRAHMS Concerto; CO, Haitink	Philips Universo 6580 087	Philips 6570 172

		UK no.	US no.
——	MOZART Concertos Nos 2 in D major K.211, 4 in D major K.218; Netherlands Chamber, Zinman	Philips Universo 6580 120	
Kreisler, Fritz	BEETHOVEN Concerto; LPO, Barbirolli	*World Records Angel H 101	COLH 11
——	BEETHOVEN Concerto; Berlin State Opera Orchestra, Blech; 'Midnight Bells'	HMV HLM 7062	
——	BEETHOVEN Sonata No.8; GRIEG Sonata No.3; SCHUBERT Sonata; Rachmaninov, piano	RCA ARM3 0295	id.
——	BRAHMS Concerto; LPO, Barbirolli	World Records SH 115	Vic 14588/92
——	KREISLER 'Caprice Viennois'; recordings from 1904–1924, misc.	Pearl GEMM 132	
——	MOZART Concerto No.4 in D major K.218; LSO, Ronald; BACH Concerto for two violins in D minor; Zimbalist, string quartet; four encores, piano accompaniment	Pearl GEMM 132	*Victor 6520/3
Kubelik, Jan (and others)	PAGANINI 'Moto perpetuo'; SARASATE 'Tarantella'; WIENIAWSKI Scherzo-Tarantella; FIBICH 'Poème'	Pearl GEMM 102	
La Salle Quartet	DEBUSSY and RAVEL Quartets	DGG 2530 235	id.
Leopold, Reginald	'An Evening at the Palm Court', Vols 1 and 2; Jack Byfield, piano, Reginald Kilby, cello	HMV CSD 1621 HMV CSD 3566	

		UK no.	US no.
——	The Palm Court Trio; Jack Byfield, piano, Reginald Kilby, cello	Music for Pleasure MFP 1300	
Lindsay Quartet	TIPPETT Quartets Nos 1–3	Oiseau-Lyre DSLO 10	
Loveday, Alan	VIVALDI *The Four Seasons*, Op.8, 1/4; Academy of St Martin-in-the-Fields, Neville Marriner	Argo ZRG 654	id.
Markov, Albert	PAGANINI Concerto No.2 in D major Op.6; Moscow Radio Orchestra, Rozhdestvensky; CORELLI/ KREISLER 'La Folia'; PAGANINI Capriccio No.7; KREISLER 'Gypsy Capriccio'; DE FALLA 'Spanish Dance'		Gershunoff M 101 A
Medici Quartet	HAYDN Quartets Nos 63–8 Op.64/1–6	HMV SLS 5077	
Melkus, Eduard	BIBER 15 Rosary sonatas and Passacaglia in G	DGG Archive 198 422/3	
——	J. S. BACH Concertos in A minor and E major; Concerto for two violins in D minor; (with Spiros Rantos); Capella Academica, Vienna	DGG Archive 2533 075	id.
——	CORELLI Sonatas Nos 1–12 Op.5; Huguette Dreyfus, harpsichord or organ; Garo Atmacayan, cello; Karl Scheidt, lute; No.7 only, Vienna Capella Academica	DGG Archive 2533 132/3	id.

		UK no.	*US no.*
Melos Quartet	SCHUBERT Quintet in C major D.956 (Op. posth. 163); Rostropovich, cello	DGG 2530 980	
Menuhin, Yehudi	J. S. BACH Concertos in A minor and E major; Concerto for two violins in D minor (with Christian Ferras); Bath Festival Chamber, Masters	HMV ASD 346	Sera S 60258
——	BARTÓK Sonata for unaccompanied violin; BLOCH Suites 1 and 2	*HMV ASD 3368	
——	BEETHOVEN Sonatas for violin and piano: No.5 in F Op.24 ('Spring'), No.9 in A major Op.47 ('Kreutzer'); Hephzibah Menuhin	HMV SXLP 30164	Capitol SG 7246
——	BERKELEY Concerto Op.59; Menuhin Festival, Boult	*HMV ASD 2759	
——	BRUCH Concerto No.1 in G minor Op.26; PO, Susskind; MENDELSSOHN Concerto in E minor; PO, Kurtz	HMV ASD 334	Capitol SG 7148
——	ELGAR Concerto; LSO, Elgar	*HMV HLM 7107	*Vic 7747/52
——	ENESCO Sonata No.3 in A minor Op.25; Hephzibah Menuhin, piano	HMV ASD 2294	
——	VIOTTI Concertos Nos 16 in E minor, 22 in A minor; Menuhin Festival	HMV ASD 3492	
——	WILLIAMSON Concerto; LPO, Boult	HMV SLS 5085	

		UK no.	US no.
Menuhin, Yehudi and Grappelli, Stephane	See under Grappelli, Stephane and Menuhin, Yehudi		
Milanova, Stoika	SCHUBERT Sonatina in A minor Op.137 No.2; SAINT-SAËNS (arr. Ysaÿe) 'Étude en forme de valse' Op.52 No.6; PROKOFIEV '5 Mélodies' Op.35; PIPKOV Sonata No.2 for solo violin Op.73	United Artists UACL 10009	
Milstein, Nathan	J. S. BACH unaccompanied violin sonatas Nos 1 in G minor, 2 in A minor, 3 in C major; violin partitas Nos 1 in B minor, 2 in D minor, 3 in E major	DGG 2709 047	id.
——	BEETHOVEN Concerto; Pittsburgh Symphony Orchestra, Steinberg	EMI MFP 2098	Capitol P 8313
——	BRAHMS Concerto; VPO, Jochum	DGG 2530 592	id.
——	MENDELSSOHN and TCHAIKOVSKY Concertos; VPO, Abbado	DGG 2530 359	id.
——	PROKOFIEV Concertos Nos 1 in D major Op.19; PO, Giulini; 2 in G minor Op.63; PO, Frühbeck de Burgos	HMV SXLP 30235	Angel S 36009
Monosoff, Sonya	GEMINIANI Sonatas for violin and continuo: Nos 2 in D minor Op.1; 10 in E major Op.1; 1 in D major Op.4; 11 in B minor Op.4 (baroque violin); James Weaver, harpsichord; Judith Davidoff, baroque cello		Musical Heritage Series MHS 3744

		UK no.	*US no.*
Mordkovich, Lydia	RAVEL Sonata; Allen Sternfield, piano	RCA RL 25166	
Morini, Erica	BRUCH Concerto No. 1 in G minor Op. 26; GLAZUNOV Concerto in A minor Op. 82; Berlin Radio, Fricsay	DGG Heliodor 2548 170	
——	TCHAIKOVSKY Concerto; LPO, Rodzinski	EMI/HMV Concert Classics SXLP 20053	Westminster in set WM 1101 WST 1401 XWN 18397
Neveu, Ginette	BRAHMS Concerto; PO, Dobrowen	EMI SLS	
——	SIBELIUS Concerto; PO, Süsskind; SUK Four Pieces Op. 17; Jean Neveu, piano	EMI	
Oistrakh, David	BARTÓK Sonata No. 1; PROKOFIEV Sonata No. 1; Richter, piano	HMV ASD 3105	
——	BRAHMS Concerto; Cleveland, Szell	HMV ASD 2525	Angel S 36033
——	BRAHMS Double Concerto for violin and violoncello; DVORAK Slavonic Dances Nos 3 and 10; Rostropovich, cello; Cleveland Orchestra, Szell	HMV ASD 3312	Angel S 36032
——	BRUCH *Scottish Fantasia*; LSO, Horenstein; HINDEMITH Concerto; LSO, Hindemith	Decca Ace of Diamonds SDD 465	Lon. CS 6337
——	FRANCK Sonata in A major; BRAHMS Sonata No. 3; Richter, piano	HMV ASD 2618	Angel S 40121

		UK no.	US no.
——	PROKOFIEV Concerto No. 2 in G minor Op. 63; (MIASKOVSKY Cello Concerto with Rostropovich); PO, Galliera	HMV SXLP 30155	Sera S 60223
——	SHOSTAKOVICH Concerto No. 1 in A minor Op.99; NPO, M. Shostakovich	HMV ASD 2936	Angel S 36964
——	STRAVINSKY Concerto; Lamoureux, Haitink	Philips Universo 6580 003	PHM 500050 PHS 900050
——	SZYMANOWSKI Concerto No. 1 Op.35; Leningrad Philharmonic Orchestra, Sanderling	HMV SLS 5058	
——	YSAŸE Sonata for unaccompanied violin No.3 Op.27	Ultraphon E 23327	
Oistrakh, David and Igor	BACH Concertos in A minor, E major; Concerto for two violins in D minor; VSO, Oistrakh/RPO, Goossens	DGG 138 820	id.
Oistrakh, Igor	CHAUSSON 'Poème' Op.25; Moscow Radio Orchestra, Rozhdestvensky	HMV ASD 2813	Angel S 40077
Perlman, Itzhak	'The Itzhak Perlman Record': BACH Concerto in E major; ECO, Barenboim; PAGANINI Caprices Nos 9, 24; SARASATE Carmen Fantasy; RPO, Foster; TARTINI (arr. Kreisler) Variations on a theme by Corelli; S. Sanders, piano; etc.	EMI SEOM 22	

		UK no.	*US no.*
——	BARTÓK Concerto No.2 in B minor; LSO, Previn	HMV ASD 3014	Angel S 37014
——	BEETHOVEN Sonatas (complete) for violin and piano; Vladimir Ashkenazy, piano	Decca D 92 D5	Lon. OSA 2501
——	BRUCH Concerto No.2 in D minor Op.44; *Scottish Fantasia*; NPO, Lopez-Cobós	HMV ASD 3310	Angel S 37210
——	FRANCK Sonata in A; Ashkenazy, piano	Decca SXL 6408	Lon. CS 6628
——	MENDELSSOHN Concerto in E minor; BRUCH Concerto No.1 in G minor Op.26; LSO, Previn	HMV ASD 2926	Angel S 33963
——	PAGANINI Concerto No.1 in D major Op.6 and Caprices; SARASATE *Carmen Fantasy*; RPO, Foster	HMV SLS 832 (2 discs)	Angel S 36836 S 36860
——	VIVALDI *The Four Seasons*, Op.8 Nos 1–4; LPO, Perlman	HMV ASD 3293	Angel S 37053
——	WIENIAWSKI Concertos Nos 1 in F sharp minor Op.14; 2 in D minor Op.22; LPO, Ozawa	HMV ASD 2870	Angel S 36903
Perlman, Itzhak and Zukerman, Pinchas	J. S. BACH Concerto in G minor (Zukerman), No.2 in E major; Concerto for two violins in D minor; ECO, Barenboim	HMV ASD 2783	Angel S 36841
Powell, Maud (and others)	'Great Virtuosi of the Golden Age', Vol.1; BEETHOVEN Minuet in G	Pearl GEMM 101	

		UK no.	US no.
——	'Masters of the Bow', Vol. I: GREIG 'To the Spring', etc.		Discopaedia MB 1005
Prague Quartet	DVOŘÁK Quartets Nos 8 (5) in E major Op. 80, 10 (3) in E flat major Op. 51	DGG 2530 719	
Ricci, Ruggiero	BRUCH Concerto No. I in G minor Op. 26; MENDELSSOHN Concerto; LSO, Gamba	Decca SPA 88	Lon. STS 15402
——	KHACHATURIAN Concerto in D minor; LPO, Fistoulari; GLAZUNOV *Stenka Razin*; Suisse Romande, Ansermet	Decca Eclipse ECS 641	Lon. STS 15240
——	MENDELSSOHN Concerto; TCHAIKOVSKY Concerto: Netherlands Radio, Fournet	Decca Phase 4 PFS 4345	Lon. CS 21116
——	PAGANINI Caprices	Decca Eclipse ECS 803	Lon. CS 6163
——	PAGANINI Concerto No. 4 in D minor; 'Le Streghe' ('Witches' Dance'); Variations on a theme by Süssmayr Op. 8; RPO, Bellugi; BOTTESINI Grand duo (with F. Petrarchi)	Unicorn RHS 304	Col. M 30574
——	SARASATE *Zigeunerweisen* Op. 20/I No. I: *Carmen Fantasy*; SAINT-SAËNS *Havanaise*; Introduction and Rondo Capriccio Op. 28; LSO, Gamba	Decca SDD 420	Lon. CS 6165

		UK no.	*US no.*
Rosand, Aaron	JOACHIM Hungarian Concerto Op. 11; HUBAY *Hejre Kati*; Radio Luxembourg, Kohler; ENESCO Prelude for solo violin Op. 9	Vox STGBY 668	Can 31064
Sammons, Albert	DELIUS Concerto; Liverpool Philharmonic Orchestra, Sargent	EMI World Records SH 224	
——	ELGAR Concerto; New Queen's Hall, Wood	EMI World Records SH 288	
Sandler, Albert	MASSENET *Thaïs: Méditation* (arr. violin and piano Marsick); Jack Byfield, piano	Columbia DX 621	
Sarasate, Pablo (and others)	'Great Virtuosi of the Golden Age', Vol. 1: SARASATE *Zigeunerweisen*, Op. 20/21: 'Tarantella'; 'Zapateado'	Pearl GEMM 101	
Smith, Stuff	Town Hall Concert, Vol. 2	Decca/London HMC 5002	
——	'Stuff Smith and his Onyx Orchestra', February-August 1936	Collector's 12–12 C 12–A/B (limited ed.)	
South, Eddie	'Continental Story', Vol. 1	Storyville SLP 1003	
Spivakov, Vladimir	MOZART Concertos Nos 2 in D major K. 211, 5 in A major K. 219; ECO	HMV ASD 3639	
Stern, Isaac	BEETHOVEN Concerto; NYPO, Bernstein	CBS Classics 61598	Col. M 31805
——	BRAHMS Concerto; Philadelphia, Ormandy	CBS Classics 61325	Col. M 31836

		UK no.	US no.
——	CHAUSSON 'Poème' Op. 25; SAINT-SAËNS Concerto No. 3; Orchestre de Paris, Barenboim	CBS 76530	Col. M 34550
——	MOZART Sinfonia Concertante in E flat major K.364 (Pinchas Zukerman, viola); STAMITZ Sinfonia Concertante; ECO, Barenboim	CBS 73030	Col. M 31369
——	PROKOFIEV Concertos Nos 1 in D major Op.19; 2 in G minor Op.63; PO, Ormandy	CBS 61796	Col. MS 6635
——	TCHAIKOVSKY and MENDELSSOHN Concertos; Philadelphia, Ormandy	CBS Classics 61029	Col. M 31835
——	BRAHMS Sonatas Nos 1–3; Scherzo in C minor; Julius Katchen, piano; (J. P. Marty, piano, etc.)	Decca Ace of Diamonds SDDA 261/9	
Suk, Josef	DVOŘÁK Concerto in A minor Op.53; Czech Philharmonic, Ančerl	Supraphon 50181	Quintessence 7112
——	FRANCK Sonata in A; J. Panenka, piano	Supraphon SUAST 50879	
——	MOZART Concertos Nos 3 in G major K.216, 4 in D major K.218; Prague CO	RCA LRL1 5046	
Szeryng, Henryk	BRAHMS Sonatas Nos 1–3; BEETHOVEN Sonatas Nos 5, 8 and 9; Arthur Rubinstein, piano	RCA SER 5701/2	LSC 2620
——	BRAHMS Concerto; LSO, Monteux	RCA Camden CCV 5052	VICS 1028

		UK no.	US no.
——	KREISLER 'Caprice Viennois', 'Liebesfreud', 'Praeludium', etc.; Charles Reiner, piano	Philips 6833 164	
——	PAGANINI Concertos Nos 1 in D major Op. 6; 4 in D minor; LSO, Gibson	Philips 9500 069	
——	TCHAIKOVSKY Concerto; BSO, Munch; TARTINI 'Devil's Trill' Sonata; C. Reiner, piano	RCA Camden CCV 5015	RCA VICS 1037
Szigeti, Joseph and Flesch, Carl	BACH Concerto for two violins and orchestra in D minor; orchestra (unnamed), Walter Goehr	HMV HQM 1127	Col. set X–90
Szigeti, Joseph	BARTÓK Portrait for violin and orchestra Op. 5; LPO, Lambert	Col LX–1531	Col ML 2213
Thibaud, Jacques	DEBUSSY Sonata for violin and piano No. 3 in G minor; Cortot (pre–1935 rec.)	*HMV DB 1322/3	*Vic 8183/4
——	FAURÉ Sonata No. 1 in A Op. 13; Cortot, piano	*HMV COLH 74	Vic 8086/8
—— (and others)	VIEUXTEMPS Serenate; BACH Gavotte	Pearl GEMM 102	
Tokyo Quartet	HAYDN Quartets Nos 44–49	DGG 2740 135 (3 discs)	2709 060
Végh Quartet	BARTÓK Quartets Nos 1–6	Telefunken FK 635023 (3 discs)	id.
——	BEETHOVEN Quartets Nos 7–11	Selecta Telefunken EX6 35041	id.
——	BEETHOVEN Quartets Nos 12–16	Telefunken FK6 35040	id.

		UK *no.*	US *no.*
Venuti, Joe	'Joe Venuti and his Orchestra 1934'; orchestral accompaniment including Louis Prima, trumpet and vocal, and possibly Frank Victor, guitar	Decca Lon. HMG 5023	
——	'Violinology'	RCA Sel. Imps Black & White 740 110	
Venuti, Joe and Grappelli, Stephane	See under Grappelli, Stephane and Venuti, Joe		
Venuti, Joe and Lang, Eddie	'Hot Strings'	RCA (F) Black & White FPM1 7016	
Vito, Gioconda de	BRAHMS Concerto; German Opera House, Kempen	*Polydor 68308/12	
Ysaÿe, Eugène (and others)	'Great Virtuosi of the Golden Age', Vol. 1: VIEUXTEMPS Rondino Op. 32; WIENIAWSKI Mazurkas Op. 19; MENDELSSOHN Concerto (finale, excerpts)	Pearl GEMM 101	
Zimbalist, Efrem	YSAŸE Sonata for unaccompanied violin No. 1		Vic. 16194/5
Zukerman, Pinchas	ELGAR Concerto; LPO, Barenboim	CBS 76528	Col. M 34517
——	TCHAIKOVSKY Concerto; LSO, Dorati; MENDELSSOHN Concerto; New York PO, Bernstein	CBS 72768	Col. MS 7313
Zukerman, Pinchas and Perlman, Itzhak	See under Perlman, Itzhak and Zukerman, Pinchas		

Index

Abbreviations:
GSM — Guildhall School of Music and Drama;
RAM — Royal Academy of Music;
RCM — Royal College of Music;
Where only city is mentioned, e.g. Brussels, Paris, Vienna, etc., Conservatoire is
   implied unless otherwise stated.

Accardo, Salvatore 310
Aeolian Quartet 299–300
Ahna, Heinrich de 295
Alard, Delphin 63; xxvi, 27; as
   representative of French School /
   edited 'Les Maîtres Classiques' 63
Albrechtsberger, Johann Georg 294
Aldrich, Richard 96, 136, 141
Alexander I, Tsar: Rode, solo violinist
   to 25
Alexander II, Tsar: Wieniawski, solo
   violinist to 70; 97
Alexander III, Tsar 97
Alexandra, Queen 112, 155
Alvin, Andrée 100
Amadeus Quartet 301–5
Amati, Andreas xxiv
Amati, Antonio xxiv
Amati, Nicola xxiv, xxv, xxvii, 42
Amaury–Duval 40
Amphion Quartet 305
Ansermet, Ernest 258
Applebaum, Sam 157
Armstrong, Louis 203
Armstrong, Sir Thomas 292
Arrau, Claudio 165
Ashkenazy, Vladimir 278

Auber, Daniel F.E. 117
Auer, Leopold 94–8; xvii, 46, 55, 66;
   as pupil of Joachim 77; founds
   Academy in New York / New York
   début at 72 / Tchaikovsky concerto
   dedicated to 96; writes *Violin Playing
   as I teach it* / influence at St
   Petersburg / forms String Quartet
   97; technique 98; establishes
   principles of tone production 101;
   107, 122, 150; as Elman's teacher
   153, 156; as Heifetz's teacher 168–9;
   as Milstein's teacher 176–7; 309

Bacciochi, Princess 39
Bach, C.P.E. 13
Bach, J.S. xxvii, xxix; composes at
   Anhalt-Köthen 12–13; 76; Joachim
   plays unaccompanied sonatas 82,
   180
Backhaus, Wilhelm 162
Baillot de Sales, Pierre 21–5; meets
   Viotti / *Méthode* and *L'Art du Violon*
   published 23; skill in old age 25; 48,
   57, 59, 63
Baltzar, Thomas xvii; as leader of
   'Twenty-four Violins of the King'

under Charles II 1

Banister, John: as Baltzar's successor 2; 288

Barbirolli, Sir John 121, 146, 191, 195, 289

Barenboim, Daniel 278, 279, 281

Barnett, John 277

Bartholomew, William 86

Bartók 165, 229–30

Bauer, Harold 124

Bazzini, Antonio 45–7; emulates Paganini 46; tries to promote Bach and Beethoven in Italy / composer of virtuoso pieces 47; performs with Joachim 75

Bean, Hugh 148–9

Becker, Carl 198

Becker, Hans 296

Becker, Hugo 105

Beckwith, Arthur 188

Beecham, Sir Thomas 112, 144–5, 147, 164, 228

Beethoven 9, 27, 28; first performance of violin concerto 31; 181

Bender, William 279

Benedetti, René 195

Bennewitz, Antonin 20, 101

Benvenuti, Giovanni 5

Bergman, Leon 300

Bériot, Charles de 57–9; xxiv, 23, 46, 49; meets Viotti in Paris / London début / execution / character 57; love affair with Malibran / professor at Brussels / publishes 'Grande Méthode' 59; 61, 63, 65, 86, 109

Berlin, Irving 20

Berlioz 46; on Vieuxtemps's compositions 66

Bernstein, Leonard 237, 281

Betti, Adolfo 297

Bianchi, Antonia 39

Biancolli, Louis 210, 289

Biber, Heinrich von 2–3; uses scordatura / as composer / 'Rosary' sonatas 3

Billington, Vincent 193

Bilse 62, 102, 109

Blinder, Naoum 249

Bliss, Arthur 184

Bloch, Ernest 164

Blom, Eric 212

Bochmann, Michael 311

Bodanski, Artur 210

Böhm, Joseph 54–5; 26, 46; as first Hungarian to pursue serious study of violin 55; 66, 75, 301

Bonavia, Ferruccio 243

Bordes, Charles 113

Bordes-Péne, Léontine 113

Borodin Quartet 299

Boulanger, Nadia 240, 262

Boult, Sir Adrian 92, 134, 146, 257, 292, 296

Brahms 61, 77; friendship with Joachim / composes violin concerto 80–1; composes double concerto 81–2; 140, 178–80; Ida Haendel on 248

Brainin, Norbert 301–5; 107

Bream, Julian 205

Bridgetower, George 27

Briggs, Christopher 296

Britten, Sir Benjamin 305

Brodsky, Adolf 96, 249, 296

Brodsky Quartet 296

Bronstein, Raphael 310

Brook, Donald 151, 157

Brosa, Antonio 297

Brosa Quartet 297

Brown, Vanna 195

Bruch 89

Bruckner 118

Brugnoli, Leonardo 5

Bruhns, Nikolaus 3

Budapest Quartet 288, 299, 300

Bull, Ole 47–52; as 'Flaxen-haired Paganini' 47; posture 47–8; meets Paganini 48; British début / fees 49; appearance / personality 51

Bunt, Belinda 185–6

Burney, Charles 2, 20, 21

Busby, Thomas 10

Busch, Adolf 220, 226, 298

Busch, Fritz 225–7

Busch Quartet 298, 300

Busoni, 164, 166

Butt, Clara 183

Byfield, Jack 191

Camden, Archie 86, 90

Campoli, Alfredo 182–6; wins prizes 182; recital début / suffers effects of slump / founds Salon Orchestra 183; plays in first Promenade Concert / activities during war / returns to classical field 184; repertoire /

technique / recordings 185; 187, 189, 191
Campoli, Romeo 182–5
Capell, Richard 290
Capet, Lucien 95, 269, 272, 274
Carmen Silva, Queen 133
Caruso, Enrico 155
Casals, Pablo 124, 129, 252, 280
Castelnuovo-Tedesco 212
Catherine the Great 18
Catterall, Arthur 90
Celi, Elvira 182
Celibidache, Sergiu 248
Cernohorsky, Bohuslav Matej 14
Chaput, Roger 204
Charles II xxii, 1–2
Charles VI 15
Chausson 109, 115
Chavez, Carlos 264
Cherubini 19, 25, 61
'Chiaretta, La' 8
Chilingirian, Levon 305
Chilingirian Quartet 305
Chinnery, Mrs 20–2
Chinnery, Walter 20
Chissell, Joan 279
Chopin 49
Chorley, Henry F. 41
Christina, Queen 1, 5
Chung, Kyung-Wha 276–87; acquires ex-Kubelik violin 137; 274–5; has lessons from Galamian / New York début 282; British début 282–5; rapport with orchestra / repertoire 285; plays Elgar violin concerto 280; personality / philosophy / development 287; 307, 309
Clavel, M. 70
Clement, Franz: plays at first performance of Beethoven's violin concerto 31
Clementi, Muzio 21, 30
Cleveland Quartet 305
Cohen, Raymond 311
Cole, Nat King 201
Colonne, Edouard 110, 129
Coogan, Jackie 225
Cooper, Martin 126
Coppett, Edward J. de 297
Corelli, Arcangelo 5–11; xvii, xxvii; in service of Ottoboni 5; lays foundation of violin playing / revolutionizes string ensemble 6; 16, 18, 19

Cortot, Alfred 129
Cortot-Thibaud-Casals Trio 129
Courcey, Geraldine de 44
Crichton, Ronald 237
Crickboom Mathieu 297
Cundell, Edric 310

Damrosch, Walter 224
Dancla, Charles 25, 207
David, Ferdinand 55–7; 33–4; friendship with Mendelssohn / advises on violin concerto 56; makes editions of old masters 56–7; takes Wilhelmj as pupil 94
David, Paul 25
Debussy 109
Delacroix 41
Delibes 118
Delius: first performance of violin concerto 146–7
'Diamantina, La' 84
Dincin, Jeanette 113
Dohnányi 235
Dont, Jacob 55, 66, 97, 122
Dorati, Antal 229, 280
Dounis, D.C. 229
Dowling, Helen 134; 269–70
Downes, Olin 125, 162, 226, 230, 234
Dressel, Dettmar 96
Dubois, Alfred 256
Dufour, M. 28
Duncan, Isadora 202
Dunn, John 288
Durand, Auguste 37
Dvořák: Maud Powell performs violin concerto in New York, 207

Eck, Franz 29, 30, 33
Ehrling Sixten 278
Einem, Gottfried von 237
Einstein, Albert 235
Eldering, Bram 298
Elgar, Charlie 199
Elgar, Edward 112; first performance of violin concerto 120; 146, 206; conducts Menuhin 227–8
Ellington, Duke 204
Ellis, Herb 201
Elman, Mischa 150–8; 55, 97, 117; at St Petersburg / British début 153;

so-called defects in playing / temperament / plays Tchaikovsky violin concerto 154; acquires Stradivari violin 155; experiences competition / character 156; opinions / 'Russian' bow hold / mellow tone 157; Hebraic quality in playing 158; 160, 218

Elman Quartet 156

Enesco, Georges 132–5; 62; composes in childhood 132; USA début 133; love of Bach 133–4; gives master classes in Paris 134; teaching methods 135; 225–6, 240, 290–1

Erdelyi, Csaba 311

Ernst, Heinrich Wilhelm 46–7; obsessive admirer of Paganini / as composer of virtuoso pieces 46; 49, 74–5; 82

Esterhazy, Prince 294

Etheridge, John 204

Evelyn, John 1, 3

Farina, Carlo 1

Fauré 133

Felton, James 223

Fernandez, Pilar 196

Fétis, François F. 22, 37, 44

Fidelmann, Alexander 153

Field, John 21, 30

Finck, Henry T. 124

Fischer, Conrad 94

Fischer-Dieskau, Dietrich 253

Fitelberg, Gregory 267

Flesch, Carl 94–107; *passim*; conditions at Paris Conservatoire 53, 60–2; criticizes Joachim's bowing 79; 83; on Sarasate 91–3; on Auer 97–8; as pupil of Marsick / professor at Bucharest 105; teaching methods / publishes *The Art of Violin Playing* 106; bowing principles / character 107; on Ysaÿe 111; on Kreisler 126; on Thibaud 129–30; on Enesco 134; on Huberman 142; on Szigeti 164; on Kubelik's influence 169; on Heifetz 172–3; 190, 196, 239–40, 242, 244–7; as Hassid's teacher 262; 266, 268; as Brainin's teacher 301; 311

Flonzaley Quartet 297

Fodor, Eugene 174–5

Fonteyn, Margot 231

Forkell, Johann 13

Francis I, Emperor 8

Franck, César 61, 109, 113

Fränzel, Ferdinand, 34

Frederick the Great 9

Frenkel, Maurice 262

Fried, Miriam 272, 274

Fuchs, Carl 296

Fujikawa, Mayumi 312

Furnberg, Baron von 294

Furtwängler, Wilhelm 105, 139–40

Gaisberg, Frederick 227–8

Galamian, Ivan 269–75; 252; trains in Moscow and Paris 272; teaches at Curtis Institute and Juilliard School / founds Meadowmount / views on practice 273; on balanced teaching / pupils' comments / on present-day standards 274; publishes *Principles of Violin Playing and Teaching* / interpretation / views on gifted pupils 274–5; 276, 280, 282, 286, 292, 311

Gallini 258

Garcia, Pauline 65

Gaubert, Philip 162

Gédalge, André 133

Geminiani, 10, 19, 21

George V 145

George, King of Hanover 77

Georgiadis, John 194–6; as orchestral player / as leader 195; light music recitals 195–6; repertoire / technique 196

Gershwin, George 203

Ghiretti, Gasparo 37

Gibbons, Carroll 193

Gibson, Alexander 264

Gibson, Alfred: plays in Joachim Quartet, 86–7

Gillespie, Dizzy 201

Ginastera 237

Gingold, Josef 269–72; on Ysaÿe 111, 113–14; on Kreisler 126–7; as leader 270; as professor at Bloomington and Meadowmount 272

Giraud-Mangin, Lionel 215

Goehr, Alexander 237

Goehr, Walter 165

Goldkette, Jean 201

Goodman, Benny, clarinettist 164–5

Goodman, Benny, violinist 198

Goossens, Eugène 147

Gorst Harold, E. 154

Graffman, Vladimir 270

Grancino, Paolo xxiv

Grappelli, Stephane 197–205; dances for Isadora Duncan / hears first live music 202; teaches himself violin and piano / plays in clubs 203; meets Django Reinhardt / forms Hot Club of France 204; plays with Menuhin 204–5; 232

Gray, Thomas 84

Grayston, Jean 19

Green, Horace 121

Greenfield, Edward 285

Grinke, Frederick 195

Gruenberg, Erich 311

Grumiaux, Arthur 255–60; 44, 185; early talent 255; attends Enesco master classes / receives Special Government prize 256; fugitive during war / gives first European performance of Walton violin concerto 257; American début / performs rediscovered Paganini concerto 258; recording with Clara Haskil 259; platform manner 260; 307

Grün, Jacob 105, 188, 210, 296, 301

Guadagnini, Giovanni Battista 42; the 'Maud Powell' violin, 210

Guarneri, Andreas, xxiv

Guarneri, Joseph del Gesù; the 'Ferdinand David' xxvi; the 'Cannon' xxvi–ii, 42; the ex-Kubelik 137

Guarneri Quartet 305

Guhr, Carl 42

Habeneck, François 25, 27; influence on French school 27; 61, 63, 86

Hadley, Henry 234

Haendel, Ida 239–48; on Flesch 106; on Enesco 135; on Huberman 139; 155, 214; London début 243; teaches herself to play 244; studies with Flesch 245–6; Paris début 246; battle with Flesch / Flesch v Enesco 247; interpretation / association with Celibidache 248; on Hassid 266–7

Haendel, Nathan 246

Hall, Marie 206–7; first British woman violinist to achieve international fame 206; studies with Ševčik / tours the world 207

Hallé, Sir Charles 85–6

Hallé, Lady see Norman-Neruda, Wilma; 85–6, 206, 211, 296

Handel, 5

Hanslick, Edward 82; astounded by 'little Neruda' 85; 89, 92, 96

Harrison, Julius 190

Hartley, Fred 194

Harty, Sir Hamilton 162, 234

Haskil, Clara 259

Hassid, Josef 262–8; Kreisler's comment 265; studies with Flesch 266; recordings / comment by Gerald Moore / British début 267; illness and death 268; 275

Hauptmann, Gerhard 235

Hauptmann, Moritz 75

Hausmann, Robert: in Joachim Quartet / plays in first performance of Brahms's Double Concerto 81

Haydn 294

Heermann, Hugo 140

Heifetz, Jascha 167–75; 55, 97, 117, 128; receives letter from Shaw 167; at St Petersburg 168; plays under Nikisch / New York début 169; appearance / execution / London début 171; tempi / temperament 172; Russian bow-hold 172–3; technique / character 173; as teacher 174, influence 175; 185, 196; Walton violin concerto written for 257

Hellmesberger, Johann, the elder 75

Hellmesberger, Joseph 118, 132, 188, 296

Hellmesberger Quartet 295

Helmholz, Hermann 14

Henry VII: employs woman fiddler, 84

Hess, Willy 298

Hiller, Ferdinand 25

Hochhauser, Victor 217, 220

Hochmann-Rosenfeld, Rosa 301

Holmes, Henry 33, 288

Holmes, Ralph 288–93; American début / training with David Martin 289; RAM recital / with Enesco in Paris 290; London recital début / stands in for Menuhin 291; studies with Galamian 292, repertoire / performs Harty Concerto in centenary year 293

Holst, Imogen 302
Holt, Harold 246, 267
Hornziel, Jan 69
Horowitz, Vladimir 177, 253
Howard, Daniel 199
Hubay, Jeno 94–105; 55, 73, 96;
    mixture in styles of / musical
    outlook 104; as player 105; Szigeti
    on 160; 193, 298
Hubay-Popper Quartet 298
Huber, Carl 96
Huberman, Bronislav 139–42;
    physical appearance / refuses to play
    for Nazis 139; individualism of /
    plays to Brahms 140; views on
    interpretation 141; musical
    pioneering 142; 210, 254
Huneker, James Gibbons 154
Hungarian Quartet 299
Hunter, Ian 230
Hurok, Sol 263, 277
Hurwitz, Emanuel 299–301

Ingres 40
Istomin, Eugène, 252, 280

Jaffa, Max 191–3; wins Gold Medal /
    plays at Lasserson's Memorial
    Concert 191; plays on liners / on
    meeting with Kreisler 193
Jansa, Leopold 85
Jeffries, Leslie 189
Jenkins, Tom 189–91; wins prizes 189;
    cinema violinist / orchestral
    experience / Grand Hotel 190;
    character / popularity 191
Joachim, Amalie (née Weiss) 77, 81
Joachim, Joseph 74–84; passim; 26, 55,
    61, 69; deputizes for Wieniawski 72;
    London début 74; influenced by
    Mendelssohn 75; at Weimar with
    Liszt, 76; involvement in
    controversy, 76–7; friendship with
    Brahms / plays Brahms violin
    concerto / disagreements 80–1;
    influence on performing standards /
    plays unaccompanied Bach sonatas
    82–3; plays Bach Double Concerto
    with Neruda 86; 91, 93–5; as teacher
    of Auer 97; as teacher of Hubay 104;
    108; meets Enesco 134; 140, 160;
    Szigeti plays for 161–2; 163, 188; as
    teacher of Emily Shinner 206, 207,

210, 217, 254; as quartet-leader
    295–6; 289, 300, 301
Joachim Quartet, formation of 81;
    Kruse plays in 206, 295
Jochum, Eugen 180
Jones, Tom 189
Juilliard Quartet 305
Jules, M. 240

Kagan, Oleg 218, 307
Kahn, Roger 167
Kalbeck, Max 140
Kang, Dong-Suk 311–12
Karl Josef, Emperor 208
Katten, Helen 155
Kaye, Milton 307
Keller, Hans 142
Kilby, Reginald 191
Kinsky, Count 15
Kitching, Frances 273
Klein, Howard 278
Klengel, Julius 296
Klimov, Valery 218, 307
Klotz, Matthias xxvii
Kneisel, Franz 171, 296
Kneisel Quartet 171, 296–7
Kocian, Jaroslav 20
Kogan, Leonid 66
Kohne, Ridley 96
Kraft, Anton 295
Krause, Ernest 215
Krebbers, Herman 307
Kreisler, Fritz 117–27, xvii, xxvi, 27,
    61, 83, 116; style of playing 117;
    tours USA with Moritz Rosenthal /
    medical studies / débuts in Vienna
    and Berlin 118; deputizes for Ysaÿe /
    hostility shown to by Americans
    120; recording royalty earnings /
    character 121; recording of Brahms
    violin concerto 121–2; friendships
    122; repertoire / as composer 124;
    the Kreisler hoax / battle with
    Newman 124–5; influences upon /
    vibrato 126; 130, 146, 153, 156; first
    hears Heifetz 169; honours Heifetz
    171; 185; advises Jaffa 193; 198, 217,
    218; on Ricci 235; 254
Kremer, Gidon 66, 307
Kreutzer, Rodolphe 26–7; 23; solo
    violin to Napoleon / composes
    'Studies' 26; Beethoven dedicates
    sonata to 27; 109

Kruse, Johann 206
Krystal, M. 266
Kubelik, Jan 136–8; xvii; snubbed by
    Ševčik 102–3; introduces Ševčik's
    'Method' / technique 136; public
    image 137; retirement 138; 160, 169,
    207
Kubelik, Rafael 103; son of Jan 137
Kunisch 29

Lackey, Elizabeth 233
Lafont, Charles 86
Lahee, Henry 52, 62, 91, 112
Lahoussaye, Pierre 16
Lalande 14
Lalo 89
Lamond Frederic 112
Lang, Eddie 201
La Salle Quartet 305
Lasserson, Sascha xvii, 55, 190, 191,
    269
Laurie, David 67
Lebel, Ludwig 193
Leclair, Jean-Marie 11
Legge, Robin 63
Legge, Walter 257, 267
Leipzig Quartet 295
Lener Quartet 299
Lener, Teno 299
Léonard, Hubert 60–3; 25, 27;
    succeeds de Bériot at Brussels /
    promoter of contemporary music 61
Leopold, Reginald 192–4; at the Savoy
    192; with Fred Hartley / Grand
    Hotel 194
Levine, Adrian 305
Lewin, Robert 187
Lewis, Sir Edward 183
Lewis, William 207
Lichnowsky, Prince 294
Lipatti, Dinu 259
Liszt 60; with Joachim at Weimar 76;
    takes Wilhelmj to Leipzig 94
Livron 38
Lobkowitz, Prince 295
Locatelli, Pietro 6, 18
Lockwood, Didier 205
Loebel, Karl 304
Lombardini Sirmen, Maddalena 15, 84
London Quartet 145
Lotto, Isidor 61
Louis XIV, King 2
Loveday, Alan 149, 288

Lovett, Martin 302
Lully 2
Lunacharsky, A. 177
Lundholm 47
Lupot, Nicolas xxvii

McCallum, David 122
McCormack, John 162
Magaloff, Prince Nikita da 164
Maggini, Giovanni Paolo xxiv
Malibran, Maria Felicita 49, 59
Malko, Nicolai 214
Mann, Sidney 273
Mar, Norman del 217, 293
Markees, Carl 140
Markov, Albert 307
Marsick, Martin 60–2; at Hochschule
    with Joachim / scandal ends career
    61; famous pupils 62, 105, 128, 133,
    140
Marteau, Henri 61, 162, 298
Martin, David 289–90, 292
Mary, Queen 145
Massart, Lambert Joseph 60–1; 27;
    performs 'Kreutzer' with Liszt 60;
    platform nerves / dedicated teacher
    61; 70, 109, 118
Massart, Rodolphe 109
Matteis, Nicolo 3
Matthews, Thomas 106, 149
Maurer, Ludwig 75
Mayer, Sir Robert 86, 92
Mayseder, Joseph 49
Medici Quartet 305
Mehta, Zubin 281
Melachrino, George 194
Melba, Dame Nellie 121, 137, 153,
    155, 162, 183
Melkus, Eduard 3; plays baroque
    violin 54
Mendelssohn 25, 34, 56, 74–6
Mengelberg, Willem 105
Menges, Isolde 97
Menuhin, Diana, née Gould 230
Menuhin, Hephzibah 224, 231
Menuhin, Yaltah 224
Menuhin, Yehudi 223–32; xvii, 23,
    132; on Enesco 135; 140; plays with
    Grappelli 204–5; 212–13; on
    Oistrakh 216, 220–2; lessons with
    Persinger 223; makes débuts in New
    York and Paris 224; meets Ysaÿe
    224–5; influenced by Enesco 225;

plays under Fritz Busch and Bruno Walter 226; studies with Adolf Busch 226–7, records Elgar violin concerto 227–8; plays Elgar under composer 228; period of doubt 228–9; meets Bartok 229; plays Bartok solo sonata 229–30; as director of Bath Festival 230–1; founds Menuhin School 231; influence 232; 233, 269–70; as member of Flesch Jury 289; 291, 298; as chairman of Carl Flesch competition 311

Mezzrow, Milton 201

Michalowicz, Mieczyslaw 140, 244, 266

Milanollo sisters 84–5

Milanova, Stoika 307, 311

Mildner, Moritz 101

Milstein, Nathan 176–81; xxv, 55; on Auer 97, 122, 156; on teachers 176; concerts with Horowitz / tours Europe 177; meets Stokowski / USA début / Egyptian début 178; British début 178–80; interpretation / recording 180; philosophy 181; 185, 218

Minchev, Mincho 311

Mitchell, Abbie 161

Monosoff, Sonya 10; plays baroque violin 54

Monteux, Pierre 145

Moore, Gerald 267, 291

Mordkovich, Lydia 307

Morini, Erica 206–11; 102, 185; wins 'Maud Powell' Guadagnini 207–8; in Ševčik's master class / plays under Nikisch 208; New York début / plays in Israel / technique 210; repertoire / opinions 211

Morrison, George 197–9; makes own violin / private studies 197: turns to jazz / meets Kreisler 198

Moscheles, Ignaz 56

Mossel, Max 206

Mostras, M. 272

Mozart, Leopold xxvii, 11

Mozart, W.A. xxvii, 9, 84

Müller, Wilhelm 295

Munch, Charles 211

Musin, Ovide 61; favours modern music / establishes school in New York 62

Napoleon 21, 26

Nardini, Pietro 23, 85

Neaman, Yfrah 289, 311

Neruda, Josef 85

Neruda, Victor 85

Neruda, Wilma see Norman-Neruda, Wilma

Neveu, Ginette 239–43; 107, 214; practising schedule 239; Paris début / meets Flesch 240; retires during war / débuts in London and New York 241; style of playing / technique / personality 242; death 243

Neveu, Jean 239

Newman, Ernest 124–5

Newman, Philippe 116

Newton, Ivor 227, 246

Nicholas II, Tsar 97, 155

Nikisch, Arthur 105, 112, 118, 162, 169, 208

Nissel, Siegmund 302

Norman, Ludwig 86

Norman-Neruda, Wilma (Lady Hallé) 84–7, 206, 211; astounds Hanslick 85; London début / technique / plays in Joachim Quartet 85–7; 296

North, Roger 3

Novotny, Bretislav 299

Nupen, Christopher 281

Odnoposoff, Ricardo 301

Oistrakh, David 213–22; xxv, 66, 156–7; 184; loyalty to Soviet 213; studies with Stolyarsky / début in Leningrad / in Wieniawski Competition 214; wins Ysaÿe Contest 215; association with Menuhin 216; Paris début under Thibaud 216–17; British début 217; New York début / as teacher 218; as violinist / as musician 219; bowing style 219–20; plays with Igor / character 220; achievements 220–2, 240, 307, 309

Oistrakh, Igor 66, 214, 217

Oistrakh, Tamara 214

Oliveira, Elmar 310

Ondříček, Karel 20, 136

Onnue, Alphonse 298

Ormandy, Eugene 104, 242

Ottey, Sarah: early professional violinist 84

Ottoboni, Cardinal 5, 7

Pachmann, Vladimir 112
Paganini, Achilles, son of Niccolò 39
Paganini, Niccolò 36–44, *passim*; 18;
meets Spohr in Vienna 32; lessons
on mandolin 36; influenced by
Durand 37; is given 'Cannon' del
Gesù 38; association with Antonia
Bianchi, 39; début in Vienna, 40;
début at Paris Opera / receives
phenomenally high fees on British
tour 41; death of 42; 'tricks' and
techniques of 43–4; Caprices show
influences of Locatelli 44; meets Ole
Bull 48; meets Vieuxtemps 66;
Caprices played by Ricci 236
Paganini Quartet 42
Papen, Count von 235
Paray, Paul 224
Parkinson, Michael 204
Pasdeloup, Jules 86
Patti, Adelina 117, 140
Patti, Carlotta 117
Pecskai, Louis 193
Pepys, Samuel 2
Peresson, Sergio 174
Perlman, Itzhak 276–87; xxv, 44, 275;
as polio victim 276; goes to USA /
visits Israel 277; British début /
partnership with Ashkenazy 278;
recording / technique 279; 309
Persinger, Louis 269–70; 113, 223–4;
233; with gifted children 269–70; as
Menuhin's teacher 270
Peterson, Oscar 204
Petri, Endre 164
Philipp, Margrave of
Hessen-Darmstadt 7
Piatigorsky, Gregor 105
Piatti, Alfredo 296
Pickeisen, Victor 218, 307
Pincherle, Marc 8
Pini, Eugène 194
Pisendel, Georg Johann 8
Pixis, Friedrich Wilhelm 20, 21, 101
Pixis, Johann Peter 55
Pizzetti 212
Pohl, C. Ferdinand 295
Popper, David 193
Porter, Cole 203
Poulenc 259
Powell, Maud 206–7; achieves

international fame / gives first
performance of Dvořák's violin
concerto in New York 207;
bequeathes violin 207–8
Prague Quartet 299
Pré, Jacqueline Du 278, 281
Previn, André 282, 285
Principe, Remy 211
Pro Arte Quartet 298
Prokofiev: dedicates first violin
concerto to Szigeti 164
Provence, Count of 19
Prume, François 25, 27
Prunières, Henri 172
Pugnani, Gaetano 11, 15, 18
Pugno, Raoul 124
Pulver, Jeffrey 36

Quantz 9

Rabin, Michael 275
Rachmaninov 122
Rasumovsky, Count 295
Rasumovsky Quartet 295
Ravel 299
Read, Ernest 290
Reicha, Antonin 66
Reinhardt, Django 204
Reinhardt, Joseph 204
Reynolds, Howard 197
Ricci, Ruggiero 232–8; 44, 220; pupil
of Persinger and Lackey 233; early
concerts / is involved in legal battle
234; British début 234–5; in army
service 235; explores
unaccompanied violin repertoire
235–6; studies Paganini / technique
236; as programme innovator / first
performances by 237; as performer /
philosophy 238; 269
Richter, Hans 105, 118
Riddle, Frederick 165; on Oistrakh
219–20
Ries, Ferdinand 33
Ries, Franz 296
Rignold, Hugo 194
Rivarde, Achille: devises vibrato
exercises 62
Robberechts, André 57; as Viotti pupil
/ influence in Belgian school / on
Viotti's principles 57; 109, 249
Robertson, Paul 305
Robinson, Eric 291

Robjohns, Sydney 300
Rochford-Davies, Joan 195
Rocklitz, Johann Friedrich 28
Rode, Pierre 25–6; 23 solo violin to
    Napoleon and Tsar Alexander I 25:
    influence 26; 30, 48, 55, 59, 63, 66
Rogeri, Giovanni xxiv, 42
Rolla, Alessandro 37
Ronald, Sir Landon 145
Ronay, Kalman 188
Rosé, Arnold 118
Rosé Quartet 118
Rose, Leonard 252
Rosenthal, Moritz 118
Rostal, Max 302, 310, 311
Roth, Henry 165, 167, 235
Roth, Nicholas 105, 131
Rubinstein, Anton: tours USA with
    Wieniawski 70
Rubinstein, Artur 112, 244, 263
Rubinstein, Ignace 244
Ruggieri, Francesco xxiv, 42
Ruppa, Alexander 141, 164, 178

Sadie, Stanley 264
Saez, Manuel Rodriguez 88
Safonov, Vassily 146
St Petersburg Quartet 97
Saint-Saëns 89
Sainton, Prosper 25, 27; influence in
    Britain 63
Salabue, Count di xxv, xxvii
Salò, Gasparo da, xxiv
Salzburg, Prince Archbishop of 2
Sammons, Albert 144–9; 121;
    employed by Beecham 145; plays
    Elgar concerto / gives first
    performance of Delius concerto 146;
    repertoire / character 147; as
    connoisseur of violins / as soloist / as
    composer / publishes Secrets of
    Technique 148; professor at RCM /
    as a teacher 149; 288
Sandler, Albert 187–9; tone 187; as
    cinema violinist / at the 'Corner
    Houses' / Grand Hotel 188;
    technique / interpretation 189
Sandor, Arpad 249
Sarasate, Pablo 88–93; xvii, 27, 61, 63;
    'Spanish Dances' of 88; changes in
    style of playing / avoids playing
    Paganini 89; fast tempi 90; technique

/ appearance 91; as composer 92;
    technique 92–3; 196; handkerchief of
    211, 254
Sarbu, Eugene 311
Sargent, Sir Malcolm 178; 190
Sassoon, Sir Philip 267
Saunders, John 145
Sauret, Emile 59, 128
Schidlof, Peter 302
Schiever, Ernst 295
Schnabel, Artur 105
Schneiderhan, Wolfgang 289
Schonberg, Harold 70
Schottky 37, 39
Schradieck, Henry 207, 288
Schuller, Günther 197
Schumann 56; hears Vieuxtemps 65,
    76
Schumann, Clara 76, 77, 82
Schumann, Elisabeth 153
Schuppanzigh, Ignaz 55, 294–5
Schurmann, Gerard 237
Schwarz, Rudolf 212
Schwarzberg, Dora 311
Scott, Cyril 151
Sechter, Simon 65
Seher, Ilona 280
Seidel, Toscha 97
Serkin, Rudolf 299
Serwaczynski 69, 74, 75
Ševčik, Otakar 94–105; 20, 73;
    professor at Kiev and Prague 101; as
    Kubelik's teacher / founds school at
    Pisek 102; principles of method 103;
    104, 107, 136, 207, 208, 210
Shankar, Ravi 232
Shaw, G.B. 110, 167
Shearing, George 204–5
Shelley, Mary 41
Shinner, Emily 206
Sibor 272
Sigal, Lubov 309
Silks, Mattie 198
Simrock, Fritz August 81
Sina 295
Siskind, Jacob 247
Sitt, Hans 296
Sivori, Camille 45–6; gives first
    British performance of Mendelssohn
    concerto 45; Paganini's only pupil 46
Smith, 'Stuff' 197–201; at Onyx Club
    in New York 199; as comedian /
    uses electric amplifier 201

Soh, Tomotada 307

Somis, Giovanni Battista 11, 15, 18

South, Eddie, 197–9; as jazz player / recordings with Grappelli and Reinhardt 199

Spalding, Albert 168–9

Spielman 296

Spivakov, Vladimir, 66, 289, 309

Spohr, Louis 28–35; 21, 25; in service of Duke of Brunswick and training with Eck 29; virtuoso career 30; friendship with Clement and Beethoven 31–2; meets Paganini in Venice 32; London début and sartorial blunder 33; facility as player / invents chin-rest / publishes *Method* 34; 48–9, 51, 53; discourages wife as violinist 86

Stadlen, Peter 264

Stainer, Jacob xxvi, xxvii

Stamitz, Johann 21, 26

Stamitz, Karl 26, 29

Stanford 28, 145

Steinberg, William 277

Stern, Isaac 249–54; 212; New York recital début 249; philosophy / as musician 251; interest in chamber music / association with Casals 252; saves Carnegie Hall 253; 280, 307, 312

Stokowski, Leopold 105, 162, 178

Stolyarsky, Pyotr 176, 213–14

Stradivari, Antonio xxiv; the 'Viotti' xxv; the 'Messiah' xxv; xxvi, xxvii, 42; modification of instruments 54; the 'Wieniawski' 73; Joachim Golden Jubilee violin / the 'De Barrau', the 'Alard', the 'Dolphin' 83; the 'Emperor' 137; the 'Hercules' 265; instruments of the Joachim Quartet 296

Stradivari, Paolo xxv

Straeten, E. van der: heard Sivori in Cologne, 45; 95

Stransky, Josef 150

Strauss, Richard 105

Strinasacchi, Regina: performs with Mozart, 84

Strungk, Nicolaus 6

Suk, Josef 293

Sullivan, Ed 277

Susskind, Walter 291

Symons, Arthur 91, 110–11, 120

Székely, Zoltan 299

Szell, Georg 184, 210, 270

Szerying, Henryk 262–5; 44, 106; Warsaw and Paris 262; on Thibaud / war service / meets Rubinstein 263; first performance of lost Paganini concerto 264; presents violin to Israel 265

Szigeti, Joseph 159–66; 117; with Hubay at Budapest 60; in theatre / circus musician / London début 161; meets Joachim 161–2; first performs Hamilton Harty concerto / meets Stokowski / USA début 162; tours Soviet 163; as player / as programme-planner / first performs Bloch's concerto 164; character / interests 165; friendship with Busoni 166; 176, 185, 220

Talluel, Mme 239

Tarisio, Luigi xxv

Tartini, Giuseppe 12–17; xxviii; 'Mystery Violinist of Assisi' 13; composes 'Devil's Trill' sonata / scientific experiments 14; eclipse by Veracini / founds 'School of the Nations' 15; letter to Maddalena Lombardini-Sirmen 15–16; composes 'The Art of Bowing' 16; 18, 57, 84

Tasca, Santa 8

Tate, Erskine 199

Taubman, Howard 218–9

Tchaikovsky 96

Teagarden Brothers 201

Telmányi, Emil 104

Tertis, Lionel 112

Theodor, Duke Carl 20

Thibaud, Jacques 128–31; 62; 117, 124; technique / personality 128; tone colour / forms Cortot-Thibaud-Casals Trio 129; repertoire / tone-levelling 130; 140–1, 153, 215; conducts Oistrakh 216, 311

Thomson, César 60–2; as leader of Bilse's orchestra / succeeds Ysaÿe at Brussels / 'fingered octaves' / as teacher 62

Thomson, Virgil 241

Tomasini, Luigi 294

Tononi, Carlo-Antonio 42
Torff, Brian 204
Toscanini, Arturo 140, 211, 270, 298
Tost, Johann von 30–1
Tourte, François: sets standards for bow-making xxviii; Viotti, one of first to use bow of 22; bow in universal use 57
Traill, Sinclair 201
Tretiakov, Victor 218
Tua, Teresina 61; as professor in Rome 211
Tureman, Horace 198

Uffenbach, von 9
Urso, Camilla 85

Van Cliburn, 174
Vaughan Williams 112, 185; 'Lark Ascending', first played by Marie Hall 207
Veczey, Franz von 104, 160
Végh Quartet 299
Végh, Sandor 299, 306–7
Venuti, Joe 197–202; teams up with Eddie Lang 201; as practical joker / influence 202
Veracini, Francesco 15, 16
Vieuxtemps, Henri 64–8; 23; 60; new ideas on violin-playing 64; meets Paganini / experience in orchestration / solo violinist to Tsar 66; 72, 82, 91; friendship with Hubay 104; as teacher of Ysaÿe 109
Vincent, Alfred 148
Viotti, Giovanni Battista 18–27; passim; xvii, xxv, xxix, 13; studies with Pugnani / rejects Catherine the Great's offer 18; employed by Marie Antoinette 19; flight to England / friendship with Chinnerys / exile 20; opens wine shop / refuses Spohr as pupil 21; character / advises Tourte on bow 22; advice to de Bériot / principles of playing / influence 23; 29, 30, 37, 55–7, 67; link with Ysaÿe 109
Vito, Gioconda De 206–12; as interpreter of classic repertoire / professor at Accademia di Santa Cecilia in Rome 211; British début playing Brahms / refuses to play contemporary music / temperament

in playing 212
Vivaldi, Antonio 5–11; enters priesthood / at Ospedale della Pietà / association with Giraud sisters 7; posthumous neglect 8; invents cadenza / character 9–10; 13, 54
Vola, Louis 204
Voltaire 19
Vuillaume, Jean-Baptiste xxv, xxvii

Wade, Jimmy 199
Wagner 2, 76–7
Wagner, Mayor 253
Wales, Prince of 27
Walker, Jimmy 234
Waller, Fats 201
Walpole, Sir Edward 17
Walter, Bruno 105, 226
Walter, Ernst 240
Walther, Johann Jakob 3
Wanami, Takayoshi 311
Watkinson, Andrew 311
Webb 296
Weingartner, Felix 191
Weiss, Franz 295
Weist-Hill, Frederick 145
Wessley, Hans 188
Whistler 91
White, Joseph 237
Whiteman, Paul 201
Widdicombe, Gillian 276, 280, 285
Wieniawski, Henri 69–73; 61, 66; technique 69; concert tours with Rubinstein 70; character / illness 72; 'Russian' hold of bow 73; 97, 109
Wieniawski, Joseph 70
Wilhelmj, August 94–6; 55; taken by Liszt to Leipzig 94; arranges 'Air' on G string / physical appearance 95; principal professor at GSM, 96; 206
Wood, Sir Henry 112, 119, 129, 184, 207, 243

Yampolsky, V. 217
Yankelevich, Yuri 307–9
Ysaÿe, Eugène 108–16; 60, 62; attends Vieuxtemps' funeral 68, 92; feared by Flesch 107; playing style 108; meets Vieuxtemps / leader in Bilse's orchestra 109; London début 110; technique / début in USA 111; London soirées / as joker 112; Franck dedicates sonata to 113; as a

teacher 114; as composer 115; as defender of Paganini 116; 117–18, 124, 128, 130, 146, 153, 215, 224–5; as teacher of Persinger and Gingold 269–70; plays in Joachim Quartet 296

Zacharewitch, Michael 102
Zimbalist, Efrem 150–1; 97, 102; wins Rubinstein Scholarship 150; style of playing / as composer / as connoisseur 151; 160, 169; honours Heifetz 171; 273
Zingarelli, Niccolò 47
Zukerman, Pinchas 276–87; 275; studies with Galamian / shares Leventritt with Chung 280; first recording 280–1; makes British début / physique and character 281; musical directing 282; 309